THE PHILOSOPHY OF
SAINT THOMAS AQUINAS

THE PHILOSOPHY OF ST. THOMAS AQUINAS

Authorised Translation from the Third Revised & Enlarged Edition of 'Le Thomisme' by Étienne Gilson

TRANSLATED BY EDWARD BULLOUGH

EDITED BY REV. G. A. ELRINGTON

DORSET PRESS
NEW YORK

This edition published by Dorset Press,
a division of
Marboro Books Corporation

ISBN 0-88029-122-2

Distributed in the United Kingdom by Bibliophile Editions

The paper used in this book meets
the minimum requirements of the
American National Standard for
Permanence of Paper for Printed
Library Materials Z39.48–1948.

Printed in the United States of America
M 9 8 7 6 5 4 3 2 1

FOREWORD

THE Hebrew story of the tower of Babel suggests to us that "a confusion of tongues" is an extreme penalty for grievous mental faults. We must bear this Hebrew wisdom in mind whilst we see around us the divided speech—the cleft palate—of modern enthusiasts for philosophy. Anyone who has sought to discuss his concepts of the universe has speedily been made numb or dumb by realising that so great an abyss has been dug between him and them that even when words are held in common, their meaning is not held in common.

The desire to spread a knowledge of the philosophical synthesis of St. Thomas Aquinas is therefore not merely a desire to win men to the truth. It is also a humble hope that men may come to use a common philosophical speech by accepting words in the meaning of a philosophical master. All the sciences, even the lowliest, owe their gradual expansion to the standardisation of terminology. Botany, without a fixed botanical nomenclature, would be little more than "the hooting of owls." If Metaphysics are given this latter name, it is because in the supreme subject matter of human discussion men have shirked the irreducible unit of discussion, to wit, an accepted philosophical language.

The present work of a French professor is a witness to a homeward march of the intellect of Europe. French clarity of logic owed more than perhaps it knew to the genius who was the chief glory of the University of Paris. Yet this razor-edge of Gallic clarity, when wielded by a Descartes, and even by a Pascal, was not always an instrument of life. France, which in the sphere of the spirit, is so often our master, is again leading us back to classical forms of thought. She is thus publicly unsaying the idealistic fallacies which Descartes originated with his philosophical doubt. Professor Gilson is a trustworthy guide in the multiple wisdom of the Dumb Ox, whose very words are constantly used in the exposition of his ideas. He is happy in his translator, who gives us the scholarship of one of our great historic English universities. The partnership of Paris and Cambridge is perhaps a harbinger of a new dawn of sound thinking. The desire of this dawn has been the motive power of this work and its translation.

Fr. VINCENT McNABB, O.P.

St Dominic's Priory,
    London.

THE AUTHOR'S PREFACE TO THE TRANSLATION

THE present revival of interest in the name and work of St. Thomas Aquinas is a fact which is bound to impress even the most superficial observer. In fact, nobody thinks of denying it; but, since it disturbs the set habits of some, the attempt has been made to give it an unfavourable interpretation in order to escape the duty to take an interest in it. It is—so it has been said—a merely artificial return to an obsolete scholasticism, a movement, political-religious rather than strictly philosophical; what has not been alleged and invented to explain a movement of ideas whose depth and vitality are sufficient to disprove so mean an origin! Indeed, who, one may ask, gives proof of the greater liberty of mind, he whom the anxiety never to be sufficiently "modern" prevents from examining a problem so evidently contemporary as this, or he who cannot consider it as solved without having first examined it? After all the following proposition contains no absurdity such as to relieve us of all discussion: a philosophical system, elaborated in the XIIIth century by a thinker of genius, can even to-day teach us something. The traveller who returns from Paestum or Pompeii to Naples or compares Notre-Dame of Paris and the Madeleine is not necessarily a simpleton because he asks himself which of these present the more harmonious conception of art and of life. It will doubtless be objected that, though there is no definitely obsolete beauty, there yet are definitely obsolete ideas, and that, since the time of Descartes, the ideas of scholastic philosophy are precisely of this kind. But the criticism of scholastic thought is nothing but an historical and in some measure contingent fact of that which constitutes the Cartesian reform; and the Cartesian spirit, surviving the particular circumstances of its birth, is the right of free examination which entitles us to call everything in question, even Cartesianism, even Kantism, and to judge philosophies by their arguments, not by their dates.

Indeed, as will be seen, Thomistic philosophy asks for no more, and it would require much ingenuousness to be surprised thereat. If Thomistic philosophy deserves to be studied still to-day, the reason for it can only be, that it presents the whole problem of Philosophy with a fullness which had never been attained to before and has never been reached since. The achievement of combining in one single synthesis the metaphysical principles of Reality, its inward structure, the nature of man, the principles of his moral and civil conduct, the solution of the problem of his destiny, may be found elsewhere partially attempted in more or less developed efforts, but nowhere so completely realised as it is presented to us in the "Summa theologica" for our study and admiration. This extraordinary structure of ideas, to which our book claims to be no more than a first guide, displays its directive principles and perspectives only by degrees; to appreciate them fully we must explore the building ourselves in all directions, after having dismissed the importunate guide with whom we had at first to bear as with a necessary evil. Only after we have mastered both the simplicity of its principles and the multiplicity of their consequences, and have seen these consequences issue from the fertility of the principles, we become conscious of the very life that animates the whole teaching, and only then the teaching will really have come to life again in us.

Shall we nevertheless pretend to ignore the most widely spread prejudice and objection, so often pleaded as an excuse for discarding every intellectual obligation towards scholasticism in general and to St. Thomas in particular; viz. that these systems are not philosophies but theologies? Thomism is indeed first and foremost a theology, but it will be seen that this theology could not have been constituted as such, unless it borrowed its technique from an underlying philosophy having its own principles. The final view of St. Thomas on this important point seems indeed to have been that man, employing nothing but his reason, should not only not have to deny any part of it, but would rather find his reason attaining to its full expansion and complete satisfaction precisely by this collaboration in a work begun by theology. However paradoxical in its terms, this view was only the concrete experience of St. Thomas himself, expressed in abstract language, and its doctrinal statement was fraught with truly incalculable philosophical, moral and religious consequences.

For the drama of Medieval Western thought which in its issue, was to determine the road followed by the whole of our civilisation, seems to have consisted in the choice which had to be made, between Christianity and Greek Humanism, represented by Aristotle. It might perhaps not be impossible to show that this drama went much further back, that it was innate in Catholicism itself and that the crisis, which set in in the XIIIth century owing to the invasion of Arabic philosophy, only carried it to its culminating point. Of the two opposing tendencies within Christian thought, radical asceticism with its negation of nature expressed in the *contemptus mundi*, and Humanism with its acceptance of nature, proclaimed as early as the 2nd century by St. Justin—was the one to stifle the other, or could they be reconciled? To sacrifice Greek Humanism to asceticism meant a break in the intellectual and moral continuity of mankind, a break in the unity of our interior life by opposing religious life in its most passionate form to the human ideal at its noblest. The sacrifice of Christian asceticism to Greek Humanism meant the neglect of the Divine lesson of the Gospels, the withering of the deepest

springs of interior life, and ultimately a civilisation of
empty and formal elegance, characteristic later on of
certain aspects of the Renaissance. St. Thomas, an
innovator when compared with the Augustinianism
of his time, yet deeply conservative if considered
as the heir to St. Justin, Lactantius or St. Clement
of Alexandria, makes his choice both for Greek
naturalism and Christian supernaturalism, fuses both
in an indissoluble synthesis, and postulates, or rather
guarantees, the perfect development of natural man
and of reason in the name of the supernatural and
of Revelation. The Renaissance was to be but
the consequence—the achievement at certain points,
at others a mere falling short—of this Christian
Humanism, set up in the mid-XIIIth century. Even
to-day it still represents, as the heir of Athens no less
than of Bethlehem and of Rome, Western thought
in its most complete form, determined to sacrifice
nothing of whatever may give man more truth, more
beauty, more love and order. This is the reason why
Thomistic Philosophy, accepting and gathering up the
whole of human tradition, legitimising and arranging
it in order, deserves still to-day that we should turn to
it for counsel; for it bears the very semblance of our
highest ideal.

In conclusion, we have to fulfil certain pleasant
duties: firstly that of thanking the Rev. Fr. Elrington,
O.P., who first initiated the idea of this translation,
and the publisher, Mr. Heffer, for his kindness in
undertaking to present it to the public. The text of
the translation is based upon a copy of the original,
revised, corrected, and, at some points, enlarged,
which we had prepared for a new French edition. We
gladly take this opportunity of thanking Mr. Edward
Bullough for the care and accuracy bestowed upon the
translation which reproduces most faithfully and in
happily chosen terms, a text by no means devoid of
difficulties. May this book, in the new form given to
it by its translator, contribute in England, as we hope
it does in France, to a better mutual understanding of

cultured minds, and to the peace fostered by such understanding. This is a hope, based upon the conviction, which we hold, that there would be no Western civilisation without the powerful moral support of Great Britain, and that there, as in France, no fruitful external action is possible except as the expression of an inward peace between thoughtful minds.

ETIENNE GILSON.

MELUN,
   June, 1924.

TRANSLATOR'S PREFACE TO THIS (SECOND) ENGLISH EDITION

THIS present edition is very considerably enlarged (by more than a third), by the insertion of two entirely new chapters, viz.: IX on "The Corporeal World and the Efficiency of Secondary Causes," and XIII on "Knowledge and Truth"; by the addition of a third section to Chapter I, on the "Christian Doctor" and of a fourth section to Chapter XV on "The Laws," as well as by minor changes in the text and notes—additions for which the students will feel deeply grateful to the author who, with his customary lucidity and ease of exposition leads them there through some of the most difficult stretches of thomistic thought.

A word of explanation seems needed concerning the somewhat puzzling mention of the third French edition as the basis of this, as well as of the former English edition. While the translation of the first English edition was in progress, the author very kindly handed to the translator a number of manuscript additions for insertion, which were intended by the author to form part of a proposed third French edition. The English version was accordingly stated to be based on that edition. The third French edition did not, however, appear until 1927 and contained then, apart from the additional matter already incorporated in the English version, the new chapters and sections mentioned. The circumstance that in the course of the last year the first English edition was completely exhausted, and the willingness of Messrs. Heffer to embark upon a new edition, make it possible now to present the enlarged French edition with all its valuable additional matter in English form.

The translator takes this opportunity of thanking many friends for pointing out errors in the previous edition which have been corrected in this.

E.B.

CAMBRIDGE,
    August, 1929.

CONTENTS

THE PHILOSOPHY OF
SAINT THOMAS AQUINAS

CHAPTER I. THE MAN AND
HIS ENVIRONMENT

ALL great philosophies present themselves at first sight and externally as closed systems uncompromisingly opposed to all concessions. The history of philosophy, however, very soon discovers in pursuing its analysis beneath that rigorously systematic appearance, a hidden spirit of conciliation. Indeed, the very concessions which a philosophy is no longer able to make once it exists, were bound to be made before it came into existence. For every philosophical system represents a more or less successful attempt to organise tendencies which, in their natural state, would have remained irreconcilable. The teaching of St. Thomas is no exception to this rule. Like all the richest philosophies, it is born of a compromise, in the mind of an epoch or of a person, between spiritual tendencies which recognise fairly each other's claims and thus order themselves in an harmonious equilibrium. The "thomistic problem" as such is the original conflict of these tendencies. It is therefore a matter of importance to define these, in order to understand the system which was designed to furnish the solution of this conflict, and to review in a general way the peculiarly complex conditions in the midst of which the system took shape.

A. THE LIFE[1] AND WORKS[2] OF ST. THOMAS

St. Thomas of Aquino was born towards the beginning of the year 1225 at the Castle of Roccasecca. The very name alone calls up the wildness and desolation of the spot where even to-day stand the ruins which indicate the site of his family seat. A little further, in the direction of Naples, lies the little village of Aquino,[3] of which his father was count; further still rises the Benedictine Abbey of Montecassino, where he was brought as an oblate by his parents in 1230. It has been supposed, not without probability, that certain family ambitions concealed themselves behind this decision. Landolf, Count of Aquino, was the nearest Lord to the Abbey; in the year preceding, 1229, he had supported the Emperor Frederic II against the Pope by assisting him in seizing the monastery to hold it to ransom. In these circumstances the idea of establishing there one of his sons with the view to his later becoming Abbot and to a participation of his family in the revenues of the Abbey, barely even deserve to be called a ruse, so evident must have been the object of the game.[4] Nor could he have discovered a more profitable way of making peace after the war which was then drawing to its close, and this, no doubt, was a consideration very present to the mind of Count Landolf. As to rearing a future saint in the Benedictine spirituality, or a future philosophical genius in a taste for science to which the austere and bare hill-top had for centuries offered a refuge, or a future theologian in the respect for the rights of the Church which the monks upheld against the Emperor and himself—that surely was an idea that never entered the head of Count Landolf; yet that was precisely what he did.[5]

The child remained for nine years in the care of his first teachers there, near a library which was almost unique at that time, covering under the guidance of excellent masters the classical road of the "trivium" and introduced to the Latin tongue by the writings of St. Gregory, St. Jerome and St. Augustine. The fact, moreover, that he remained from the age of five to fourteen under the influence of a Benedictine environment in which humanism, science and religion formed an indivisible whole, cannot have failed to leave deep traces upon his mind.[6] In 1239 this happy existence came to an end. Frederic II, still engaged in war against Gregory IX, expelled the monks from Montecassino in order to

break the opposition which these uncompromising supporters of the Papacy offered to his designs. The boy
had to return to his parents and to put off the Benedictine habit; he remained at home until the autumn of
that same year, when he proceeded to the University
of Naples which Frederic II had just founded.[7]

Accurate information of what the University milieu
was like and of the directions which the new student
may have received from his teachers there, would be
most valuable; unfortunately none is available or at
least so sparse that it would be very unwise for us to
draw any definite conclusions from it. It is of little
use to be told that a certain Master Martin there taught
the "trivium" or that Peter of Ireland gave instruction
in the "quadrivium."[8] What biographers tell us of the
successes achieved by the young student, does not go
beyond the simplest conjectures. On the other hand,
it is certain that the Neapolitan student world was
open to the scientific and philosophical works recently
translated from the Greek and Arabic, and was eminently suited to awaken the curiosity of a mind like
that of the boy.[9] We should gain little by exchanging
this modest certainty for the study of hypotheses
which recent years have shown to have yielded perhaps but little profit.

In the course of the year 1244 a decisive change occurred in the life of St. Thomas. Of age by now, since he
was in his twentieth year, and free since the death of his
father on December 24th, 1243, the young man decided
to enter the Order of St. Dominic. The meaning of this
decision is clear, if we bear in mind the examples which
had inspired it. The Dominicans, established right in
the centre of University life, at Naples as well as in
Paris, presented the wholly new spectacle of religious
whose special vocation it was to cultivate the sciences
and to teach them publicly. Men whom previously
one had been accustomed to find within massive walls
of fortress-like Abbeys, were here mixing freely in the
crowd of teachers and students, learning from the
former in order to teach the latter in their turn. The

Dominican vocation, born in the midst of a medieval University, is, therefore, above all the resolve to serve God by teaching and in absolute poverty. To be a religious and a Doctor, such remains until the last months of his life, the ideal of St. Thomas of Aquino.

In taking the Dominican habit, the young man definitely disappointed a family hope: he renounced the dignity of Abbot of Montecassino. Anticipating opposition on the part of the family, the Master-General of the Order, John the Teuton, decided to take him away at once to Bologna, where he had to attend a General Chapter, and to send him to the University of Paris, which was then the most important centre of University studies, not only of France but of the whole Christian world. It was during this journey that the famous incident occurred when his brothers attacked him and locked him up, in anger at his decision to enter the Dominican Order. After having been kept in confinement for about a year, which he spent in prayer and studies, St. Thomas, having defeated all the schemes and wearied the obstinacy of his persecutors, recovered his freedom towards the autumn of 1245 and was at last able to proceed to Paris.

The young Dominican stayed there for a first period from 1245 till the summer of 1248,[10] and came under the influence of Albert of Cologne, the famous teacher who later was to be called Albert the Great. That the impression made by such a teacher upon such a student must have been deep and lasting admits of no doubt; much more difficult, however, than one thinks, is it to know precisely in what it consisted. In a general way, it is held that the genius of Albert the Great, possessing as he did a prodigious power of assimilation, was then collecting the materials, and was beginning to sketch the outline of a doctrinal synthesis which he was never to complete; and that the young Thomas of Aquino, gifted with a genius, if less extensive in its curiosity, yet more constructive and better ordered, and, as it were, supported and carried along by the efforts of his master, immediately grasped the plan of the latter's work and

undertook its realisation.[11] This is a view which certainly
contains an element of truth but requires a good deal of
modification. What the pupil found in such a teacher
was no doubt an erudition which was the vastest as
well as the deepest that the 13th century had known;
and again, a taste for science and the right feeling of
what a rational explanation means and, lastly, perhaps
the most precious gift of all, the powerful impetus
which a mature and fully developed mind can impart
to a young and budding genius. But it is by no means
certain that the thomistic system was more necessarily
preformed in the teaching of Albert the Great than in
that of Alexander of Hales, for instance, or that, in
consequence, the work of Albert the Great can be
considered as a sketch, of which that of St. Thomas is
to be taken as the finished picture.[12] To define and
measure exactly the influence of the master upon the
pupil will no doubt remain for ever an inaccessible ideal
of history; we are lacking too much information to lay
any claim to be able even to approach it. At any rate,
the effect of Albert the Great upon the young Thomas
was certainly very deep. On leaving Paris in order to
set up in Cologne a "studium generale," i.e. a centre of
theological studies for a whole province of the Order,
the celebrated master took his disciple with him in
order to keep him under his direction for another four
years. It may be said that in these six years of intensive
work and in daily intercourse with Albert the Great,
St. Thomas assimilated the essential parts of all the
materials which had been amassed by the encyclopae-
dic erudition of his master and was to be recast in turn
by him in a new philosophical and theological system.

In 1252 St. Thomas returned to Paris, where he passed,
though not without incidents, through the regular
stages leading to the degree of Master in Theology. He
therefore commented on the Bible (1252–1254), then on
the Sentences of Peter the Lombard (1254–1256) and
obtained the degree of Licentiate in Theology.[13] He was
then a young man with his future before him, even then
enjoying the esteem of his equals and of his superiors.

The friar's habit concealed a gentleman of noble birth, a fact which had not been forgotten;[14] he led a life of perfect regularity; as to his erudition, he knew all that was known at his time. The licentiate, whom Alexander IV described in the foregoing terms, had every claim to aspire to the degree of Master, i.e. to form part of the body of Masters teaching in the University of Paris. The disputes which at that time were raised by the secular Masters against the mendicant Orders, delayed only for a very short time St. Thomas' attainment to the standing of Master in Theology, since he performed his "principium" in the course of that same year, 1256; nor did they trouble his activity as teacher, since he continued his teaching for the three academic years, up to the summer vacations of 1259.

After this date, St. Thomas returned to Italy to teach almost uninterruptedly at the pontifical curia, under the Popes Alexander IV, Urban IV and Clement IV, from 1259 till 1268. In the autumn of this year he was recalled to Paris to teach again Theology. The University had by then become a battlefield, where the struggle between corporations had given way to the bitterest doctrinal disputes. It is during this period that St. Thomas began the struggle, on the one hand, against Siger of Brabant and the Latin Averroists and, on the other, against certain Franciscan theologians who were anxious to maintain intact the teaching of Augustinian theology. Recalled from Paris, St. Thomas went back to Italy and resumed in November, 1272, his theological instruction in Naples. He left this town for the last time to take part in the general Council of Lyons, on the invitation of Pope Gregory X. In the course of this journey he fell ill and died, on March 7, 1274, at the Cistercian monastery of Fossanuova, near Terracina.

His works, the bulk of which is very considerable, especially if we remember the shortness of the author's life (1225–1274), are catalogued in a writing of 1319, and other documents of a similar kind have, on the whole, confirmed this list. There is therefore no room for doubt about the authenticity of the great works which are attributed to St. Thomas by tradition. The question of their chronology, on the contrary, is still much debated. We therefore begin by giving a list of his principal works, grouping them according to their method of exposition or according to their subject-matter. The most probable chronological order is given for the writings within each group.[15]

1. *In Boetium de Hebdomadibus* (about 1257–1258, M).
2. *In Boetium de Trinitate* (unfinished, same date, M).
3. *In Dionysium de divinis nominibus* (about 1261, M).
4. On Aristotle: Physics
5. —   Metaphysics[16]   } 1261–1264, G.
6. —   Ethics
7. —   *De anima*   From 1265
8. —   *De sensu et sensato*   } or earlier to
9. —   *De memoria et reminiscentia*   1268, M.
10. —   Politics, 1272, G.
11. —   *Analytica posteriora*
12. —   *De causis*, 1268, G.
13. —   *Metereologica*   } 1269–1271,
14. —   *Perihermeneias*   } M; G.
15. —   *De coelo*   } 1272–1273,
16. —   *De generatione et corruptione*   } M; 1272, G.
17. *In IV lib. Sententiarum* (1254–1256, M).
18. *Compendium theologiae ad Reginaldum* (1260–1266, M; G).
19. *Summa theologica.*
    Prima pars, 1267–1268, M.
    Prima secundae, 1269–1270, M.   } 1265–1272, G.
    Secunda secundae, 1271–1272, M.
    Tertia pars, 1272–1273, M; 1271–1273, G.
    Unfinished; the *Supplementum* is by Reginald of Piperno.
20. *Summa contra gentes*, 1258–1260, M; 1259–1264, G.
21. *De rationibus fidei contra Saracenos, Graecos et Armenos*, 1261–1268, M.
22. *Contra errores Graecorum*, 1263, M; G.
23. *De emptione et venditione*, 1263, M.
24. *De regimine principum ad regem Cypri*, 1265–1266, M. (Only the first Book and the second Book, up to Chapter IV. inclusive, are by St. Thomas.)
25. *De principiis naturae*, 1255, M.
26. *De ente et essentia*, 1256, M.
27. *De occultis operationibus naturae*, 1269–1272, M.
28. *De aeternitate mundi contra murmurantes*, 1270, M; G.
29. *De unitate intellectus contra Averroistas*, G, 1269–1272; M, 1270.
30. *De substantiis separatis* (after 1260, G; 1272, M).
31. *De mixtione elementorum* (1273, M).

32. *De motu cordis* (1273, M).
33. *De natura verbi intellectus.*[17]
34. *De intellectu et intelligibili.*[18]
35. *Quaestiones quodlibetales* (disputations, held twice every year, at Christmas and at Easter, on questions of any kind).
    Quaest., 7, 9, 10, 11, 8. Italy, 1263–1268, M[19]; 1272–1273, G.
    Quaest., 1 to 6. Paris, 1269–1272, M; G.
36. *Quaestiones disputatae* (more detailed discussions of theological and philosophical problems; generally once every fortnight).
    De veritate, 1256–1259, M; G.
    De potentia, 1259–1263, M; 1256–1259, G.
    De spiritualibus creaturis, 1269, Jan.-June, M.
    De anima, 1269–1270, M. ⎫ 1260–1268,
    De unione Verbi incarnati, 1268, Sept.-Nov., M. ⎬ G.
    De malo, 1263–1268, M. ⎭
    De virtutibus, 1270–1272, M; 1269–1272, G.

EDITIONS OF THE WORKS OF ST. THOMAS.

I. *Sancti Thomae Aquinatis D.A. Opera omnia*, Romae, Typis Riccardi Garroni, actually published 13 Vols. in fol; 1882–1918.
   Vol. 1. Commentaries on the *Perihermeneias* and the *Analytica posteriora*.
   2. Commentary on *Physics*.
   3. *De coelo et mundo; De generatione et corruptione; In lib. Meteorum.*
   4–12. *Summa theologica.*
   13. *Summa contra Gentes*, lib. I. and II.
   Cf. on this edition the masterly study of A. Pelzer, *L'édition léonine de la Somme contre les Gentils*, Rev. néo-scolast. de phil., May, 1920, p. 217–245.
   II. For the works not yet published in the above edition, consult: *S. Thomae Aquinatis opera omnia*, ed. E. Fretté and P. Maré, Paris, Vivès, 1872–1880, 34 Vols. in 4°.
   III. For practical purposes and as easily accessible the following may be mentioned:
   Summa theologica, Torino, P. Marietti, 6 vols., 1894; 11th ed., 1913.
   Summa contra Gentiles, ibid., 1 vol., 12th ed., 1909, and Paris, Lethielleux, *ed. nova*, w.d.
   Summa theologica, texte and French translation, Paris, *Revue des Jeunes*, 1925 onward.
   Quaestiones disputatae et quaestiones duodecim quodlibetales, nova editio, 1914, 5 vols., Torino, P. Marietti. Also published by Lethielleux, Paris, in 3 vols.
   Opuscula selecta theologica et philosophica, Paris, Lethielleux, 4 vols., w.d.

BIBLIOGRAPHIES AND LEXICA.

I. BIBLIOGRAPHIES:

F. Ueberwegs, *Grundriss der Geschichte der Philosophie der patristischen und scholastischen Zeit*, 10th ed. by M. Baumgartner, Berlin, E.S. Mittler, 1915 (cf. for editions of St. Thomas, p. 479–482; for works on St. Thomas, the bibliographical appendix, p. 166–178).—P. Mandonnet et J. Destrez, *Bibliographie thomiste* (Bibliothèque thomiste, vol. I., published by the Rev. des sciences phil. et théol.), Le Saulchoir, 1921. Indispensable for research. The Bibliography covers works published since the beginning of the XIXth cent.

II. LEXICA:

L. Schütz, *Thomaslexikon; Sammlung, Übersetzung und Erklärung der in sämtlichen Werken des hl. Thomas von Aquin vorkommenden Kunstausdrücke und wissenschaftlichen Aussprüche*, Paderborn, 1881; 2nd ed., 1895.

GENERAL WORKS ON THE PHILOSOPHY OF
ST. THOMAS OF AQUINAS.

Johannes a S. Thoma, *Cursus philosophiae thomisticae*, 3 vols. in 4°, Paris, 1883.—Ch. Jourdain, *La philosophie de saint Thomas d'Aquin*, 2 vols., Paris, 1858.—A.-D. Sertillanges, *Saint Thomas d'Aquin*, 2 vols., Paris, 1910, Alcan (Les Grands Philosophes).—P. Rousselot, *L'intellectualisme de saint Thomas*, Paris, 2nd ed., 1924.—M. Grabmann, *Thomas v. Aquin. Eine Einführung in seine Persönlichkeit und Gedankenwelt*, Kempten u. München, 1912. Italian transl. (*Profili di Santi*, 1920); French transl. (Bloud et Gay, 1921).—J. Durantel, *Le retour à Dieu par l'intelligence et la volonté dans la philosophie de saint Thomas*, Paris, Alcan, 1918.

A selection of the most useful works for consultation on particular questions will be given in connexion with each chapter.

B. ST. THOMAS AND ARISTOTELIANISM.

A reference to the period of the philosophical "Dark Ages" which followed upon the last efforts of Hellenistic speculation, is almost a platitude. With Plotinus the great lineage of Greek philosophers came to an end. The system which he elaborated undoubtedly presents a clearly marked religious character, but it is after all a real philosophy, a vast syncretistic system in which elements taken from Plato, Aristotle and even the Stoic philosophers were fused. It is a monistic system of the Universe in which we see how all things proceeded

from the ONE and how, in ecstasy, we are able to reach
back to the One and find union with It. The Greek
philosophical speculation reaches its completion with
Porphyrius, the disciple of Plotinus, who gives a still
stronger relief to the religious element in the doctrine
of his master.

It may be said that all philosophical speculation
vanishes at that point for a long time to come. If philosophy is taken to mean a natural interpretation of
the universe, a general view of things taken from the
point of view of reason, there is no philosophy between
the end of the 3rd century after Christ, which saw the
death of Porphyrius, and the middle of the 13th century, which witnessed the appearance of the "Summa
contra Gentiles." Does this mean that humanity passed
through ten centuries of ignorance and darkness? It
is possible to maintain this only by the confusing of
intellectual activity with philosophical speculation. In
reality and on closer examination, this apparently obscure period is found to be employed upon the fruitful
work which is about to lay the foundations of medieval philosophy. The characteristic feature, in fact, of
the patristic period is the substitution of religious for
philosophical thought. Catholic dogma is finally elaborated and organised. Numerous elements have for this
work been borrowed from the Greek philosophers;
traces of Hellenistic culture have been alleged even in
St. Paul. In any case, and even without going back
so far, Hellenistic culture is obvious in Origen, St.
Clement of Alexandria, St. Augustine. The aim, however, which these thinkers pursue is not philosophical.
What they express in philosophical formulæ, are religious conceptions, and it is a theological system which
they intend to build up. Against the tireless imagination of heretics, these Fathers affirm and maintain the
existence of one God, one in three persons, the creator
of the world, distinct from creation as the infinite
is from the finite, incarnated in Jesus Christ, true God
and true man, who has given Himself for the world in
order to save it. They affirm that the end of man is

knowledge of the eternal and the love of God for all time; a love and a vision face to face, reserved for the elect, for those who with the necessary help of Divine Grace, will follow the commandments of God and of His Church. To establish these fundamental truths, to express them in the least inadequate form, to defend them against the incessant attacks from all sides— that is the work achieved by the Fathers from Origen to St. Augustine, passing through Athanasius, Gregory of Nyssa, St. Ambrose and Cyril of Alexandria. When we come to the death of St. Augustine, we find ourselves in the middle of the 5th century. The two hundred years of theological speculation since the time of Plotinus, have produced the "De Trinitate" and the thirteen books of the "Confessions," that is to say, one of the most perfect monuments which Christian theology can boast and one of the masterpieces of the human mind.

Then and only then, and for a relatively short time only, a general stagnation of intellectual activity seems to set in. Three centuries elapse, laboriously occupied in building up a new civilisation on the wreckage of the Roman world, between the 5th century and the first stammerings of the new philosophy. The restoration of the Empire and of Roman Law is the great achievement of that epoch; and even then, in the midst of so great a darkness, men are to be found who outlined a new synthesis as St. John of Damascus, or salved what could be rescued from the wreck. With Boëthius, Isidore of Seville, and the Venerable Bede we reach Alcuin, and with him the Carlovingian renaissance. The difficult pass is overcome. Philosophical speculation is about to be reborn, to develop down to modern times without any real break in its continuity.

The road covered from the 9th to the 13th century is considerable. Leaving aside a system outlined by a thinker such as John Scotus Erigena and confining ourselves to such works as prepared the birth of the Thomistic philosophy, we find in that period three important acquisitions assured to philosophy: the progressive determination of the relation of reason and faith; conceptualism; and the so-called scholastic method.

Concerning the relation of reason and faith, a way was found to let them live peaceably side by side without allowing one to stifle the other or preventing the legitimate development of both. This result had not been achieved, of course, without endless difficulties. The dialecticians who wished to force dogma and Scripture into the form of syllogisms, were confronted, by an inevitable reaction, with those teachers of the inward life who considered the time spent on philosophical speculation as so much time lost for salvation. Between Anselm the Peripatetic, and St. Peter Damian[20] a middle course gradually opened out. It came to be admitted more and more that reason and faith cannot be in contradiction, since both come from God; that, therefore, reason should render faith credible, by exposing the hidden flaws in the arguments of its enemies. "Fides quaerens intellectum": this is the programme which it is hoped henceforth to realise.

Moreover, the long and subtle controversy on the nature of universals ends in Abelard and John of Salisbury by restoring the Aristotelian doctrine of abstraction. Universals are concepts "cum fundamento in re." As opposed to the philosophers who keep more or less to the Platonic theory of ideas, the tendency is to think that the intellect abstracts from the individual the universal which is contained in it. With the demonstration of the sensory origin of concepts, philosophical thought takes possession of a principle of which the Thomistic system is largely the metaphysical justification and consistent application.

Lastly, and this last progress is also not without importance, the scholastic method of exposition and argument takes shape. After the incomplete attempts, such as the "Sic et Non" of Abelard, the final solution is reached with Alexander of Hales. At least, as far as our present state of knowledge allows us to form an opinion, it is he who first employs the form of argument which became classical from the second half of the 13th century onwards: the enumeration of the arguments *contra*; the exposition of the proposed solution, and the criticism of the objections previously set out.

Nevertheless, despite these advances and despite all those which might be added, philosophical speculation of the 12th and early 13th centuries displays grave defects. The gravest of these, and the root of all the others, consists in the lack of co-ordination. With the exception of the attempt, so original, although so far so little known, of Guillaume d'Auvergne, that period, when more than one thinker proved his capacity to explore and discuss with skill and insight certain special problems, produced no single general system having any pretension to give a rational explanation of the universe. Without doubt, the fault was, that philosophical thought, deprived of the great works of antiquity, was unable to draw out of itself the substance of a new philosophy; but, as has been very truly observed,[21] the fault also lay in that the scholastics of that time made use simultaneously of philosophical systems which were not only misunderstood but were moreover mutually contradictory. Wavering, as they were, without reaching a definite position between Aristotle and Plato, and possessing a very imperfect knowledge of both, how could they have succeeded in drawing a truly coherent system from principles which were mutually exclusive?

This is the internal defect, which, hidden in the philosophical speculation of the 12th century, prevented its reaching a complete development. But at this point a revolution is about to set in: a revolution determined by the influx of the works of Greek and Arabic philosophy.

The Middle Ages had all along been in possession of part of Aristotle's works. The 12th century possesses the whole of the "Organon." From that time onwards certain parts of Aristotelian Physics are known in the

scholastic circles of Chartres[22]; but although it is true
to say that the infiltration of Aristotelian natural
philosophy has henceforth begun, it remains also true
that "the scholastics of the first centuries saw in
Aristotle nothing but a logician."[23] The situation in
which we find the philosophers of the early 13th
century is quite different.[24] The Physics and Metaphysics of Aristotle, the abbreviated form of these by
Avicenna and the commentaries of Averroës are translated from Arabic into Latin, thanks mainly to the
translators of the College of Toledo. Therewith the
imperfect philosophical attempts of the end of the 12th
century are confronted by a complete and systematically elaborated philosophy; and this is all the more
serious as the doctrine, especially in the interpretation
of Averroës, harmonises badly at more than one point
with the traditional teaching of the Church. The
most clear-sighted witness to this opposition between
the peripatetic philosophy and Christianity is St.
Bonaventure.

According to this doctor,[25] the fundamental error of
Aristotle consists in his rejection of the Platonic doctrine of ideas. Since, according to Aristotle, God does
not possess in Himself, like so many models, the ideas
of all things, it follows that God knows only Himself
and is ignorant of the particular. From this first error
springs the second, namely, that God, ignorant of all
things, possesses no prescience and exercises no providence in regard to things. But, if God exercises no
providence, it follows that everything happens either
by accident or by necessity of fate. And as events cannot be the result of a simple accident, the Arabs concluded that everything is necessarily determined by the
movement of the spheres, viz. by the intelligences
which move them. Such a conception obviously annuls
the disposition of events of this world with a view to
the punishment of sinners and the glory of the elect.
Hence we find that Aristotle never mentions either
the devil or the future beatitude. The error is therefore threefold, namely, a failure to understand first,

exemplarism, then Divine providence and lastly the disposition of this world with a view to the other.

This threefold failure is the root of a threefold blindness. The first concerns the eternal existence of the world. Since God is ignorant of the world, how can He have created it? All the commentators, whether Greek or Arabic, are accordingly agreed on this point. Aristotle has never taught that the world has had a beginning and an origin. This first blindness entails a second: for, if the world is assumed as eternal, the true nature of the soul is obscured. On such an assumption we are driven to the choice of one of the three following errors: if the world is eternal an infinite number of human beings has existed, and therefore an infinite number of souls, unless either the soul is corruptible, or the same soul passes from one body to another, or there exists, for all human beings, but a single intelligence. If we follow the interpretation of Averroës, Aristotle would seem to have decided for this last error. Now, this second blindness leads necessarily to a third: since there exists only one soul for all men, there is consequently no personal immortality, and, therefore, there cannot be after this life either punishment or reward.

Let the reader imagine what the state of mind of the theologians and the Christian philosophers must have been when confronted with such a doctrine. We may leave aside all those who, on principle, maintained an attitude of irreconcilable suspicion to all philosophical speculation. This attitude, which in the 11th century had inspired the resistance to the dialectic movement, had lost none of its strength in the 13th and had never perhaps a better opportunity for display. But the great majority of theologians had not the slightest intention of denying the usefulness of philosophical speculation and among these a twofold tendency appears. The one, the smaller party, was so profoundly impressed by the Averroist Aristotelianism that they saw in this doctrine the final and complete truth. They accepted it, therefore, with all its inherent consequences and there were clerics who actually taught at Paris that there is no providence, that the world is eternal, that there is but a single intelligence for the whole human race and that, in short, there is for man neither freedom nor immortality. Such were Boëthius of Dacia and especially Siger of Brabant. The others, far more numerous, felt a repugnance, which varied much according to each mind, against these damnable innovations, and they entrenched themselves more strongly than ever behind the Platonic-Augustinian philosophy which, at that moment, was the only traditional philosophy of the Church. The most remarkable personality which we find among this party, is without a doubt St. Bonaventure. We saw how energetically this doctor maintained the Platonic exemplarism against Aristotle; he, and the whole Franciscan school with him, also maintained the Augustinian doctrine of illumination against the Aristotelian doctrine of abstraction; he affirmed the hierarchic plurality of forms against the unity of substantial form which seemed to him to compromise the immortality of the soul. Thus the attitude of St. Bonaventure remained in opposition to the doctrine of Aristotle, even though Aristotelian thought had at several points coloured his own thought unwittingly to himself.

But a third attitude yet remained possible. The doctrine of Aristotle—and this was evident to any Christian thinker—showed serious lacunae in its metaphysical parts. To say the least, this philosophy left the two problems of the creation and of the immortality of the soul in the air. On the other hand, the strictly physical and natural part of the doctrine presented a system incomparably superior to the fragmentary and little coherent solutions proposed by the older schoolmen. This superiority of the Aristotelian physics was so crushing that in the eyes of clear-sighted minds it could not fail to obtain the assent of reason and to secure the ultimate triumph of the doctrine. Was it therefore not an act of grave imprudence to persist in maintaining positions which were foredoomed to fall?

The triumph of Aristotle was inevitable, and wisdom urged that steps should be taken to make this triumph a help to Christian thought, rather than a menace. In other words, the task to be undertaken was to Christianise Aristotle: to re-introduce exemplarism and the creation into the system, to maintain providence, to reconcile the unity of substantial form with the immortality of the soul; to show, in short, that even accepting the Aristotelian physics, the great truths of Christianity remained unshaken; better still, to show that these great truths find in the physics of Aristotle their natural support and their strongest foundation. Such was the problem which it became a matter of urgency to solve.

It is impossible to doubt that the problem presented itself from this point of view to several of the theologians of the 13th century, for one need but consult their works to convince oneself that each in his own manner was pursuing its solution. On the other hand, it is very hard to discover what could have put the young Thomas of Aquino on the road to the very personal answer which he was to supply.

The simplest hypothesis, and consequently the most tempting, concerning the genesis of thomistic thought would be to look for the origin of it in the direction of theology. Since the point was to secure the accord of Aristotelian teaching with Faith, why should we not assume that a theologian like St. Thomas would have simply formulated the question in this way: What changes are necessary in Aristotelianism in order to harmonise it with the Christian dogma? At first sight this seems a very plausible hypothesis; but it encounters two very serious historical objections.

In the first place, it is very difficult to account by preoccupations of an exclusively theological nature for the genesis of a system which was bound to appear to the pure theologians as a dangerous innovation. If the young Thomas, essentially a theologian as he was and always remained, had not been actuated by more complex preoccupations, how would he ever have conceived the idea of reconstructing the entire system of theology on the foundations provided by a new philosophy? For the fact is that the thomistic reform was to proceed along the lines of the greatest theological resistance. Did it not mean consciously to run counter to the bitterest theological opposition to force upon the partisans of the traditional Augustinianism the notion that philosophy could be a science distinct from theology, without thereby endangering its legitimacy; to accustom the minds of his contemporaries to think along the lines of Aristotle instead of along those of Plato, when the great theological authority of St. Augustine seemed indissolubly linked with the platonic tradition; to abandon the conception of innate ideas and therewith every proof *a priori* of the existence of God, to define the human soul as a form, and as the unique form of the body, at the risk of being suspected of compromising thereby the immortality of the soul; to recast, finally, the whole system of the traditional theological truths without losing anything of the substance of any of them, while at the same time the formulation of all of them had to be modified? Indeed, having early become suspect in the eyes of the Augustinian partisans, attacked by the Franciscan John Peckham in 1270, declared suspect by the General Chapter of the Order in 1282, he is involved in the condemnation of the 219 Averroist and peripatetic articles which is passed by Etienne Tempier, Bishop of Paris, in 1277. Assailed by two mutually hostile parties, the Masters of the Faculty of Arts who had been won over to Averroism, and the Masters of the theological Faculty, who were the champions of traditionalism, we find him constantly engaged in maintaining against the partisans of Augustinianism what he considered true in the system of Aristotle, and in maintaining against the absolute Aristotelians the Christian truths unknown to Aristotelianism. This is the narrow ridge on which St. Thomas moves with incomparable sureness. The brilliant execution of his task masks for us to-day too easily the extreme difficulty he had to face, in maintaining his position, and the psychological improbability of a pure theologian ever attempting to take it up.

But such an interpretation would raise a second, still more serious difficulty. To present St. Thomas as a simple adaptor of Aristotle to theology, would imply, to start with, that he found Aristotle ready to hand— which would be a misconception of the characteristic form in which the whole problem presented itself to St. Thomas' contemporaries. Albert the Great has formulated it with delicious humour at a time when it was already more than half solved: all the Aristotelians are agreed that Aristotle has spoken the truth, but they all disagree about what Aristotle has said, and each interprets him in his own manner.[26] This is a complication the causes of which history enables us to lay bare; but it is important to bear it in mind in order to estimate at its proper value the work accomplished by St. Thomas.

It is a well-known fact that Aristotle presented himself to the medieval thinkers in the disguise of Arabic interpretations. At first sight there seemed to be no reason for removing this disguise.[27] The famous prohibition of Robert de Courçon in 1215 to comment on the Physics and Metaphysics of Aristotle "nec summae de eisdem"[28] is evidently aimed at works in which the thought of the philosopher was often confused with that of Averroës. But what has emerged only from recent researches on the 13th century is the capital rôle played by Avicenna and the extreme difficulty which the western thinkers experienced, of liberating themselves from his influence.[29] Imbued as he was with neoplatonic and even Christian notions quite as much as with Aristotelianism, this Arab philosopher presented under the name and authority of Aristotle an original system, expounded in a series of connected writings, not merely of commentaries, which produced a profound impression upon his Christian readers. Strange errors, it is true, could not fail, at first sight, to shock them and to repel them from a system which was so manifestly contrary to Faith; but the whole Plotinianism which inspired Avicenna adapted itself so easily to that form of it which had

formerly inspired St. Augustine and was so familiar to
them, that the possibility of reconciling the Aristotle
of Avicenna with the Christian Faith forced itself upon
their acceptance as an evident proposition. It may be
said that down to the time of St. Thomas, not excepting
even Albert the Great himself, the western philosophers
lived on the idea that Avicenna, but for a few gross but
easily removable errors, was on the right road. A substantial soul, mistress of the body of which it was only
secondarily the form, illuminated by the influence of
God, the first cause of our contingent Universe, was
not all this the essence of what a Christian philosophical
thought might require? With many different shadings
and in very different degrees, Guillaume d'Auvergne,
Alexander of Hales, St. Bonaventure, Roger Bacon and
Albert the Great certainly held this view with conviction.

Only later and through the influence which he had
increasingly acquired in the Faculty of Arts in Paris,
Averroës succeeded in inducing the theologians to devote
serious attention to an Aristotle different from that of
Avicenna. The impossibility of accepting the doctrine
as it stood, was even more evident here than in the other
case, and it has been explained above how this disagreement with Faith struck everyone. All the same Averroës
offered both a text of Aristotle together with his commentaries and not merely, like Avicenna, treatises inspired by Aristotle. Averroës' commentaries might be
systematic and tendencious, but he presented at the
same time the text and left readers free to compare text
and commentary. Now, it was impossible to compare
them without observing that Averroism and Avicennism
corresponded to two possible types of Aristotelianism,
but nevertheless remained wholly distinct from it;
other interpretations were conceivable, as legitimate as,
and possibly more so than, those which the Arabic
philosophers had championed. It is precisely this, the
original thought of Aristotle that the young Thomas of
Aquino seems to have set himself to reach, behind and
beyond the mass of commentary which obscured it.
We find him, all through his life, bent upon translation

direct from the Greek text of Aristotle itself as the subject-matter of his thought[30]; as regards the commentaries to it which he composed, there again his chief care is to recover the order of ideas, the technical sense of terms and the authentic meaning of the teaching that mainly inspired it. The chief object of St. Thomas appears to have been to understand rather than reconstruct, and the freedom of thought which benefited his own doctrine, was the result of his effort to eliminate all intermediaries between Aristotle and himself.

It is indeed remarkable to note that St. Thomas seems to have laid so great a stress upon the actual letter of Aristotle only in order to disentangle once and for all the spirit of him and freely to appropriate it for himself. Unfortunately the history of his own intellectual development is unknown to us and we have no means of formulating with certainty the problem upon the solution of which he must early have come. From the time of the "Commentary on the Sentences," we find him, except for an occasional detail and the sometimes rather Augustinian tone of his expression, in full possession of the fundamental principles of his philosophical teaching, so that the initial phases of his thought will probably for ever elude us. But many facts allow us to suppose that, in all probability, it was the dialectic arguments directed by Aristotle against Plato which early arrested the attention of the young friar. Nowhere better than in the First Book of the Metaphysics could the original spirit of Aristotelianism reveal itself to him with its assertion of a sensible world, endowed with reality, stability and intelligibility, as against Platonism which leaves to things only the appearance of being and confines intelligibility to a world from which we are excluded. It would not be impossible to show that, in more than one respect, the thomistic philosophy is the continuation and amplification in the 13th century of the struggle which Aristotle originally began against Plato. Plato is the objective of St. Thomas' attacks behind Avicenna, Ibn Gabirol and even St. Augustine[31]; it is in opposition to him that he denies innate ideas, rejects the proofs *a priori* of the existence of God, denies the need of a special illumination of the intellect by divine ideas, refuses to consider the soul as a substance subsisting *per se* and independently of the body to which it is bound, maintains the efficacy of secondary causes in a universe whose very texture is made up of the relations of a real causality between beings. The universe of Plato remains for St. Thomas one in which we shall one day be called to live; but he refuses to see in it that in which we live now. By a reform converse to that carried out by his master, he places into heaven the Ideas which Aristotle had brought down upon earth, but he leaves sensible things in possession of their forms as real participations of the Ideas.

This is an essentially philosophical change of perspective which cannot be said to have been unprepared and yet can be said to have been accomplished only by St. Thomas. Many works anterior to him might have suggested this new orientation of his mind towards it. Not only Abelard and Gilbert de la Porrée in the 12th century,[32] but also the masters immediately preceding him against whom he reacted, could not but suggest to him a new solution of the problems that had engaged their attention. Guillaume d'Auvergne, Alexander of Hales and Albert the Great are indeed visibly interested to maintain against the Arabs the substantiality and efficacy of secondary causes, of which the individual human beings are only a special case.[33] But what they failed to see and what St. Thomas saw immediately, was that it was impossible to make an effective defence against the Arabs by relying on St. Augustine, because Augustinianism and Arabic thought both rested in their common foundation upon the same philosophy, that of Plato. St. Augustine might, it is true, furnish weapons against the enemies of Divine efficacy; but he himself was poorly protected against the enemies of the efficacy of secondary causes. What, in short, was needed, was the construction of a doctrine of the Real beyond all authorities and local scholastic traditions. The young Thomas of Aquino presents himself therefore, first and foremost, as a philosopher who, taking the part of Aristotle against Plato, was inevitably bound to depart from St. Augustine. Perhaps the greatest difficulty for us is to understand how this philosopher was by the very fact a Christian philosopher, without however ceasing to be himself, or more exactly precisely because he had to be Christian in order to be fully himself.

C. THE CHRISTIAN DOCTOR.

The personality of St. Thomas exceeds the limits of this study in three of his most important aspects. The saint that he was, belongs properly to hagiography; the theologian would require a special treatment, conducted on its own appropriate method, the result of which would by rights occupy the first place in a comprehensive study of St. Thomas; the mystic and his inner life elude very largely our grasp; the only aspect that concerns us here, is the intelligence and activity which he placed at the service of philosophy. Fortunately it happens that one of the aspects of his life involves almost equally all the activities of this many-sided personality and seems to represent the most central point of view which we can take up in respect to it. The most evident and most constant element of his personality, the form under which there is the greatest likelihood that he thought of himself, is that of the "Doctor."[34] The saint was essentially a Doctor of the Church; the man was a Doctor of theology and philosophy; the mystic, lastly, never separated entirely his meditations from his teaching which drew its inspiration from them. We shall, therefore, run but little risk of losing our way in looking in that direction for one of the principal sources of the doctrine which is the object of our study.[35]

Man can choose only between two kinds of life: the active and the contemplative life.[36] What imparts to the activities of the Doctor their outstanding dignity, is that they involved both kinds of life, lived in the order of their precise subordination. The proper function of a "Doctor" is to teach: but teaching ("doctrina") consists

in communicating to others the truths which have been
the subject of one's previous meditation,[37] which involves
both contemplative reflexion in order to discover the
truth, and the functions of the professor in order to
convey to others the results of these discoveries. But
the most remarkable feature in this complex activity is
that the higher function precisely takes precedence over
the lower, contemplation over action. Thus the function
of a Doctor, as just defined, is naturally orientated
towards a twofold object, interior and exterior, according
as it is directed to the truth which the Doctor meditates
and contemplates within himself, or to the pupils whom
he instructs. Hence of the two sides of his life the former
is the better, which it is his task to direct.

Now we see that the function of the Doctor is not
simply an artificial adjunct to his contemplative life; it
derives, on the contrary, from it as from its source and is, as
it were, its outward unfolding. His teaching, as well as
his preaching which is its kindred action, belong indeed
to the work of the active life, but they flow in some
manner from the very abundance of his contemplation.[38]
Hence his teaching cannot even be regarded as in any
sense a real interruption of his contemplative life. A
man who withdraws himself from the meditation of
intelligible realities which feed his contemplative
thought, to turn to works even though good, yet purely
external, makes a complete break in his contemplation.
It is an excellent thing to distribute alms or to entertain
strangers, but to do so, nevertheless, makes all meditation, properly so-called, impossible. To teach, on the
contrary, is to utter outwardly the inner contemplation,
and if it is true that a soul truly free from temporal
interests, preserves in each of its outward acts something of the freedom acquired, there is certainly no other
activity where this freedom can more perfectly be
preserved than in the act of teaching.[39] To combine in
this manner the active with the contemplative life means
not a subtraction but an addition. It is, moreover,
evident that in no other manner can the balance more
perfectly be kept between these two kinds of life, to

maintain which must needs be the object of our actual human state.[40] To teach the truth which meditation has shown to us, is a relaxation of contemplation without any loss of it, but on the contrary with an increase of its best part.

Several important consequences follow from this which enable us to determine the precise part which St. Thomas assumed in taking upon himself the high function of a Christian Doctor. This is a function, indeed, peculiarly appropriate to the religious state[41] and specially to an Order which was at the same time a teaching and a contemplative Order, like that of St. Dominic. St. Thomas has never tired of defending against all the attacks of seculars the legitimacy of the ideal to which he had devoted his life, that of a mendicant and teaching friar. If anyone contested the right to absolute poverty, he called to witness the example of the ancient philosophers who renounced all riches to devote themselves all the more freely to the contemplation of truth. How much more urgent was not such a renunciation for him, who wished to follow not only wisdom, but Christ, according to the saying of St. Jerome, addressed to the monk Rusticus: "Christum nudum nudus sequere"?[42] If anyone attacks the legitimacy of accepting an honour such as that of Mastership or a title such as Master, St. Thomas replies with much common-sense that a Mastership is not an honour but a charge,[43] and that, the title of Master not being taken but given, it would be difficult to prevent others from giving it to you.[44] If lastly it was urged that the true religious is bound to do manual work which in its requirements goes badly with the requirements of meditation and teaching, St. Thomas has plenty of distinctions to suggest in order to free himself from so evidently subordinate an occupation and to replace it by the "oral work" of teaching and preaching.[45] Nothing could, in his eyes, be more legitimate than a religious Order both contemplative and teaching.

Nor could anything be more legitimate, nor even more desirable for a member of such an Order than to aim at the activities of a Doctor and to spend his life in carrying them into effect. Doubtless, the part of a Master is not without its dangers. There are those who teach all their life for mere vainglory, instead of for the good of others, and who, therefore, lead a life unworthy of the true religious.[46] But he who is conscious of giving his teaching as an act of kindness and true spiritual charity, need have no scruples in desiring to lead such a life. An objection which was constantly raised by the seculars against the religious, aspiring to the position of Master, was: How can you reconcile the humility of the friar with the claim to authority?[47] St. Thomas disposed of it in perfect accordance with the position occupied by the Masters of the University of Paris and by distinguishing carefully between the situation of a candidate to a professorial chair and that of a candidate to a bishopric. He who aspires to an episcopal place, desires a dignity which is not yet in his possession: but a person on whom a professorial chair is conferred, does not, in fact, receive a new dignity, but merely an opportunity of communicating his knowledge to others; to grant a licentiate to someone does not in any sense mean to grant him knowledge, but the right to teach what he knows. A second difference between the two instances is that the knowledge required for the occupation of a professorial chair is a perfection of the individual person possessing the knowledge, whereas the episcopal power adds to the dignity of its possessor in respect to others. A third difference is that a man is fitted to receive the episcopal dignity foremost by Divine Grace, while it is knowledge which fits a person for the office of teacher. Hence the radical difference between the two cases cannot fail to be clear to anyone: it is praiseworthy to desire one's own perfection, therefore, also knowledge and teaching for which one is fitted by it, whereas it is bad to desire power over others without knowing whether one is in possession of the Grace needed for its exercise. On the other hand, the desire to teach, that is to communicate to others the knowledge one has, is merely the desire to perform an act of charity: nothing could therefore be

more praiseworthy than the wish to be authorised to do
so, always provided that one is really capable of it.
Again, as regards this latter point, the position is clear
and defined. No one can know of certain knowledge
whether or no he possesses the Grace which is wholly
in the gift of God; but anyone can know for certain
whether or no he possesses the knowledge required for
the legitimate exercise of teaching.[48] It is, therefore,
with the full assurance of possessing the necessary
knowledge and from love of the minds he desires to
enlighten that St. Thomas devoted the whole of his life
to the activity of teacher. The contemplation of truth
by thought uttered for the sake of charity and communicated: such is the life of the Doctor, the least unfaithful,
however deficient, human imitation of the very life of
God.

Withal, we have to beware of a possible equivocation
which might blur the precise sense of St. Thomas' words.
Whenever he speaks of the Doctor or the Master, we
think first of the philosopher, whereas his first thought is
of the theologian. The "Master" *par excellence* cannot but
teach the wisdom *par excellence*, i.e. the science of Divine
things, which is essentially theology. This is also the
only Mastership to which a religious can legitimately
aspire. When, therefore, St. Thomas sings the praises of
a life divided between teaching and the contemplation
which inspires it, he thinks primarily of this; it is for its
sake that he demands the manifold Graces needful to the
Doctor[49]: a full knowledge of the Divine things on
which he is to instruct others conferred on him by Faith;
power of persuasion and demonstration in order to convince others of the truth, assisted by the gift of Wisdom;
aptitude to develop his ideas and to express them in a
form suited to the instruction of others, aided by the
gift of Knowledge[50]: wisdom and knowledge directed
above all else to the understanding of Divine things and
placed at the service of their teaching. If we wish,
therefore, to look for the Doctor of philosophical truth
in the complex personality of St. Thomas, it is only
in the theologian that we can hope to find him.

In thus going back to the definition which he himself has given of his own function, we find on last analysis nothing but a philosopher inseparable from a theologian. This is an abstract formula, inadequate through its very indefiniteness, since the most diverse doctrines have been able to appeal to it with perfect justice; yet it is a formula which needs to be considered first in all its bareness, with all the demands it implies, in order to avoid certain serious errors concerning the meaning of thomistic thought.

A religious, St. Thomas considers, can legitimately aspire to the title and functions of a Master, but since he teaches nothing but Divine things, secular science can be of interest to him only in reference to these. This is the demand, in fact, made by the very essence of the contemplative life whose direct prolongation into the sphere of the active life constitutes teaching. Contemplation is the highest form of human life on condition that it is centred upon the object, the knowledge of which is the end of that life; knowledge and contemplation which in the future life will be perfect and will give us full beatitude, cannot but be imperfect in this life and can carry with them only the beginnings of beatitude. Yet it is best for us to enjoy it, and the use of philosophy is both legitimate and necessary as a condition of this supreme contemplation. Now, we shall have to observe that in the actual conditions of man, all knowledge rests fundamentally on the order of sensible things: hence the Doctor of theology must start inevitably from a scientific and philosophical knowledge of the universe, in order to rise to his proper object, which is the contemplation of God; but it is only in proportion as this knowledge can give him access to the higher wisdom that it is permissible for him to labour at acquiring it.[51] We may, therefore, say that a philosophy is a strict requirement for the Christian Doctor, but that, however useful, this philosophy cannot itself be its own end.

What then is this philosophy? St. Thomas has never practised or conceived it, except in its proper place within the hierarchic structure of Christian Wisdom,

and therefore, no doubt, it never occurred to him to
detach it from it and to give it a special name. Yet it might
have a name, because it existed and had a name long
before St. Thomas transformed it and marked it so
deeply with his impress: it is the "Christian Philosophy."[52]
We mean by this a philosophy which intends to be a
rational interpretation of data, but considers as the
essential element of these data the religious Faith, the
object of which is defined by the Christian revelation.
Within such a doctrine the rôle assigned to reason and
the place assigned to philosophy may vary endlessly:
St. Augustine, St. Bonaventure, Pascal will incline to
treat secular knowledge with suspicion and to expect
from this handmaid a service kept under strict surveil-
lance; Clement of Alexandria, John Damascene, Albert
the Great, St. Thomas of Aquino, Roger Bacon will, on the
contrary, give it wider scope; but all are agreed on the
essential point, namely, that there is a Christian philosophy, that is to say, a philosophy directed towards an
object which eludes its grasp, but from which, knowing
that it exists, it cannot turn away. Destined to fall short
of its object, it will find a foothold, in some manner,
upon the prolongation of the ideal roads which lead to
it. Without consenting to deform in any way the
natural aspect of things and still less the true knowledge
which we have of them, it claims to possess in the little
that it can grasp of an object actually inaccessible, a
principle of selection and of order for that knowledge
which reason supplies.

Such at least, it seems to us, must be the point of
view to be adopted, unless we are prepared to turn two
grave historical problems into as many insoluble riddles:
how did St. Thomas conceive the work which it was his
mission to accomplish? What is the thomistic philosophy?

Upon the first point, it is impossible to pursue research honestly to its last consequences without coming
to the conclusion that the philosophical problems which
St. Thomas undertook to examine, were and always remained for him strictly philosophical problems; and yet

we should have to run counter to his most express statements and his clearly stated intentions, if we denied that his whole philosophy is consciously ordered towards the sphere of revelation and of Faith. As regards the second point, it is clear that St. Thomas recognised in the strictest possible manner the real distinction between philosophy and theology. Nothing is easier than to sketch the ideal plan of a pure philosophy such as St. Thomas himself has conceived, approximately such as Aristotle had already carried out[53]; and yet St. Thomas never troubled to realise it himself or to carry out the plan he had drawn so well. It has therefore all the appearance as if St. Thomas had had the idea of constituting a system of purely rational truths which, precisely because rational, fit of themselves into the doctrinal structure of Revelation. Thence flows for the historian the important consequence that, to present under the name of thomistic philosophy a system which St. Thomas has neither known nor intended, because it would have proved to be built upon the plan of a pure philosophy, would mean not only to present a mere phantom in place of an historical reality, but also to misconceive the original inspiration of Thomism in its most intimate and deepest elements. It would mean to forget what St. Thomas was and consciously wanted to be: a Christian Doctor.

In what manner a philosophy can be Christian without ceasing *pro tanto* to be a philosophy, must be the next object of our study.

NOTES TO CHAPTER I.

1. Concerning the biography of St. Thomas we follow the chronology of P. Mandonnet, *Chronologie sommaire de la vie et des écrits de saint Thomas*, Rev. des sciences phil. et théol., 1920, p. 142–152. Cf. *Bibliographie thomiste*, Introduction, p. ix–xi. For a series of important articles by P. Mandonnet on the life of St. Thomas cf. Rev. thomiste and Rev. des Jeunes, May, June, 1919; 25 Jan., 10 March, 1920.

2. As regards the works of St. Thomas (authenticity and chronology), cf. especially P. Mandonnet, *Des écrits authen-*

tiques de saint Thomas d'Aquin, Fribourg, 1909, 2nd ed., 1910. Some of his conclusions have been contested by M. Grabmann, *Die echten Schriften des hl. Thomas von Aquin*, Beiträge Cl. Baeumker, XXII, 1-2, Münster, 1920; A. Birkenmayer, *Kleinere Thomasfragen*, Phil. Jahrb. Bd. 34, H. 1, p. 31-49. The whole question has been taken up afresh, from the methodological point of view, by Fr. Pelster, *Zur Forschung nach den echten Schriften des hl. Thomas von Aquin*, Phil. Jahrb., Bd. 36; H. 1, p. 36-49. The problem of the Quodlibets is the subject of an important comprehensive study by P. J.-A. Destrez, *Les disputes quodlibétiques de saint Thomas d'après la tradition manuscrite*, Mélanges thomistes (Bibl. thomiste, III), Le Saulchoir, Kain, 1923. Cf. also Bibl. thomiste, nos. 556, 557. As to works dealing with the Summa theol., see nos. 526ff.

3. Roccasecca lies at kilom. 121 on the railway from Rome to Naples; Aquino, the home of Juvenal before it became that of St. Thomas, lies at kilom. 126; a little further, on the top of a bare ridge, one sees the Abbey of Montecassino,. 138 km. from Rome and 111 km. from Naples.

4. Legend has chosen an hermit, fra Buono, as the mouthpiece of popular opinion, in making him prophesy, at the birth of the child, that his parents would entertain this scheme: "ad magnos ipsius monasterii reditus pervenire." See L.-H. Petitot, *Saint Thomas d'Aquin. La vocation. L'œuvre. La vie spirituelle.* Ed. by the Rev. des Jeunes, 1923, p. 14-16.

5. The presentation of a child of 5 years by his parents as an oblate monk ("Pater dicti fr. Thomae *monachavit* eum puerum," says Bartolomeo of Capua) in a Benedictine Abbey may seem curious. St. Thomas always considered that his father had an absolute right to do so: "quia pueri quousque ad annos discretionis pervenerint, sunt secundum jus naturale in potestate parentum." Quodlib., III, art. 11, concl. He even considered that it was an excellent thing for the child's soul: "considerandum est pueros etiam infra annos pubertatis in religionem recipi non esse secundum se malum, immo est expediens et fructuosum, quia illud quod a pueritia assuescimus, semper perfectius et firmius tenemus," Quodlib., IV, art. 23, concl. For the same reason, he thinks (*ibid.* ad *Sed quod ulterius*), that it is not only right but praiseworthy that the child should bind itself by a vow: "Cum ergo bonum sit quod pueri ad religionem veniant, multo melius est quod eorum voluntas sit ad hoc firmata, quod fit voto vel juramento." It is, of course, not a question here of solemn vows, but of a simple vow to enter religion. Cf. *Summa theol.*, IIaIIae, qu. 189, art. 2, ad 1um; and *ibid.*, art 1 on the whole question.

6. Cf. L.-H. Petitot, *op. cit.*, pp. 17-19.

7. Cf. Denifle, *Die Universitäten des Mittelalters bis 1400*, Berlin, 1885, p. 453. The establishment of a studium generale at Naples by Frederic II goes back to 1224. Concerning the teachers of St. Thomas at the University, cf. Cl. Baeumker, *Petrus de Hibernia, der Jugendlehrer des Thomas von Aquino und seine Disputation vor König Manfred* (Sitzgsber. d. Bayer. Akad. d. Wissensch. philos. phil. u. hist. Kl., 1920, Abh. 8). An Italian translation has appeared in Rivista di filosofia neo-scolastica, 1921, fasc. 2 and 5.

8. This, in fact, is all we know. Baeumker has found in a "determinatio" of Peter of Ireland the proof that he interpreted Aristotle on the lines of Averroes rather than of Avicenna; whence he draws the conclusion (*op. cit.*, pp. 35–40), that St. Thomas received the first suggestion to abandon the Avicennism professed by Albert the Great from his first teacher. But this "determinatio," if it is really that of St. Thomas' teacher, dates from a time about 15 years after he had him as pupil, i.e. from a time when St. Thomas had already written his *Commentary on the Sentences*, his *De ente et essentia* and was working at his *Contra gentes* (*op. cit.*, p. 10, 34–35). Between 1244 and 1260 the Averroist interpretation of Aristotle had become sufficiently general to make the assumption more probable that Peter of Ireland was simply following the general movement at the same time as his former pupil. The fact that St. Thomas has written an extract from the Sophistici elenchi (p. 35, note 1) immediately after the interruption of his Neapolitan studies, merely proves that he had even then been taught the logic of Aristotle (which had been called in question), and nothing more. The tendency to think that the most recently discovered unedited writing must solve necessarily all sorts of important questions, is only natural; the fact that the "disputatio" published by Baeumker is later than 1244 detracts from it as a source of information about the teaching which St. Thomas received at Naples.

9. Later, towards 1263, King Manfred, King of Sicily, presented to the University of Paris a number of philosophical writings recently translated by his order (cf. Denifle-Chatelain, *Chartularium*, t. I, pp. 435–6). On the influence of the Hohenstaufen on the dissemination of the works of Aristotle, see Amable Jourdain, *Recherches critiques sur l'âge et l'origine des traductions latines d'Aristote*, ed. 2, Paris, 1843, pp. 50–51, 152–165.

10. Fr. Pelster, S. J., in his *Kritische Studien zum Leben u. zu den Schriften Alberts des Grossen*, Freiburg i. Breisg., Herder, 1920, pp. 62–84, admits on the contrary that St. Thomas went

direct from Italy to Cologne, where he heard Albert the Great before the latter's departure for Paris. He himself is said to have come to Paris only in 1252. On this view, which accords with the evidence of ancient biographers, but raises, nevertheless, a number of difficulties, see Paulus de Loë, O.P., *De vita et scriptis B. Alberti Magni*, Analecta Bolland., 1900, T. 19, p. 259, No. 2; Petitot, *op. cit.*, p. 36, note.

11. P. Mandonnet has repeatedly defined this point of view, *Siger de Brabant. Etude critique*, Louvain, 1911, pp. 39–42. *Saint Thomas d'Aquin. Le disciple d'Albert le Grand*, Rev. des Jeunes, 25 Jan., 1920, p. 153–155. We have ourselves also dealt with it in *La philosophie au moyen-âge*, Paris, 1922, t. II, pp. 4–5.

12. Cf. sect. B, p. 20.

13. *Chartularium Universitatis parisiensis*, ed. Denifle-Chatelain, t. I, p. 307. The letter of Alexander IV, praising Aymery, the Chancellor, for having conferred the licentiate on fr. Thomas is dated 3 March, 1256. An earlier letter, actually lost, urged the Chancellor to do so.

14. "Delectabile nobis est auditu percipere ... quod dilecto filio fratri Thome de Aquino Ordinis Praedicatorum, viro utique nobilitate generis et morum honestate conspicuo ac thesaurum litteralis scientie per Dei gratiam assecuto, dedisti licentiam in theologica facultate docendi, priusquam illuc nostre littere pervenirent, quas tibi super hoc specialiter mittebamus" (*ibid*).

15. The letter M after a date means a date suggested by P. Mandonnet, the letter G a date proposed by Mgr. Grabmann.

16. Mgr. Grabmann has since put the writing of the Commentary on the Metaphysics back to 1266; Augustin Mansion, *Pour l'histoire du commentaire de St. Thomas sur la métaphysique d'Aristote*, Rev. néoscolast. de phil., Aug., 1925, pp. 274–295, places it in the year, 1271–1272.

17. The treatise, rejected by P. Mandonnet, but retained by Mgr. Grabmann, seems to us not only authentic, but a fundamental text for the thomistic epistemology.

18. Cf. Fr. Pelster, Phil. Jahrb., 1923, vol. 36, p. 42. This treatise, rejected by P. Mandonnet and Mgr. Grabmann, appears to us, as to Fr. Pelster, undoubtedly authentic.

19. Cf. Destrez, *op. cit.*, p. 74.

20. Cf. J.-A. Endres: *Petrus Damiani und die weltliche Wissenschaft*, Beitr. z. Gesch. d. Phil. d. Mitt., VIII, 3, Münster, 1910; *Forschungen zur Gesch. d. frühmitt. Philosophie*, *ibid.*, XVII, 2–3, 1914.

21. Cf. M. de Wulf, *Histoire de la phil. médiévale*; 4th ed., pp. 141–147.

22. Cf. Duhem, *Du temps où la scolastique latine a connu la physique*

d'Aristote, Rev. de phil., 1909, pp. 162–178.

23. De Wulf, *op. cit.*, p. 156.

24. On this point, see esp. Mandonnet, *Siger de Brabant et l'averroisme latin*, "Les Philosophes belges," t. VI, pp. 1–63, Louvain, 1911; M. Grabmann, *Forschungen über d. lat. Aristoteles Übersetzungen des XIII. Jahrhdts*, Beitr., XVII, 5–6, Münster, 1916.

25. *In Hexaemeron*, collatio VI, *Opera omnia*, ed. Quaracchi, t. V, pp. 360–361. Mandonnet, *op. cit.*, p. 157, note, refers also on this point to Henry of Ghent: *Quodlibeta*, IX, qu. 14 and 16. Cf. E. Gilson, *La philosophie de saint Bonaventure* (Études de phil. méd., IV), Paris, Vrin, 1925, p. 99.

26. Albertus Magnus, *De anima*, lib. III, tr. 2, cap. 3; in *Opera omnia*, ed. Jammy, t. III, p. 135.

27. Amable Jourdain, *op. cit.*, pp. 193 and 199.

28. Denifle-Chatelain, *Chartularium*, t. I, pp. 78–79.

29. Cl. Baeumker, *Petrus de Hibernia*, *op. cit.*, pp. 31–32.

30. The whole series of translations of Aristotle by the Dominican William of Moerbeke marks a fundamental date in the history of medieval Aristotelianism. Now St. Thomas himself seems to have been the prime mover in the matter; cf. Amable Jourdain, *op. cit.*, pp. 67–75.

31. See on the point the decisive text in *De spiritualibus creaturis*, art. X, ad 8m.

32. Dehove, *Qui praecipui fuerint labente XII° sec. ante introductam Arabum philosophiam temperati realismi antecessores*, Lille, 1908.

33. Apart from Christian thought, a special place must be reserved, among the sources of St. Thomas, to the influence of Moses Maimonides. On a good many points the position of the "Rabbi Moses" prepares that adopted by Thomism and their respective interpretation of Aristotle is often analogous. Maimonides is opposed to the Arabic "motecallemin" (theologians) just as St. Thomas opposes the Augustinian traditionalists; their mental attitude, positive and full of common-sense, is singularly akin and the study of their relationship would be worthy of an exhaustive treatment. Cf. J. Guttmann, *Das Verhältnis des Thomas von Aquino zum Judentum*, Göttingen, 1891; L.-G. Levy, *Maimonide* (Les Grands Philosophes), Paris, 1911, pp. 265–267.

34. St. Thomas himself has declared, in adopting a saying of St. Hilary, that his main business in life is to speak of God: "Ut enim verbis Hilarii (*De Trin.*, I, 37) utar, ego hoc vel praecipuum vitae meae officium debere me Deo conscius sum, ut eum omnis sermo meus et sensus loquatur," *Contra Gent.*, I, 2.

35. Cf. on this A. Touron, *La vie de St. Thomas d'Aquin* . . .

avec un exposé de sa doctrine et ses ouvrages, Paris, 1737; esp. bk. IV, chap. ii and iii: Portrait of the perfect Doctor according to St. Thomas. On the mystical side of his personality, cf. *Saint Thomas d'Aquin. Sa sainteté, sa doctrine spirituelle*, "Les Grands Mystiques," ed. of the *Vie spirituelle*, Saint-Maximin. Joret, O.P., *La contemplation mystique d'après saint Thomas d'Aquin*, Desclée, Lille-Bruges, 1924. This is a very penetrating study equally useful concerning his personality as concerning his mysticism. Also consult *Bibliographie thomiste*, pp. 70–72.

36. See on this point, Chapter II.

37. "Ergo quod aliquis veritatem meditatam in alterius notitiam per doctrinam deducat...," *Sum. theo.*, IIaIIae, qu. 181, art. 3,3a obj. Cf. *ibid.* on what follows.

38. "Sic ergo dicendum est, quod opus vitae activae est duplex: unum quidem, quod ex plenitudine contemplationis derivatur, sicut doctrina et praedicatio...; et hoc praefertur simplici contemplationi: sicut enim majus est illuminare quam lucere solum, ita majus est contemplata aliis tradere, quam solum contemplari." *Sum. theol.*, IIaIIae, 188, 6, concl.

39. *Sum. theol.*, IIaIIae, 182, 1, concl. and ad 3m. See esp. the conclusion of the article: "Et sic patet quod cum aliquis a contemplativa vita ad activam vocatur, non hoc fit per modum subtractionis, sed per modum additionis."

40. On the diversity of natural aptitudes for the active and contemplative life, see *Sum. theol.*, IIaIIae, qu. 182, art. 4, ad 3m.

41. *Sum. theol.*, IIaIIae, 188, 6, ad *Resp.* It is there shown that the contemplative and teaching Orders are of a dignity superior to the merely contemplative Orders, and take their place, in the ecclesiastical hierarchy immediately after the bishops, because "fines primorum conjunguntur principiis secundorum."

42. *Sum. theol.*, IIaIIae, 186, 3, ad 3m.

43. *Contra impugnantes Dei cultum et religionem*, cap. II: "Item hoc falsum est, quod magisterium sit honor; est enim officium, cui debetur honor."

44. *Ibid.*, cap. II, ad *Ita, cum nomina* and *Restat ergo dicendum*.

45. *Sum. theol.*, IIaIIae, 187, art. 3, ad 3m. *Quaest. quodlib.*, VII, art. 17 and 18. *Contr. impug. Dei cult. et rel.*, cap. II, ad *Item, sicut probandum est*, where teaching is counted as spiritual almsgiving and a work of mercy. Cf. cap. V.

46. The following curious question was put to St. Thomas: Can a teacher who has always taught out of sheer vainglory recover a claim to his halo by doing penance? Answer: Penance gives a claim to the reward which one deserves; but he who teaches out of vainglory has not deserved a halo;

hence no penance would confer on him the claim to recover it. *Quodlib.*, XII, art 24.

47. *Quodlib.*, III, qu. IV, art. 9: "Utrum liceat alicui petere licentiam pro se docendi in theologia."

48. "Nam scientia, per quam aliquis est idoneus ad docendum, potest aliquis scire per certitudinem se habere; charitatem autem, per quam aliquis est idoneus ad officium pastorale, non potest aliquis per certitudinem scire se habere." *Quodlib.*, III, art. 9, ad *Resp.* Cf. ad 3m: "Sed pericula magisterii cathedrae pastoralis devitat scientia cum charitate, quam homo nescit se per certitudinem habere; pericula autem magisterii cathedrae magistralis vitat homo per scientiam, quam potest homo scire se habere."

49. *Sum. theol.*, IaIIae, 111, 4, ad *Resp.* Cf. *In evang. Matth.*, c. V.

50. On this see *Sum. theol.*, IIaIIae, 177, 1, ad *Resp.*

51. *Sum. theol.*, IIaIIae, 180, 4, ad *Resp.*

52. This is the expression used by P. Touron, who had so precise as appreciation of thomistic thought. See *op. cit.*, p. 450.

53. See on this point the observation of P. Mandonnet in Bulletin thomiste, Nov., 1924, pp. 135–6.

CHAPTER II. FAITH AND REASON
THE OBJECT OF PHILOSOPHY

IF our analysis had for its object a modern philosophical system, our first task would be to determine the concept of human knowledge held by our philosopher. The task is not quite the same when we begin the study of a philosophical theologian of the Middle Ages. For St. Thomas, as for all the Christian doctors—one might add, for the Arabic and Jewish doctors as well—another problem takes precedence over that of human knowledge: namely, the problem of the relations between Reason and Faith. Whereas the philosopher as such professes to draw truth from the spring of Reason alone, the philosophical theologian draws truth from two different sources: from Reason, and—since he is a theologian—from Faith in the truth revealed by God, and its interpreter, the Church. Hence an initial difficulty has to be faced: what are the respective spheres of Reason and of Faith? Must the one be sacrificed to the other or can they be harmonised?

Nothing is easier than to distinguish from an abstract point of view philosophy and theology, the one consisting in the pursuit of truth by means of Reason, the other taking as point of departure a fact independent of Reason, viz. the Revelation given by God to the human mind of truths superior to Reason, i.e. truths which unaided Reason would be unable to reach, or even understand once it possessed them, or consequently justify. In practice, when beginning the study of St. Thomas, considerable difficulties have to be surmounted. Of the same texts different historians, when asked to distinguish the philosophical from the theological matter, neither retain nor abandon always the same points.

The explanation is that two attitudes are possible behind which lies, more or less skilfully hidden under the cloak of historical impartiality, a philosophical thesis of a, strictly speaking, dogmatic kind.

The one attitude, very widespread in certain circles and almost popular, is simply to neglect St. Thomas, because, since he is *also* a theologian, the conclusion is drawn that whatever philosophical matter his work contains, must necessarily therefore be tainted. This *a priori* assertion, based on the demands of an uncompromising rationalism, assumes that the philosopher cannot come into contact nor especially collaborate with the theologian, without being discredited by that very fact.

Another attitude, opposed to the former, but perhaps no less widespread, though held in different circles, consists in admitting that the philosophy of St. Thomas, *de jure* and *de facto*, exists in and by itself, independently of the theological speculation with which it may eventually be associated. We are told, that if Thomism is true, this can only be for exclusively philosophical reasons with which dogma has nothing whatever to do. When in an exposition of his teaching, a dogma appears on the sky-line or elements belonging to Revelation are introduced, the well-known warning is uttered: you misunderstand the true thought of St. Thomas, you confuse philosophy and theology. It is, of course, easy to see that this second attitude, though in practice opposed to the first, argues all the same from the same principle.

One might, at least provisionally, adopt a third attitude, and, without attempting to judge, enquire what are the relations of philosophy and theology in the system of St. Thomas. When he took up this problem himself, a solution of it had for some time back been prepared by the Catholic doctors[1]; but the answer which he himself gives offers some very original features and as soon as we analyse the grounds on which he rests his solution, we shall see some of the principles at work on which his whole system is based.

First, what is the object of metaphysics which is still called "the first philosophy" or "wisdom"? Following the common usage, a "sage" is one who can arrange things as they ought to be arranged and can handle them well. To arrange and handle a thing well, means to dispose it with a view to its end. Hence we find that in the hierarchy of arts, one art governs another and furnishes, in a sense, its principle, when the immediate end of the first constitutes the ultimate end of the second. Thus medicine is a principal and directive art in relation to pharmacy, because health, which is the immediate end of medicine, is at the same time the end of all the remedies prepared by the pharmacist. These principal and directive arts receive the name of "architectonic" arts, and the man who exercises them is called a "sage." But he deserves the title of "sage" only in respect of the very things which he is able to handle in view of their end. His wisdom, bearing on particular or partial ends, is only a particular or partial wisdom. If we imagine, on the contrary, a sage who proposes to consider not such and such a particular end, but the end of all things: he would not be called a sage in such and such an art, but an absolute sage. He would be the sage *par excellence*. The real object of wisdom, or of the first philosophy, is therefore the end of the universe, and, since the end of an object is the same as its principle or cause, we meet again the definition of Aristotle: the first philosophy has for its object the study of first causes.[2]

Let us now consider which is the first cause or the final end of the universe. The final cause of a thing is evidently that which its author, in making it, or the first mover, in moving it, has in view. Now, it will be shown that the first Author and first Mover of the universe is an intelligence; the end, therefore, which he has in view in creating or setting in motion the universe, must be the end or good of intelligence, i.e. truth. Thus truth is the final end of the universe, and, since the object of the first philosophy is the ultimate end of the universe, it follows that its proper object is truth.[3] But here we must beware of a confusion. Since it is the philosopher's business to attain to the ultimate end and consequently the first cause of the universe, the truth in question cannot be just *any* truth; it can be only *that* truth which is the first source of all truth. Now, the disposition of things in the order of truth is the same as that in the order of being (*sic enim est dispositio rerum in veritate sicut in esse*), since being and truth are equivalent. A truth which is to be the source of all truth can be found only in a being which must be first source of all being. The truth, therefore, which forms the object of a first philosophy, should be that truth which the Word, made flesh, manifested to the world, according to the words of St. John: "Ego in hoc natus sum et ad hoc veni in mundum, ut testimonium perhibeam veritati."[4] In one word, the true object of metaphysics is God.[5]

This determination set out by St. Thomas at the opening of the "Summa contra Gentiles" in no way contradicts that which leads him elsewhere to define metaphysics as the science of being and of its first causes.[6] If the immediate matter upon which the enquiry of the metaphysician is directed, is indeed "being in general," it constitutes none the less its true end. The object to which philosophical speculation tends, beyond "being in general," is the first cause of all being: *Ipsa prima philosophia tota ordinatur ad Dei cognitionem sicut ad ultimum finem; unde et scientia divina nominatur.* Therefore, when St. Thomas speaks in his own name, he leaves aside the consideration of being as such and defines metaphysics from the point of view of its supreme object: the first principle of being which is God.

What are our means to attain to this object? We have, first—and this is obvious—Reason at our disposal. The question is whether our Reason is an instrument sufficient to reach the goal of metaphysical enquiry, namely, the Divine essence. Let us say at once that natural Reason, left to itself, allows us to attain to certain truths concerning God and His nature. Philosophers are able to establish by demonstration that God exists, that He is one, etc. But it must also appear as evident that certain forms of knowledge concerning the Divine nature exceed by far the forces of human understanding. This is a point which it is important to establish in order to silence unbelievers who consider as false all assertions in respect of God which our Reason is unable to establish. Here the Christian sage must join forces with the Greek sage.

All possible demonstrations of this thesis aim ultimately at throwing into relief the disproportion between our finite understanding and the infinite essence of God. The line of argument which leads us perhaps most deeply of all into the thought of St. Thomas is drawn from the nature of human knowledge. Perfect knowledge, if we accept Aristotle, consists in deducing the properties of an object by using its essence as the principle of the demonstration. Accordingly, the mode in which the substance of each thing is known to us, determines *ipso facto* the mode of the knowledge which we can have of the thing. Now, God is a purely spiritual substance; our knowledge, on the contrary, is only such as a being composed of a soul and a body can reach. It originates necessarily in sensation. The knowledge which we have of God is, therefore, only such as a person starting from sense-data, can acquire of a being which is purely intelligible. Thus, our understanding, resting upon the testimony of our senses, can indeed infer that God exists, but it is evident that a mere examination of sensory objects, which are the effects of God and therefore inferior to Him cannot bring us to a knowledge of the Divine essence.[7] There are, consequently, truths about God which are accessible to Reason; and there are others which exceed it. Let us examine, in either case, the particular function of Faith.

Let us first state that—speaking abstractly and absolutely—wherever Reason can find a foothold, Faith has no place. In other words, one cannot both know and believe the same thing at the same time: *impossibile est quod de eodem sit fides et scientia.*[8] According to St. Augustine, the proper object of Faith is precisely that to which Reason does not attain; whence it follows that all rational knowledge, based analytically on first principles, falls at the same time outside the sphere of Faith. This is legitimate truth. In practice, Faith must replace Reason in a large number of our affirmations. It may, in fact, not only happen that certain truths are *believed* by ignorant people and *known* by the learned, but it also occurs often that, owing to the feebleness of our understanding and to failures of our imagination, error is introduced into our enquiries. There are many who fail to understand the conclusiveness of an argument and consequently remain uncertain concerning the best established truths, and the discovery of dissension between men of acknowledged wisdom about the same questions finally leads them astray. It is therefore salutary that providence imposed as articles of Faith even such truths as are accessible to Reason, to enable all to participate easily in the knowledge of God, without fear of either doubt or error.[9]

If we consider, on the other hand, the truths which exceed our Reason, we shall see no less clearly that they had to be offered to the acceptance of our Faith. For the end of man is none other than God; but this end manifestly exceeds the limits of our Reason. Again, man must possess some knowledge of his end to be able to order his intentions and actions in relation to it. The salvation of man, therefore, demanded that the Divine Revelation should bring to his knowledge a certain number of truths which are incomprehensible to his Reason.[10] In short, since man needed knowledge concerning the infinite God who is his end, this knowledge, going beyond the limits of his Reason, could not but be offered to the acceptance of his Faith. Nor can we see in Belief any violence done to our Reason. On the contrary, Faith in the incomprehensible confers upon rational knowledge its perfection and crowning completion. We do not, for example, know God truly, unless we believe Him to be superior to all that man may think. Now, it is evident that to expect us to accept incomprehensible truths about God, is the surest means to implant in us the knowledge of His incomprehensibleness.[11] Moreover, the acceptance of Faith represses in us presumption, the mother of error. There are some who believe themselves able to measure Divine nature with the ell of their Reason; to propose to them truths superior to their understanding in the name of Divine authority, is a means to recall them to the just sense of their own limitations. In this manner the discipline of Faith profits Reason.

Can we, however, admit that, apart from this purely external and merely expedient harmony, it may be possible to establish between Faith and Reason an internal accord, from the point of view of truth? In other words, can we assert an accord of such truths as exceed our Reason, with those which Reason can grasp? The answer to this question depends on the value given to the grounds of credibility which Faith can claim. Admitting, as one must, that the miracles, prophecies and the wonderful effects of Christian religion prove sufficiently the truth of Christian Revelation,[12] one is bound also to admit that Faith and Reason cannot contradict each other. Only the false can be contrary to the true. Between a true Faith and a true knowledge, accord is established of itself, and, so to speak, by definition. But it is possible to give a purely philosophical proof of the harmony. When a teacher instructs a pupil, the knowledge of the teacher contains what he instils into the pupil's mind. Now, the natural knowledge which we possess of principles comes to us from God, since God is the author of our nature. These principles are, therefore, also contained in the wisdom of God. Whence it follows that whatever is contrary to these principles, is contrary to Divine Wisdom and consequently cannot come from God. Between Reason, which comes from God, and a Revelation, which comes from God, accord must be of necessity.[13] Let us therefore rather say: Faith may teach truths which *seem* contrary to Reason; than: Faith teaches propositions which *are* contrary to Reason. The yokel thinks it contrary to Reason that the sun should be larger than the earth, but this proposition seems reasonable to the learned man.[14] Let us therefore also believe that the apparent incompatibilities between Reason and Faith are reconciled in the infinite wisdom of God.

We are, moreover, not reduced to such an act of general belief in an accord which escapes altogether our direct perception; many facts open to observation can be satisfactorily interpreted only on the assumption of the existence of a common source of these our two orders of knowledge. Faith dominates Reason, not so much as a mode of knowledge, for it is, on the contrary, an inferior type of knowledge on account of its obscurity, but insofar as it places human thought in possession of an object which reason would be incapable of grasping naturally. Hence, Faith gives rise to a whole series of influences and actions, the consequences of which are of the utmost importance within Reason itself, which yet does not cease to be pure Reason. Faith in Revelation does not result in destroying the rationality of our knowledge, but, on the contrary, in allowing it to develop more completely; just as Grace does not destroy our nature, but fertilises, exalts and perfects it, so Faith, by its influence upon Reason as such, promotes the development of a rational activity of a more fruitful kind.[15]

This transcendent influence of Faith upon Reason is an essential fact which it is important to understand, if the true features of Thomistic philosophy are to be preserved. Many of the criticisms directed against it, are based precisely on the alleged discovery of the mixture of Faith and Reason in it. But it is as inaccurate to say that St. Thomas has isolated these two spheres by a watertight compartment, as to say that he has confused them. We shall later on have to raise the question whether he has confused them, for the moment it is clear that he has not isolated them, but has kept them in contact in a manner which does not oblige him to confuse them ultimately. This enables us to understand the admirable unity of the philosophical and the theological work of St. Thomas. It is impossible to pretend that a mind of this temper is not fully conscious of its aim. Even in the commentaries on Aristotle, his mind always knows where it is going, and there too, it works towards the doctrine of Faith, not as an explanation, but as a completion and counterpoise of mental balance. And yet one may say that St. Thomas works in the full and clear consciousness of never appealing to arguments not strictly rational, for if Faith acts upon Reason, his Reason, supported and fertilised by his Faith, does not, for all that, cease to perform purely rational operations and to assert conclusions, based only on the evidence of first principles common to all human minds. The fear betrayed by some of his commentators of a possible contamination of his Reason by his Faith, is wholly un-Thomistic; to assert that he is unaware of, or opposed to, this beneficial influence, is to present as fundamentally inexplicable the accord which, in point of fact, his reconstruction of philosophy and theology ultimately reaches, and suggests an uneasiness which St. Thomas himself would certainly not have understood. Aquinas is too certain of his thought to be afraid of anything of this kind. His thought proceeds under the helpful impulse of his Faith, as indeed he recognises; but he notes that in following the road of Revelation Reason easily finds and, as it were, recognises the truths which it might have run some risk of mistaking. The traveller who has been led by a guide to the summit, is none the less entitled to the spectacle which unfolds itself from there, and the view is none the less true, because an external assistance has led him to it. No one can study St. Thomas for any time without being convinced that this vast system of the world which his doctrine presents, took shape in his mind in proportion as his doctrine of Faith was formed; and when he assures others that Faith is a salutary guide to Reason, the memory of the rational gain which he himself realised by Faith, is still vividly present to his mind.

It is therefore no matter for surprise that, as far as theology is concerned, there should be room for philosophical speculation, even when it is a question of revealed truths which exceed the limits of our Reason. Undoubtedly—and this is obvious—speculation cannot claim to demonstrate or even to understand them, but, emboldened by the superior certitude that there is there a hidden truth, it enables us to catch a glimpse of it with the help of well-founded analogies. The sense-objects which form the point of departure of all our knowledge, have retained some traces of the Divine nature which has created them, since the effect always bears a resemblance to its cause. Reason can, therefore, even in this life, and thanks to the starting-point offered by Faith, set us to some extent on the road to the understanding of the perfect truth which God will show us in our Home.[16] This statement marks the limits of Reason, when it undertakes an apologia of the truths of Faith. Nothing could be more imprudent than to attempt their proof; to try to demonstrate the indemonstrable is but to confirm the incredulous in their incredulity. The disproportion between the theses which we believe to have established, and the false proofs adduced in their support, is so evident that instead of serving Faith by such arguments, we run the risk of exposing it to ridicule. Still, it is possible to explain, to interpret and to bring home to us what it is impossible to prove: we should therefore lead our opponents by the hand in face of these inaccessible truths, and we can show them on what probable reasons and on what authorities in this world they rest.

But we must go further and, gathering the fruit of the points previously set forth, we must assert that there is room for demonstrative argument even in matters of truths inaccessible to Reason, and, further, for theological intervention even in matters apparently reserved to pure Reason. We have seen that Revelation and Reason cannot be in contradiction. If it is certain that Reason cannot demonstrate revealed truth, it is equally certain that any so-called rational proof which claims to establish the falsity of Faith, can only be a mere sophism. Whatever the subtlety of the arguments adduced, we must hold firm to the principle that truth cannot be divided against itself, and that Reason cannot therefore be right as against Faith.[17] We can always look for a sophism in a philosophical thesis which contradicts the teaching of Revelation, for it is certain that it must contain at least one. The revealed texts are never a philosophical proof of the falsity of a doctrine, but they are the proof for the believer that the philosopher, maintaining the doctrine, is mistaken, and it is the business of philosophy alone to furnish the proof of this. *A fortiori*, the resources of philosophical speculation must be employed by Faith, when it is a question of religious truths which are at the same time humanly demonstrable. That body of philosophical doctrines which in its fullness the human mind can rarely grasp with nothing but the resources of Reason, is easily reached, if it is pointed out by Faith, although the mind may rest these doctrines on a purely rational foundation. As a child understands what he could not have discovered himself, unless the master had taught him, so the human intellect grasps without difficulty a system, the truth of which is guaranteed by a superhuman authority. Hence the extraordinary firmness and certainty with which the intellect meets errors of all kinds, bred by unbelief or ignorance. It can always oppose conclusive proofs to its adversaries which will reduce them to silence and re-establish the truth. Finally, we must add that even the purely scientific knowledge of sense-objects cannot leave theology wholly indifferent. Not that there is no knowledge of created things valid in itself and independent of all theology: science exists as such and, provided it does not exceed its natural limits, remains untouched by any interference of Faith. But Faith, on its part, is bound to take science into account. Once science has been constituted as such, theology cannot fail to be interested in it, in the first place, because the study of creation is useful for the interpretation of Faith, and secondly, because, as we have seen, natural knowledge is at least able to destroy errors concerning God.[18]

Such being the intimate relations between theology and philosophy, the fact still remains that they form two distinct, autonomous and formally separate spheres. In the first place, they do not coincide, though their domains are in some measure co-extensive. Theology is the science of the truth necessary for our salvation; but not all truths are necessary for that purpose. Hence there was no need for God to reveal to us what we are capable of discovering by ourselves concerning created things, as long as such knowledge was not required to ensure our salvation. There is consequently room, outside theology, for science which considers things in themselves and is divided into different parts according to the different kinds of natural things, whereas theology considers them under the aspect of our salvation and in reference to God.[19] Philosophy studies fire in itself; the theologian sees in it an image of Divine elevation. There is then room for the attitude of the philosopher side by side with that of the believer (*philosophus, fidelis*), and there is no cause to reproach theology for passing over in silence a great number of the properties of things, such as the shape of heaven or the nature of its movement; these things belong to the philosopher who alone has the task of explaining them.

Even where the two disciplines have common ground, they retain specific features which assure their independence. They differ first and foremost in their principles of demonstration and this feature definitely makes their confusion impossible. The philosopher draws his arguments from the essences and consequently from the proper causes of things, as we shall constantly do in the sequel. The theologian, on the contrary, argues by always referring to the first Cause of all things which is God, and appeals to three different orders of arguments which are in no case considered satisfactory by the philosopher. Sometimes the theologian affirms a truth in the name of the principle of authority, because it has been transmitted and revealed by God; or again, because the glory of an infinite God demands that it should be so; or, lastly, because the power of God is infinite.[20] It does not follow therefrom that theology should be excluded from the sphere of science, but rather that philosophy occupies a sphere belonging properly to itself which it exploits by purely rational methods. As two sciences may establish the same fact, each science in the way proper to it, so the philosopher's proofs, being exclusively rational, differ *toto genere* from the theologian's proofs, which are always drawn from authority.

A second, less profound difference lies, not in the principles of the demonstration, but in the order which it adopts. For in philosophical speculation which is concerned with the consideration of created things in themselves and endeavours to work upwards from created things to God, the consideration of creatures comes first, and that of God comes last. In doctrines of Faith, on the contrary, which considers created things in relation to God, the consideration of God comes first and that of creation afterwards. Herein it follows, moreover, an order which in itself is more perfect, since it follows the model of the knowledge of God who, knowing Himself, knows all things.[21]

Such being the position *de jure*, it remains to determine what we mean when we speak of the "philosophy" of St. Thomas. We do not find in any of his works a body of his philosophical conceptions set out for their own sake and in their rational order. There is indeed a series of writings composed by St. Thomas according to the philosophical method: these are his commentaries on Aristotle and a small number of minor works. But the smaller works give us only a fraction of his ideas and the commentaries on Aristotle, following patiently the meanderings of an obscure text, enable us to guess only imperfectly what a "Summa" of the Thomistic *philosophy* might have been like, if it had been systematised by St. Thomas himself with that lucidity of genius which dominates his *Summa theologica.*[22] And there is a second group of writings of which the "Summa theologica" is the most perfect specimen; this contains his philosophy, demonstrated according to the *principles* of philosophical argument, but presented according to the *order* of theological argument. An ideal Thomistic philosophy would have to be reconstructed by taking the best from these two groups of works and re-arranging the arguments of St. Thomas according to the needs of a new order. But who would venture upon the attempt of such a synthesis? And who, in particular, could guarantee that the order of the philosophical demonstration adopted would correspond to that which the genius of St. Thomas might have been able to select and realise? Who especially could give us the assurance that we would not thereby lose that by which St. Thomas perhaps set the greatest store of all: the tangible proof of the benefit reaped by Philosophy from its intercourse with Faith, and the joy felt by Reason discoursing in the same order in which the Intelligences contemplate, thanks to the guiding thread given to it by Revelation? In the absence of such a synthesis, carried out by the philosopher himself and in our uncertainty whether he has not deliberately avoided it in order to follow the natural progress of Christian thought, it is a matter of elementary prudence to reproduce his thought in the order adopted by himself and in the most perfect form given to it, viz. that of the two "Summæ."

It does not by any means follow from this that the value of a philosophy arranged in the order of theological argument is necessarily subordinated to criteria of Faith which from the very start appeals to the authority of a Divine Revelation. The philosophy of St. Thomas presents itself as a system of truths rigorously demonstrable and is justifiable, precisely *quâ* philosophy, by Reason alone. When St. Thomas speaks as philosopher, his demonstrations alone are under discussion, and it matters little whether the thesis he upholds occupies the place assigned to it by Faith, since he never introduces Faith into the argument and does not ask us to introduce it into the proofs of what he considers as rationally demonstrable. Between the assertions of the two disciplines, even when they bear upon the same subject-matter, an absolutely strict formal distinction is maintained, which rests upon the heterogeneity of their principles of demonstration. There is a generic difference between theology which founds its principles on the articles of Faith, and philosophy which for such knowledge of God as it can give us, appeals to Reason alone: *theologia quae ad sacram doctrinam pertinet, differt secundum genus ab illa theologia quae pars philosophiæ ponitur.*[23] And it is easy to show that this generic distinction is not stated by St. Thomas as an ineffective principle which need not be further taken into account, once it has been recognised. An examination of his teaching, considered in its historical significance and in comparison with the Augustinian tradition of which St. Bonaventure is the most distinguished representative, shows what profound recastings, what incredibly bold changes he did not hesitate to take upon himself to meet the demands of Aristotelian thought, whenever he considered them identical with the demands of Reason.[24]

Herein precisely lies the truly philosophical value of the Thomistic system, and this is what makes it a turning-point in the history of human thought. With a full consciousness of all the consequences of such an attitude, St. Thomas accepts simultaneously both his Faith and his Reason, each with all the demands proper to it. His thought, therefore, does not aim at achieving as economically as possible a superficial harmony wherein the doctrines most easily reconcilable with the traditional teaching of theology may find room, but he insists that Reason should develop its own content in full liberty and should set out its demands in their utmost stringency; the value of his philosophy lies not in the fact that it is Christian, but in the fact that it is true. He does not, therefore, follow passively the regular current of Augustinian tradition, but develops a new theory of knowledge, shifts the foundations on which the proofs for the existence of God rested, submits the concept of creation to a fresh criticism and founds or entirely reorganises the structure of traditional ethics. In this lies the whole secret of Thomism, in this immense effort of intellectual honesty to reconstruct philosophy on a plan which exhibits the *de facto* accord with theology as the necessary consequence of the demands of Reason itself, and not as the accidental result of a mere wish for conciliation.

Such appear to us the points of contact and the distinctions between Reason and Faith in the system of St. Thomas of Aquino. Faith and Reason can neither contradict each other, nor ignore each other, nor be confused. Reason may well try to justify Faith: it will never transform Faith into Reason, for as soon as Faith were to abandon authority for proof, it would cease to believe; it would know. And Faith may well move Reason externally or guide it internally; Reason will never cease to be itself, for once it renounced the proof of its assertions, it would deny itself and would vanish to make room for Faith. It is, therefore, the inalienability of their proper essences which permits them to act upon each other without contaminating each other. A mixed state, composed of prudent doses of knowledge and belief, in which so many mystic minds took delight, is considered by St. Thomas as contradictory and monstrous: it is as chimerical a thing as an animal composed of two different species. It is, therefore, intelligible that, in distinction to Augustinianism for instance, Thomism has room, by the side of a theology which should be nothing but theology, for a philosophy which should be nothing but philosophy. For this reason, St. Thomas of Aquino, together with his master, Albertus Magnus, is the first, and not the least, of modern philosophers.

Lastly, it is clear that, considered under this aspect and as a discipline which grasps of God all that human thought can conceive, even in this world, the study of philosophy appears to St. Thomas as the most perfect, the most sublime, the most useful and also as the most consoling of studies. The most perfect, because man, in proportion as he devotes himself to the study of philosophy, shares already here in the true beatitude. The most sublime, since man raises himself at least a little towards Divine resemblance, as God founded all things in wisdom. The most useful, since it leads us to the eternal Kingdom. The most consoling, because, according to the word of Scripture (*Wisd.* VIII., 16), her conversation has no bitterness, nor her company any tediousness, but joy and gladness.[25]

Without doubt, certain minds, susceptible only or chiefly to logical certitude, will be inclined to contest this superiority of metaphysical enquiry. They will prefer the certain deductions of physics or mathematics to the researches which yet declare themselves not wholly powerless even in face of the incomprehensible. But the value of a science is constituted not only by its certitude, but also by the status of its object. It is vain to offer to minds, tortured by the thirst for the Divine, the most certain knowledge concerning the laws of numbers or the disposition of the universe. Straining after an object which eludes them, they will try to raise a corner of the veil, only too happy to catch sometimes even in dense darkness some reflexion of the eternal Light which will illumine them one day. To such the least knowledge concerning the highest realities seem more desirable than the fullest certitude of lesser things.[26] At this point we find the reconciliation of the extreme distrust of human Reason, of the contempt even which St. Thomas sometimes displays towards it, with the keen taste he always retained for dialectical discussions and arguments. For when it is a question of attaining to an object which its very essence renders inaccessible to us, our Reason shows itself powerless and defective in all respects. No one was ever more convinced of this insufficiency than St. Thomas. And if, nevertheless, he untiringly applies this feeble instrument to the highest objects, the reason is that the most obscure knowledge, even such as barely deserves the name of knowledge, ceases to be contemptible, when it has for its object the infinite essence of God. It is from poor conjectures, from analogies, at least not wholly inadequate, that we derive our purest and deepest joy. The supreme happiness of man in this world is to anticipate, however confusedly, the vision face to face of unchanging Eternity.

NOTES TO CHAPTER II.

1. To mention only the principal writers, cf. on the attitude of St. Augustine and St. Anselm, M. Grabmann, *Geschichte der scholastischen Methode*, I. 116–143 and 258–339. Cf. also Heitz, *Essai historique sur les rapports entre la philosophie et la foi, de Bérenger de Tours à saint Thomas d'Aquin*, Paris, 1909; of the same, *La philosophie et la foi chez saint Thomas*, Rev. des sciences phil. et théol. 1909, p. 244–261; L. Laberthonnière, *Saint Thomas et les rapports entre la science et la foi*, Ann. de phil. chrét., CLVIII., 1900, p. 599–621; E. Gilson: *Études de philosophie médiévale*, Strasbourg, 1921: p. 1–29; 30–50; 76–124.
2. *Cont. Gent.*, I. 1; *Sum. theol.*, I. 1, 6, ad *Resp.*
3. *Cont. Gent.*, I. 1.
4. *Joann.*, XVII. 37.
5. *Cont. Gent.*, I. 1 and III. 25, ad *Quod est tantum. In II Sent.*, *Prolog.*
6. *In IV. Metaphys.*, lect. I., med. Cf. all the necessary references in Sertillanges, *Saint Thomas d'Aquin*, I. p. 23–26.
7. *Cont. Gent.*, I. 3.
8. *Qu. disp. de Veritate*, qu. XIV., art. 9, ad *Resp.* and ad 6[nm].

9. *Cont. Gent.*, I. 4, St. Thomas' source is here Maimonides, as appears from *De Veritate*, qu. XIV., art. 10, ad *Resp.*
10. *Sum. theol.*, I. 1, 1, ad *Resp. de virtutibus*, art. X., ad *Resp.*
11. *Cont. Gent.*, I. 5.
12. *Cont. Gent.*, I. 6. *De Verit.*, qu. XIV., art. 10, ad 11.
13. *Cont. Gent.*, I. 7.
14. *De Verit.*, qu. XIV., art 10, ad 7.
15. *De Verit.*, qu. XIV., art. 9, ad 8^m, and art. 10, ad 9^m.
16. *Cont. Gent.*, I. 7; *de Verit.*, qu. XIV., art. 9, ad 2^m. This is the echo of the *fides quaerens intellectum* of the Augustinian school; but in distinction to Augustinianism this is not St. Thomas' definition of Philosophy.
17. *Cont. Gent.*, I. 1; I. 2 and I. 9.
18. *Cont. Gent.*, II. 2, and esp. *Sum. theol.*, I. 5, ad 2^m.
19. *Cont. Gent.*, II. 4.
20. "Fidelis autem ex causa prima, ut puta quia sic divinitus est traditum, vel quia hoc in gloriam Dei cedit, vel quia Dei potestas est infinita." *Cont. Gent.*, II. 4.
21. *Cont. Gent.*, II. 4.
22. Hence the advice given by J. De Rohellec in Rev. thomiste, 1913, XXI., p. 449, to follow rather the Commentaries than the Summa for mapping out courses of neo-scholastic philosophy may well be adopted by the philosophers to whom it is given; the historian, on the contrary, cannot accept it without being led to the purely hypothetical reconstruction of a doctrinal edifice which in fact has never existed. It is hardly necessary to point out that the *Contra Gentes*, which is constantly called a *Summa philosophica*, in contrast to the *Summa theologica*, in no sense deserves that name as far as the order of demonstration is concerned. Cf. *Cont. Gent.*, II., 4 and 5. *In Boët. de Trinitate*, qu. II., art. 2, ad *Resp.*
23. *Sum. theol.*, I. 10, ad 2^m.
24. We have developed this point in greater detail in our *Études de philosophie médiévale*, Strasbourg, 1921: *La signification historique du thomisme*, p. 95–124.
25. *Cont. Gent.*, I. 2.
26. *Sum theol.*, I. 1, 5, ad 1^m; *ibid.*, Ia, IIae, 66, 5, ad 3^m.

CHAPTER III. THE ALLEGED EVIDENCE FOR THE EXISTENCE OF GOD

It is said with justice, St. Thomas asserts, that if a person wishes to learn, he must begin by believing his teacher; for he would never attain to perfect knowledge unless he accepted the truth of such doctrines as may be offered to him at first, the justification for which he cannot, at that time, discover for himself.[1] This observation is especially true of the Thomistic theory of knowledge. We encountered it already in the preceding chapter; we shall see that it is the presupposition of all the proofs of the existence of God; it governs further all our affirmations concerning His essence. St. Thomas Aquinas does not hesitate to burden it with the weight of some of its most important consequences, long before he offers the slightest justification of the theory itself.

One feels sometimes tempted to fill what appears a gap, and to suggest, by way of Prolegomenon, a theory of knowledge which the rest of the doctrine would merely show in application. But, if we place ourselves at the truly Thomistic point of view, such a proceeding would be neither necessary nor quite satisfactory. The view that a theory of knowledge must necessarily be placed at the beginning of the system, attributes to it a function which our philosopher did not assign to it. His philosophy is in no sense a critical philosophy.[2] Undoubtedly the analysis of our faculty of knowing involves as a consequence a limitation of its range, but St. Thomas does not dream of denying it the power to apprehend being as such. What reservations he makes, apply solely to the nature of the being which our reason can apprehend immediately, and to the mode in which it apprehends. Hence, since our reason is always competent with regard to being, though not equally so with regard to *all* being, nothing prevents us from applying it straightway to the infinite being which is God, and to ask what information it can furnish of such an object. In other words, the problem whether it is necessary to start with a theory of knowledge, has at this point only a purely didactic interest; it may be convenient to explain this theory to begin with, but there is nothing obligatory about such an order of arrangement. Moreover, there are reasons for not adopting it. Let us note, in the first place that, if the full understanding of the proofs of the existence of God presupposes an exact determination of our faculty of knowing, this determination remains impossible without some preceding knowledge of the existence and the essence of God. In the mind of St. Thomas, the mode of knowing is the direct result of the mode of being; it is therefore impossible to establish what is man's mode of knowing before having assigned to man his place in the order of thinking beings. In consequence, in either case, we must inevitably make use of certain propositions before they have been proved. This being the case, there can be no doubt about the preference of St. Thomas: the order which he follows is always the synthetic order. He takes as his point of departure not the principles which, from the point of view of the subject condition the acquisition of all other knowledge, but the Being which, from the point of view of the object, conditions both all being and all knowing. The only obligation which St. Thomas imposes upon himself is not to make any use of his reason which might appear as illegitimate, once the time for analysis has come. With this reservation, he avails himself—and we shall avail ourselves—of a theory not yet proven. To proceed in this manner implies no *petitio principii*; it means to leave to reason the care of proving its value and the conditions of its functioning by the wealth and coherence of the results it obtains.

Our task is to examine the proof of the existence of God. It is true that some philosophers consider this

a self-evident truth. We shall therefore have first
to consider their arguments, which, if well founded,
would relieve us of the need of all further proof.

One way of establishing that the existence of God
is a self-evident truth, consists in showing that we
possess a natural knowledge of it, "self-evident,"
in this sense, meaning something which has no need
of being proved.[3] This would indeed be so, if the
existence of God were a truth naturally known to us
like that of the first principles. Now, St. John
Damascene asserts that the knowledge of the existence
of God is naturally instilled in the human heart:
the existence of God is consequently something known
of itself.[4] The argument might be presented in
another form by saying that, since the desire of man
naturally tends towards God as man's ultimate end,
the existence of God must of necessity be known of
itself.[5]

It is not difficult to recognise the doctors whose
arguments St. Thomas here reproduces.[6] They are
either his predecessors, like John of La Rochelle,[7] or his
contemporaries, like St. Bonaventure, for whom all
the other proofs had little more than the value of
dialectical exercises. Only the intimate knowledge
of God's existence can give us evident certitude of it:
*Deus praesentissimus est ipsi animae et eo ipso cog-
noscibilis.*[8] St. Thomas is consequently prepared to
challenge the Augustinian school on this point. He
straightway denies in the first place that we possess
an innate knowledge of the existence of God. What
is innate in us is not this knowledge, but only the
principles which will allow us to work back to God,
as first Cause, by reasoning from His effects.[9] We
shall find the justification of this reservation, when
we come to study the origin of our knowledge. And
if the reply is made on the other side, that we know
God naturally, since we tend towards Him as to
our end,[10] we must admit this in a certain sense. It is
true that man tends naturally towards God, since he
tends towards his beatitude which is God. We must,

however, distinguish: man tends towards his beatitude and his beatitude is God; but he may tend towards his beatitude without knowing that God is his beatitude. In point of fact, many consider wealth as the supreme Good; others pleasure. It is consequently in a quite confused manner that we can be said to tend towards God and to know God naturally. To know that a man is coming along is not knowing Peter, although it may be Peter who is coming along; in the same way knowing that there is a supreme Good, does not mean knowing God, although God is the supreme Good.[11]

Having disposed of the philosophers who consider the existence of God as a matter of natural knowledge, we meet those who base it upon a self-evident reasoning, i.e. upon the simple application of the principle of non-contradiction. Such are all the doctors who argue from the idea of truth as their starting-point. It is self-evident that truth exists, we are told, for to deny that truth exists, is to concede its existence. Indeed, if truth does not exist, it is true that truth does not exist; but if anything true does exist, then truth necessarily exists. Now, God is truth itself, according to the words of St. John: *Ego sum via, veritas et vita.* Consequently it is self-evident that God exists.[12] Moreover, it is self-evident that God has always existed; for of everything that is, it was first true that it was to be. Now, truth exists; consequently it was first true that truth had to exist. Now, God is the truth; it is, therefore, impossible to think that God has not always existed.[13] These proofs the first origin of which seems to have been an argument used by St. Augustine against the sceptics[14] had been propounded by Alexander of Hales in his "Summa theologica."[15] St. Thomas opposes to these arguments a categorical verdict of "non-suited." They all rest on the same equivocation, in arguing from any truth to the First Truth which is the source of all truth. What is self-evident is that, in a general way, truth exists, like being exists; and especially the first argument succeeds in demonstrating this

But it proves by no means that this truth—and, since truth rests on being, this being—which cannot be conceived as non-existent, is the first Being, the Cause of all being. We cannot know it, unless faith leads us to believe it or reason proves it to us. But it is in no way self-evident. The same applies to the second argument: it is valid, if it refers to an indeterminate truth, not if it refers to God. Assuming, *per impossibile*, that at a given moment nothing had existed; at that moment there would not have been any being, and yet there would have been matter for truth. Non-being, can, in fact, offer matter for truth as well as being, since one can speak the truth about non-being no less than about being. Whence it follows that at that moment there would have been matter for truth, but not truth itself. It is consequently possible to conceive that truth has not always existed. This is not the road whereby we can make our way to God.

Another way remains, however, still open to us. Truths are called self-evident when it is sufficient, in order to know them, to know their terms. If, for instance, I know what a "whole" is and what a "part" is, I know at the same time that the whole is greater than the part. Now, the truth that God exists, is a truth of this kind. We mean, in fact, by the term "God" something than which we cannot conceive anything greater. But something that exists at the same time in our mind and in reality, is greater than something existing in our mind only. Hence, since, when we understand the word "God," we form the idea in our mind, and therewith God exists in our mind, it follows that God also exists in reality. Consequently it is self-evident that God exists.[16] The reader will have recognised St. Anselm's argument. Alexander of Hales seems to have taken it up on his own account,[17] and St. Bonaventure still defended it against the objections raised by Gaunilon.[18] St. Thomas aims here again at the Augustinian philosophy and this proof, according to him, contains in fact two main flaws.

The first is to suppose that everyone necessarily means by the term "God" a being than which no greater can be conceived. Now, many of the ancients considered that our universe was God, and among all the interpretations enumerated by St. John Damascene, there is none which amounts to the definition under discussion. For all such minds the existence of God could not be evident *a priori*. Secondly, even granting that by the word "God" everybody understood a being than which no greater could be conceived, the real existence of such a being would not necessarily follow. If we grasp in our mind the meaning of these words, it does not follow that God exists, except in our mind. The necessary existence of a being than which no greater can be conceived, is therefore necessary only in our mind, and only after the above definition has been accepted; but it follows by no means that this being, so conceived, possesses a real and *de facto* existence. There is therefore no contradiction in asserting that God does not exist. As long as the real existence of a being than which no greater can be conceived is not conceded, we can always conceive a being greater than any given being, either in our mind or in reality.[19] But since, *ex hypothesi*, our opponent denies God's existence, we shall find it impossible, by this argument, to force him to admit it.

The attitude adopted by St. Thomas in face of all the *a priori* proofs is particularly significant. It enlightens us perhaps but little concerning the intentions of their authors, but throws a vivid light upon the Thomistic idea of proof and indicates the conditions which according to St. Thomas have to be met by any valid proof of the existence of God. Let us note in the first place that all the arguments criticised by our doctor are presented as leading up to the same conclusion: viz. that the existence of God is a truth known of itself, i.e. a truth which requires no proof in the strict sense of the term. One conceives the possibility of interpreting in this sense the assertion of an innate knowledge of the existence of God. In the case of Bonaventure, for instance, it is not so much a proof as rather the final confirmation of all proofs; it adds inner certitude to the logical conviction produced by arguments. The proof drawn from the idea of truth and that of St. Anselm present themselves, on the contrary, as proofs in the proper sense of the term, sufficient of themselves to force us to assent to them. What reason can St. Thomas have for his refusal to recognise them as such? The reason is that he interprets, from the Thomistic point of view, proofs formulated from the Augustinian point of view.

The three aforesaid arguments rest upon a conception of intellectual knowledge which St. Thomas cannot accept. The postulate on which they are based is that we could have no idea either of God, or of a subsistent truth, or of a being than which no greater can be conceived, unless these ideas had been implanted in us by God, or rather unless they were that very being and that very truth, shared in a finite mode by our human understanding. On such an hypothesis, the *a priori* proofs do not involve any transition from the idea to being; for it is being which is the starting-point of the argument. Underlying St. Thomas' criticisms, however, we find an entirely different postulate, namely that all our knowledge originates from sensory intuitions. The being which we apprehend directly is the idea realised in matter; it is therefore a sophism to try and prove that the very being we apprehend is none other than God. Thus emptied of its realistic content, the argument of St. Anselm is no longer the analysis of an essence: it has turned into the analysis of a simple abstract notion. The only problem in that case is to know whether our conception of God or of truth is such as to allow us to discover the link which, in God Himself, unites essence and existence. Now, according to St. Thomas, it neither is nor can it be such.

To admit that such a knowledge of God is accessible to man in this world, is equivalent to supposing that our reason is naturally capable of apprehending what is in

itself purely intelligible; and moreover, that the more
an object is in itself intelligible, the more must it be
so to us. Bonaventure argued in this sense that, if
the mountains could give us the strength to carry
them, we should be able to carry the higher mountains
more easily than the smaller.[20] But there is a fallacy
in this: the analysis of our faculty of knowing shows
that the apprehension of the purely intelligible is
impossible for a being which is, like ourselves, at the
same time material and spiritual. The object which
possesses the highest degree of intelligibility—and this
is the case of God, since in Him essence and existence
are identical—may consequently remain perpetually
present without our ever apprehending it. There is a
disproportion, a lack of adaptation between our understanding, attuned as it is to sensory things, and such
an object: in the same way the eye of the owl cannot
see the sun. What would, accordingly, be needed for
the existence of God to appear to us as self-evident?
We should need to be delivered from our body to
apprehend this purely intelligible being which is His
essence; then we should at once discover that His
existence is necessarily implied in it. Thus when we
shall be able to contemplate the essence of God in
our blessed state, His existence will be known to us
much more evidently than the principle of contradiction
is known to us now.[21]

The existence of God is, therefore, not an evident
truth. Those who think so have been led into error
by their long established habit of believing that God
exists, as well as by the natural illusion which leads them
to think that a truth evident of itself is also evident to
us.[22] But does it follow therefrom, as some believed,
that the existence of God is an undemonstrable truth?
Already Maimonides knew that kind of religious mind
which, holding that this truth was neither evident nor
demonstrable, claimed to hold it only on faith.[23]
Such an attitude is unquestionably not without justification. Some of the proofs of the existence of God
are so feeble that they raise a doubt whether any good

proofs can be found. On the other hand, philosophers show that in God essence and existence are identical; that therefore to know His existence means to know His essence. But His essence remains unknowable to us; hence it should be the same with His existence. Lastly, is it not true, as we have suggested, that the principles of proof originate in sense-perception? And does it then not follow that all that exceeds the sense and sensible world, is unamenable to proof?[24] Yet we are assured of the contrary by the word of the Apostle: *Invisibilia Dei per ea quae facta sunt, intellecta, conspiciuntur.*[25] It is indeed incontestable that in God essence and existence are identical. But this is true of the existence in which God subsists eternally in Himself; not of the existence to which our finite mind can rise when, by demonstration, it establishes that God is. We are consequently able without attaining to the essence of God or the fullness of the infinite being which He possesses, to demonstrate this existence, expressed in the conclusion: God exists.[26] Again it is certain that God exceeds all our senses and all sensible objects; but His effects, whence we start to establish His existence, are, on the contrary, sense-objects. The fact accordingly remains that our knowledge of the supersensible takes its origin in the sensible. But we must remember that in the arguments whereby we prove the existence of God, we cannot take as principle the essence or quiddity of God, which is unknown to us. The proof *propter quid* being impossible, we are left with the proof *quia.*[27] The only road which can lead us to a knowledge of the Creator must be cut through the things of sense. The immediate access to the Cause being barred to us, it remains for us to divine it with the help of its effects.

NOTES TO CHAPTER III.

1. *De Verit.*, qu. XIV., art. 10, ad *Resp.*
2. The term "critical" is here used in the definite Kantian sense. Even if St. Thomas' teaching were arranged on the lines of pure philosophy, such an exposition would not set out with the enquiry under what conditions mathematical physics are possible.
3. *Cont. Gent.*, I. 10.
4. *Sum. theol.*, I. 2, 1, ad 1'''.
5. *Cont. Gent.*, I. 10.
6. For the identification of the writers whom St. Thomas opposed on the question of the proofs of the existence of God, cf. esp. Grunwald, *Geschichte der Gottesbeweise im Mittelalter bis zum Ausgang der Hochscholastik*, Münster, 1907; Cl. Baeumker, *Witelo, ein Philosoph und Naturforscher des XIII. Jahrhunderts*, Münster, 1908, p. 286–338.
7. Cf. Manser, *Johann von Rupella*, Jahrb. f. Phil. u. spek. Theol., 1911, Bd. XXVI., H. 3, p. 304.
8. Bonav., *De mysterio Trinitatis*, quaest. disp., IX., 1a, concl. 10. See other refs. in E. Gilson, *La philosophie de Saint Bonaventure*, Paris, 1924, pp. 119–140.
9. *De Verit.*, qu. X., art. 12, ad 1'''.
10. Cf. St. Augustine, *De lib. arbitr.*, 1, II., c. 9, no. 26; P. L., XXXII., col. 1254.
11. *Sum. theol.*, I. 2, 1, ad 1'''; *Cont. Gent.*, I. 11, ad 4'''; *De Verit.*, X. 12, ad 5'''.
12. *Joann.*, 14, 6; *Sum. theol.*, I. 2, 1, ad 3'''; *De Verit.*, X., art. 12, ad 3'''.
13. *De Verit.*, X., art. 12, ad 8'''.
14. *Soliloq.*, 1, II., c. 1, n. 2; P. L. XXXII., col. 886.
15. I., qu. 3, membr. 1. Cf. the texts in Grunwald, *op. cit.*, p. 97–98.
16. *Sum. theol.*, I. 2, 1, ad 2'''; *Cont. Gent.*, I. 10.
17. See Grunwald, *op. cit.*, p. 98–100.
18. *Sent.*, 1, dist. III., p. 1, qu., 1, concl. 6.
19. *Cont. Gent.*, I. 11; *Sum. theol.*, I. 2, 1, ad 2'''.
20. *Sent.*, I. dist. 1, art. 3, qu. 1, ad 2'''.
21. *Cont. Gent.*, I. 11; *De Verit.*, X. 12, ad *Resp.*
22. *Cont. Gent.*, I. 11; *Sum. theol.*, I. 2, 1, ad *Resp.*
23. *De Verit.*, qu. X., art. 12, ad *Resp.*
24. *Cont. Gent.*, I. 12.
25. *Rom.*, I. 20.
26. *Cont. Gent.*, I. 12.
27. *Cont. Gent.*, I. 12; *Sum. theol.*, I. 2, 2, ad *Resp.*

CHAPTER IV. THE FIRST PROOF OF THE EXISTENCE OF GOD

THE Thomistic proofs of the existence of God are formulated in the "Summa theologica" and in the "Summa contra Gentiles."[1] In both works the proofs are substantially the same; but they differ in the manner of their exposition. In a general way the proofs of the "Summa theologica" are presented in a very succinct and simplified form (we must remember that the "Summa" is addressed to beginners, "*Sum. theol.*" *prolog.*); they also attack the problem in its most metaphysical aspect. In the "Summa contra Gentiles," on the contrary, the philosophical demonstrations are developed with great minuteness and may be said to take up the problem in a more physical form and to appeal more frequently to sense-experience. We shall deal with each proof successively in both forms of its exposition.

Although, according to St. Thomas, the five proofs which he gives of the existence of God, are all conclusive, they do not, in his opinion, all possess the same evidential character. From this point of view the proof based on the consideration of movement is superior to the other four.[2] Hence St. Thomas is at pains to elucidate it with all completeness and to prove its minutest propositions.

The first beginnings of the proof may be found in Aristotle.[3] Of course it remained unknown as long as Aristotle's Physics itself, i.e. till towards the end of the XIIth century. If we take it as the characteristic feature of the proof that it starts from the consideration of cosmic movement and establishes the principle "Nothing is set in motion of itself" on the conceptions of act and potency (*actus, potentia*)[4], we may say that it appears for the first time in the work of Adelhard of Bath. It recurs in its complete form in

Albertus Magnus who propounds it as an addition to the proofs of Peter the Lombard and borrows it, without doubt, from Maimonides.[5]

The "Summa theologica" sets out the proof in the following form: It is certain—and our senses witness to the fact—that there is movement in the world; everything that moves is set in motion by something. Nothing, in fact, is in motion unless it be in potency with regard to that towards which it is moved; and nothing *per contra*, moves anything except as it is in act*. To set a thing in motion means to cause it to pass from potency to act. Now, a thing can only be brought from potency to act by something which is in act. For instance, it is heat in act (for example fire) which makes the wood, which is only potentially hot, actually hot, and to that extent, moves and alters it. But it is impossible for a thing to be both in act and in potency at the same time in reference to the same things. Thus an actually hot thing cannot at the same time be actually cold, but only potentially cold. It is therefore impossible for a thing to be, at the same time and in reference to the same things, both mover and moved, i.e. set in motion by itself. Whence we see that everything that is in motion, is moved by something else. If, on the other hand, that by which a thing is moved, is itself in movement, the reason is that it is, in its turn, set in motion by some other mover, which is again moved by another thing and so on. But it is impossible to regress in this way *ad infinitum*, because, in that case, there would be no first mover, nor consequently other movers, for the second mover imparts movement only because the first set it in motion, as a stick moves only because the hand imparts movement to it. To explain movement it is consequently necessary to regress to a first mover which is itself not set in motion by anything, i.e. to God.[6] The reader will have noticed the very general form given here to the idea of movement.[7]

---

* See for explanation of the terms "potency" and "act," the explanatory note at the end of this Chapter.

It is reduced to the conceptions of act and potency, transcendental conceptions which divide all being. What forms the basis of the whole proof in the "Summa theologica" is presented in the "Summa contra Gentiles"[8] as only one of the possible foundations of the proof; and this proof itself appears there in two forms, the one direct, the other indirect.

The direct proof, propounded by Aristotle, can be summarised as follows: Everything that is set in motion, is so moved by something else. Now, it is a matter of sense-experience that there is movement; for instance, the movement of the sun. Consequently the sun moves, because something sets it in motion. But that which sets it in motion is either itself set in motion or it is not. If it is not, we have reached our conclusion, viz. the necessity of positing an immobile mover which we call God. If it is moved, there must be another mover that imparts movement to it. Therefore we must either regress to infinity or posit an immobile mover; now the regress to infinity is impossible: consequently we must assume a first immobile mover.

In this proof, two propositions require to be established, first, that everything in motion receives movement by some other thing, and secondly, that we cannot regress to infinity in the series of things moved and moving.

Aristotle proves the first of these propositions by three arguments. The first presupposes in its turn three hypotheses. First: for a thing to be in motion of itself, it must contain in itself the principle of its movement; otherwise it is evidently set in motion by some other thing. Secondly: the thing must be moved *in toto*, i.e. it must be in motion in respect of its whole and not in respect of one of its parts, as an animal is moved by the movement of its feet; in which case it cannot be said that the whole thing moves itself, but only that one part of the whole moves another part. The third hypothesis is that the thing in question must be divisible and have parts, since, according to Aristotle, everything that is in motion is divisible.* With these assumptions, we can prove that nothing can set itself in motion. That which we assume to be moving itself, is moved *in toto*, hence the repose of one of its parts implies the repose of the whole.[9] Indeed, if one part remained at rest, while another is in motion, it would no longer be the whole which is set in motion *in toto*, but one part which is in motion, while the other would be at rest. Now, nothing the repose of which depends on the repose of another thing, moves of itself. If, in fact, the repose of one thing depends on the repose of another, of necessity its movement also depends on the movement of another, and consequently, it does not set itself in motion. And since the thing which we assume to be in motion does not set itself in motion, it follows necessarily that everything in motion is moved by another thing.

The second proof of Aristotle is an induction. Everything that is moved by accident does not set itself in motion; its motion in fact depends on another thing. The same is also evident of everything that undergoes a violent movement or is set in motion by its nature or contains the principle of its movement in itself, such things for instance as animals which are moved by their soul, or all those things which are moved by their nature without containing in themselves the principle of their movements, such as heavy

---

* *Phys.*, VIII. 5. The proof of this is to be found in *Phys.*, IV., 4, for "motion" and "mutation" are the same thing. Aristotle is here speaking of *continuous* motion, therefore strictly of local motion, and of other kinds of motion (such as change) only insofar as they are continuous, as St. Thomas points out in his commentary on this passage (*lect.* 5, par. 16). In such continuous movement the moving thing does not pass instantaneously from the sphere AB to the sphere CD, but partly relinquishes the sphere AB, as it partly reaches the sphere CD. Thus it is in AB and CD at the same time—not completely in both, for this is impossible—but part of it is in AB and part in CD. The motion is completed when all the parts have left AB and are in CD. Therefore anything that moves by continuous motion has parts and is divisible (cf. *ibid.*, *lect.* 5, par. 16).

or light bodies which are moved by their places of origin.* Now, everything that is in motion is set in motion either by itself or by accident. If moved by accident, it does not set itself in motion; if it sets itself in motion, it is moved either by violence or by nature; if it is moved by nature, it is moved either by its own nature like the animal, or by another, like the heavy or light bodies. Thus all that is in motion is moved by something else.

The third proof of Aristotle is the following: nothing is at the same time, in reference to the same things, both in act and in potency. But everything is in potency in as far as it is set in motion, for movement is the actualising of that which is in potency, in as far as it is in potency. Now all things which impart movement are insofar in act, since nothing acts except it be in act. Consequently nothing is at the same time and in respect of the same things, both mover in act and moved: therefore, nothing moves of itself.

There remains our second proposition, viz. that an infinite regress in the series of things moved and moving is impossible. Here again Aristotle gives three arguments.

The first is as follows: if you regress *ad infinitum* in the series of things moved and moving, you must assume an infinite number of bodies, for everything that is in motion is divisible and consequently a body. Now, every body which moves and is moved, is in motion simultaneously imparting movement. Hence, all this infinite number of bodies which impart movement because themselves set in motion, must move simultaneously, if one of them moves. But each of them must, as it is in itself a finite body, move in a finite time, therefore the infinite number of bodies moving simultaneously, must be in motion in a

* A heavy body tends to find its natural position by moving downwards, a light body by moving upwards. Therefore the former moves downwards when its support is removed, and the latter upwards when it is released. Their natural positions are therefore indirectly the cause of their movements.

finite time. But this is impossible. It is therefore impossible to regress *ad infinitum* in the series of things moved and moving.

Moreover, the impossibility of an infinite number of bodies being in motion in a finite time, is proved by Aristotle in this way: the thing that gives and the thing that receives motion must be together, as can be shown inductively by reviewing all the kinds of movement. But bodies can be together only by continuity or contiguity. Since therefore all the things moved and moving are necessarily bodies, they must form, as it were, a single moving object, the parts of which are in contiguity or continuity. And thus a single infinite thing would have to be in motion in a finite time,—a proposition which Aristotle has proved to be impossible.

The second argument, showing the impossibility of infinite regress, is as follows: if a series of things moved and moving are arranged in order, i.e. if they form a series in which each thing gives movement to the next, it is inevitable that, if the first mover disappears or ceases to move, none of the following things will be either moving or moved: it is in fact the first mover that imparts the power of movement to all the others. Now, if we deal with an infinite series of things moved and moving, there will be no first mover and all the things will function as intermediate movers. Consequently, in the absence of a first mover, nothing will be moved and there will be no movement in the world.

The third argument amounts to the same as the preceding, except that the order of the terms is inverted. We begin with the superior term and argue thus: the intermediate moving cause cannot impart movement, unless there be a primary moving cause. But in an infinite regress of a series of moved and moving things, all are at the same time moved and moving. Therefore only intermediate moving causes exist, and, since there is no primary moving cause, there will be no movement in the world; unless, indeed, we should ever observe an axe or saw operating without the action of the carpenter.

This is the proof of the two propositions which, as we saw, form the foundation of the first proof by which Aristotle establishes the existence of a first immobile mover.

The same conclusion can also be established indirectly, i.e. by showing that the proposition "Whatever imparts motion is set in motion by another" is not a necessary proposition.* If, indeed, everything that imparts motion, is set in motion, and if this proposition is true only by accident, it is not necessary. It is therefore possible that none of the things that impart movement are themselves in motion. But our opponent admits that a thing that is not itself in motion, does not set another in motion; if therefore it is possible that nothing is in motion, it is also possible that nothing imparts movement and that, consequently, there is no longer any movement. Now, Aristotle holds it to be impossible that movement should cease at any moment. It follows that our starting-point is inacceptable, i.e. that the proposition "Whatever imparts motion, is set in motion by another," is not true by accident.

Again, the same conclusion may be reached by an appeal to experience. Aristotle asserts[10] that if two properties are joined in a subject by accident, and one of these may be found to occur without the other, it is probable that the second may also be found without the first. If, for example, we find both "white" and

---

* In a "necessary" proposition the predicate is contained in the very notion of the subject and the truth of the proposition is absolute and universal. In an "accidental" or "contingent" proposition the predicate is not included in the notion of the subject, though not repugnant to it, and the proposition is true only in particular cases. Thus: "Man is a rational animal" (a necessary proposition) is true absolutely and universally of all men. "Men are learned" (an accidental proposition) is true only of some, not of all.

"musician" in Socrates, and in Plato we find "white" without "musician," it is likely that in another subject "musician" may be found to occur without "white." If therefore the properties of mover and moved are found together by accident in one thing, and if we find somewhere the property of "being in motion" without finding that of "mover," it is probable that we may find elsewhere a mover which is not in motion.[11] The conclusion in this case goes in fact beyond its objective. In proving that this proposition, "Whatever imparts motion is set in motion by another," is not true by accident, we prove at the same time that, if the relation between mover and moved object were accidental, the possibility or rather the probability of a first mover is by that very fact established.

The proposition, "Whatever imparts motion is set in motion by another," is accordingly not true by accident. Is it true *per se*? If it is true *per se*, again an impossibility results. The mover may receive either a motion of the same kind as the one it imparts, or a motion of a different kind. If the movement is of the same kind, it follows that everything that produces a change, is itself changed, everything that heals is itself healed, everything that instructs, is instructed, etc., and all this in reference to the same things (the same science, etc.). But this is impossible; for, if he who instructs must, indeed, possess the science he teaches, it is no less necessary that he who learns that science, should not possess it. If, on the other hand, it is a question of a movement of a different kind, so that (for instance) something which imparts a movement of change, itself receives a movement affecting its position in space, and that which moves another locally, itself receives a motion of change in volume, and so forth, it would follow, since the kinds and forms of movement are finite in number, that a regress *ad infinitum* would be impossible, and thus again we must find a first mover which itself is not set in motion by any other.

The objection will perhaps be raised that, after having passed through all kinds and manners of movement, we must come back to the first kind and close the circle—so that the thing which moved another in space, was itself changed, and that which changed it, was increased in volume, and that which increased the other in volume, was in its turn, moved in space. But we should always come back to the same conclusion: that which sets up a movement of a certain kind, is itself set in motion in the same manner; the only difference is that it would be moved indirectly instead of directly. In either case, the same impossibility forces us to posit a first mover, not set in motion by anything outside itself.

The conclusion reached is accordingly as follows: this proposition, "Whatever imparts motion is set in motion by another," is true neither by accident nor *pe se*. Consequently there must be a mover which is not set in motion from outside. The preceding argument had proved, in the first place, that, in the order of secondary things, everything that is in motion, is set in motion by something else. St. Thomas therefore opposed this thesis that it is possible to find movement without a mover, but only to show that a first mover must be assumed at the beginning of every movement. Here, on the contrary, he does not confine the bearing of the principle *omne movens movetur* to the order of secondary things. He gives it, by hypothesis, an absolute value, and if he in the present context criticises it, it is not so much because this principle allows us to affirm that there is no movement without mover in secondary things as, because it might be taken to deny the proposition "there is no first immobile mover."

At the same time the distinctive character of this new line of argument is evident. St. Thomas places himself at the point of view of a hypothetical opponent, asserting: everything that moves, is set in motion. If it is logically impossible to conceive of a mover which is not itself in motion, then there cannot be God, i.e. a first Mover, Himself immobile. But if, on the contrary, this proposition, taken absolutely, possesses neither accidental nor necessary truth, it follows that the contrary proposition is necessarily true: there is a first Mover who is not in motion.

Our second demonstration is, however, still in-incomplete. It does not follow from the fact that there is a first Mover, unmoved from outside, that there exists a first Mover who is absolutely immobile. Hence Aristotle points out that the expression "a first Mover, not set in motion" is ambiguous. It can, in the first place, mean an absolutely immobile first Mover; in that case our conclusion holds. But it can also mean that this first Mover receives no movement from outside, while conceding that it may move itself and may not, therefore, be absolutely immobile. But is this being which moves itself, set in motion as a whole, by the whole of itself? Then we relapse into our former difficulty, viz. that the same being is teaching and taught, in potency and in act at the same time and in the same respects. Should we say, *per contra*, that only a part of this being is the mover, while another part is set in motion? Then we reach again our conclusion: there is a mover which is nothing but mover, i.e. which is entirely immobile.

Such are, in their essential elements, the proofs of the existence of the first Mover propounded in the "Summa contra Gentes" (I. 13). It is easy to see that, in the mind of St. Thomas the conception of a first Mover coincides with that of God. In the "Summa theologica" he is of opinion that, if we speak of a first Mover not set in motion by anything else, everyone will understand that we mean God.[12] Not that St. Thomas expects us to accept this conclusion as pure and simple evidence: we shall get the full proof when he developes all the Divine attributes which human reason can apprehend, from the conception of a first immobile Mover. In particular the "Compendium theologiae" shows the development of the notions of eternity, simplicity, aseity, unity and, in short, of all the attributes, characteristic of the essence of God, from this single principle.[13]

The reader will also have noticed in the preceding demonstration the absence of all reference to any beginning of movement in time. The proof in no way considers movement as a present reality the existence of which requires an efficient cause in the past, which is God. It aims simply at establishing that in the universe as actually given, movement, as actually given, would be unintelligible without a first Mover communicating it to all things. In other words the impossibility of an infinite regress must not be taken as an infinite regress *in time*, but as applying to the present consideration of the universe.[14] The point might also be stated by saying that nothing would be changed in the structure of the proof, if the false assumption of the eternity of the movement were admitted. St. Thomas knows this and states it expressly.[15] If we admit, in accordance with Catholic dogma, that the world and movement have had a beginning in time, we should be in much the most favourable position to prove the existence of God. For if the world and movement have had a beginning, the necessity of positing a cause which has produced movement and the world, is self-evident. Everything, in fact, which is produced, requires a cause originating the new thing, since nothing can transfer itself from potency to act, or from non-being to being. As easy as a proof of this kind is, as difficult is it, if we assume the eternity of the world and of movement. Yet we find St. Thomas giving preference to this relatively difficult and obscure form of proof. The explanation is that in his opinion a proof of the existence of God from the necessity of a creator producing movement and everything else within time, would never be a conclusive proof from the strictly philosophical point of view. We shall see that, from the point of view of simple reason, it is impossible to prove that the world has had a beginning. On this score St. Thomas is immovably opposed to the

Franciscan school and up to that point adopts Aristotelianism. To demonstrate the existence of God
ex suppositione novitatis mundi, would, when all is said
and done, make the existence of God a truth of Faith,
dependent on the credence given to the account of
Genesis; it would no longer be a philosophical truth,
proved by demonstration. By taking up this position
and by proving the existence of God on the assumption
of an eternal movement, St. Thomas proves it *a fortiori*
on the hypothesis of a universe and movement which
have had a beginning. His proof accordingly remains
unassailable and coherent with the whole of his teaching.

Lastly, it is important to explain why an infinite
regress at the present moment when we consider the
universe, would be an absurdity. The reason is that
the causes, on the series of which we argue, are hierarchically arranged; i.e. that, in the assumption on
which the proof from the first Mover rests, everything
that is in motion is given motion by a moving cause,
superior to it, and which consequently is the cause both
of its own movement and of its moving power. What
the superior cause has to account for, is not only the
movement of an individual thing of any degree (for
another individual of the same degree would suffice
to explain it, as one stone moves another stone), but
the movement of the whole species. It is true that,
taking our standpoint *within* a species, we see without
difficulty the sufficient reason of the individuals or of
the movements in question, once the species is given;
but each individual or each moving cause, having *ex
hypothesi* received from another its nature and power of
movement, can no longer be considered as being itself
the cause of its nature or its power. But the problem
presents itself in the same manner for each individual of
the species under discussion, since, for each, the nature
defining it, has been received from outside. The sufficient reason for the efficacy of the individuals must
therefore be sought outside or above the species.[16] Consequently we must either suppose that whatever receives its nature, is at the same time the cause of it and

therefore the cause of itself—which is absurd; or that everything which acts by virtue of a nature received, is only an instrumental cause, leading back, through superior causes, to a first cause: *oportet omnes causas inferiores agentes reduci in causas superiores sicut instrumentales in primarias.*[17] In this sense it may be said not only that the ascending series of hierarchically arranged causes is not infinite, but even that its terms are not very numerous: *Videmus enim omnia quae moventur ab aliis moveri, inferiora quidem per superiora; sicut elementa per corpora coelestia, inferiora a superioribus aguntur.*[18] The proof from the first Mover displays its full significance only on the assumption of an hierarchically ordered universe.

NOTES TO CHAPTER IV.

* The principle of the real distinction between *Act* and *Potency* is one of the most fundamental and far-reaching principles in Thomistic philosophy, having for St. Thomas an even wider application than for Aristotle from whom it emanated. The two notions are complementary and are practically synonymous with "being determined" and "being determinable." In this context "potency" represents "passive potency," as distinct from "active potency" or "faculty." It is a principle or aptitude of receiving or becoming. St. Thomas defines it as "principium per quod alicui competit ut moveatur vel patiatur ab alio" (*Comm. Met.*, V., lect. 14). The realisation of this aptitude or capability is known as "act." As St. Thomas says: "Just as the *action* is the complementary perfection of an active potency, so that which corresponds to the passive potency, as its perfection and completion, is called *act.*" (*Comm. Sent.*, I., dist. XLII., qu. I., art. 1, ad 1ᵐ.)

In God there is no passive capability at all. He is Pure Act, i.e. He has—or more correctly, He *is*—every possible perfection. But in all other beings there is passive potency of some kind. In the pure spirits the distinction must be drawn between their "essence," which has the capability of being, and their "existence," which is the actualisation of that capability. In material beings there is yet a further capability resulting from the nature of matter. This may be the capability of coming to be or of passing away, or that of local movement. The latter is included in the former, though not necessarily vice-versâ. Man has both these potencies, but the celestial bodies, the potency of whose matter is completely actualised by their form from the first moment of their existence, have only that of local motion.

In the more detailed application of "potency" and "act," as

in the distinction between the soul and its faculties, between the active and the possible intellect, in short, wherever there is a determination of something hitherto undetermined, the general doctrine here given, will serve as a guide. The scope of its application can be seen in the following dictum: *Actus et potentia dividunt ens et quodlibet genus entis.*

1. A convenient work is: E. Krebs, *Scholastische Texte.* I. *Thomas von Aquin. Texte zum Gottesbeweis, ausgewählt und chronologisch geordnet,* Bonn, 1912. The various texts of the Thomistic proofs are there collected in chronological order.

2. *Sum. theol.,* I, 2, 3, ad *Resp.*

3. *Phys.,* VIII. 5, 311a, 4ff.; *Metaph.,* XII. 6, 1071b, 3ff. Cf. E. Rolfes, *Die Gottesbeweise bei Thomas von Aquin und Aristoteles,* Köln, 1898.

4. See Baeumker, *Witelo,* p. 332ff.

5. *Guide,* tr. Munk, Vol. II., p. 29–36; L.-G. Lévy, *Maimonide,* p. 126–127. 6. *Sum. theol.,* I. 2, 3, ad *Resp.*

7. "To be in motion" means simply "to change," whatever order of change may be in question: "Quod autem se aliter habet nunc quam prius, movetur." *Cont. Gent.,* II., 33. ad *Adhuc quandocumque.*

8. S. Weber, *Der Gottesbeweis aus der Bewegung bei Thomas von Aquin auf seinen Wortlaut untersucht,* Freiburg i/B., 1902.

9. We follow the reading *sequitur,* as *non sequitur* seems quite inacceptable. Concerning this textual controversy see Grunwald, *op. cit.,* p. 136, where all the necessary references can be found. The reading is moreover adopted in the Leonine edition, Vol. XIII., p. 31.

10. *Phys.,* VIII., 5, 256b, 20.

11. This argument had already been adopted by Maimonides, *Guide to the Erring,* tr. Munk, II., p. 36, and by Albertus Magnus, *De caus. et proc. universit.,* I., tr. 1, c. 7; ed. Jammy, Vol. V., p. 534b, 535a. See also on this point and the various examples quoted, Baeumker, *Witelo,* p. 326.

12. *Sum. theol.,* I. 2, 3, ad *Resp.* 13. *Op. cit.,* I. 5–41.

14. *Cont. Gent.,* II., 38, ad *Quod etiam quinto.*

15. *Cont. Gent.,* I. 13.

16. *Cont. Gent.,* III. 65, ad *Item nullum particulare.*

17. *Cont. Gent.,* II. 21. The term "instrument" is moreover the precise technical term to designate an intermediary mover, both moved and moving: "est enim ratio instrumenti quod sit movens motum" (*ibid.*). See also the text of the *Comment. in Phys.,* VIII., cap. 5, lect. 9, which insists on this point: "Et hoc (*scil.* the impossibility of an infinite regress) magis manifestum est in instrumentis quam in mobilibus ordinatis, licet habeat eamdem veritatem, quia non quilibet consideraret secundum movens esse instrumentum primi"; and the profound observation of St. Thomas indicating the source of the doctrine, *Sum. theol.,* Ia., IIae., 1, 4, ad 2ᵐ.

18. *Comp. theol.,* I. 3.

CHAPTER V. THE FOUR OTHER PROOFS OF THE EXISTENCE OF GOD

THE proof from the first Mover is not only the most evident but also the most fertile in consequences concerning our knowledge of the Divine essence. Still, there are other ways open to us which lead to the same conclusion that God exists, and unfold to us new points of view of His infinite essence.

THE SECOND PROOF

The second proof of the existence of God is drawn from the conception of efficient cause, *ex ratione causae efficientis*.[1] Its origin is to be found in Aristotle,[2] who held an infinite regress to be impossible in the four kinds of causes: material, efficient, final and formal,* and concluded that we must always come back to a first beginning. Aristotle does not, however, infer from this directly the existence of God. But Avicenna,[3] then Alain of Lille,[4] and lastly Albertus

---

* The four kinds of causes may be arranged and illustrated as follows:

External causes $\begin{cases} \text{efficient.} \\ \text{final.} \end{cases}$

Internal causes $\begin{cases} \text{formal.} \\ \text{material.} \end{cases}$

(a) An *efficient* cause is the external agent by whose operation a thing comes to be: a father is the efficient cause of his son, or a craftsman the efficient cause of an article of furniture.

(b) A *final* cause is the end for which the thing exists: beatitude is the final cause of man; or use is the final cause of a chair.

(c) A *formal* cause is the intrinsic active principle whereby a thing is of a certain definite nature: the soul of man is his formal cause.

(d) A *material* cause is the intrinsic passive principle out of which a thing is made: the body is the material cause of man.

Magnus,[5] make use of Aristotle's argument for this purpose. Of the various forms given to the proof by these thinkers, that of Avicenna is particularly interesting, because it comes very near to the Thomistic proof. Yet the similarities are not such as to exclude the probability[6] that St. Thomas had discovered it directly by a deeper personal study of the Aristotelian text. We shall therefore proceed at once to consider the proof.

Let us consider the objects of sense-experience, the only possible starting-point for a proof of the existence of God. We observe in them an order of efficient causes. On the other hand, there neither is nor can be found a being which is the efficient cause of itself. The cause being necessarily anterior to the effect, a being, to be its own efficient cause, would have to be anterior to itself—which is impossible. Again, it is impossible to regress *ad infinitum* in the series of efficient causes. For we have established that there is an order of efficient causes, i.e. that they are arranged in such a manner that the first is the cause of the second, and the second, etc. of the last. This statement remains true, whether it is a question of a single intermediate cause connecting the first with the last, or a number of intermediate causes. In both cases, and whatever the number of intermediate causes, the first cause is the cause of the last effect, so that, if we suppress the first cause, we suppress the effect, and that, if there is no first term in the series, there will be no intermediate or last terms either. Now, if the series of causes so arranged were infinite, there would be neither intermediate efficient causes nor a last effect. But we note that there are such causes and such effects in the world: consequently we must posit a first efficient cause—which everybody calls God.[7] The text of the proof in the "Contra Gentes" is almost identical with that of the "Summa theologica"; the only differences are in the form of expression; it is therefore unnecessary to insist.

On the other hand, it is well to note the close relation

between the second Thomistic proof of the existence
of God and the first; in both cases, the necessity of a
first cause rests on the impossibility of an infinite
regress in an ordered series of causes and effects.
Nowhere is one more strongly tempted to admit the
thesis, recently put forward, that there are not five
proofs, but one single proof of the existence of God
divided into five parts.[8] But if by this is meant that
the five demonstrations of St. Thomas condition each
other—and one critic has gone so far as to assert that
the proof from the first Mover is merely the prepara-
tion of the proof,—this contention is inacceptable.
Each proof is self-contained and self-sufficient, and
this is eminently true of the proof from the first
Mover: *prima et manifestior via*. Yet it is true to say
that the five proofs of St. Thomas have the same
structure, and even that they mutually complete each
other; for, though each of them is sufficient to establish
that God exists, yet each starts from a different order
of effects and consequently throws light on a different
aspect of Divine causality. Whereas the first proof
shows us God as the cause of cosmic movement and of
all movements dependent on it, the second presents
Him as the cause of the very existence of things. We
have found that God is the moving Cause; now we
know that he is the efficient Cause. In a system of
knowledge which in respect of the Divine essence
subordinates the determination of the *quid est* to that
of the *an est* the multiplicity of convergent proofs
could not be a matter of indifference.

It is lastly necessary to point out that, if the proof
from the efficient Cause rests like that from the first
Mover on the impossibility of an infinite regress in
the series of causes, the reason is, here too, that the
essentially ordered causes are hierarchically arranged.
An infinite series of causes of the same degree is
not only possible, but, on the Aristotelian hypothesis of the eternity of the world, necessary. One
man can beget another man, who in his turn begets
a third, and so on *ad infinitum*; the explanation

is that such a series has no inner causal order, since
one man begets another in his quality as man, not
as the son of his father. If, on the contrary, we wish
to find the cause of his form as such, i.e. the cause by
virtue of which he is a man and capable of begetting
another man, then the cause will be found not within
the status of man, but in a being of higher status;
and as this superior being explains at the same time
the existence and causality of the being subordinated
to it, so it has received its causality from a being, in
turn superior to it. Hence the necessity of a first
term is inevitable: this first term will, in fact, virtually
contain the causality of the whole series and also of each
term composing it.[9] In the system of St. Thomas
there is not *one* efficacy only, but there is only one
source of the efficacy for the whole world: *nulla res
dat esse nisi in quantum est in ea participatio divinæ
virtutis*: and therefore, as we have to posit a final
supreme degree in the order of moving causes, so we
must also posit a final supreme degree in the order of
efficient causes.

THE THIRD PROOF

This can easily be verified again by indicating the
third way, the starting-point of which is the distinction between the Possible and the Necessary. Two
premisses may be considered as the basis of this proof.
The first is that the Possible is contingent: i.e. that
it may or may not be. Hence its opposition to the
Necessary. The second premiss is that the Possible
has its existence not in itself, viz. from its essence,
but from an efficient cause which imparts existence to
the Possible. These propositions and the principle
just established that there can be no regress *ad
infinitum* in the series of efficient causes, supply the
elements of the proof.

In considering the Possible as not having its existence
of itself, this third proof assumes the distinction
between essence and existence in created things.
This distinction which is to be found in St. Augustine

and Boethius, and is fully set out by the Arabic philosophers and especially by Alfarabi, was a universally accepted thesis at the time of St. Thomas. Indeed we find as early as Avicenna a complete proof of the existence of God, based on the above-mentioned principles. This proof, slightly altered, occurs again in Maimonides, who no doubt had it from Avicenna himself,[10] and we find it again in St. Thomas, who, as has been pointed out by Baeumker, follows the Jewish thinker step by step in his demonstration.[11] Maimonides starts from the fact that there are beings,[12] and admits a threefold possibility: (*a*) no being is either born or perishes; (*b*) all beings are born and perish; (*c*) some beings are born and perish and some beings neither are born nor perish. The first possibility need not be discussed, since experience shows us that there are beings which are born and perish. The second will not stand scrutiny. If all beings could be born and could perish, it would follow that at a given moment all beings had necessarily perished; for in the case of an individual a possibility may or may not be realised; but in respect of a species it must necessarily be realised[13]: unless this were so, "possible" would be a mere empty word. Therefore, if disappearance constituted a real possibility for all beings, considered as forming a single species, they would have disappeared already. But if they had vanished into nothingness, they could never have returned to existence of themselves, and consequently, still to-day nothing would exist. Now, we see that something does exist: therefore the third hypothesis has to be accepted as the only true one, viz. that some beings are born and perish, but that there is one Being beyond all possibility of destruction and endowed with necessary existence, namely the First Being, which is God.

This proof is not inserted in the "Summa contra Gentiles," but it forms, almost in the same words, in the "Summa theologica," the third possible demonstration of the existence of God. There are, says

St. Thomas, things which come into existence and die, and which consequently can or cannot be. But it is impossible that things of this kind should always exist, because, when the non-existence of a thing is possible, there must have been a moment when it did not exist. If therefore the non-existence of all things were possible, there would have been a moment when nothing existed. But if it is true that there was such a moment, even now nothing would exist, because whatever does not exist, cannot come into existence without the intervention of something that is. If, therefore, at this moment, no being existed, it is absolutely impossible for anything to have begun to exist, and nothing ought to exist any more—which is evidently false. Consequently the existence of all beings cannot be only possible, and we must recognise the existence of something which exists of necessity. This necessarily existing being may have the necessity of its existence either from itself or from some other being; but it is impossible to start on an infinite regress in the series of beings which are endowed with the necessity of their existence from another being, just as one cannot start on an infinite regress in the series of efficient causes, as has already been shown. It is accordingly, necessary to posit a being, which, necessary of itself, does not receive the cause of its necessity from another, but is, on the contrary, the cause of the necessity for all the others, and such a being all call God.[14]

St. Thomas' third proof of the existence of God is related to the first in assuming—and more evidently assuming—the thesis of the eternity of the world. The Jewish and the Christian philosophers both admit that, if the non-existence of all things were possible, a moment would necessarily have occurred when nothing existed; for they argue that, on the hypothesis of an infinite duration of the world, a Possible—if that word is to have any sense—cannot fail to be actualized. Of course, as we have observed earlier in the case of St. Thomas, they do not really admit the eternity of the world, but, in the words of Maimonides, they wish "to establish the existence of God in our belief by a demonstrative method which could not possibly be contested, so as not to rest this dogma, true and of so great an importance, upon a foundation which anyone might shake and which some might even consider non-existent."[15] Maimonides and St. Thomas are in complete accord on this point. It is easy to estimate the new gain secured by this third proof: God whom we know already as the moving Cause and the efficient Cause of all things, is known to us henceforth as necessary. This is a conclusion which we shall have to recall more than once.

THE FOURTH PROOF

The fourth proof of the existence of God rests on the consideration of the degrees of being. None of the Thomistic proofs has given rise to so many different interpretations. In the first place we will consider the two expositions given by St. Thomas, and then explain in detail the difficulties offered by the texts, and lastly attempt to solve them.

St. Thomas informs us in the "Contra Gentes" that another proof might be drawn from the teaching of Aristotle in Book II. of his Metaphysics.

Aristotle teaches[16] that the things which possess the highest degree of truth, possess also the highest degree of being.[17] Again, he shows elsewhere[18] that a supreme degree of truth exists. Of two false statements, one is always less false than the other, whence it follows, that of the two one is truer than the other. But greater or lesser truth as such is defined by an approximation to what is supremely and absolutely true. Hence it may be concluded that something exists which is being supremely and at its highest degree, and this very thing is what we call God.[19]

In the "Summa theologica" St. Thomas states that he proposes to draw his proof from the degrees which are observable in things. For we notice that there are things more or less good, more or less noble, more or less true, and so on for all the kinds of perfection. But the "more or less" can only be applied to things according as they approximate in different degrees to that which in the particular kind of thing is its supreme degree. Something, for instance, is hotter as it approximates to the highest degree of heat. Consequently something exists which is true, good, noble, etc. at their highest degree, and which, therefore, is the highest degree of being. For, according to Aristotle, that which possesses the highest degree of truth, possesses also the highest degree of being.[20] On the other hand, whatever is considered as constituting the highest degree in a kind, is the cause of all that belongs to this kind: for instance, fire which is the highest degree of heat, is the cause of all heat. Consequently there must exist some other thing which is the cause of being and of goodness and of all the perfections of whatever kind which are found in all things, and this precisely is what we call God.[21]

As we have said, the interpretation of this proof has led to many controversies. The explanation is that, in distinction to the others, it presents a conceptual and somehow a fairly marked ontological appearance. In consequence, a number of philosophers may be quoted who have regarded it with some suspicion. Staab[22] accords it an only probable value. Grunwald[23] remarks that the proof passes from the abstract concept to the assertion of being. It has been said, moreover, that it was the sense of this inconsistency which led St. Thomas to modify this proof in the "Summa theologica." By appealing, in the second version, constantly to sense-experience, by quoting the examples of fire and heat, he endeavoured—it is suggested—to establish his demonstration on a more empirical basis. And this "modulation," designed to bring the proof down from the heights of idealism

to the firm ground of Thomistic realism, is said to be
noticeable by the simple comparison of the two texts.
On the other side, there are numerous historians who
express whole-hearted admiration for this proof and,
more Thomistic than St. Thomas on this point, give
it even the preference over the others.[24] These
differences of appreciation are interesting because they
are symptomatic of differences of interpretation.

No difficulty can arise about the observation that
there are degrees of truth and of being in things.
But it is not so with the conclusion drawn by St.
Thomas: "Therefore a supreme degree of truth exists."
The question has been asked whether this is to be taken
in a relative or an absolute sense. Kirfel[25] takes it in
the relative sense, i.e. as the highest degree actually
realised in each kind. Rolfes[26], on the contrary, takes
it in the sense of the highest degree possible, that is,
in the absolute sense. And Father Pègues writes in
the same strain: "It is first and foremost a question of
the being which exceeds all others in perfection; but,
by that very fact, we reach the most perfect conceivable."[27]

The interpretation which takes *maxime ens* in the
relative sense is easily intelligible; its object is to
eliminate from the Thomistic proof every trace of what
is believed to be ontologism. St. Thomas argues:
there are degrees of error and of truth, hence there is
a supreme truth and consequently a supreme Being
which is God. But would this not amount to passing,
like St. Anselm, from thought to being, from the realm
of knowledge to that of reality? Nothing could be
less Thomistic than such an attitude. In order to
avoid this difficulty St. Thomas is credited with an
induction which from the supreme relative degree
observed in every order of reality as actually given,
should carry us to the supreme absolute degree of
being, i.e. to the highest being that we can conceive.

On this assumption we can further understand the
important addition which distinguishes the proof
as given in the "Summa theologica." The "Contra

Gentes" concludes the proof by affirming the existence
of a *maxime ens*, identified directly with God; the
"Summa theologica" adds the further argument that
the *maxime ens* is also universal cause, and therefore,
cannot but be God. Why this addition? If we take
maxime ens in the relative sense, it is easy to understand. In that case it is, indeed, not immediately
evident that this supreme degree of being is God; it
may be a very high degree which yet is finite and intelligible to us. By identifying it, on the contrary,
with the universal and supreme Cause, we establish
the fact that the *maxime ens* is God. If, however,
this expression is taken in the absolute sense, it is
evident that this supreme being is identical with God,
and it becomes incomprehensible that St. Thomas
should have uselessly prolonged his proof, especially
in a work which, like the "Summa theologica," aims
at clearness and brevity.[28]

These arguments are ingenious, but they substitute
inextricable difficulties for one difficulty which perhaps
is not inextricable after all. The first of these difficulties is that, if *maxime ens* is to be understood in a
purely relative sense, the argument in the "Contra
Gentes" is a crude paralogism. St. Thomas argues
thus: that which is supreme truth is also supreme
being; now, there is a supreme truth; hence there is a
supreme Being which is God. If *maxime verum* and
maxime ens have a relative sense in the premises,
how can an absolute sense be given to *maxime ens* in
the conclusion? Yet this is what the proof demands,
since it argues directly to God.[29] If we are referred
on this point to the supposedly fuller form in the
"Summa theologica," we find that the letter of the
text itself fits in badly with such an interpretation.
The example of the more or less hot, which St. Thomas
uses there, must not mislead us: it is a simple comparison, a *manuductio* meant to help us in understanding the main thesis. Undoubtedly, *maxime calidum*
is a purely relative supreme degree; at a pinch one
might argue about the *maxime verum* and *maxime*

nobile; but it seems difficult to argue about the *maxime ens*. It is possible to conceive a relative supreme degree in any order of perfection, but not in that of being. The moment St. Thomas posits a supreme truth which is also the supreme being, either the expression he uses has no conceivable sense, or he posits purely and simply the supreme degree of being which is God. As regards the appeal to the principle of causality at the end of the proof in the "Summa theologica," its object is by no means to establish the existence of a supreme Being; that conclusion is already secured. Its object is simply to lead us to recognise in this first Being which we posit as above all beings, the cause of all the perfections which appear in secondary things. This consideration adds nothing to the proof as such, but gives greater precision to the conclusion.

The fact therefore remains that St. Thomas seems to have argued directly from the consideration of the degrees of being to the existence of God. Can such an argument be considered as a concession to ontologism? The very sources of the proof seem to make it probable. When this proof occurs for the first time, we find, side by side with Aristotle, the famous passage from the "City of God," where St. Augustine praises the Platonists for having seen that in all changeable things the form whereby a being—of whatever nature it may be—is what it is, can only come to it from Him who Is, truly and immutably: *Cum igitur in eorum conspectu, et corpus et animus magis minusque speciosa essent et, si omni specie carere possent, omnino nulla essent, viderunt esse aliquid ubi prima esset species incommutabilis, et ideo nec comparabilis: atque ibi esse rerum principium rectissime crediderunt, quod factum non esset, et ex quo facta cuncta essent.*[31] But to conclude from the Platonic inspiration of the proof to its ontological character, and to say with Grunwald that it is a useless waste of labour to reduce this idealistic argument to the truly Thomistic attitude of moderate realism,[32] is perhaps a little hasty. The criticisms which St. Thomas directed against the *a priori* proofs of the existence of God led precisely to this conclusion that it is impossible to start our proofs from the consideration of the Divine essence, and that we must, therefore, necessarily rely on the consideration of sense-objects. But "sense-object" does not mean only "material" object. St. Thomas has the unquestionable right to take sense-object in its complete form and with all the conditions which are laid down by his doctrine. Now, as we shall see later, a sense-object is constituted by the union of the intelligible and the material, and though the purely intelligible idea does not come directly within the range of our understanding, it is nevertheless true that our understanding can abstract from sense-objects the intelligible involved in them. Viewed from this aspect, the beautiful, the noble, the good and the true—for there are degrees of truth in things—constitute realities which we can grasp; from the fact that their Divine exemplars escape us, it does not follow that their finite participations escape us also. But, if this is the case, nothing prevents us from taking them as the starting-point of a new proof; the movement, the efficacy and the being of things are not the only realities demanding an explanation. Whatever good, noble and true there is in the universe also requires a first Cause and in searching for the origin of the perfections hidden in the things of sense, we are not in any way exceeding the limits which we had previously set ourselves.

Undoubtedly such an enquiry could not be carried on without the intervention of the Platonic and Augustinian idea of participation. But we shall see that exemplarism is one of the essential elements in the system of St. Thomas. He has never changed his opinions on the point that the inferior degrees of perfection and of being presuppose an essence in which the perfections and the being are to be found in their supreme degree. He also admits without discussion that "to possess a perfection incompletely" and "to hold it from some other cause" are synonymous expressions; and, as a cause can only confer what it possesses itself, it follows necessarily that that which does not possess a perfection of itself and possesses it only incompletely, must have it from something else which has it of itself and in the supreme degree.[33] But it does not follow therefrom that this proof of St. Thomas amounts to nothing more—as has been asserted—than to a purely abstract and conceptual deduction. All the proofs assume simultaneously two things: the use of rational principles transcending sense-experience, and a solid foundation, supplied by the sense-objects themselves, on which the principles that are to lead us towards God can rest. This is precisely the case here, since the very intelligibility of things is due to the fact that they resemble God: *nihil est cognoscibile nisi per similitudinem primae veritatis.*[34] This is why the conception of an universe hierarchically ordered according to the degrees of being and perfection is involved in the proofs of the existence of God from the first Mover and the efficient Cause. If, therefore, this new proof were to be considered as essentially Platonic, we should have to concede as a matter of logic that the same is true of the earlier proofs. And they are indeed Platonic, to the extent to which St. Thomas had borrowed from the Platonic philosophy his conception of a participation of things in God by resemblance. It was this that led him to consider the universe as hierarchically ordered according to different possible degrees of a finite participation in the causality of the Cause, in the actuality of the immobile Mover, in the goodness of the Good, the nobility of the Noble and the truth of Truth.

THE FIFTH PROOF: THE SYNTHESIS OF THE PROOFS

The fifth and last proof rests on the consideration of the Government of things. There is no need to determine the philosophical origin of this proof, since the idea of God as ruler of the universe was the common property of Christian theology, and the texts in Scripture on which it could be based, are very numerous. St. Thomas, however, himself refers us to St. John Damascene,[35] who seems to have supplied the model for his argument. It is impossible for opposed and disparate things to be harmonised and reconciled in one and the same ordered arrangement, whether always or generally, unless there is a being to govern them and to direct all together and each one separately towards a definite end. Now, we observe that in the world things of different natures are harmonised in one order, not now and then and by accident, but always or for the greater part of time. There must therefore exist a being by whose providence the world is governed, and this being we call God.[36] The "Summa theologica" argues in exactly the same manner, but adds the observation that the providence ordering the world, whereby all things are disposed in view of their end, is an intelligence; and one might, eventually, arrive at the same conclusion by different ways, notably by reasoning on the analogy of human action.[37] Whatever is the road followed by the argument, it is clear that the proof and the conclusion drawn from it have the same value as the preceding proofs. To admit that things order themselves by accident, is to admit that there is room in the universe for an effect, namely their very order, without cause. For if the form proper to each body, is sufficient to explain the particular function of that body, yet it by no means explains why the different bodies and their different functions arrange themselves in a harmonious whole.[38] We find therefore in the proof from finality as in all the earlier proofs, a sense-datum which, seeking its sufficient reason, finds it only in God; the thought inherent in things is explained, as are the things themselves, by the imitation, from afar, of the thought of the Divine providence that rules them.

The different roads, followed by St. Thomas to attain to the existence of God are evidently distinct when considered each by itself, yet no less evidently linked by an affinity when considered all together and in their relations to each other.[39] To begin with, each proof rests upon an empirical statement of fact, because an existence can be inferred only by starting from another existence. From this point of view, all the thomistic proofs stand opposed to the Augustinian proofs from

Truth, or to the proof of St. Anselm from the idea of God: movement exists, there exist reciprocal actions, beings which come into existence and die, more or less perfect things, there is order in things; and because all this exists, it is possible to assert of its cause that it too exists. The empirical basis is therefore the first feature common to the five proofs of the existence of God.

A second characteristic trait is the use which they make of the principle of causality. At bottom, indeed, there is not one of the proofs that does not demonstrate God to be the sole conceivable cause of the sense-experience from which the proof has set out. The reason is that the principle of causality is for St. Thomas a first principle, i.e. directly known by the natural light of reason as soon as reason awakens on contact with experience. Each proof therefore adds to the empirically given fact a rational and necessary element which imparts to it its own evidentialness while at the same time allowing it to transcend the datum itself. *Ex nihilo nihil fit*; therefore: all movement presupposes a mover, every effect presupposes a cause; every contingent being a being *per se*; every series a first term; all order an orderer.

To these two features a third characteristic must be added. With the exception of the proof from finality, all the others presuppose that the effects on which the argument rests are disposed in a series of more and more perfect causes. This aspect of thomistic thought, very evident in the fourth, is no less so even in the first, viz. the hierarchic subordination of essentially ordered causes and effects which renders an infinite regress in the series of cause impossible and allows reason to assert the existence of God. It must, however, be noted to avoid all misunderstanding that this hierarchy of causes under a first term posited by St. Thomas, is required by him not so much as an ascent leading up to God, as to enable him to consider the entire series of intermediary causes as a single secondary cause of which God is the First Cause. Without doubt, St.

Thomas' imagination loves to mount up these steps, but his metaphysical reason sees in them but a single step, since the efficacy of each intermediary cause presupposes the actual realisation of the complete series of its preconditions. And thus we meet again the first general feature of the proofs: the necessity to start from an actual existence, for in order to prove the existence of God it is enough to reveal the complete sufficient reason of any single existence, given in experience.

NOTES TO CHAPTER V.

1. On this proof, see A. Albrecht, *Das Ursachgesetz und die erste Ursache bei Thomas von Aquin*, Philos. Jahrb., Bd. 33, H. 2, p. 173–182.
2. *Metaph.* II. 2, 994a, 1; of St. Thomas, II. 2, ed. Cathala, art. 299–300. For the history of this proof, see Baeumker, *Witelo*, p. 326–335. Cf. the important note of S. van den Bergh, in *Epitome der Metaphysik des Averroes*, Leiden, 1924, p. 150–152.
3. See texts in Baeumker, *op. cit.*, p. 328–330.
4. *Ars fidei*, Prol. P. L. CCX., p. 598–600.
5. *De caus. et proc. universit.*, I., t. 1, c. 7; ed. Jammy, V., p. 534.
6. Cf. Grunwald, *op. cit.* p. 151. The fundamental difference between the two proofs is that St. Thomas interprets in terms of creation (*i.e.* as absolute production of being) what Avicenna interprets as natural action (*i.e.* the eduction of a form from a matter by means of movement). See below Chapter VII., A: *Creation*, p. 108, note 8.
7. *Sum theol.*, I. 2, 3, ad *Resp.*
8. A. Audun, *A proposito della dimostrazione tomistica dell' esistenza di Dio*, Rivista di filos. neo-scolast., IV., 1912, p. 758–769. See the criticism of this article by H. Kirfel, *Gottesbeweis oder Gottesbeweise beim hl. Thomas v. Aquin?* Jahrb. f. Phil. u. spek. Theol., XXVII., 1913, p. 451–460.
9. *Sum theol.*, I. 46, 2, ad 7^m, and I. 104, 1. Cf.: "Quod est secundum aliquam naturam tantum, non potest esse simpliciter illius naturae causa. Esset enim suiipsius causa. Potest autem esse causa illius naturae in hoc, sicut Plato est causa humanae naturae in Socrate, non autem simpliciter, eo quod ipse est creatus in humana natura." *Cont. Gent.*, II. 21.
10. Carra de Vaux, *Avicenne*, Paris, 1900, p. 266ff.
11. *Witelo*, p. 338.
12. *Guide to the Erring*, tr. Munk, II., ch. 1, p. 39ff. Cf. Lévy,

Maïmonide, p. 127–128.

13. "An Aristotelian conception," writes Baeumker, p. 128, n. 2. See in Lévy, p. 128, n. 1, the explanation which Maimonides himself gave when consulted by the translator Ibn Tibbon on the passage: "Si nous posons que l'écriture est une chose possible pour l'espèce humaine, dit-il, il faut nécessairement qu'à un moment donné il y ait des hommes qui écrivent; soutenir que jamais un homme n'a écrit ni n'écrira, ce serait dire que l'écriture est impossible à l'espèce humaine."

14. *Sum. theol.*, I. 2, 3, ad *Resp.*

15. *Guide*, I., ch. LXXI., p. 350.

16. Cf. on this proof the study of R. Joly, *La preuve de l'existence de Dieu par les degrés de l'être: "Quarta via" de la Somme théologique. Sources et exposés*, Gand, 1920.

17. *Met.*, II. 1, 993b, 19–31.

18. *Met.*, IV. 4, *sub fine*. St. Thomas does not seem to have known the fragment of the *De philosophia*, preserved by Simplicius in his commentary to *De coelo*, which contains precisely the proof which he himself has reconstructed with the help of the *Metaphysics* (fr. 1476, t. 22–24): "In general, wherever a better is to be found, there also the best is to be encountered. Therefore, since among beings one is better than another, there must also exist a perfect being, which is the divine being." Simplicius adds that Aristotle had borrowed this proof from Plato, which shows that the remains of Platonism in the first Aristotelianism allowed St. Thomas to feel that he was in agreement with these two philosophies on this fundamental matter.

19. *Cont. Gent.*, I. 13.

20. *Met.*, *loc. cit.*

21. *Sum. theol.*, I. 2, 3, ad *Resp.*

22. *Die Gottesbeweise in der katholischen deutschen Litteratur von* 1850–1900, Paderborn, 1910, p. 77.

23. *Op. cit.*, p. 155.

24. Th. Pègues, *Commentaire litt. de la Somme théol.*, Toulouse, 1907, Vol. I., p. 105.

25. See *Der Gottesbeweis auf den Seinstufen*, Jahrb. f. Phil. u. spek. Thoel., XXVI., 1912, p. 454–487.

26. *Op. cit.*, p. 207 and 222. Cf. his reply to the article by Kirfel in Phil. Jahrb., XXVI., 1913, p. 146–159.

27. *Commentaire*, I., p. 106.

28. Kirfel, *op. cit.*, p. 469.

29. Rolfes, Phil. Jahrb., XXVI., p. 147–148.

30. *Met.*, II. 1, 993b, 24, and IV. 4, 1008b, 31–1009a, 5. The *locus classicus* in *De potentia*, qu. III., art. 5, ad *Resp.* expressly attributes this conception to Aristotle and gives it even as the specifically Aristotelian reason of creation:

"Secunda ratio est quia, cum aliquid invenitur a pluribus diversimode participatum oportet quod ab eo in quo perfectissime invenitur, attribuatur omnibus illis in quibus imperfectius invenitur.... Et hacc est probatio Philosophi in II. Metaph." See the above quoted text. However, St. Thomas was fully aware of keeping in this matter as close to Plato as his own system and that of Aristotle allowed. Cf. the following note.

31. *Civitas Dei*, lib. VIII., c. 6.
32. *Op. cit.*, p. 157.
33. *Cont. Gent.*, I. 28, ad *In unoquoque*, and II. 15, ad *Quod alicui*. Cf. ... "Quidam autem venerunt in cognitionem Dei, ex dignitate ipsius Dei; et isti fuerunt Platonici. Consideraverunt enim, quod omne illud quod est secundum participationem, reducitur ad aliquid quod sit illud per suam essentiam sicut ad primum et ad summum; sicut omnia ignita per participationem, reducuntur ad ignem, qui est per essentiam suam talis. Cum ergo omnia quae sunt, participent esse, et sunt per participationem entia, necesse est esse aliquid in cacumine omnium rerum, quod sit ipsum esse per suam essentiam, idest quod sua essentia sit suum esse; et hoc est Deus, qui est sufficientissima et dignissima et perfectissima cause totius esse, a quo omina quae sunt, participant esse." *In Joannem evangelistam expositio*, Prologus.
34. *De Verit.*, qu. XXII., art. 2, ad 1ᵐ. This enables St. Thomas to make some room for the augustinian proofs from the idea of truth. Cf. *In Joannem evangelistam*, Prologus, ad: "Quidam autem venerunt in cognitionem Dei ex incomprehensibilitate veritatis." St. Augustine considers this proof as the most evidential of all, because he argues solely from the intrinsic character of truth; while St. Thomas, who bases his arguments only on sensible and empirically given true, anxious as he is to start from existences, necessarily regards truth as less manifest to the senses than movement. Hence the secondary part which this proof plays in the transposition of it which he gives.
35. *De fide orthodoxa*, I. 3; in *Patr. gr.*, vol. XCIV., col. 795.
36. *Cont. Gent.*, I. 13; and II. 16, ad *Amplius, quorumcumque*. Cf. *In II. Phys.* 4, 7, 8.
37. *Sum. theol.*, I. 2, 3, ad *Resp.*; *De Verit.*, qu. V., art 1, ad *Resp.*
38. *De Verit.*, qu. V., art. 2, ad *Resp.*
39. Cf. on this: Garrigou-Lagrange, *Dieu, son existence et sa nature*, 3rd ed. Paris, 1920, Appendix I., p. 760–773; E. Rolfes, *Die Gottesbeweise bei Thomas von Aquin*, Philos. Jahrb., Bd. 37, p. 329–338.

CHAPTER VI. THE DIVINE ATTRIBUTES

A. THE KNOWLEDGE OF GOD BY NEGATION

HAVING proved the existence of a First Being which we call God, we have now to examine His nature, i.e. to enquire into the properties of this Being. A complete examination into everything pertaining to the Godhead would have to set itself a threefold task: an inquiry into, first, the unity of the Divine essence; secondly, the Trinity of the Divine persons; and thirdly, the effects produced by the Godhead.[1] But the Trinity of the Divine persons is not an object falling within the purview of the philosopher as such. We are not forbidden to endeavour to grasp it as far as we can; it is, however, a teaching of God imposed upon Christian Faith and exceeding the limits of human understanding.[2] The two objectives of enquiry remaining are accordingly the essence of God and His effects.

Before examining the Divine essence in itself, we must determine to what extent and under what conditions this essence is knowable for us. Whenever we wish to define an object, we begin by assigning it to a particular *genus* and we determine thereby its essence in general: *quid est in communi*. We then add to the *genus* the differences which allow us to distinguish this object from all the others and in this way we acquire the most complete knowledge attainable concerning the nature of the object in question. But when we set out to know the Divine nature, we must needs proceed differently. It is impossible to take the quiddity or essence as *genus* and to define this *genus* by the addition of a number of differences, distinguishing it from all others.

It is, to begin with, impossible to take as our point of departure the consideration of the Divine essence, by assigning to it the rôle usually played by the *genus* in every definition. For the Divine essence exceeds in its immensity everything that the human mind can grasp; we cannot therefore claim to know this essence, nor, consequently, start from it in our enquiry. We are, however, for all that not reduced to complete silence. If we cannot attain to what the essence of God *is*, we can endeavour to ascertain what it is *not*. Instead of starting from the essence which is inaccessible to us, and adding positive differences which would allow us to know progressively better and better what it is, we can collect a more or less considerable number of negative differences which determine more and more accurately what it is not. The question will perhaps be raised whether in this way a true knowledge can be attained. The answer must be: yes. Undoubtedly, a knowledge of this kind is imperfect, for the only perfect knowledge of an essence is that which gives us a knowledge of the essence in itself. Still, it is, after all, a knowledge of some sort and worth more than sheer ignorance. Indeed, in the case of positive differences, each difference defines the other, so that each additional difference brings us nearer and nearer to the complete definition of the object. In the same way, each negative difference, by distinguishing the unknown essence from an increasingly greater number of other essences, determines also with increasing precision the preceding difference and brings us nearer to the real nature of the object. For example: by saying that God is not an accident, but a substance, we distinguish Him from all possible accidents; but if we add that God is not a body, we determine with greater accuracy the place which He occupies in the *genus* of substances. And thus proceeding in order and distinguishing God from everything that is not He, we shall by such negations reach a knowledge, if not exhaustive, at least true, of his substance, inasmuch as we shall know it to be different from all else.[3] We shall therefore follow this road as far as it will take us: when its usefulness is exhausted, then will be the time to try a new path.

In order to determine, even negatively, the conditions of the Divine essence, we must have a starting-point. In point of fact, we have as many as we have proofs of the existence of God, and in the "Summa contra Gentiles," St. Thomas takes delight in linking up, with extraordinary dialectical virtuosity, the Divine attributes with the most diverse principles of the proofs. It is, however, not difficult to see in which direction his preferences incline: the deductions in the "Contra Gentiles" and those in the "Compendium theologiae" are drawn most frequently from the conception of the First Mover, i.e. the proof which St. Thomas considers as the first and most evident. We shall accordingly start from this same principle.

It is easy, in the first place, to discard from the Divine essence the notion of time. In the first proof, "immobile" was, in fact, taken in the widest sense, like movement itself. Now, as the absence of movement amounts to the absence of all change, we can substitute "unchangeable" for "immobile" and argue thus: everything that comes to exist or ceases to exist, undergoes a movement or a change. Now, we have established that God is unchangeable: hence He has neither beginning nor end and is, consequently, eternal.[4]

The knowledge of the Divine eternal existence allows us further to discard from God all purely passive power. Since God is eternal, He cannot not be; and since He cannot not be, it follows that there is nothing in Him which is merely in potency; for whatever is in potency can either be or not be, and in proportion as God contained in Himself some passive power, He could either be or not be. Consequently, there is nothing in God which is only in potency,[5] and this means that He is pure act. But this conclusion enables us at once to reach a further negative difference, namely, that God is not matter. For matter is that which is in potency, and since God is wholly act, He must be also immaterial.[6]

If there is in God neither matter nor potency, there cannot be in Him any composition whatever. God is accordingly simple, and this conclusion will be seen to contain a number of subordinate consequences. Let us first establish that God is simple. We have already seen that God is pure act[7]; now everything composite contains both potency and act. A number of objects cannot be combined in a pure and simple unity, unless some of them are in act and others in potency. A number of objects, all in act, cannot form in combination anything but a sort of bundle or heap of things, not a true unity. For objects to constitute by their union truly *one* thing, they must be capable of uniting and must potentially possess unity before they possess it actually. In other words, they are actually one (united in act) only after being potentially unifiable. Now, there is nothing potential in God; His essence consequently contains no composition.[8]

But if God is simple, we discover immediately this first corollary that He contains nothing forcibly imposed or foreign to His own nature. For everything that contains in itself anything forcibly imposed or superadded to its nature, presupposes an addition and consequently a composition; for whatever belongs to the substance of a thing, cannot be either forcibly imposed or superadded.[9] God, therefore, contains nothing forcibly added or imposed. A second corollary of the simplicity of God is that God is not a body. For every body is continuous and therefore composite and contains parts. Now, we have shown that God is not composite;[10] He is consequently not a body;[11] and therewith all the idolatrous pagans are refuted who imagined God in a bodily form, as well as the Manicheans and Greek philosophers who substituted celestial bodies for the elements for God. A third corollary of the Divine simplicity is that God is His own essence. In everything which is not its own essence, a composition will, in fact, be observed. For, in everything, its own essence may first be found, and if nothing is added to its essence, the whole of the thing is its own essence. If therefore a thing is not its own essence, something superadded to its essence must of necessity be found in it, and, consequently, the thing contains a composition. This, by the way, is the reason why in all composite things, the essence in never more than a part of the composition; such is humanity in man. Now, we have shown that there is nothing composite in God. God, consequently, is His own essence.[12] But if God is His own essence, we may go further and assert that God is His own being. For, in the same manner, as something which contains fire without being itself fire, is ignited by participation, so something which possesses being and yet is not being, has being only by participation. Now, we know that God is His essence; if therefore He were not His being, He would possess being only by participation, not by essence. He would therefore not be the First Being—which assertion is absurd. God, accordingly, is not only His essence, but also His being.[13] It might also, in short, be argued that, if God does not admit of any composition, it is impossible to distinguish in Him being from essence and the *quod est* is identical in Him with the *quod aliquid est*.[14]

And still another consequence follows from this conclusion: namely, that nothing can occur in God which is added to His essence by way of accident. For a being which is being itself, cannot participate in anything whatever which does not derive from its essence. Any particular thing can perfectly well participate in some other thing, but, since there is nothing more formal or simple than being, something which is being itself cannot participate in anything else, since whatever it were to participate in would necessarily again be a being. But the Divine substance is being itself; it therefore possesses nothing which does not spring from its own substance;

consequently the Divine substance cannot contain any accident.[15] Nor would it be possible to define this substance by the addition of any substantial *difference*, or to subsume God as a *species* under any *genus* whatever. For every *species* presupposes a *genus* to which the *difference* defining the *species* must be added, since it is the *difference* added to the *genus* which constitutes the *species*. But as the being of God is being itself, purely and simply, He contains nothing added to Himself, for whatever might be added, belongs to the order of being and consequently is already contained in Him by right. God, consequently, cannot admit of any substantial *difference* nor constitute any *species*.[16] But neither is God a *genus*. For the absence of any substantial *difference* which prevents His constituting a *species*, prevents *a fortiori* His forming a *genus*. The *genus* "animal" cannot exist, unless there are animals characterised by the *difference* "rational" and "non-rational." To posit God, therefore, as a *genus* which yet is not defined in its own being by *differences*, would be to attribute to Him who is being itself, an only incomplete and potential being—which is manifestly absurd.[17]

Thus the Divine being is neither *genus*, nor *difference*, nor *species*. This is a conclusion of the greatest importance, readily recognised in principle, but its logical consequences are not always drawn with sufficient consistency. Indeed, if God falls outside the range of *genus* and *difference*, it is evident that He cannot be defined, since all definitions are reached by way of *genus* and *differences*. It is also evident that no proof of God can be given, except from His effects, for the beginning of all proof is the definition of whatever is to be the object of the proof. We were therefore entirely right to reject all the proofs *a priori* of the existence of God,[18] and though it is hard to believe that their supporters had lost sight of the transcendence of the Divine being, yet they certainly seem to have forgotten the logical conditions required for any valid proof of the existence of God.

Such is the absolute simplicity of God, considered in itself. But it would be no less erroneous to imagine this simple being as forming part of a composite union with other beings. Yet this error was committed more than once. It may be found in three main forms. Some persons have thus posited God as the soul of the world, as appears from the words of St. Augustine,[19] and from the same source springs the error of the philosophers who asserted that God was the soul of the first Heaven. Others have contended that God is the formal principle of all things, an opinion attributed to the Amauritians.[20] There is, lastly, the foolish error of David of Dinant, who maintained that God was identical with primary matter.[21] But it is impossible, in any manner whatever, for God to form part of anything, either as a material or a formal principle. For the form★ of a body is not itself the being of that body; it is one of the principles of its being. But, God is being itself: He is, consequently, not the form of a body.[22] We can therefore reject the opinion of those who consider God to be the soul of the world or of the First Heaven, as well as of those who see in Him the formal being of all things. We can, moreover, refute it in a way which disposes at the same time of the opinion which confuses God with primary matter. For it has been demonstrated that God is the first efficient Cause. Now, an efficient cause is not numerically identical with the form of created individual things; these things are identical only from the point of view of the species, as one man begets another man. Consequently God, who is the efficient Cause, cannot again be the form of individual beings.

★ Form is here used in the special sense of "active essential principle of being," *i.e.* the intrinsic principle whereby a thing is of a particular nature and whereby it exists. From a slightly different point of view it is the same as "formal cause." For the various uses of "form," Aristotelian, scholastic and modern, cf. "Dictionary of Philosophy and Psychology," Baldwin, s.v. Form, Matter and Form.

But if the efficient Cause is not identical with the form in each individual created thing it cannot be identical with matter, either in the individual or the species, because matter is in potency, while the efficient Cause is in act.[23]

We have excluded from God everything that is not reducible to being as such, that is, all the conditions which make created being an incomplete and defective being. But it may be feared that in proceeding thus, we have followed a dangerous path. Does not the denial of everything which defines a being as within such and such a particular existence, amount to suppressing, one after another, all its perfections? The things which possess being and life are more perfect than those which possess only being; by restricting God to being only, have we not, by dint of negations, emptied the Divine essence of all content? By no means. God who is nothing but His being, is yet the most universally perfect being. And, St. Thomas adds, I call universally perfect the being which is not lacking in any kind of nobleness and perfection.[24] By entering deeper into the matter at this point, we reach the very heart of the Thomistic conception—and we may add, the scholastic conception—of being.

For this being from which we have excluded all the imperfections of created things, is far from being thereby reduced by our understanding to an abstract idea of what is common to all things and to a sort of empty form; it is, on the contrary, identical with supreme perfection. Nor must we take it in the sense that being is reduced to a particular kind of perfection, but, conversely, in the sense that every kind of perfection reduces itself to the possession of a certain degree of being. Let us take, for example, the perfection of "wisdom": to possess wisdom, for man, is to *be* wise. The fact is that, because man, in becoming wise, has achieved a degree of being, he has also achieved a degree of perfection. For everything is said to be more or less noble or perfect in the measure in which it *is* a particular, more or less high mode of perfection. If we, therefore, assume some one thing which possesses total being, this being will also be total perfection, since all perfection is nothing but a certain manner of being. Now we know one thing which in this way possesses all being; it is the very thing of which we predicated that it *is* its own being. A thing which is its own being, i.e. the essence of which has its being of itself and not from outside, is necessarily also the whole being, or, in other words, possesses the power of being at its highest degree. A white thing, for instance, cannot be perfectly white because it is not itself "whiteness"; it is therefore white, only because it participates in whiteness, and its nature may be such as to prevent it participating in complete whiteness. But if there existed "whiteness" in itself, the nature of which consisted precisely in being white, it would evidently not lack any degree of whiteness. The same applies to being. We have already proved that God is His own being; He therefore does not receive it from outside. But we know that "to be a thing imperfectly" is the same as "to receive being imperfectly": God who is His being, is therefore the whole being which lacks no perfection. And since God possesses all perfection, He has no defects. In the same manner, in fact, in which everything is perfect in the measure of its being, every thing is also imperfect in the measure in which, in some way, it lacks being. But, since God possesses being completely, He is absolutely free from non-being, for a thing is free from non-being in the measure of its possessing being. God, consequently, has no defect and He possesses all perfections; that is to say, He is universally perfect.[25]

What, we ask, is the source of the illusion that, by denying to God a certain number of modes of being, we believe the degree of His perfection to be diminished? Simply an equivocation on the meaning of words. Without doubt, a thing which only *is*, is less perfect than one that is alive; but the fact is that we are reasoning in this case no longer about the being which *is its* being. It is a question of imperfect and participated beings which gain in perfection as they gain in being, *secundum modum quo res habet esse est suus modus in nobilitate,* and it is therefore easy to see that that which is only the perfection of the body, is inferior to that which is, in addition, the perfection of life. The expression "is only" consequently means nothing else but an inferior mode of participation in being. But when we say of God that He is only His being, without adding that He is matter, or a body, or a substance, or an accident, we mean that He possesses absolute being, and we exclude everything which might contradict the supreme degree of being and the plenitude of perfection.[26]

Hence, lastly, we understand why St. Thomas can define God by being, purely and simply, without ever confusing Him with all given beings or leaving any opening for pantheistic conceptions of the universe. When we conceive in the abstract of a being common to all existing things, we cannot conceive of it as realised without adding to or withdrawing from it something, in order to define it as such and such a particular being. Besides being in itself, there must be an essence, with its place within a genus and a species, for a real and existing object to be constituted. But it is not the same with the being that God is. His condition is such as to exclude all additions; He is neither in a species nor in a genus; He has not even an essence, since His essence is none other than His being: *Deus nor habet essentiam, quia essentia ejus non est aliud quam suum esse.* We are therefore far from confusing Him with creation; what distinguishes the Divine Being from all other being, is His absolute purity and His perfect simplicity.[27] Between the Being of God and the participated being which we are, no common measure can be found, and we might say, using the Augustinian formula, that while the creature *has* its being, God *is* His being. A strictly infinite distance separates these two modes of existence, and so far from fearing any confusion, henceforth impossible, we shall call God by the name which He gave Himself: "He Who Is,"[28] being certain of applying thus to Him a name which fits Him as no other name could, because it designates nothing but the being which is above all essence and all form: an infinite ocean of substance.[29]

B. THE KNOWLEDGE OF GOD BY ANALOGY

The preceding conclusions were, despite their often affirmative appearance, nothing but disguised negations. For an absolutely simple or completely immaterial being cannot constitute an object proportionate to our human understanding. When we say: "God is simple," we have no interior conception of this absolutely simple being; and when we say: "God is eternal," we cannot grasp with our changing thought this perpetual present which is eternity. Even when we describe God as the absolute and supereminent being, we do not claim in any way to apprehend Him as such. We have, therefore, faithfully followed the negative path which we had mapped out for ourselves. Let us now examine whether it might not be possible to acquire some positive knowledge, however imperfect, concerning the infinite essence of God.

There is doubtless no affirmation which can be applied in the same sense to God and to creatures; and we can easily see the reason. All judgments applied to both the Divine and the human nature, employ the copula "est." But it has been established that God "is" not in the same sense in which creatures "are." The created being owns such perfections as it may possess, inasmuch as it has received them, while, on the contrary, in God there is nothing which is not His own being.[30] We must consequently expect to find that every proposition about the nature of God, even when it conveys some positive knowledge, retains a good deal of negative meaning. When we apply to a man the term "wise," we indicate thereby a perfection distinct from the essence, the power and the being of the man. But when we apply this term to God, we mean to express nothing distinct from His essence and His being. Accordingly, the word "wise," applied to man, professes in a certain measure to describe and to contain the reality it signifies; but, in speaking of God, it fails to contain or even to grasp the reality signified by it. We express this negative aspect of all our judgments concerning the Divine nature, by saying that nothing can be predicated of God and the creatures in an univocal sense.[31]

Are we therefore to conclude that a proposition about a creature loses necessarily all meaning when applied to God? Such a conclusion would be inaccurate, and moreover dangerous. For to accept it would be tantamount to admitting that, taking our starting-point from creatures, we can know nothing of God nor prove anything concerning him without continual equivocations. We must accordingly admit, a certain analogy or proportion[32] between the creature and the Creator, the basis of which is not hard to discover.[33] Effects which are inferior to their causes, cannot be described in the same terms as the causes, nor especially in terms of the same meaning. Nevertheless, a certain resemblance between cause and effect must be conceded. Every productive thing produces naturally its like, since each thing produces or acts inasmuch as it is in act. Consequently, in a cause superior to its effect, the form of the effect may be traced in a certain sense, but not in the actual mode in which it occurs in the effect; hence such a cause is called an "equivocal" cause. For example, the sun causes the warmth of inferior bodies, acting accordingly as it is in act. The warmth, caused by the sun, possesses therefore some resemblance to the active power of the sun, which causes the warmth in these bodies; hence we may say that the sun is warm, although it is warm not in the same sense in which terrestrial things are warm. For the same reason, and because God confers upon all things all their perfections, we are able to discover in all things their resemblance and unlikeness to God.[34] We have emphasised these differences sufficiently not to be accused of believing that God resembles His creatures. It is the creature which, inasmuch as it holds everything it possesses from God, resembles its Creator. But this resemblance is none the less real, and would suffice to prevent our assertions concerning God from being completely equivocal. In speaking of God and of created things in the same terms, we use these terms in a sense of at least partially common meaning, since they signify in the first case the cause, and in the second, the effect.[35]

Accordingly, our statements about God and creatures are not used in an univocal sense but neither are they used in a purely equivocal sense: they must therefore bear an analogical sense. Here a final difficulty must be removed. As long as we confine ourselves to negation, we clearly run no risk of breaking up the unity and perfect simplicity of the Divine being. For these negations aimed mainly at excluding from the Absolute Being everything that might divide and thereby limit it. Will this danger not arise and, indeed, become inevitable when we affirm of God positive analogical perfections, such as are displayed by creatures? In that case, the perfections will be either conceived by us as identical, and the terms applied to God will in that case be pure synonyms, or the terms represent distinct perfections, and then the Divine essence will lose its eminent simplicity. Perhaps, however, we may escape from the horns of this dilemma. The attempt to secure the perfect idea of the Divine unity by means of a number of concepts would evidently be self-contradictory. On the other hand, a direct intuition of this intelligible unity is denied us in this world. Now, it is a fundamental principle of Thomistic philosophy that, if we are unable to attain to the Oneness and Simplicity, we should endeavour to imitate it in some way by multiple means. Thus the universe, this defective image of God, imitates by its diverse forms the one and simple perfection of God. In the same way, again, our intellect, by gathering up the various essences and perfections which it finds in things, forms in itself the resemblance of this inaccessible unity by means of multiple conceptions. Our assertions about the Divine essence are, therefore, not purely synonymous, for our intellect invents different names signifying different conceptions to attribute them to God; and yet they do not introduce into God any diversity, because our intellect aims at designating by these different terms a reality which is absolutely one. In short, the intellect does not necessarily attribute to things the mode according to which it understands them. Therefore, if the intellect affirms the unity of an object by complex propositions, whatever is diverse and complex in the propositions must be referred to the intellect making them, but the unity described by them, must be referred to the object.[36] Bearing in mind these reservations we can apply to God terms which describe the perfections of creatures; and in the first place, we may assert His goodness.

Let us take as our starting-point our last conclusion, i.e. the absolute perfection of God. Each being may be said to be good by reason of its own virtue. For the proper virtue of each being makes the being that possesses it good, and equally good the function that each being fulfils. On the other hand, a virtue is a certain kind of perfection, for each being is said to be perfect in proportion as it attains to its own virtue. If, therefore, the goodness of a being is reducible to its virtue and its virtue to its perfection, a being is good in proportion as it is perfect, and for that reason also each being tends towards its perfection as to its own good. Now, we have shown that God is perfect: therefore He is good.[37] Moreover, His *is* His own goodness, as is evident from what has been said about His perfection. It has been proved that the perfections of the Divine being are not properties superadded to His being, but that the Divine being itself, considered as such and in His sole plenitude, is perfect. The goodness of God consequently cannot be a perfection added to His substance; it is the substance of God which is His own

goodness.[38] In affirming this conclusion, we distinguish radically the Divine being from all created
things. For the goodness of created things is a participated goodness. God alone is good by His essence;
an infinite distance separates the Being which is
good, and the being which possesses some goodness by
reason of which it is good.[39] Whence we see lastly
that God is the good of all things and the supreme
Good. For, since the goodness of each thing is
reducible to its perfection, and since God, as pure and
simple perfection, contains within Himself the perfections of all things, it follows that His goodness
contains all goodnesses: God is therefore the good of
all that is good.[40] Thus each thing holds its goodness
from the Divine goodness, as the first exemplary,
efficient and final Cause of all goodness. And yet
everything possesses its own goodness, inasmuch as
it is said to be good by resemblance to the Divine
goodness inherent in it. There is, therefore, one
single goodness for all things and yet many particular
goodnesses; still there is no contradiction between
them.[41] For the goods are ordered in a hierarchy,
culminating in the universal Good, i.e. the Good
in essence or supreme Good, below which the particular
and participated goods are arranged in descending
degrees.[42] Moreover this relation causes no complexity
in the infinitely simple essence of God, for the relation
by reason of which anything is asserted of God relatively to the creatures, has no reality in God, but only in
the created things.[43] To posit God as the supreme
Good, does not mean that He is the sum of particular
goods, or that He would not be defined in His supreme
degree even without the existence of created goods, but
on the contrary it means that the finite and limited
goods are defined by reference to Him, as participated
and falling short of His perfect goodness. Here again
the relation is unilateral: it is valid only as from the
creature to the Creator.

If God is the supreme Good, it follows that God is
unique. For it is not possible for two supreme Goods

to exist, since the supreme Good, being by definition the superabundance of Good, can exist in only one being. Now, God is the supreme Good: hence He is unique. We can draw the same conclusion by starting our argument from Divine perfection. It has been shown that God is absolutely perfect; if therefore several gods existed, several absolutely perfect beings, free from all imperfections, would exist. Now, this is impossible, for if none of them were lacking in the slightest perfection and no imperfection of any sort were contained in their essence, we should fail to see how these diverse beings could be distinct from each other. It is consequently impossible to posit the existence of several gods.[44]

We have argued from the Divine perfection that God is good and that He is unique; we can also deduce from it that He is infinite. Everything that by its nature is finite, must fall within the definition of some *genus*. Now, God does not come under any *genus*: He is consequently infinite.[45] It may be objected that by excluding all limits of Divine perfection we leave the argument by analogy and relapse into that by negation; but this objection rests simply on an equivocation about the idea of infinity. In the case of spatial or numerical quantity the nature of which requires limits and an end, infinity, i.e. the lack of limits, must be considered as a privation and defect. An indeterminate dimension or a number are therefore infinite only by the withdrawal of what they ought by nature to possess. In God, on the contrary, infinity is not a privation but the negation of such limits as would contradict His absolute perfection; and this negation itself is intended to express an eminently positive content, namely, the existence in God of all the perfections to be found in created things but possessed by Him, in the plenitude of His being, in the supreme degree.[46] Among these perfections, three deserve particular attention, since they constitute the highest perfections of the most perfectly earthly creature: viz. intelligence, will and life.[47]

The intelligence of God might be argued directly from His infinite perfection. Since we attribute to the Creator all the perfections found in the creature, we cannot but attribute to Him the noblest of all perfections by which one being can in a certain sense identify himself with all beings: in short, intelligence.[48] But it is possible to base it upon a deeper reason, drawn from the very nature of Divine being. In the first place, it can be observed that every being is intelligent in proportion as it is lacking in matter.[49] It can further be noted that beings endowed with knowledge, are distinguished from those having no knowledge by the fact that these latter are confined to their own form, whereas the former are capable of apprehending also the form of other beings. In other words—the power of knowing corresponds to an increasing amplitude and extension of the being having knowledge; the privation or lack of knowledge corresponds to a narrowing limitation and, as it were, restriction of the being not having knowledge. This is the meaning of Aristotle's remark: *anima est quodammodo omnia*. A form, accordingly, will be the more intelligent, the more it is able to become a greater number of other forms; it is only matter, that restricts and limits the extension of the form, and hence it may be said that the more immaterial forms are, the more they approximate to a kind of infinity. It is therefore evident that it is the immaterialness of a being that confers knowledge upon it, and that the degree of knowledge depends upon the degree of immaterialness. A rapid induction will bring final conviction; plants are lacking in knowledge by reason of their materialness. Sense, on the contrary, is already endowed with knowledge because it apprehends the sensory species* free from matter. The

---

* The word "species" may mean *either* a universal classification of individuals of the same nature, *or* that image or representation of an object of knowledge, whether it be sense-knowledge or intellectual knowledge, which results from the abstraction from objective matter by the faculty of a medium

intellect is capable of a still higher degree of knowledge, as furthest separated from matter. Accordingly, its proper object is the universal, not the particular, since the principle of individuation is matter. We finally reach God who is entirely immaterial, as we demonstrated earlier; He is accordingly also supremely intelligent: *cum Deus sit in summo immaterialitatis sequitur quod ipse sit in summo cognitionis.*[50]

By combining this result with the conclusion that God is His own being, we discover that the intelligence of God is identical with His essence. Knowing is, in fact, the act of an intelligent being. Now, some acts of a being can pass from this being to another being, external to it: the act of heating, for example, passes from that which heats to that which is heated. Certain other acts remain, on the contrary, immanent in their subjects, and the act of knowing is of this kind. The knowable or intelligible suffers no change by being known, but the intelligence achieves thereby its act and perfection. When, therefore, God knows, His act of intelligence remains immanent in Him; for we know that all that is in God, is the Divine essence. The intelligence of God is consequently identical with the Divine essence and therefore with the Divine being and with God Himself; for God is His essence and His being, as has been shown.[51] We further see that God understands Himself perfectly, for if He is, as has been shown above, the supreme intelligence, He is also the supremely intelligible. For a material thing becomes intelligible only if separated from matter and material conditions by the light of the active intellect. Consequently we can assert of the intelligibility of things all that can be asserted of their immaterialness. In other words, the immaterial is in and by itself intelligible. On the

whereby knowledge is alone possible to corporeal beings. It is in this latter sense that the word is here used. Species of one kind or another are necessary for all knowledge, except the Divine, though in the case of purely intellectual beings, such as are the angels, these species are innate and not acquired by abstraction.

other hand, everything intelligible is apprehended inasmuch as it is one in act with the intelligent being; now, the intelligence of God is identical with His essence and His intelligibility is also identical with His essence; the intelligence is, therefore, here one in act with the intelligible, and consequently God, understands perfectly Himself because in Him the supreme degree of knowledge is joined with the supreme degree of knowableness.[52] Further: the only object which God knows, of itself and directly, is Himself. For it is evident that to know directly in itself some other object, God would necessarily have to turn away from His immediate object which is Himself, in order to attend to this other object. But this other object could only be inferior to the former, and Divine knowledge would thereby suffer in its perfection—which is impossible.[53]

God knows perfectly Himself and knows directly only Himself. This does not mean that He knows nothing but Himself. Such a conclusion would be in absolute contradiction with what we know of the Divine intelligence. Let us start from the principle that God knows perfectly Himself, a principle which is, by the way, evident without proof, since the intelligence of God is His being and His being is perfect. It is further evident, that to know a thing perfectly, we must know perfectly its power, and in order to do so, we must know the effects of which it is capable. But the power of God extends to things other than God Himself, since He is the efficient Cause of all things. It follows therefrom that God, in knowing Himself, knows necessarily also everything else. And this will be more evident if we add that the intelligence of God, as First Cause, is identical with His being. Whence it follows that all effects which pre-exist in God, are to be found in the first place in His intelligence, and that all exists in Him in its intelligible form.[54] This, a truth of fundamental importance, requires a more precise definition.

To begin with, it is important to note that by

extending Divine knowledge to all things, we do not make it dependent on any one thing. God sees Himself in Himself, for He sees Himself in His essence. As regards the other things, however, He sees them not in themselves, but in Himself, inasmuch as His essence contains in itself the image of all that is not He. Knowledge, in God, owes its specification to nothing but the very essence of God.[55] Accordingly the real difficulty does not lie here; it is rather to determine under what aspect God sees other things. Is the knowledge which He has of them general or particular? Is it limited to the real or does it extend to the possible? Are we to include in it even future contingencies? These are the points in dispute on which we must take up a position all the more decidedly as they were the burden of the gravest errors of the Averroists.

For it has been maintained that God knows things by general knowledge, i.e. *quâ* beings, but not by distinct knowledge, i.e. insofar as they constitute a number of objects, each endowed with its own reality. It is needless to insist on this point, for such a doctrine is manifestly incompatible with the absolute perfection of Divine knowledge. The nature proper to each thing consists in a certain mode of participation in the perfection of the Divine essence. God accordingly would not know Himself, unless He knew distinctly all the modes under which His own perfection could be imitated. He would not even know perfectly the nature of being unless He knew perfectly all the modes of being.[56] The knowledge by God of things is therefore a proper and determinate knowledge.[57] Are we then to say that this knowledge extends to the particular? This has been disputed not without some show of reason. For to know a thing amounts to knowing the constituent principles of the thing. Now, every particular essence is constituted by a determinate matter and by a form individualised in this matter. Knowledge of the particular as such presupposes therefore a knowledge of matter as such. But we observe that in man the only faculties capable of apprehending the material and particular are imagination and sense, or other faculties similar to these by reason of their employing similarly material organs. The human intellect on the contrary, is an immaterial faculty, whence we see that its proper object is the general. But the Divine intellect is evidently much more immaterial than the human intellect; His knowledge must consequently be still further removed than human knowledge from all particular objects.[58] But the principles of this argument are incompatible with the conclusion to be drawn from them. It is true that they allow us to assert that he who knows a determinate matter and the individualised form in this matter, knows the particular object constituted by this form and this matter. But the Divine knowledge extends to the forms, the individual accidents and to the matter of each being. Since His intelligence is identical with His essence, God inevitably knows everything that is, in any manner whatever, in His essence. Now everything that possesses being in any way or degree, is in the Divine essence as in its first source; but matter is a certain mode of being, since it is potential being; accident too is a certain mode of being, as it is *ens in alio*; matter and accidents accordingly, as well as form, are within the essence of God and, therefore, within His knowledge. This means that the knowledge of particulars cannot be denied Him.[59] Thereby St. Thomas openly took up a position against the Averroism of his time. A thinker like Siger of Brabant, for instance,[60] interpreting the doctrine of Aristotle on the relation of God to the world in its strictest sense, saw in God only the final Cause of the universe. According to him, God was the efficient Cause of physical beings neither in their material nor their formal constitution, and, since He was not their Cause, there was no need for Him to rule them providentially or even to know them. It was therefore the denial of Divine causality which led the Averroists to deny to God the knowledge of particulars, as it was the affirmation of the universal Divine causality which prompted St. Thomas to attribute it to Him.

God, then, knows all real beings, not only as distinct from each other, but also in their very individuality, with the accidents and the matter which make them into particular beings. Does He also know possible beings? There is reasonably no room for doubt. That which does not actually exist, but can exist, possesses already a certain degree of existence, without which it would be undistinguishable from nothingness. Now, it has been shown that God knows all that exists, whatever the kind of existence; God, therefore, knows possible beings. If it is a question of possible things which, though not existing actually, either have existed or will exist, God is said to know them because He has in respect of them the knowledge of vision. If it is a question of possible things which might be, but are not, have not been and will not be, God is said to know them by the knowledge of simple intelligence. But, in any case, they do not escape the perfect understanding of God.[61] Moreover, our conclusion extends even to that class of possible things of which it is impossible to say whether they should or should not be, the so-called future contingents. For a future contingent may be viewed in two ways, either in itself and as actually realised, or in regard to its cause and as capable of realisation. For instance: Socrates may sit or stand; if I see Socrates sitting, this contingency is actually present and realised. But, if I see simply in the concept "Socrates" the possibility of his either sitting or standing, I view the contingency in the form of a future as yet indeterminate. In the first case, there is matter for certain knowledge; in the second case, no certitude is possible. Consequently, knowing a contingent effect only in its cause, is having a merely conjectural knowledge. But God knows all future contingents, both in their causes and in themselves as actually realised. For, although future contingents are realised successively, God knows them not successively. We have

already established that God is outside time; the
standard of His knowledge, as of His being, is eternity;
now, eternity which exists simultaneously, comprises
the whole of time in a changeless present. God,
therefore, knows the future contingents as actually
present and realised,[62] yet the necessary knowledge
which He has of them, in no way invalidates the
character of their contingency.[63] Here again, St.
Thomas departs from Averroism and even from the
most authentic Aristotelianism.[64] According to Averroes and Aristotle, the essential character of a future
contingent is that it may or may not occur; it is
therefore impossible to conceive how it can be an
object of knowledge for anyone at all, and, as soon
as a contingent is known as true, it ceases to be
contingent and immediately becomes necessary. But
the authority of Aristotle is unable to prevail against
the truth of dogma. To deny to God the knowledge
of future contingents is tantamount to rendering
Providence impossible. On this point, as on all
others which touch the Divine essence, we must
abandon the Greek philosopher to follow the teaching
of St. Augustine.

After determining in what sense intelligence is
attributable to God, we have finally to settle in what
sense we are to ascribe will to Him. For from the
fact that God knows we can argue that He also wills;
because the good, inasmuch as known, constitutes
the proper object of the will, it follows necessarily
that the good, as soon as known, must also be willed.
Whence it follows that the being which knows the
good, must, by that very fact, be endowed with will.
Now, God knows the good. Since, as has been shown,
He is perfectly intelligent, He knows being at the
same time under its aspect of being and under its
aspect of good. God, therefore, wills by the mere fact
that He knows.[65] And this consequence is valid not
only for God, but for all intelligent beings. For the
relation of every being to its natural form leads the
being to tend to its form, if it does not possess it,

and to rest in it once it has reached it. Now, the natural form of the intelligence is the intelligible. Every intelligent being, therefore, tends towards its intelligible form, if it has not already attained to it, and rests in it, on securing it. But both this tendency and this repose of contentment spring from the will; we can therefore conclude that in every intelligent being will must be found. Now, God possesses intelligence; hence He also possesses will.[66] But we know also, that the intelligence of God is identical with His essence; since therefore He wills insofar as He knows, His will must also be identical with His essence. Consequently, in the same way as His knowing is His being, so His willing is His being.[67] And so no sort of composition is caused in God by His will, any more than by His intelligence.

Conclusions, parallel to those which were deduced concerning the intelligence of God, follow from this principle. The first is that the Divine essence constitutes the first and principal object of God's will. The object of the will, we said, is the good, apprehended by the intellect. Now, what the Divine intellect apprehends directly and in itself, is nothing but the Divine essence, as has been shown. The Divine essence is accordingly the first and principal object of the Divine will.[68] Herein we find a fresh confirmation of the certitude that God does not depend on anything external to Himself. It follows that God wills nothing but Himself. The will, in fact, follows from the intelligence. Now, the immediate object of the Divine intelligence is God; but we know that in knowing Himself, God knows all other things. In the same way, God wills Himself as immediate object, and He also wills all other things by willing Himself.[69] But the same conclusion can also be established on a deeper principle, leading to the discovery of God's creative activity itself. Every natural being has not only an inclination tending towards its own good, when it does not possess it, or causing it to rest in it when it attains to the good; but every being also inclines to expand, as far as it can, and to diffuse its own good in other beings. For this reason, every being endowed with will, tends naturally to communicate to others the good which it possesses. This tendency is eminently characteristic of the Divine will, whence, as we know, all perfection is derived by resemblance. In consequence, if natural beings communicate to others their good to the extent to which they possess some perfection, it is, *a fortiori*, characteristic of the Divine will to communicate to other beings His perfection by way of resemblance, and to the extent to which it is communicable. Thus God accordingly wills to exist Himself, and He wills others to exist; but He wills Himself as end, and the others only by reference to their end, i.e. in the measure in which it is proper for other beings to participate in the Divine Goodness.[70]

By placing ourselves at the point of view just defined, we see at once that the Divine will extends to all particular goods just as the Divine knowledge extends to all particular beings. It is not necessary in order to keep the simplicity of God intact, to admit that He wills other goods only in general, that is, inasmuch as He wills the principle of all the goods which spring from Him. There is nothing to prevent the Divine simplicity from being the principle of a multitude of participated goods, or to prevent God from remaining simple, even while willing such and such particular goods. As soon as the good is known by the intelligence, it is, *ipso facto*, willed. Now, God knows the particular goods, as has previously been shown. His will accordingly extends also to the particular goods.[71] It equally extends to the merely possible goods. For, since God knows the possible things, including the future contingents, in their proper nature, He also wills them in their proper nature. Now, their proper nature consists in that they should or should not be realised at a definite moment in time; it is therefore thus that God wills them, and not merely as existing eternally within the

Divine intelligence. This does not mean, by the way, that God creates them by willing them in their proper nature; for willing is an action performed within the person that wills. God, in willing temporal creatures, does not, therefore, confer *ipso facto* existence upon them. Such existence is theirs only by reason of Divine actions aiming at an effect external to God Himself, viz. by the acts of producing, creating and governing.[72]

Having defined the objects of the Divine will, let us consider the various modes in which it is exercised. In the first place: Are there things which God cannot will? The answer to this question must be in the affirmative. But we must at once limit this assertion. The only things which God cannot will are such as are, at bottom, not things at all; namely, all such things as contain within themselves some contradiction. For example, God cannot will that man should be an ass, for He cannot will a being that should be endowed with, and at the same time deprived of, reason. To will that the same thing should at the same time and under the same aspects be itself and its opposite is tantamount to willing that it should be and should not be; it would consequently mean willing something that is in itself contradictory and impossible. We must, moreover, bear in mind the reason for which God wills things. He wills them, as explained earlier, insofar as they participate in His resemblance. But the first condition to be fulfilled by things, in order to resemble God, is to *be*, since God is the First Being, the source of all being. God therefore would have no reason for willing what would be incompatible with the nature of being. But to posit self-contradiction, is to posit a being which is self-destructive; it is to posit at the same time being and non-being. God, accordingly, cannot will the self-contradictory,[73] and this is the only limitation which must be set to His omnipotent will.

Let us consider further what God is able to will, i.e. all that deserves the name of "being" in any degree whatever. In dealing with the Divine Being, considering it in its infinite perfection and supreme goodness, we must say that God wills necessarily this being and this goodness and that He cannot will whatever is contrary to them. It has been shown earlier that God wills His own being and goodness as the principal object of His will, and as the ground for His willing the other things. Consequently in all that God wills, He wills His being and His goodness. But it is, on the other hand, impossible for God not to will something by His actual will, for in that case His will would be merely in potency, which is impossible, since His will is also His being. God, therefore, wills necessarily His own being and His own goodness.[74] But the case is different in respect of the other things. God wills them only insofar as they are ordered towards His own goodness as to their end. Now, if we will a certain end, we do not necessarily also will the things relevant to this end, unless their nature is such that we cannot do without them in order to achieve the end in view. If, for example, we wish to preserve our life, we must necessarily wish for food; and if we wish to cross the sea, we must needs wish for a ship. But we do not necessarily will something without which we can secure our object: if, for instance, we wish to make an excursion, nothing obliges us to wish for a horse, for we can make our excursion without one. And this applies all round. Now, the goodness of God is perfect; nothing existing outside it can in the slightest degree increase His perfection. Therefore, God, who wills necessarily Himself, is in no way forced to will anything else.[75] The fact remains that, if God wills other things, He cannot not will them, for His will is unchangeable. But this purely hypothetical necessity involves no real and absolute necessity, i.e. constraint, in Him.[76]

It might lastly be objected that, if God wills the other things of His own free will, without any constraint, He yet does not will them without reason, since He wills them with the view to their end which is His own goodness. Are we then to say that the

Divine will remains free to will things, but that, if God wills them, we may assign a cause to His will? To say this would be misleading, for the fact is that the Divine will has in no sense a cause. This is easy to understand, if it is remembered that the will springs from the understanding and that the causes prompting a being endowed with will, are of the same order as those which induce knowledge in a being endowed with intelligence. As far as knowledge is concerned, if an intelligence understands separately the principle of an argument and the conclusion, the knowledge acquired by the conclusion, is caused by the understanding of the principle; but if this intelligence apprehends the conclusion *within* the principle itself, thus understanding both in a single intuition, the knowledge of the conclusion would not be caused in him by the understanding of the principle, for nothing can be its own cause; yet he would understand that the principles are the cause of the conclusion. The same applies to the will: the end is to the means what the principles are to the conclusion in the case of understanding. If therefore someone willed, by a separate act, the end, and by another act the means relevant to this end, the act of willing the end would be the cause of the act willing the means. But if he wills both end and means by a single act, this does not hold, for it would mean positing the same act as a cause of itself. Yet it remains true to say that this will wills the means in view of their end. In the same manner just as God by a single act knows the things in their essence, so He wills all things in His goodness in a single act. In the same way, therefore, as in God the knowledge which He has of the cause is not the cause of the knowledge which He has of the effect, though He knows the effect within the cause, so His willing the end is not the cause of His willing the means, though He wills the means as ordered in view of their end. He, therefore, wills the means to be for the sake of the end; but His willing the end is not the cause of His willing the means.[77]

Intelligent and free, God is also a living God. He is so, in the first place, by reason of the very fact that He has intellect and will, for to know and to will without living is impossible; but He is living, for a more direct and deeper reason which derives from the very notion of life. Among the diverse beings, those to which we attribute life, possess an internal principle of movement. This is so far true that we even extend this attribution to inanimate things as long as they present at least the appearance of spontaneous movement: thus the water which leaps from a spring is to us "living" water, in contrast to the "dead" water of a cistern or a pond. Now, to know and to will belong to those acts whose principle is internal to the thing that performs them, and speaking of God it is even more evident that such acts spring from the innermost depth of this being, since, being the First Cause, He is eminently also the cause of His own operations.[78] Thus God appears as a living spring of efficacy whose acts flow eternally from His being, or, to speak more accurately, whose operations are identical with His very being. What, in fact, is meant by the term "life," is for a being the very fact of being alive, considered in its abstract form, just as the term "a run" signifies the concrete act of running; and this for an even better reason, since the life of a being is that very principle which causes it to exist. In applying this to God, the conclusion holds in an even more absolute sense, because His is not only His own life in the way in which particular beings are that life which they have received, but is His own life as a being which lives *per se* and causes the life of all other things.[79] From this eternally productive life of an intelligence always in act, the divine beatitude flows of which our beatitude can be no more than a participation.

The term "beatitude" is itself inseparable from the conception of intelligence, since to be happy means the knowledge of the possession of one's proper good.[80] But the proper good of a being consists in the most perfect possible performance of its most perfect operation, and the perfection of an operation depends on four main factors each of which is eminently realised in the life of God. In the first place, the operation must be self-sufficient and be performed wholly within the being that performs it. Why this requirement? Because an operation taking place wholly within a being, is in the last resort wholly accomplished for that being's advantage, since the result achieved remains within its power and represents a positive gain, the benefit of which goes entirely to the being itself.[81] On the contrary, operations which are accomplished outside of their author benefit less himself than the work performed and cannot constitute a good of the same order as an operation previously described. What constitutes, therefore, God's beatitude must be an operation immanent to God. The second feature of such a beatific operation is that it must be performed by the highest power of the being in question. In the case of man, for instance, his beatitude could not consist in an act of merely sensible knowledge, but only in the act of perfect and assured intellectual knowledge. But further account must be taken of the object of the operation: thus, speaking again of ourselves, beatitude presupposes the intellectual knowledge of the supreme intelligible. This constitutes its third requirement. The fourth consists in the manner in which the operation is performed: it must be easy, perfect and enjoyable. This precisely and in the highest degree is the operation of God: He is pure intelligence, totally in act; He is His own object, which amounts to saying that He knows perfectly the supreme intelligible; finally being Himself the act by which he knows Himself, He performs it with ease and joy: God is therefore, indeed blessed.[82] Here again we should rather say that God is His own beatitude, since He is blessed by an act of the intelligence and this act is His own substance; it is a beatitude which is not only of the greatest perfection, but actually outside any common measure with other beatitudes. For to enjoy the Supreme Good is assuredly happiness; but to grasp oneself as being the Supreme Good means not merely to participate in beatitude, but to *be* it.[83] Hence of this attribute as of all the others, it may be said that it belongs to God in a unique sense: *Deus qui singulariter beatus est*. It is because He *is* beatitude, that the creature *has* it.

The foregoing reflections bring us to that point where we leave the Divine essence to turn to the consideration of its effects. Such an enquiry would be impossible, if we had not previously determined as far as possible the principal attributes of God, the efficient and final Cause of all things. But whatever the importance of the results so far obtained, if we consider them from the point of view of our human knowledge, we must not forget their extreme shortcomings compared with the infinite object on which they claim to enlighten us. It is unquestionably a precious gain for us to grasp the eternity of God, His infinity and His perfection; to know His intelligence and His goodness. But if this poor knowledge were to make us forget that the Divine essence remains for us in this world unknown, it were better never to have attained even to that knowledge. Our intellect can be said to know a thing only if it can define, i.e. if it can apprehend it in a form which corresponds at all points to that which it is. But we must not forget that all that our intellect has been able to conceive of God, has been conceived only in a defective manner which is the reason why the Divine essence escapes our grasp. We can conclude with Dionysius the Areopagite,[84] by affirming that the fullest knowledge vouchsafed to us in this life of the Divine nature is the certitude that God remains beyond all that we may think concerning Him.[85]

NOTES TO CHAPTER VI.

1. *Comp. theol.*, I. 2.
2. *Comp. theol.*, I. 36.
3. *Cont. Gent.*, I. 14.
4. *Cont. Gent.*, I. 15; *Sum. theol.*, I. 10, 2, ad *Resp.*; *Comp. theol.*, I. 5.
5. *Cont. Gent.*, I. 16.
6. *Cont. Gent.*, I. 17; *Sum. theol.*, I. 3, 2, ad *Resp.*
7. *Cont. Gent.*, I. 16.
8. *Cont. Gent.*, I. 18; *Comp. theol.*, I. 19.
9. *Cont. Gent.*, I. 19.

10. *Cont. Gent.*, I. 18.
11. *Cont. Gent.*, I. 20; *Sum. theol.*, I. 3, 1, ad *Resp.*
12. *Cont. Gent.*, I. 21; *Sum. theol.*, I. 3, 3, ad *Resp.*
13. *Sum. theol.*, I. 3, 4, ad *Resp.* and 3°.
14. *Comp. theol.*, I. 11; *Cont. Gent.*, I. 22.
15. *Sum. theol.*, I. 3, 6, ad *Resp.* and 2°.
16. *Comp. theol.*, I. 12; *Cont. Gent.*, I. 24 and 25; *Sum. theol.*, I. 3, 4, ad *Resp.*
17. *Comp. theol.*, I. 13; *Cont. Gent.*, I. 24.
18. *Cont. Gent.*, I. 25.
19. *Civit. Dei.*, lib. VII., cap. 6.
20. On Amaury de Bènes and his partisans, see de Wulf, *op. cit.*, p. 246–250.
21. *Sum. theol.*, I. 3, 8, ad *Resp.*
22. *Cont. Gent.*, I. 27.
23. *Sum. theol.*, I. 3, 8, ad *Resp.* and 1°.
24. *Cont. Gent.*, I. 28.
25. *Cont. Gent.*, I. 28; *Sum. theol.*, I. 4, 2, ad *Resp.* and 2°.
26. *Cont. Gent.*, I. 28.
27. *De ente et essentia*, c. 6.
28. *Exod.*, III. 13.
29. *Sum. theol.*, I. 13, 11, ad *Resp.* and 2°.
30. *Cont. Gent.*, I. 32 ad *Si aliquis.*
31. *Sum. theol.*, I. 13, 5, ad *Resp.*; *Cont. Gent.*, I. 32; *Comp. theol.*, I. 27; *De Potentia*, qu. VII., art. 7.
32. *Sum. theol.*, I. 13, 5, ad *Resp.*
33. See F.–A. Blanche, *Sur le sens de quelques locutions concernant l'analogie dans la langue de Saint Thomas d'Aquin.* Rev. des sciences phil. et théol., 1921, p. 52–59. B. Desbuts, *La notion d'analogie d'après saint Thomas d'Aquin*, Ann. de phil. chrét., 1906, p. 377–385. B. Landry, *La notion d'analogie chez saint Bonaventure et saint Thomas d'Aquin.* Louvain, 1922.
34. *Cont. Gent.*, I. 29; *Sum. theol.*, I. 47, 2, ad 2^m.
35. *Cont. Gent.*, I. 33.
36. *Cont. Gent.*, I. 35 and 36.
37. *Cont. Gent.*, I. 37; *Sum. theol.*, I. 6, 1, ad *Resp.*; *De Verit.*, qu. XXI., art. 1, ad 1^m.
38. *Cont. Gent.*, I. 38.
39. *Sum. theol.*, I. 6, 3, ad *Resp.* and ad 3^m; *De Verit.*, qu. XXI., art. 5, ad *Resp.*
40. *Cont. Gent.*, I. 40.
41. *Sum. theol.*, I. 6, 4, ad *Resp.*
42. *Cont. Gent.*, I. 41.
43. *Sum. theol.*, I. 6, 2, ad 1^m.
44. *Cont. Gent.*, I. 42; *Sum. theol.*, I. 11, 3, ad *Resp.* and 2°; *Comp. theol.*, I. 15; *De Potentia*, qu. III., art. 6, ad *Resp.*
45. *Cont. Gent.*, I. 43.
46. *Cont. Gent.*, I. 43; *Sum. theol.*, I. 7, 1, ad 2^m.

47. A more detailed study would have to reserve for special discussion the conception of "Life" on which St. Thomas has laid great stress. Cf. on this point M. Grabmann, *Die Idee des Lebens in der Theologie des hl. Thomas v. Aquin*, Paderborn, 1922.
48. *Cont. Gent.*, l. 44.
49. *Cont. Gent.*, l. 44, ad *Ex hoc.*
50. *Sum. theol.*, I. 14, 1, ad *Resp.*; *De Verit.*, qu. II., art. 1, ad *Resp.*
51. *Cont. Gent.*, l. 45.
52. *De Verit.*, qu. II., art. 2, ad *Resp.*; *Cont. Gent.*, l. 47; *Sum. theol.*, I. 14, 3, ad *Resp.*
53. *Cont. Gent.*, l. 48.
54. *Sum. theol.*, I. 14, 5, ad *Resp.*
55. *Sum. theol.*, I. 14, 5, ad 2^m and 3^m.
56. *Cont. Gent.*, l. 50; *Sum. theol.*, I. 14, 6, ad *Resp.*
57. *De Verit.*, qu. II., art. 4.
58. *Cont. Gent.*, l. 63, 1a obj.
59. *Cont. Gent.*, l. 65; *Sum theol.*, I. 14, 11 ad *Resp.*; *De Verit.*, qu. II., art. 5, ad *Resp.*
60. See Mandonnet, *op. cit.*, I., p. 168; II., p. 76.
61. *Sum. theol.*, I. 14, 9, ad *Resp.*
62. *Sum. theol.*, I. 14, 13, ad *Resp.*; *Cont. Gent.*, l. 67; *De Verit.*, qu. II., art. 12, ad *Resp.*
63. *Sum. theol.*, I. 14, 13, ad 1^m.
64. Mandonnet, *op. cit.*, I., p. 164–167; II., p. 122–124.
65. *Cont. Gent.*, l. 72.
66. *Sum. theol.*, I. 19, 1, ad *Resp.*; *De Verit.*, qu. XXIII., art. 1, ad *Resp.*
67. *Sum. theol.*, I. 19, 1; *Cont. Gent.*, l. 73.
68. *Cont. Gent.*, l. 74.
69. *Cont. Gent.*, l. 75.
70. *Sum. theol.*, I. 19, 2, ad *Resp.*
71. *Cont. Gent.*, l. 79.
72. *Cont. Gent.*, l. 79.
73. *Cont. Gent.*, l. 84.
74. *Cont. Gent.*, l. 80.
75. *Sum. theol.*, I. 19, 3, ad *Resp.*; *Cont. Gent.*, l. 81 and 82.
76. *Cont. Gent.*, l. 83.
77. *Sum. theol.*, I. 19, 5, ad *Resp.*
78. *Cont. Gent.*, l. 97, ad *Adhuc vivere.*
79. *Cont. Gent.*, l. 98.
80. "Cujuslibet enim intellectualis naturae proprium bonum est beatitudo." *Cont. Gent.*, l. 100.
81. Such are the operations which St. Thomas calls "immanentes," viz. seeing, knowing, etc., in distinction to the so-called "transitive" operations, whose effect is external to the being which causes them, as building, healing, etc.
82. *Cont. Gent.*, l. 100, ad *Amplius, illud.*

83. "Quod per essentiam est, potius est eo quod per participationem dicitur; ... Deus autem per essentiam suam beatus est, quod nulli alii competere potest. Nihil enim aliud praeter ipsum potest esse summum bonum...; et sic oportet ut quicumque alius ab ipso beatus est, participative beatus dicatur. Divina igitur beatitudo omnem aliam beatitudinem excedit." *Cont. Gent.*, I. 102.
84. *De mystica theolog.*, I. 1.
85. *De Verit.*, qu. II., art. 1, ad 9^{m}.

CHAPTER VII. CREATION

A. THE NATURE OF THE CREATIVE ACT

WE saw that, according to St. Thomas, the sole object of all Philosophy is God. Its first object is therefore His nature; its second object is His effects. We must accordingly address ourselves to this second problem; but before considering His effects, i.e. all creatures in their hierarchic order, we must determine the mode in which these creatures issue from their first principle.[1]

The mode in which every created thing issues from its universal cause—which is God—goes by the name of "creation." Hence the importance of defining the nature of creation. We speak of creation whenever something which was not, begins to be. In other words, there is creation wherever a transition occurs from non-being to being, in other words, from nothingness to being. Applying this notion to all existing things, we may say that creation, which is the emanation of all being, consists in the act whereby all things pass from non-being or nothingness to being.[2] This is the meaning of the expression that God has created the world from nothing. But it is important to note that in this assertion the preposition "from" signifies in no way the material cause; it means simply a sequence. God has not created the world from nothing in the sense that He caused it to issue from nothing as from a sort of pre-existing matter, but in the sense that, after the nothing, being appeared. "Creating from nothing," in short, means "not creating from something." This expression, far from putting any matter at the beginning of things, systematically excludes all conceivable matter,[3] in the same way as when we say that someone is sad about nothing, we mean that his sadness has no cause.[4]

Such a conception of the creative act encounters at once certain objections of philosophers whose whole habits of thought run counter to it. For the student of physics, for instance, an act is, by definition, a change, i.e. a sort of movement. But everything that passes from one place to another, or from one state to another, presupposes an initial place or state which is the point of departure of the movement or change, so that, where such a point of departure is lacking, the very notion of change would be inapplicable. For example: I move a body; it was consequently in a certain place, whence I have caused it to pass to another. Or I alter the colour of an object; the object must therefore have been of a certain colour in order that I should have been able to give it another. But in the case of creation, as just defined, it is just this point of departure which is lacking. Without the creation, there is nothing; after the creation, there is something. Is not then this passage from nothingness to being a contradictory notion, since it supposes that something which does not exist, nevertheless changes its condition, and that something which is nothing, becomes something? *Ex nihilo nihil fit*: such is the initial objection of the philosopher against the very possibility of creation.

Yet this is an objection which holds only in proportion as you concede its starting-point. The student of physics argues from the notion of movement; he observes that the requisite conditions for the existence of movement are not met by the case of creation; hence he concludes that creation is impossible. In point of fact, the only legitimate conclusion of his argument is that creation is not a movement. In that case the argument would be quite legitimate. For it is perfectly true that every movement is the change of condition of a being, and if we talk of an act which yet is not a movement, we do not know how to picture it to ourselves. Whatever effort we may make, in consequence, we shall always *imagine* creation *as if it were* a change, a pictorial representation which makes it into something self-contradictory and impossible. In reality, creation is something quite else, something for which we have even no name, because it lies so entirely outside the range of human experience. To say that creation is the gift of being, is still a deceptive expression, for how can anything be given to something which is nothing? To say it is acceptance of being, is no better, for how can something which is nothing accept anything? However—let us say that in some manner it is the acceptance of being, without attempting to picture it to ourselves.[5]

If such is indeed the mode of production signified by the term "creation," it is evident that God can create and is alone capable of creating. For it has been established that God is the universal Cause of all being. Now, the workman when he manufactures something, uses a matter not produced by him—wood, for example; this matter is produced by nature, and moreover produced only as to its form, not as to its matter. But if God created merely by using some pre-existing matter, this matter would not be caused by Him. Therefore, to say that God is the universal Cause of all being, taken in its totality, is to affirm that God is capable of creating.[6] Are we to add that He alone is capable of creating? This is denied by the Arabic philosophers, notably by Avicenna. The latter, though admitting that creation is the action proper to the universal Cause, nevertheless considers that certain inferior causes, acting by virtue of the First Cause, are capable of creating. Avicenna in particular teaches that the first separate substance, created by God, creates then the substance and the soul of that sphere, and that thereupon the substance of this sphere creates the matter of the inferior bodies.[7] In the same way the Master of the Sentences[8] asserts that God can communicate to the creature the power of creating, but only by delegation, not by right of its own authority. Now, it must be plain that the conception of a creative creature is self-contradictory. All creation by a creature must evidently presuppose the existence of that creature. But we know that the creative act presupposes nothing anterior to itself, and this is as true of the efficient Cause as of matter. It simply causes being to follow upon non-being. Creative power is consequently incompatible with the condition of the creature which is on the contrary incapable of acting except by means of being and of the powers previously received.[9] God, on the contrary, as Being *per se*, can also cause being; and as He is the only being *per se*, He is also the only one who can produce the very existence of other beings. Corresponding to this unique mode of being, there is a unique mode of causality: creation is the act proper to God.

It is interesting, by the way, to look for the secret motive which led the Arabic philosophers to attribute the power of creation to the creature. The reason is that according to their view, a single and simple cause can produce only a single effect. One thing only can issue from one thing; consequently a succession of single causes must be admitted, each producing a single effect, in order to explain how a multitude of things can have sprung from the first, single and simple Cause, which is God. It is, indeed, true that from some one and simple principle only one thing can come; but this is true only in the case of whatever acts by the necessity of its nature. The reason, therefore, why the Arabic philosophers admitted the existence of creatures which were also creative, was at bottom, that they considered creation as a necessary production. A complete refutation of their doctrine involves therefore the question whether God created things by necessity of nature and how His simple and single essence could be the source of the multiplicity of beings.

St. Thomas' answer to these two questions is contained in a single sentence. We maintain, he says, that things proceed from God by means of knowledge and intelligence, and in this mode a multitude of things can proceed directly from a single and simple God whose wisdom contains in itself the universality of beings.[10] What implications does this assertion contain and what deeper significance does it impart to the conception of creation?

There are three reasons which compel us to hold firmly that God has brought creatures into being out of His own free will and without any natural necessity. The first is as follows: we must admit that the universe is ordered with a view to a certain end; if it were otherwise, the universe would be the result of chance. God therefore set Himself an end in creating it. Now, it is true enough that nature can, like the will, act towards an end; but nature and will tend towards their ends in quite different ways.[11] For nature knows neither the end, nor the reason of the end, nor the relation of means to the end; nature cannot consequently either set itself an end, nor move towards it, nor arrange or direct its actions with a view to the end. On the contrary, a being, acting by will, possesses all this knowledge which nature lacks; he acts for the sake of an end in the sense that he knows it, sets himself this end, moves towards it, so to speak, of his own account, and orders his actions in relation to this end. In short: nature tends towards an end only because it is moved and directed to it by a being endowed with will and intelligence; as an arrow tends towards the aim because the direction is given to it by the archer. Now, whatever is by or through something else, is always posterior to something existing of itself. If, therefore, nature tends towards an aim assigned to it by an intelligence, the first being who gave it its end and its disposition in view of this end, must have created it, not out of the necessity of His nature, but out of His intelligence and will.

The second argument is that nature operates always, unless prevented, in the same invariable way. And the reason is that everything acts according to its nature, so that, as long as it remains the same thing, it acts in the same way; but everything acting by nature, is determined to a single mode of being; nature, therefore, performs always one and the same action. But the Divine being is in no way determined to a single mode of being; we have seen, on the contrary, that He contains in Himself the total perfection of being. If, therefore, He acted by necessity of nature, He would produce a sort of infinite and indeterminate being; but two simultaneous infinities are impossible[12]; it is consequently self-contradictory that God should act by necessity of nature. Now the only action possible, apart from natural necessity, is voluntary action. We conclude therefore that things proceed, as so many determinate effects, from the infinite perfection of God, according to the determination of His intelligence and of His will.

The third argument is drawn from the relation of effects to their cause. Effects pre-exist in their cause only according to the mode of being of the casue. Now, the Divine being is His very intelligence: His effects pre-exist therefore in the intelligible mode of being; they also proceed according to the intelligible mode of being and therefore in the last resort by the will. For the inclination of God to accomplish what His intelligence has conceived, falls into the sphere of His will. Consequently, it is the will of God that is the first Cause of all things.[13] The question remains how a multitude of particular things can spring from this single and simple Being. For God is the infinite being from whom all that exists has its being; but, on the other hand, God is absolutely simple and all that is in Him is His own being. How can the diversity of finite things pre-exist in the simplicity of the Divine intelligence? The theory of ideas will help us to solve this difficulty.

By "ideas" are meant forms considered as having existence apart from the things themselves. Now, the form of a thing can exist apart from the thing in two distinct ways: either because it is the exemplar of that of which it is said to be the form, or because it is the principle which enables us to know the thing. In either case, we must assume ideas to exist in God. In the first place ideas are in God in the shape of exemplars or models. In the case of every production which is not the result of a mere accident, the form of whatever is produced, evidently constitutes the end of the productive process. Now, the agent in this process could not act with a view to this form, unless he had in himself the resemblance to, or the model of, the form. But

he may have it in two ways: in some beings, the form
to be realised pre-exists according to its natural being;
this is the case of those that act by nature; thus man
begets man and fire begets fire. In other beings, on the
contrary, the form pre-exists in a purely intelligible
mode; this is the case in those who act by intelligence;
in this manner, the resemblance or the model of a house
pre-exists in the mind of the architect. Now, we
know that the world is not the result of accident; we
know further that God does not act by natural necessity;
we must consequently admit the existence in the Divine
intelligence of a form in resemblance to which the world
has been created. This is precisely what is called an
"idea."[14] Let us go further. Not only one idea of the
created universe exists in God, but a plurality of ideas,
corresponding to the various beings constituting the
universe. This proposition will be evident, if we consider that, when any effect whatever is produced, the
ultimate object of this effect is precisely whatever the
producer had mainly intended to achieve. Now, the
ultimate end in view of which all things are disposed,
is the order of the universe. The real intention of God
in creating all things, was therefore the order of the
universe. But if the intention of God has indeed been
to create the order of the universe, it follows necessarily
that God has in Himself the idea of the universal order.
Now, it is impossible to have the idea of a whole without having also adequate ideas of the parts composing it.
Thus, the architect cannot really conceive the idea of a
house, unless he forms also in himself the idea of each of
its parts. It follows therefore of necessity that the
proper ideas of all things must be contained in the mind
of God.[15]

But we can see at the same time why this plurality
of ideas does not conflict with the Divine simplicity.
The alleged difficulty here rest on a simple equivocation. For there are two kinds of ideas: those which
are copies, and others which are models. The ideas
which we form in resemblance to objects, belong to
the former kind: they are the ideas *by means of which*

we know the forms that cause our intellect to pass from potency to act. It is of course evident that, if the Divine intellect were composed of a plurality of ideas of this kind, His simplicity would be *ipso facto* destroyed. But this consequence does not follow, if we assume all ideas to be in God in the shape in which the idea of the work is in the mind of the craftsman. This idea is no longer that *by which* the intellect knows, but *that which* the intellect knows and by which the intelligent being is able to accomplish his work. Now, a plurality of such ideas introduces no composition into the intellect in which they are: on the contrary, their being known is implied in the knowledge which God has of Himself. For, we said that God knows perfectly His own essence; He therefore knows it under the modes by which it is knowable. But the Divine essence can be known not only as in itself, but also as imitable in a certain manner by created things. Each creature possesses its own being which is merely a manner of participating in the resemblance to the Divine essence, and the proper idea of this creature represents simply this particular mode of participation. Accordingly, inasmuch as God knows His essence as imitable by such and such a particular creature, He has the idea of this creature. And the same applies to all others.[16]

We know that creatures pre-exist in God in the shape of intelligible being, i.e. in the shape of ideas, and that these ideas introduce no complexity in the mind of God. Nothing, therefore, prevents us now from seeing in Him the single and direct author of the diverse beings of which the universe is composed. But perhaps the most important result of the preceding considerations is to show, how inadequate and vague our first definition of the creative act was. In saying that God has created the world *ex nihilo*, we excluded from the creative act the conception of a resemblance to the activity of a craftsman utilising some pre-existing matter for his work. But if we take this expression in a negative sense, as it has been shown that we must, it leaves the first origin of things completely unexplained. It is certain that nothingness is not the original matrix whence all creatures spring; being can only issue from being. We now know from what First Being all other beings come; they exist only because all essence is derived from the Divine essence: *omnis essentia derivatur ab essentia divina.*[17] This formula in no way violates the real thought of St. Thomas; for no being would exist, unless God were virtually all beings: *est virtualiter omnia*; and it adds nothing to the assertion often repeated by the philosopher that each being is perfect in the very measure in which it participates in the Divine perfection.[18]

It may perhaps be asked how creatures can be derived from God without either fusing with Him or being superadded to Him. The solution of this problem need not detain us. Creatures have no goodness, no perfection, no particle of being which they do not hold from God; but we know already that none of all these are in the creature in the same mode as in God. The creature *is not* what it merely *has*; God *is* what He has; He *is* His being, His goodness, His perfection, and therefore creatures, though they derive their being from God since He is Being absolutely, hold it merely in a participated and defective manner which keeps them at an infinite distance from the Creator. As a pure *analogue* of Divine being, the created being can neither form an integral part of God, nor be added to, nor subtracted from Him. There is no common measure between two quantities not of the same order. The whole problem is consequently a false problem; it vanishes as soon as the question has been rightly framed.

There remains the question why God has wished to realise outside Himself these particular and diverse beings which He knew as possible. In Him and taken in its intelligible being, the creature is fused with the Divine essence; or, more exactly, the creature, *as* idea, is nothing but the creative essence.[19] How comes it that God should have projected outside Himself a part of His ideas or that He at least should have projected outside Himself a reality, the whole being of which consists in imitating some of the ideas He thinks in thinking Himself? We have already seen the only explanation which the human mind can offer: that good tends naturally to diffuse itself beyond itself; its characteristic feature is to seek to communicate itself to other beings to the extent to which they are capable of receiving it.[20] What is true of every good being in proportion as it is good, is eminently true of the Supreme Good which we call God. The tendency to propagate and communicate itself, expresses then nothing but the superabundance of an infinite Being whose perfection overflows and spreads over a hierarchy of participating beings: thus the sun, without having to reason or to choose, illuminates, by the mere presence of its being, all that shares in its light. But this comparison used by Dionysius, requires some explanation. The internal law governing the essence of the good and causing it to communicate itself, must not be taken as a natural necessity which God is constrained to follow. If creative action resembles the illumination of the sun in so far as God, like the sun, leaves no being untouched by His influence, it yet differs from it, since the sun is devoid of will.[21] The proper object of the will is the good: consequently the goodness of God, in so far as it is desired and loved by Him, is the cause of the creature. But it is so only by the intermediate action of the will.[22] Thus, we assume that there is in God an infinitely powerful tendency to diffuse and communicate Himself outside Himself, and at the same time that He diffuses and communicates Himself only, by an act of His will. These two assertions, far from contradicting, rather confirm each other.

The act of the will is, in fact, nothing but the inclination to the good apprehended by the understanding: God, who knows His own goodness in itself and as imitable by creatures, wills it therefore both in itself and in the creatures capable of sharing it. But from the fact that such is the will of God, it does not follow that God is subject to any necessity whatever. The

Divine goodness is infinite and complete; the entire creation could therefore not increase this goodness in the slightest degree, and, conversely, even if God did not communicate His goodness to any being, His goodness would not in the least be decreased.[23] Consequently created being in general, does not introduce any necessity into the will of God. Are we to say, at least, that, if God *meant* to realise creation, He had necessarily to realise what He has realised? Not by any means. And the reason is still the same. God wills necessarily His own goodness, but this goodness is in no way increased by the existence of creation; neither would it be diminished by its disappearance. Consequently, just as God manifests his goodness by the things now existing actually, and further by the order established within these things, so He might manifest it by other creatures disposed in a different order.[24] The actual universe, being the only one in existence, is *ipso facto* the best there *is*, but it is not the best that *might be*.[25] And just as God could or could not create a universe, so He could create a better or a worse, without His will being in either case subject to any necessity.[26] The fact is that all the difficulties that can arise on this point, spring from one and the same confusion. They all assume that creation brings God into a relation to created things as to His object; whence the attempt naturally follows to see in created things the determining cause of the Divine will. But in reality creation establishes in God no relation to the creature; here again the relation is unilateral and holds only between the creature and the Creator as between being and its principle.[27] We must accordingly hold firmly to this conclusion, that God wills Himself, and necessarily wills only Himself; and that, if the super-abundance of His being and of His love leads Him to will and to love Himself even in the finite participations of His being, we must see therein nothing but a free gift and nothing even remotely resembling a necessity.

To push the enquiry further would exceed the limits

of the knowable, or, to be more accurate, attempt to know what has no existence. For the only question that might be raised is this: why did God, who was able not to create the world, nevertheless will to create it? Why, if He was able to create other worlds, did He create this one? But such a question admits of no answer, unless we are satisfied with this: that it is so because God willed it. We know that the Divine will has no cause. No doubt, all effects which presuppose another effect, do not depend solely on the will of God; but the first effects depend on the Divine will alone. For instance, we may say that God gave man hands to be the obedient instrument of his intellect in carrying out his wishes; that He willed man to be endowed with intellect because this was necessary for his being a man; and that He willed men to be for the greater perfection of the universe and because He wishes that such creatures should exist to rejoice in Him. But to assign an ulterior cause to this last will, remains absolutely impossible; the existence of the world and of creatures capable of rejoicing in their Creator has no other cause but the pure and simple will of God.[28]

Such is the true nature of the creative act, at least as far as we are able to determine it. There remains the consideration of its effects. But before examining these in themselves and according to their disposition in the hierarchic order which they received from God, we must raise two general problems, the solution of which affects created nature in its totality: viz. at what moment have things come into existence and whence arise their distinctions and inequalities?

B. THE BEGINNING

The problem of the beginning of the world is one of the obscurest questions that the philosopher can attack. Some profess to prove that the world has always existed; others, on the contrary, set out to show that the world has necessarily had a beginning in time. The upholders of the first thesis appeal to the authority of Aristotle. but the writings of that thinker are not explicit on this point. In the eighth book of the "Physics" and the first book of "De Coelo" his object seems to have been to establish the eternity of the world only in order to refute the teaching of certain ancients who attributed to the world an inacceptable mode of beginning. He tells us, moreover, that there are some dialectical problems for which we have no demonstrative solution, such, for example, as the question whether the world is eternal.[29] Aristotle's authority, therefore, which by the way would by no means suffice to settle the question, cannot be appealed to on this point.[30] As a matter of fact, we meet here a clearly marked Averroist[31] doctrine which the Bishop of Paris, Etienne Tempier, had condemned as early as 1270; *quod mundus est aeternus* and *quod nunquam fuit primus homo*. Among the numerous arguments on which the doctrine professed to rest, one is particularly worthy of our consideration, for it leads to the very heart of the difficulty, since it claims the all-powerful causality of the Creator as its foundation.

To posit an efficient cause means positing *ipso facto* the effect. Every cause not immediately resulting in its effect is a non-sufficient, because imperfect, cause; that is to say, it requires something in order to produce its effect. Now, God is the sufficient cause of the world, either as final Cause, since He is the supreme Good, or as exemplary Cause, since He is supreme Wisdom, or as efficient Cause, since He is Omnipotence. On the other hand, we know that God exists from all eternity; the world, like its own sufficient Cause, therefore exists also from all eternity.[32] Moreover, it is evident that the effect proceeds from its cause by reason of the action exercised by the cause. But the action of God is eternal, otherwise we should have to admit that God, originally in potency in respect of His action, changed from potency to act under the impulse of some anterior agent—which is impossible,[33] or we should lose sight of the fact that the action of God, is His own substance, which is eternal.[34] It follows, therefore, necessarily that the world has always existed. If we, further, consider the problem from the point of view of creatures, we see that we are driven to the same conclusion. For we know that there are incorruptible beings in the world, like the celestial bodies and intellectual substances. Now, the incorruptible, i.e. that which is capable of existing always, cannot be conceived as existing sometimes and sometimes not, for it exists as long as it has the power to exist. Now, everything that begins to exist, falls into the class of things which sometimes exist and sometimes not; consequently, nothing incorruptible can have had a beginning, and we may conclude that the universe, outside which incorruptible substances would have neither place nor justification for being, also exists from all eternity.[35] Finally, we can deduce the eternity of the world from the eternity of movement. For nothing begins to be in motion except for the reason that either the mover or the thing moved is in a different state from that in which it was at the moment preceding the movement. Or, in other words, a new movemen cannot be produced without a preceding change in either the mover or the thing set in motion. But to change is nothing but to move; consequently there is always a movement anterior to that which sets in, and therefore, however far we ascend the chain of this series, we shall always find movement. But if motion has always existed, it follows that a thing moved has always existed, for movement exists only in the thing moved. The universe has therefore always existed.[36]

These arguments are all the more seductive in appearance as they seem to rest on the most authentic principles of Peripatetic philosophy. Nevertheless, they cannot be considered as truly conclusive. In the first place, we can eliminate the last two arguments by a simple distinction. From the fact that there has always been motion, it does not by any means follow that there has always been a thing moved. The only legitimate conclusion of the argument is simply that there has always been movement as soon as a thing in motion existed; but this thing in motion can only have come into existence by way of creation. Aristotle sets out this argument in the eighth book of his "Physics" against those who admitted the eternal existence of things in motion, and yet denied the eternity of movement. The argument, therefore, proves nothing against us, as we hold that, ever since things in motion existed, movement has also existed. The same observations apply to the argument from the incorruptibility of celestial bodies. It must, of course, be conceded that a thing naturally capable of always existing, cannot be conceived as existing sometimes and sometimes not. But it must not be forgotten that, to be able to exist always, a thing must first exist, and that incorruptible substances could not be such before coming into existence. The argument of Aristotle set out in the first book of "De Coelo," does not, therefore, simply conclude that incorruptible beings have never begun to exist, but that they have not come into existence by way of natural generation, like being susceptible to generation and corruption. The possibility of their creation is therefore, perfectly safeguarded.

Are we, on the other hand, necessarily driven to admit the eternity of a universe which we know to be the effect of an eternal sufficient Cause and of an eternal action which in their turn are the omnipotent efficacy and eternal activity of God? There is nothing to force us to this conclusion, if it is true to say, as was shown earlier, that God does not act by natural necessity but of His own free will. We might, indeed, at first sight think it self-contradictory that an omnipotent, immovable and unmoved God, should have willed to confer existence at a given point in time upon a world which did not exist before. But this difficulty reduces itself to a simple illusion which is easily dispelled by explaining again the true relation between the duration of created things and the creative will of God. We found already in explaining the production of created things, that we must distinguish between the production of a particular creature and the "exodus" by which the whole universe issued from God. For, in speaking of the production of a particular creature, we can show a reason why this creature is such as it is, either by reference to some other creature, or to the order of the universe, in respect of which each creature is ordered as a part in respect of the whole. If, on the contrary, we consider the coming into existence of the whole universe, it becomes impossible to seek the reason why the universe is as it is, in another created reality. For, since the reason for any particular arrangement of the universe cannot be found in the power of God which is infinite and inexhaustible, nor in the Divine goodness which is self-sufficient and has no need of any creature, the only remaining reason for the choice of such a universe, is the pure and simple will of God. If we apply this conclusion to the selection of the moment fixed by God for the coming into existence of the world, we must say, that, just as it depended on the simple will of God that the universe was of a particular extent in point of dimension, so it depended on His will alone that the universe should have a particular extent of duration, all the more as time is a quantity really extrinsic in respect of the nature of the enduring thing, and completely indifferent as regards the will of God.

It may be objected that a will may be delayed in doing what it intends to do only as the result of some modification undergone by it and causing it to do at a particular moment of time what it had intended to do at another. Consequently, if the immovable will of God wills the world, it follows that it willed it always, and accordingly the world has always existed. But such an argument subjects the action of the first Cause to the conditions governing the action of particular causes acting in time. The particular cause is not the cause of the time within which its action takes place; God, on the contrary, is Himself the cause of time, for time is comprised in the totality of the things created by Him. Therefore, in speaking of the manner in which the being of the universe has issued from God, we have no need to ask why God has willed to create this being at that moment rather than at another; such a question would assume that time pre-existed to creation, whereas in point of fact it is subordinated to it. The only question we can raise concerning the creation of the world, is not why God has created the world at that moment of time, but why He has assigned this extent to the duration of this time. Now, the extent of this time depends solely on the Divine will, and since, on the other hand, Catholic faith teaches us that the world has not always existed, we can admit that God has willed to fix a beginning of the world and to assign a limit to its duration, as He assigned a limit to its spatial extent. The words of Genesis[37]: *In principium creavit Deus coelum et terram*, are consequently acceptable to reason.[38]

We know then that the eternity of the world cannot be demonstrated. Let us see whether it is not possible to go further and to prove its non-eternity. This position, usually adopted by the followers of the Augustinian philosophy is considered by St. Thomas as logically untenable. A first argument, which we encountered before as used by St. Bonaventure against the Averroists, was the assertion that, if the world had existed from all eternity, there must actually exist an infinite number of souls. For, since the human soul is immortal, all those that have existed since an infinite time, must still exist to-day; therefore an infinite number must necessarily exist; but this is impossible; therefore, the world has at some time begun to exist.[39] But it is easy to reply to this argument that God may have created the world without man and without souls, and that, moreover, it has never been proved that God could not create an actually infinite number of simultaneously existing beings.[40] The creation of the world in time has also been proved by the argument that it is impossible to exceed the infinite; now, if the world has not had a beginning, an infinite number of revolutions of the celestial bodies must have taken place so that in order to arrive at the present day, the universe must have passed through an infinite number of days, which the premiss states to be impossible. The world has, therefore, not always existed.[41]

But this reasoning is not conclusive, for, even if it is granted that an infinite number of simultaneous beings is impossible, the fact remains that an infinite number of successive beings is possible, because every infinite series, in its succession, is in point of fact terminated by its present term. The number of celestial revolutions which would have taken place in a universe the existence of which in the past was eternal, would be, strictly speaking, a finite number, and no impossibility would be involved in the world exceeding this number in order to reach the present moment. Moreover, taking all the revolutions together, it must be admitted that in a universe which has always existed, no single revolution could be the first; now, every transition presupposes two terms, the point of departure and the point of arrival, and since in an eternal world the first term would be lacking, the question whether the transition from the first day to the present day is possible, cannot even arise.[42] Lastly, the eternity of the world has been based on the proposition that it is impossible to add to the infinite, on the ground that whatever is added to, becomes thereby larger, and nothing larger than the infinite can exist. But if the world has not had a beginning, it must necessarily have had an infinite duration and nothing can be added to it. But, this assertion is manifestly false, since every day adds a celestial revolution to the preceding revolutions; the world can therefore have always existed.[43] But the distinction, previously established, is sufficient to solve this new difficulty; for nothing prevents an infinity from being added to at the end, so to say, at which it is, in fact, finite. It follows from the assumption of an eternal extent of time at the beginning of the world, that this time is infinite in the past, but finite at its present end, for the present is the end of the past. The eternity of the world, considered from this point of view involves therefore no impossibility.[44]

The fact is that the non-eternity of the world is similarly a truth which cannot be established by argument. This truth is like the Mystery of the Trinity which also cannot be proved by reason and must be accepted by faith. Even the probable arguments alleged as a basis for them must be disproved to prevent the Catholic Faith from seeming to be supported by empty reasonings, instead of being founded on the unshakeable teaching given to us by God.[45] The creation of the world cannot be deduced of necessity either from the consideration of the world itself or from that of the will of God. For the principle of every proof is contained in the definition of the essence from which the properties are deduced. Now, essence in itself is irrelevant to time and place—which is the reason why universals are said to exist everywhere and always. The definitions of man, of heaven or earth do not in any way imply that these beings have always existed, but neither do they imply that such beings have not always existed.[46] Still less can the proof be furnished by starting from the will of God, for that will is free and without cause; we cannot consequently prove anything about it, except concerning the things which it is necessarily obliged to will. But the Divine will may manifest itself to man by Revelation whereon Faith is founded. We can, therefore, believe, even if we cannot know, that the world has had a beginning.[47]

Thus the position to be taken up in respect of this difficult question lies midway between that of the Averroists and that of the Augustinians. Against the former, St. Thomas maintains the possibility of a beginning of the world in time, but maintains also, even *contra murmurantes*, the possibility of its eternity. There is no doubt that to solve the problem of creation our philosopher has availed himself of the results of his predecessors, notably of Albertus Magnus and Moses Maimonides. The position adopted by him is not, however, identical with that of any one of his predecessors. Maimonides admits the creation of the world only on the authority of Revelation[48]; St. Thomas, on the contrary, bases it on demonstrative arguments. But both philosophers agree that it is impossible to prove the beginning of the world in time, and further that it is always possible to deny the eternal existence of the world.[49] Albertus Magnus, on the other hand, admits with Maimonides that the creation of the world *ex nihilo* can be known only by Faith; St. Thomas, keeping on this point closer to the Augustinian tradition than his master, considers this capable of proof. *Per contra*, the creation of the world in time is, according to St. Thomas, incapable of proof; but, according to Albertus Magnus, following here the Augustinian tradition more closely than his pupil, the beginning of the world in time can be proved, once the postulate of creation is admitted. Against both these philosophers, St. Thomas maintains therefore the possibility of proving the creation *ex nihilo* of the universe, wherein he is, as we saw, resolutely opposed to Averroës and his followers; but, in conceding, like Maimonides, the logical possibility of a universe created from all eternity, he refuses to confuse the truths of faith with those which can be the objects of proof. In this way he achieves in his teaching the harmony which he sets out to establish between the authentic doctrine of Christianity and whatever undoubted truth is contained in the philosophy of Aristotle.

C. THE DISTINCTION OF THINGS—EVIL

Let us assume that the moment has come when the merely possible things which, once realised, are to constitute the universe, issue from God to pass into being; the problem then presents itself why and how a multiplicity of distinct beings is produced by the Creator, instead of one single being. The Arabic philosophers and especially Avicenna, whose opinion we have encountered earlier, attempt to explain the plurality and diversity of things by the necessary action of the first efficient Cause which is God. Avicenna supposes that the first Being understands Himself and that, in so far as He understands and knows Himself, He produces a single and unique effect which is the first intelligence. Granting this assumption, it is inevitable—and St. Thomas would follow Avicenna on this point—that the first intelligence should fall below the simplicity of the First Being. For this intelligence is not its own being, and possesses being only because it receives it from another; it is accordingly in potency in respect of its own being and the potency begins at once to mingle with its actuality. If, on the other hand, we consider this first intelligence in so far as it is endowed with knowledge, we see that, first of all, it knows the first Being, and by that very fact an intelligence, inferior to the first, flows from it. It knows forthwith all the power it has in itself, and from this knowledge comes into being the body of the first heaven, which this intelligence controls and moves. Lastly, it knows its own action and from this springs the soul of the first heaven. Continuing in this manner, we should see how the diverse beings have been brought forth by a multitude of intermediate causes, starting from the first Being which is God.[50] But this position is untenable. A first argument which would be conclusive in itself, is that Avicenna and his followers attribute to creatures a creative power which belongs only to God; as this point has been established earlier, it is superfluous to revert to it. The second reason is that the doctrine of the Arabic commentators and of their disciples amounts to placing chance at the beginning of the world. On their assumption, the universe would not be the result of the intention of the first Cause, but the result of a combination of a number of causes producing cumulative effects—which is precisely what is meant by the word "chance." The doctrine of Avicenna amounts accordingly to the assertion that the multiplicity and diversity of things which by their multiplicity and diversity contribute to the completion and perfection of the universe, are the result of chance; and this is manifestly impossible.[51]

The first origin of this multiplicity and diversity of things lies therefore not in chance, but in the intention of the first Cause which is God. It is moreover not impossible to indicate the practical reason which prompted the Creator to produce a multiplicity of creatures. Every being which acts, tends to induce its likeness in the effect which it produces, and it succeeds the more perfectly, the more perfect it is in itself. For it is evident that the more heat a being possesses, the more heat can it give out and that the better artist a man is, the more perfect is the artistic form imparted to his material. Now, God is the supremely perfect agent. It is, therefore, in conformity with His nature to induce perfectly His likeness in the things created, i.e. as perfectly as the finite nature of created things permits. Now, it is evident that a single species of creatures would not succeed in expressing the likeness to the Creator. Since in this case the effect, belonging to finite nature, is not of the same order as the cause, which is of an infinite nature, the effect of a single and solitary species would express only in the obscurest and most defective manner the cause from which it springs. For a creature to represent as perfectly as possible its Creator, it would have to be equal to Him: but this is a self-contradiction. We know of one instance, and only one, where God is the source of a unique person who yet expresses Him completely and perfectly: this is the case of the Word. But this is not a question of a creature nor of the relation of cause and effect: it remains within God. In the case, on the contrary, of created and finite things, a multiplicity of such beings is necessary to express under the greatest possible number of aspects the simple perfection whence they flow. The reason for the multiplicity and variety of created things is, therefore, that this multiplicity and variety were necessary in order to express as perfectly as created things can, the resemblance to their God and Creator.[52]

But to posit creatures of different species means necessarily to posit creatures of unequal perfection. For wherein can many and different things which all express the Divine resemblance, differ from each other? They can differ only in their matter or in their form. The distinctions arising from a difference of form, divide them into distinct species; the distinction arising from their diverse matter, constitutes individuals numerically distinct from each other. But matter exists only in view of its form, and the beings which are numerically distinct through their matter, are thus distinct only to enable the formal distinction to appear which differentiates their species from the others. Of incorruptible beings, there exists only one individual of each species, i.e. there is neither numerical distinction nor matter, for the individual, being incorruptible, suffices to ensure the preservation and differentiation of the species. In the case of beings which can propagate and die, a multiplicity of individuals is necessary to secure the preservation of the species. Beings exist, therefore, within a species, as numerically distinct individuals, only to enable the species to continue as formally distinct from the other species. The true and fundamental distinction to be found in things, lies in their formal distinctness. But, no formal distinctness is possible without inequality. The forms which determine the various natures of beings, whereby things are what they are, are nothing else, in the last resort, but different amounts of perfection. Therefore we may say with Aristotle that the forms of things are like numbers: for all that is needed to change the species of numbers is to add or to subtract a unit. God, since it was impossible to express in a sufficiently perfect manner His likeness in a single creature, wishing to impart being to a plurality of formally distinct species, was therefore bound to produce unequal species. Therefore we find in natural things that the species are arranged hierarchically and ordered in degrees. As mixed compounds are more perfect than elements, so plants are more perfect than minerals, animals more perfect than plants, and man more perfect than other animals. In this progressive series, each species is more perfect than the preceding one. The reason prompting Divine wisdom to produce the inequality of beings, is therefore the same as that which inclines it to will their distinction, viz. the highest perfection of the universe.[53]

Here it would, indeed, not be impossible to raise a difficulty. If creatures can be arranged hierarchically according to their unequal perfections, it is not at first sight obvious how they can have issued from God. An excellent being can will only excellent things, and between really excellent things it would be impossible to note degrees of perfection. Therefore, God, who is excellent, must have willed that all things should be equal.[54] But this objection rests merely on an equivocation. When an excellent being acts, the effect produced by it must be on the whole excellent; but it is not necessary that every part of the effect must be in itself excellent; it is enough that the part be excellently proportioned to the whole. Now, this proportion may demand a merely mediocre excellence of certain parts. The eye is the noblest part of the body, but the body would be ill-constituted if every part had the dignity of the eye, or still more so, if every part of it were an eye, for the other parts have severally their own functions to perform, which the eye, despite all its excellence, would be incapable of performing. The same difficulties would arise, if all the parts of a house were roofs; for such an habitation could not attain its perfection nor fulfil its end which is to protect its inhabitants against heat and rain. Far from contradicting the excellence of the Divine nature, the inequality, therefore, which we find in things is an evident sign of its supreme wisdom. It does not mean that God has necessarily willed the finite and limited beauty of his creatures; for we know that His infinite goodness cannot in any way be increased by creation. But we would simply say that it harmonized with the order of His wisdom that the unequal multiplicity of the creatures should ensure the perfection of the universe.[55]

The reason for a difference in the degrees of perfection of the various orders of creatures is, therefore, manifest. But we may still legitimately raise the question whether this explanation absolves the Creator from having willed a universe within which evil cannot fail to occur.

We may say, in effect, that the perfection of the universe requires the inequality of beings. The infinite perfection of God could be suitably imitated only by a multiplicity of finite beings, and it was accordingly

necessary that all degrees of goodness should be represented in things for the universe to form a sufficiently
perfect image of its Creator. Now to possess so excellent
a perfection as to make it impossible to fall short of it,
is a certain degree of goodness; it is another degree of
goodness to possess a perfection of which it is possible
to fall short in certain circumstances. We accordingly
find both these degrees of goodness represented in
things: certain things are so constituted that they can
never lose their being; such are the incorporeal and
incorruptible creatures. Certain others can lose their
being such as the corporeal and corruptible beings.
Thus, by the very fact that the perfection of the universe
requires the existence of corruptible beings, it also
requires that certain beings should be able to fall short
of their degree of perfection. But falling short of a
certain degree of perfection, and consequently the
deficiency in a certain good, constitutes the very definition
of evil. The existence in the world of corruptible
beings brings inevitably in its train the presence of evil;[56]
and to assert that it was in harmony with the order of
Divine wisdom to will the inequality of beings, is the
same as to assert that it harmonized with it to will evil.
But would such an assertion not imperil the infinite
perfection of the Creator?

In one sense, this objection confronts the human
mind with an insoluble problem. It is incontestable
that the production of any order whatever of creatures
was inevitably bound to lead to the existence of a subject
and, as it were, a ground of imperfection. This was
not merely a matter of convenience, but of real necessity.
A creature as such is characterised by a certain deficiency
in the degree and mode of being: *Esse autem rerum
creatarum deductum est ab esse divino secundum quamdam
deficientem assimilationem.*[57] Creation is not only an
"exodus," but also a "descending from": *Nulla creatura
recipit totam plenitudinem divinae bonitatis, quia perfec-
tiones a Deo in creaturas per modum cujusdam descensus
procedunt,* [58] and we shall have to observe a continuous
series of descending gradations of being in proceeding

from the noblest to the lowliest creatures; still this deficiency will be apparent even in the very first degree of created things, and will moreover appear from the first as an infinite degradation, since it represents the distance between what is Being in itself and what possesses being only as received. Undoubtedly—and we shall see the reason of it further on—a finite being is not a bad being, if no defect is to be found in its proper essence, but we know also that a universe composed of finite beings requires a multiplicity of distinct essences, i.e. in the last resort, a hierarchy of unequal essences, of which some are incorruptible and outside the range of evil, whereas others are subject to evil and are corruptible. But to determine why God has willed these imperfect and defective creatures, is an impossible quest, as we have explained. We may refer as a reason to the Divine goodness which wills its own diffusion outside itself among finite participations of its supreme perfection; but we can assign no cause to it, because the will of God is the first Cause of all beings, and consequently no being can in respect of it play the part of cause. But if we simply ask how it is metaphysically possible for a limited and partially bad universe to have come from a perfect God, without the corruption of the creature falling back upon the Creator, we raise a question which the human mind cannot leave without an answer. In point of fact, this apparently formidable problem rests on nothing but a confusion.

Are we, like the Manicheans, to appeal to an evil principle which is alleged to have created whatever the universe contains in the way of corruptible and defective things? Or are we to conceive the first Principle of all things as having ordered the degrees of being by introducing into the universe, within each essence, the requisite admixture of evil to limit its perfection? This would overlook the fundamental truth expressed by Dionysius: *Malum non est existens neque bonum.*[59] Evil has no existence. We have previously encountered the thesis that everything that is desirable is a good. Now, every nature desires its own existence and its own perfection; the perfection and the being of every nature are therefore truly good things. But if the perfection and the being of all things are goods, it follows that the opposite to good, i.e. evil, has neither perfection nor being. The word "evil" means, accordingly, a certain lack of good and of being, for being as such is a good and therefore the lack of the one entails necessarily the lack of the other.[60] Evil is, therefore, if we may so express it, a purely negative reality; more correctly, it has no degree of either essence or reality. To set out this conclusion more in detail: what we call an evil in the substance of a thing, reduces itself to the lack of a quality which it ought naturally to possess. If we note that man has no wings, we do not believe that this is an evil, because the nature of the human body does not permit of wings; again, we see no evil in a man not having fair hair, because, though fair hair is compatible with human nature, it is not necessarily linked with it. *Per contra*, it is an evil for a man to be without hands, though this would be no evil for a bird. Now, the term "deprivation," taken strictly and in its proper sense, signifies precisely the absence or lack of something that a being ought naturally to possess. Evil reduces itself to a deprivation in this sense;[61] it is therefore a pure negation within a substance; it is neither an essence nor a reality.[62]

Hence we also see that, if evil has nothing positive about it and precisely because it is nothing positive, its presence in the universe would be unintelligible in the absence of positive and real subjects to be its vehicle. This conclusion looks admittedly somewhat paradoxical. Evil is not a being; all good, on the contrary, belongs to being. Is it not strange to assert that non-being requires a being in which to subsist as in its subject? This objection holds, however, only against non-being taken as a simple negation; and in that case it is absolutely irrefutable. The pure and simple absence of being cannot require any subject to support it. But, as just explained, evil is *negation within a substance*, viz. the lack of some part of the substance, and, in short, a *deprivation*. There would consequently be no deprivation and therefore no evil, without the existence of substances or subjects within which the deprivation can find a place. Thus, it is not true that every negation requires a real and positive subject, but this is, nevertheless, true in the case of those special negations which we call deprivations, because *privatio est negatio in subjecto*. The true and only support of evil is the good.[63]

The relation between evil and the good supporting it, is, however, never such that evil can consume and, as it were, exhaust the good completely; for if this were so, evil would consume and exhaust itself. For as long as evil subsists, there must always be a subject within which evil can subsist. Now, the subject of evil is the good; there remains therefore always some good over.[64] Better still: we can assert that evil has, in a certain measure, a cause, and that this cause is none other than the good. For, everything that subsists in some other thing as in its subject, must necessarily have a cause, and this cause must ultimately be found in the principles of the subject itself or in some external cause. Now, evil subsists in the good as in its natural subject: it has therefore necessarily a cause.[65] But it is evident that only a being can act as cause, for in order to act, it must be. Now, all being as such is good; the good remains, therefore, the only possible cause of evil. It is easy to verify this proposition by examining the four kinds of causes.

It is, to begin with, evident that the good is the cause of evil in the sense of material cause. This conclusion follows from the principles previously set out. For it has been shown that the good is the subject within which evil subsists; that is to say, that it is the real matter of evil, though it is so merely by accident. As regards the formal cause, it must be conceded that evil has no such cause, for it is reduced rather to a mere deprivation of form. The same applies to the final cause, for evil is merely the deprivation of order in the disposition of means to their end. But we may, on the contrary, assert that evil often leaves room for an accidental efficient cause. This may be clearly seen if we distinguish between the evil which finds its way into the actions which different beings perform, and the evil which is to be found in the effects of their actions. Evil may arise in an action by reason of a defect in one or other of the principles which are the cause of the action; thus, the defective movement of an animal may be put down to the weakness of its motor-faculty, as happens in the case of infants, or to the malformation of one of its limbs, as in the case of a lame man. If, on the other hand, we consider the evil as it may be found in the effects of efficient causes, it may occur, in the first place, in an effect which is not the proper effect of the causes: in that case the defect is due either to the active power or to the matter on which it acts. The former is the case, when the efficient cause is unable to attain its full form without damaging another form. Thus, the presence of the form of fire entails the deprivation of the form of air and of water; the more perfect the form of the fire and the more successfully it imparts its form to the matter on which it acts, the more completely will it destroy the contrary forms it encounters. The evil, and the destruction of air and water, find their cause, accordingly, in the perfection of the fire; but they result from it only by accident. The end towards which fire tends, is not to deprive water of its form, but to impart its own form to the matter on which it operates, and only because it tends to this end, does it happen to be the origin of an evil and of a deprivation. If we lastly consider the defects which may occur in the effect proper to fire, for example its failure to heat, the origin of this defect will necessarily be found either in a failure of the active power of the fire, already discussed, or in an inadequate disposition of the matter, badly prepared, let us say for instance, to receive the action of the fire. But none of these defects can rest upon anything but a good, for it is the property of the good and of being alone, to act and to be a cause.

We may, therefore, legitimately conclude that evil has no other but accidental causes, but that, with this reservation, the only possible cause of evil is its contrary: the good.[66]

Lastly, we may proceed to this final conclusion to which we must hold firmly, however strange it may appear: viz. the cause of evil lies always in some good, and yet, God, who is the Cause of all good, is not the cause of evil. For it follows clearly from the preceding considerations, that, when evil is reducible to a defect in some act, its cause is always a defect in the being that acts. Now in God there is no defect, but, on the contrary, supreme perfection. The evil caused by a defect in the acting being could not, therefore, have God for its cause. But if we consider the evil which consists in the corruption of certain beings, we must on the other hand, assign its cause to God. This is equally evident in the case of beings which act by nature and those which act by will. For we have asserted that when a being by its action causes a form, the production of which entails the destruction of another form, its act must be considered as the cause of this deprivation or defect. Now, the main form which God evidently has in view in creation is the good of the universal order. But the order of the universe requires, as we saw, that some of the things should be defective. God is therefore the cause of the corruptions and defects of all things, but only in consequence of his will to bring about the good of the universal order, and as it were, by accident.[67] In short, the effect of a defective secondary cause may be attributed to the first Cause which is free from all defect, in respect of whatever being and perfection is present in it, but not in respect of whatever evil or defectiveness it contains. In the same manner as whatever movement is observed in the gait of a lame man is attributable to his motor-faculty and whatever haltingness to the malformation of his leg, in like manner whatever being and action is observable in a bad act, is attributable to God as to its cause, but whatever defectiveness is contained in the act, is attributable to the defective secondary cause, and not to the almighty perfection of God.[68]

Thus, from whatever angle we approach the problem, we always come back to the same conclusion. Evil as such is nothing. It is, therefore, inconceivable that God could be its cause. If asked, further, what is its cause, we must reply that it reduces itself to the tendency of certain things to return to non-being. It is undoubtedly not impossible to conceive finite and limited beings in whom yet no evil is to be found. In fact there are in the world incorruptible beings which never lack in anything belonging to their nature; but good exists also in those beings of lesser perfection, such as the corruptible beings, and if we note their presence in the world, the reason is that it pleased the Divine wisdom to form a more perfect image of itself, by expressing itself in unequal creatures, some of which should be corruptible and others not. But we see in both only goodness, being and perfection. In that descending scale, issuing from God, we see but the effusion and transmission of being. Even the vilest creature, the infinitesimal perfection of which is almost entirely swallowed up by evil, still enriches with its minute fragment the total perfection of the universe; even in its wretched degree of being, it still expresses something of God. We shall therefore proceed to examine this hierarchy of created goods which God, of His free and causeless will, has formed in His image, and we shall first consider the supreme degree of this hierarchy, the creature wholly free from all matter, the angel.

NOTES TO CHAPTER VII.

1. See on this question the articles by J. Durantel, *La notion de la création dans saint Thomas*, Ann. de phil. chrét. February, March, April, May, and June numbers, 1912; Rohner, *Das Schöpfungsproblem bei Moses Maïmonides, Albertus Magnus und Thomas von Aquin*, Beitr. z. Gesch. d. Phil. des Mittelalters, XI., H. 5, Münster, 1913. On the question of the eternity of the world, cf. Th. Esser, *Die Lehre des hl. Thomas von Aquin über die Möglichkeit einer anfangslosen Schöpfung*, Münster, 1895; Jellouschek, *Verteidigung der Möglichkeit einer anfangslosen Weltschöpfung durch Herveus Natalis, Joannes a Neapoli, Gregorius Ariminensis und Joannes Capreolus*, Jahrb. f. Phil. u. spek. Theol., 1911, XXVI., p. 155–187 and 325–367; Fr. M. Sladeszek, *Die Auffassung des hl. Thomas von Aquin in seiner Summa theologica von der Lehre des Aristoteles über die Ewigkeit der Welt*, Phil. Jahrb., XXXV., p. 38–56; A. D. Sertillanges, *L'idée de la création dans saint Thomas d'Aquin*, Rev. de théol. et phil., avril, 1907.

2. *Sum. theol.*, I. 44, 1, ad *Resp.*; *De Potentia*, qu. III., art. 1, ad *Resp.*

3. *Sum. theol.*, I. 44, 1, ad 3^m.

4. *De Potentia*, qu. III., art. 1, ad 7.

5. "Creatio non est factio quae sit mutatio proprie loquendo, sed est quaedam acceptio esse." *II Sent.*, 1, 1, art. 2, ad *Resp.* and ad 2^m. Cf. *De Potentia*, III., 2; *Sum. theol.*, I. 45, 2, ad 2^m and 3^m.; *Cont. Gent.*, II. 17.

6. *Sum. theol.*, I. 45, 2, ad *Resp.*

7. Cf. Mandonnet, *op. cit.*, I., p. 161; II. p. 111–112.

8. *Sent.*, IV., 5, 3, ed. Quaracchi, 1916, II. p. 776.

9. *Sum. theol.*, I. 45, 5, ad *Resp.*; *Cont. Gent.*, II. 21.

10. *De Potentia*, qu. III., art. 4, ad *Resp.*

11. *Ibid.*

12. *Sum. theol.*, I. 7, 2, ad *Resp.*

13. *Sum. theol.*, I. 19, 4, ad *Resp.*; *De Potentia*, qu. III., art. 10, ad *Resp.*

14. *Sum. theol.*, I. 15, 1, ad *Resp.*

15. *Sum. theol.*, I. 15, 2, ad *Resp.*

16. *Sum. theol.*, I. 15, 2, ad *Resp.*; *De Verit.*, qu. III., art. 1, ad *Resp.*

17. *De Verit.*, III. 5, ad *Sed contra*, 2; "Sicut sol radios suos emittit ad corporum illuminationem, ita divina bonitas radios suos, id est, participationes sui, diffundit ad rerum creationem"; *In II Sent.*, *Prolog.*; *Sum. theol.*, I. 6, 4, ad *Resp.*; for the formula quoted above, see *Cont. Gent.*, II. 15, ad *Deus secundum hoc*. The term "virtualiter" implies, of course, no passivity on the part of the Divine substance; it means that the Divine being contains, by reason of its perfect actuality itself, the sufficient reason for the analogous being of things; it contains them as the mind of the artist contains his works: "Emanatio creaturarum a Deo est sicut exitus artificiatorum ab artifice; unde sicut ab arte artificis effluunt formae artificiales in materia, ita etiam ab ideis in mente divina existentibus fluunt omnes formae et virtutes naturales." *In II Sent.*, 18, 1, 2, ad *Resp.*

18. To avoid all ambiguity, it must be remembered (1) that the created things are deduced from God in as far as they find in Him their exemplaries: "omne esse ab eo exemplariter deducitur" (*In Div. Nom.*, I. 4); and (2) that, in the language of St. Thomas, "to participate" does not mean to be a thing, but *not* to be it; "to participate in God" means not to be God (*Sum. theol.*, I. 75, 5, ad 1^m and ad 4^m). Here, as everywhere in his system, the concept of analogy is fundamental.

19. *De Potentia*, qu. III., art. 16, ad 24^m.

20. *Sum. theol.*, I. 19, 2, ad *Resp.*

21. *De Potentia*, qu. III., art. 10. ad 1^m.

22. *Ibid.*, ad 6^m.

23. *De Potentia*, qu. III., art. 10, ad 12^m.

24. *De Potentia*, qu. I., art. 5, ad *Resp.*; *Sum. theol.*, I. 25, 5, ad *Resp.*

25. *De Potentia*, qu. III., art. 16, ad 17^m.

26. *Sum. theol.*, I. 25, 6, ad 3^m.

27. *Sum. theol.*, I. 45, 3, ad *Resp.* and ad 1^m; *De Potentia*, qu. III., art. 3, ad *Resp.*

28. *Sum. theol.*, I. 19, 5, ad 3^m; *De Potentia*, III., 17, ad *Resp.*

29. *Topic.*, I. 9.

30. *Sum. theol.*, I. 46,1 ad *Resp.*

31. Horten, *Die Hauptlehren des Averroes*, p. 112; Mandonnet, *op. cit.*, I., p. 168–172.

32. *Sum. theol.*, I. 46, 1, 9; *Cont. Gent.*, II. 32, ad *Posita causa*, and *De Potentia*, III, 17, 4.

33. *Cont. Gent.*, II. 32, ad *Effectus procedit*, and *De Potentia*, III. 17, 26.

34. *Sum. theol.*, I. 46, 1, 10.
35. *Sum. theol.*, I. 46, 1, 2; *De Potentia*, III. 17, 2.
36. *Sum. theol.*, I. 46, 1, 5; *Cont. Gent.*, II. 33, ad *Quandoque aliquid.*
37. I. 1.
38. *De Potentia*, III. 17, ad *Resp.*; *Sum. theol.*, I. 46, 1, 5, ad *Resp.*; *Cont. Gent.*, II. 35, ad *Ex his etiam.*
39. Cf. St. Bonaventure, *Sent. II*, dis. 1, p. 1, art. 1, qu. 2, ad *Sed ad oppositum*, 5°.
40. *Sum. theol.*, I. 46, ad 8; *Cont. Gent.*, II. 38, ad *Quod autem*, and *De aeternitate mundi contra murmurantes*, sub. fin.
41. St. Bonaventure, *ibid.*, 3a propos.
42. *Cont. Gent.*, II. 38, ad *Quod etiam tertio*, and *Sum. theol.*, I. 46, 2, ad 6.
43. St. Bonaventure, *loc. cit.*, 1a propos.
44. *Cont. Gent.*, II. 38, ad *Quod etiam quarto.*
45. *Cont. Gent.*, II. 38, ad *Has autem rationes.*
46. *Sum. theol.*, I. 46, 2, ad *Resp.*
47. *De aeternitate mundi*, per tot.; *De Potentia*, III. 14, ad *Resp.*
48. L.-G. Lévy, *Maïmonide*, p. 71–72.
49. *Op. cit.*, p. 72–74.
50. *De Potentia*, qu. III., art. 16, ad *Resp.*
51. *De Potentia*, *loc. cit.*; *Sum. theol.*, I. 47, 1, ad *Resp.*
52. *Cont. Gent.*, II. 45, ad *Quum enim*, and *Sum. theol.*, I. 47, 1. ad *Resp.*
53. *Sum. theol.*, I. 47, 2, ad *Resp.*
54. *Sum theol.*, I. 47, 2, ad 1ᵐ.
55. *De Potentia*, III. 16, ad *Resp.*
56. *Sum. theol.*, I. 48, 2, ad *Resp.*
57. *In lib. de Divin. Nomin.*, c. I., lect. 1.
58. *Cont. Gent.*, IV. 7, ad *Nulla creatura.*—We keep on purpose the term "exodus" against one of our critics who finds in it a disquietingly pantheistic flavour, for the term is authentically thomistic: "Aliter dicendum est de productione unius creaturae, et aliter de *exitu* totius universi a Deo." (*De Potentia*, III. 47, ad *Resp.*)
59. *De Divin. Nomin.*, c. IV.
60. *Sum. theol.*, I. 48, 1, ad *Resp.*
61. *Cont. Gent.*, III. 6, ad *Ut autem.*
62. *Cont. Gent.*, III. 7, ad *Mala enim.*—Cf. *De Malo*, I. 1, ad *Resp.*; *De Potentia*, III. 6, ad *Resp.*
63. *Cont. Gent.*, III. 11, per tot.; *Sum. theol.*, I. 48, 3, ad *Resp.* and ad 2ᵐ; *De Malo*, I. 2, ad *Resp.*
64. *Cont. Gent.*, III. 12, ad *Patet autem*, and *Sum. theol.*, I. 48, ad *Resp.*
65. *Cont. Gent.*, III. 13, ad *Quidquid enim.*
66. *Sum. theol.*, I. 49, 1, ad *Resp.*

67. *Sum. theol.*, I. 49, 2, ad *Resp.*
68. *Sum. theol.*, *ibid.*, ad 2^m; *Cont. Gent.*, III. 10, ad *Ex parte quidem.*

CHAPTER VIII. THE ANGELS

THE order of creatures in whom the highest degree of created perfection is realised, is that of the pure spirits, usually called angels.[1] Very frequently the historians of St. Thomas either pass over in complete silence this part of his system or are content with a mere allusion to it. Such an omission is all the more to be regretted as the thomistic Angelology does not constitute in the mind of its author an enquiry of a specifically theological kind. The angels are creatures whose existence can be proved and, in exceptional cases, observed; their suppression would render the universe, taken as a whole, unintelligible; and lastly, the nature and the operations of inferior creatures such as man can be perfectly understood only by comparison with, and often by opposition to, those of the angels. In short, in a doctrine which bases the ultimate reason of beings so constantly upon the place occupied by them in the universe, it is impossible to omit the consideration of a whole order of creatures, without seriously endangering the equilibrium of the entire system. It must be added that the Angelology of St. Thomas is the final stage of a slow evolution of ideas, in the course of which heterogeneous elements converge, some of strictly speaking religious, others of purely philosophical origin.

It is known nowadays[2] that three sources have contributed to this part of the thomistic system. In the first place, there were the astronomical theories on certain spiritual substances, considered as the causes of the movements of the spheres and of the stars. Secondly, metaphysical speculations on the pure spirits, considered as degrees of being, and marking, so to say, definite stages in the "exodus" by which the multiplicity of things have issued from the One. Lastly, conceptions of biblical origin concerning angels and demons. The astronomical data just mentioned, originated from Aristotle who in this matter was himself under the influence of Plato. According to Aristotle, the first immovable mover imparts movement, inasmuch as he is loved and desired; but love and desire presuppose knowledge: hence the celestial spheres can be set in motion only by an intelligent substance, considered as the moving force. Again, Plato already had identified the soul of the world with the principle of universal order and had considered the stars as set in motion by divine souls. The successors of the two philosophers side with one or other of these views. But while the strict Platonists attribute a real soul to the stars, the Fathers and Doctors of the Church observe a greater reserve on this question; none of them admit this view directly; some consider it as possible, most of them deny it. The Aristotelian teaching which seems to have confined itself to affirming moving intelligences without attributing actual souls to the stars, was interpreted in the Middle Ages in different ways. Among the Eastern commentators some, like Alfarabi, Avicenna and Algazel, ascribed the principle of astronomical movement to real souls, while others located the principle of this movement either in a soul deprived of all sensory function and reduced to its purely intellectual part, as did Maimonides, or in a pure and simple intelligence, as did Averroës. This is the position adopted, in opposition to that of Avicenna, by all the great scholastic philosophers. They do not consider the celestial bodies as being themselves the cause of their own movement, as in the case of the elements. Neither do they consider the spheres as directly set in motion by God, but they ascribe the origin of astronomical movements to pure Intelligences created by God.

The metaphysical speculations about the hierarchic degrees of being—which requires here to be specially emphasised—originated in the Neoplatonic doctrine of emanation. As early as Plotinus, besides the four degrees which mark the "exodus" of things outside the One, a differentiation begins to take shape within the first degree itself, viz. the Intelligence. The "ideas" of Plato assume here a proper subsistence and a kind of individuality: they arrange themselves in an hierarchic order, analogous to that which disposes the species under the genera, and the particular sciences under Science taken as whole. This organisation will be found complete in the successors and disciples of Plotinus: Porphyrius, Iamblicus and especially Proclus. To this last we owe the final formulation of the doctrine of Intelligences: their absolute incorporealness and simplicity, their subsistence outside time, the nature of their knowledge, etc. Moreover, from ancient times onward, there is a tendency to identify the pure Intelligences, as the intermediaries between the One and the rest of creation, with beings of quite different origin: namely, with the angels to whom the Bible attributes often the function of messengers sent by God to men. Philo already speaks of pure spirits peopling the air, who are called demons by the philosophers and angels by Moses. Porphyrius and Iamblicus reckon the angels and archangels among the demons; Proclus classes them with the demons in the strict sense of the term, and with heroes, to form a triad bridging the gap between the gods and men.[3] Again in Proclus the doctrine is taking shape which was eventually to prevail in scholasticism, concerning the knowledge of angels, presenting it as simply illuminative, not as discursive knowledge. It was for the Pseudo-Dionysius the Areopagite to gather up these data and to reach a final synthesis of the biblical conception of angel-messengers with Neoplatonic speculation; patristic and medieval philosophy did little more than accept and elaborate his teaching.[4] Henceforth, the angels are more and more conceived as pure spirits; gradually the Neoplatonic conception of the absolute incorporealness of the angels prevails over the first hesitation of the patristic period,[5] and though some of the scholastics maintain the distinction of matter and form within the angelic substances, it is no longer a question of any corporeal matter, even of a luminous or ethereal matter, but of mere potentiality and the principle of change. The Pseudo-Dionysius not only transformed the angels of the Bible into pure spirits, but he also ordered them in an elaborate classification,[6] dividing them into three hierarchies, each again divided into three orders. This arrangement passed bodily over into the system of St. Thomas. The task remained to identify the angels, thus conceived, with the intelligences charged by the philosophers with the guidance of the movements of the spheres. *A priori* this identification was in no way necessary, and apart from a few indications in certain Neoplatonic thinkers, it was the oriental philosophers who finally effected it.[7] The Arabs and the Jews identified certain orders of angels from the Koran and the Bible, either with the intelligences that set the stars in motion, or with the souls of the stars dependent upon these intelligences, and the influence of Avicenna and Maimonides ultimately decided the issue. Western Scholasticism was, however, far from simply accepting their conclusions. Albertus Magnus, for instance, refused categorically to identify the angels with the intelligences; neither St. Bonaventure nor St. Thomas accept this assimilation which at bottom could be wholly satisfactory only to the Averroists; it is therefore only among these latter that it can now be found.

Such are the historical elements, various and of very different origins, which St. Thomas succeeded in combining in a synthesis, both coherent and in many respects original. The existence of angels, i.e. of an order of entirely incorporeal creatures, is attested by Holy Scripture:[8] *Qui facis Angelos tuos spiritus*; and nothing meets more satisfactorily the needs of reason than this affirmation, for reflection leads necessarily to the assumption of the existence of incorporeal creatures. The principal object aimed at by God in the creation is the supreme good which is the assimilation to God; as we saw earlier, this is the only *raison d'être* of the universe. Now, an effect can be perfectly assimilated to its cause only by imitating that whereby the cause produces this particular effect: thus the warmth of a body resembles the warmth which in the first instance warmed it. But we know that God created the creatures by intelligence and by will; the perfection of the universe accordingly demands the existence of intellectual creatures. Now, the object of the intellect is the universal; the body, however, *quâ* material, as well as all corporal virtue, is on the contrary, determined by nature to a particular mode of being; truly intellectual beings cannot therefore be other than incorporeal, which means that the perfection of the universe demands the existence of beings possessing neither matter nor bodies.[9] Moreover, the general plan of creation would display a manifest gap, if there were no angels. The hierarchy of beings is continuous; every nature of a superior degree is contiguous by whatever is least noble in it, with whatever is most noble in the next inferior degree. Thus, intellectual nature is superior to corporeal nature, and yet the order of intellectual natures is contiguous with the order of corporeal natures at the point of the least noble part of intellectual nature, which is the rational soul of man. On the other hand, the body united with the rational soul, is by the very fact of this union, placed at the highest degree in the order of bodily natures; the order of nature, to preserve proportion, must reserve therefore a place for intellectual creatures superior to the human soul, i.e. for the angels who are not united to bodies.[10]

It may, indeed, seem at first sight that an argument such as this amounts to no more than a mere reason of convenience and harmony; but it would be a mistake to think of it as subservient to a purely logical and abstract desire for symmetry. If it is reasonable to admit the existence of intelligences freed from bodies, who are to the souls united with a body, as the bodies ennobled by the union with the soul are to bodies without souls, the reason is that there is no discontinuity in the hierarchy of created perfections, and this very lack of discontinuity is a profound law governing the emanation of beings outside God. St. Thomas refused to break up the creative activity in the manner of the Arabic philosophers and of their Western disciples; but though he will not admit that each superior degree of creatures imparts being to the next inferior degree, he yet maintains firmly the hierarchic multiplicity of degrees. A single and simple creative power produced and maintains the whole creation, but though it does not spring forth afresh like a new force at each stage of creation, it none the less does not cease to flow through all of them. Hence the effects of Divine power are naturally ordered in a continuous series of decreasing perfections, and the order of created things is such that to flow from one end to another, this power must necessarily pass through all the intermediate stages. Below the celestial matter, for instance, is ranged immediately fire, below which comes air, below which is water, below which finally lies the earth, all the bodies being thus ordered by degrees of decreasing dignity and tenuousness. Now, at the supreme degree of all things we find a being, absolutely simple and one, which is God. It is consequently not possible to place immediately below God a corporeal substance, eminently composite and divisible; we must, on the contrary, assume a multitude of middle terms to descend from the sovereign simplicity of God to the complex multiplicity of material bodies. Some of these intermediate terms will be formed by intellectual substances combined with bodies; others by intellectual substances freed from all union with matter, and these precisely we call angels.[11]

The angels are consequently wholly incorporeal. Can we go further and consider them as wholly immaterial? There are many philosophers and doctors who deny this. Though the excellence of the angelic nature appears henceforth to all as entailing their incorporealness, it is more difficult to acquiesce in attributing to them so great a simplicity as to make it impossible to distinguish in them a simple combination of matter and form. By matter in this case must be understood, not necessarily a body, but, in the widest sense, any potency combined with an act in the constitution of a given being. Now, the only existing principle of movement and of change is to be found in matter; there must consequently be matter in everything capable of being set in motion. But a created spiritual substance is mobile and movable, for God alone is naturally immovable. Consequently there is matter in every created spiritual substance.[12] In the second place, we must assume that nothing is active and passive at the same time and under the same aspect; and further, that nothing acts, except by its form, and is passive, except in its matter. Now, the created spiritual substance, viz. the angel, is active in so far as it illumines the next inferior angel, and is passive in so far as it is illumined by the next superior one. The angel is therefore necessarily composed of form and matter.[13] Lastly, we know that everything existing is either pure act or pure potency or composed of act and potency. But the created spiritual substance is not pure act, for God alone is such. Neither is it pure potency, as is self-evident. It is, therefore, composed of potency and act, which means that it is composed of matter and of form.[14]

These arguments, however seductive, were unable to prevail in the mind of St. Thomas over the first principle which governs all creation. We know that the necessity for positing such incorporeal creatures as the angels rests in the thomistic system upon the necessary existence of an order of pure intelligences, placed immediately below God. Now, the nature of pure intellectual substances must be suited to their operation, and the operation proper to intellectual substances is that of knowing. It is equally easy to determine the nature of this action by starting from its object. Things tend to be intelligible in proportion as they are free from matter; the forms united to matter, for example, are individual forms which, as we shall see, cannot be apprehended as such by the intellect. The intelligence, the object of which is the immaterial as such, must therefore be on its part also free from all matter; the complete immaterialness of the angels is consequently required by the very position they occupy in the order of creation.[15]

This means that the objection raised on the ground of the mobility and mutability of the angels cannot be considered as decisive. The modifications to which they may be subject, affect in no way their being itself, but only their intelligence and their will. To explain these changes it is therefore sufficient to admit that their intellect and their will may pass from potency to act, but there is no need to assume a distinction of form and matter within their essence which remains unchanged.[16] The same applies to the alleged impossibility of simultaneous activity and passivity; the illumination received and transmitted by an angel supposes an intellect which is sometimes in act and sometimes in potency; it by no means assumes a being composed of form and matter.[17] There remains the last objection: viz. a spiritual substance which is pure act, would be identical with God; therefore a mixture of potency and act, i.e. in the last resort, a mixture of form and matter, must be assumed in the angelic nature. In a certain sense, the whole of this argument may be conceded. It is incontestable that, placed as the angel is immediately below God, he must all the same be distinct from Him, as the finite is from the infinite; his being, therefore, necessarily admits of a certain measure of potency which limits and confines his actuality. If therefore "potency" is taken as synonymous with "matter," it is impossible to deny that the angels are in some degree material; but this identification of potency and matter is not forced upon us, and an examination of material things will show the reason why. For in every material substance we can distinguish a twofold composition. In the first place, we see that it is composed of form and of matter, and by reason of this each thing constitutes a nature. But if we examine this nature itself, thus composed of matter and form, we observe in addition that this nature is not, in respect of itself, its own being. Considered in regard to the being it possesses, this nature is in the same position as every potency is in regard to its act. In other words again; even abstracting from the hylemorphic composition of a created being, it is always possible to find in it the composition of its nature or essence with the existence conferred upon it by the Creator. But what is true of any material nature, is equally true of a separate intellectual substance such as the angel. If we suppose a form of a determinate nature, subsisting by itself outside all matter, this nature is still in respect of its being in the relation of potency to act; it is therefore at an infinite distance from the first being which is God, pure act and comprising within Himself the total plenitude of all being. This means that it is not necessary to introduce any matter into the angelic nature to keep it distinct from the creative essence; though pure intelligence, simple form, free from all matter, it yet has but a limited quantity of being, and must be admitted not to *be*, but only to *have* that very being which it possesses.[18]

The certitude thus acquired concerning the absolute immaterialness of the angels allows us to solve the much controverted problem of their distinctness. The doctors who insist on introducing matter into the angelic substances were led to do so by their wish to make their distinctness intelligible. For it is matter alone which constitutes the numerical distinction of beings within each species; if therefore the angels are pure forms without being limited and individualised by matter, it is impossible to see how they can be distinct from each other.[19] The answer is simply that there exist no two angels of the same species[20]; and the reason of this is obvious. The beings belonging to the same species, but differing numerically, as distinct individuals of the same species, possess a similar form, but different matter. If therefore the angels have no matter, it follows that each of them is *specifically* distinct from the others, the individual as such constituting in this case the species.[21] Nor can this conclusion be contested on the ground that by rendering the multiplication of individual angelic natures within each species impossible, we thereby impoverish the total perfection of the universe. That whereby each being is specifically distinct from others, viz. its form, is evidently of greater dignity than the material principle of individuation which assigns to this being its place within the species, by making it into a particular being. The multiplication of species is consequently a greater addition of nobility and perfection to the universe than the multiplication of individuals within the same species; now, the universe owes its perfection above all to the separate substances it contains; substituting a multiplicity of different species for a multitude of individuals of the same species, would therefore in no way diminish the total perfection of the universe, but would, on the contrary, increase, and so to say, multiply it.[22]

We have therefore to deal with a certain number of angels, all specifically different, a number probably enormous and considerably larger than that of material things, if we assume that God must have created in much greater abundance the more perfect creatures, in order to ensure the higher excellence of the whole universe.[23] We know, on the other hand, that species differ like numbers, i.e. that they represent greater or lesser quantities of perfection and being. The problem therefore presents itself, according to what order this innumerable multitude of angels is arranged and distributed.[24] If each angel constitutes a species by himself, it must in fact be possible to descend from the first angel—*natura Deo propinquissima*[25]—by a steady transition to the last, whose perfection is contiguous with that of the human species. It is, however, but too evident that our thought would lose itself in attempting to follow such a multiplicity of degrees, all the more as we are debarred in this life from an individual knowledge of the angels[26]; the only chance which we have is to attempt a general classification by orders and hierarchies according to the diversity of their action. The proper action of pure intelligences is evidently intelligence itself or, if such an expression is allowed, the act of intellecting. It is, therefore, according to the differences in their several modes of intelligence that the angelic orders can be distinguished.

The whole angelic hierarchy, taken collectively, is, from this point of view, radically different from the human order. Undoubtedly the first origin of knowledge is the same for angels as for men. In both cases Divine illuminations enlighten the creatures, but angels and men perceive these illuminations in very different ways. While, as we shall see later, men extract the intelligible from sense-experience which contains it, the angels perceive the intelligible immediately, and in its intelligible purity; they thereby make use of a mode of knowledge, exactly proportionate to the place they occupy in the whole creation, i.e. intermediate between that which belongs to man and that which belongs to God alone. The angelic being, placed directly below God, is, however, distinct from Him in that the essence of the angel is not identical with his existence; this difference, characteristic of the creature, recurs in his mode of knowing. The intelligence of God is identical with His essence and His being, because the Divine being, as sheer infinite being, contains in Himself the totality of being; but the angel, as a finite essence, endowed by God with a certain being, cannot extend by right his knowledge to all being.[27] On the other hand, the angel is a pure intelligence, i.e. not naturally united with a body; he cannot consequently apprehend the sensible as such. For sensible things are apprehended by sense, as intelligible things are apprehended by the intellect. But every substance which extracts its knowledge from the sensible is naturally united to a body, since sensible knowledge requires the senses and therefore bodily sense-organs. The angelic substances cannot consequently use sensibles as means to knowledge.[28] Thus the very nature of the being conferred by God upon the angels entails a mode of knowing proper to them. This can in no way resemble abstraction by which man discovers the intelligible hidden in sense-experience; neither can it be anything like the act by which God *is* the intelligible and at the same time apprehends it; it can only therefore be a knowledge acquired by means of species the reception of which illumines the intelligence, but they are at the same time purely intelligible species, i.e. species adapted to a purely incorporeal being. To meet these requirements, we should have to say that the angels know things by means of species which are con-natural to them, or by means of innate species.[29] All intelligible essences which pre-existed eternally in God in the shape of ideas, issued from Him at the moment of creation along two distinct yet parallel lines: on the one hand, they individualised themselves in material beings whose form they constitute; on the other, they flowed into the angelic souls, thus conferring the knowledge of things upon them. It may consequently be asserted that the intellect of angels is superior to that of men in proportion as the being, complete and endowed with its form, is superior to unformed matter. And if our intellect may be compared to a "tabula rasa," that of the angel would be comparable to a canvas covered with its painting, or better still, a canvas reflecting the luminous essences of things.[30]

This innate possession of intelligible species is common to all the angels and characteristic of their nature; but not all of them possess in themselves the same species, and hereon their distinction is based. The relative superiority of created beings is constituted by their greater or lesser proximity and resemblance

to the one first being which is God. Now, the whole
plenitude of intellectual knowledge, possessed by God,
is concentrated for Him in one point, namely the
Divine essence in which God knows all things. This
intellectual plenitude is to be found again in created
intelligences, but in an inferior mode and with less
simplicity; the intelligences inferior to God know
therefore by many different means what God knows
in one unique object, and the more subordinate the
nature of a given intelligence is, the more numerous
must be the means employed in knowing. In short,
the superiority of the angels increases in proportion
as the number of species required by them in order to
apprehend the universality of intelligibles decreases.[31]
We know, moreover, that, as regards the angels, each
individual constitutes an original degree of being.
The simplicity of knowledge is accordingly continually degraded and broken up in descending from
the first angel to the last. Still, three distinct main
stages may be observed in this series. At the first
stage are the angels who know the intelligible essences,
inasmuch as they proceed from the first universal
principle which is God. This mode of knowing
pertains properly to the first hierarchy, ranged immediately round God, of which it may be said, with
Dionysius,[32] that it dwells within the vestibule of the
Godhead. At the second stage are the angels who
know intelligibles in so far as they are subject to the
most universal of created causes; this mode of knowing
pertains to the second hierarchy. Lastly, the third
stage is occupied by the angels knowing intelligibles
as applied to particular beings and dependent on
particular causes; these angels constitute the third
hierarchy.[33] There is consequently a decreasing
generality and simplicity in the distribution of angelic
knowledge: some, turned wholly to God, are concerned
entirely with the contemplation within Him of intelligible essences; others contemplate them in the
universal causes of creation, i.e. in a plurality of objects;
others, lastly, consider them in the determinate form

of particular effects, i.e. in a multiplicity of objects, equal to the number of created beings.[34]

In defining in detail the mode according to which the separate intelligences apprehend their object, we are led to observe three different orders within each hierarchy. For it was said that the first hierarchy contemplates the intelligible essences within God Himself; now God is the end of all creatures; the angels of this hierarchy contemplate, therefore, as their peculiar object, the supreme end of the universe which is the goodness of God. Those who apprehend it with the utmost clearness are called Seraphim, because they burn and are, as it were, aflame with love for that object of which they possess the most perfect knowledge. The other angels of the first hierarchy contemplate Divine goodness, no longer directly and in itself, but according to the wisdom of Providence. They are called Cherubim, i.e. "plenitude of wisdom," because they have a clear vision of the first operating virtue of the Divine models of things. Immediately below these are the angels who consider the disposition of Divine judgments; and as the throne is the symbol of judiciary power, they have received the name of Thrones. This does not mean that the goodness of God, His essence and His knowledge by which He knows the disposition of beings, are in Him three distinct things; they are simply three aspects under which finite intelligences, such as the angels, are able to envisage His perfect simplicity.

The second hierarchy knows the reason of things, not in God Himself as in a single object, but in the plurality of universal causes: its proper object is therefore the general ordering of means in view of the end. Now this universal ordering of things presupposes the existence of many ordering minds: these are the Dominations whose name signifies authority, because they order what others are to execute. The general directions given by these angels are received by others, multiplying and distributing them according to the diverse effects to be produced. These latter angels have the name of Virtues, because they impart to the general causes the necessary energy to preserve them from failure in the accomplishment of their numerous operations. This order therefore presides over the operations of the entire universe, and we may therefore reasonably ascribe to it the movement of the celestial bodies, as the universal causes whereby all the particular effects in nature are produced.[35] It falls also within the province of these angels to carry out the Divine effects which interrupt the ordinary course of nature and are usually in direct dependence on the stars. Lastly, the universal order of Providence, already existing in its effects, is preserved from all confusion by the Powers whose office it is to protect it against all evil influences likely to disturb it.

With this last class of angels we reach the third hierarchy which knows the order of Divine Providence no longer in itself, nor in the general causes, but insofar as it is knowable in the multiplicity of particular causes. These angels are therefore directly charged with the ordering of human affairs. Some of them are particularly concerned with the common and general good of nations and cities: on account of this position, they have been given the name of Principalities. The distinction of kingdoms, the passing of a temporal supremacy to this nation rather than to that, the conduct of princes and nobles, are matters of their direct competence. Within that very general class of goods, there is one that concerns the individual taken in himself, but at the same time also a multitude of individual persons: these are the truths of Faith to be believed, and the Divine cult to be observed. The angels whose special objects are these goods, at the same time general and particular, bear the name of Archangels. It is they also who carry the most solemn messages entrusted to them by God to man: such was the Archangel Gabriel who came to announce the Incarnation of the Word, the only Son of God, the Truth which all men are bound to accept. Lastly, we find a yet more particular good, which concerns each individual in himself and particularly. This order of good is in the hands of the Angels, strictly so called, the guardians of men and messengers of God to carry intimations of lesser importance.[36] These Angels complete the inferior hierarchy of separate intelligences.

It is easy to see that the foregoing distribution observes the continuity of a universe wherein the last beings of a superior degree border on the first beings of an inferior degree, as the least perfect animal is contiguous with the plants. The first and highest order of being is that of the Divine Persons, closing with the Holy Ghost, i.e. the Love proceeding from the Father and the Son. The Seraphim, united in their most ardent love to God, have therefore a close affinity with the Third Person of the Trinity. But the third order of this hierarchy, the Thrones, has no less affinity with the highest degree of the second, the Dominations; for it is they who transmit to the second hierarchy the illuminations needed for the knowledge and execution of the Divine decrees. In the same manner the order of the Powers is in close relation with the order of Principalities, for the distance is very small between those who render particular effects possible and those who actually produce them.[37] The hierarchic arrangement of the angels presents, accordingly, a continuous series of pure intelligences, illumined from end to end by the Divine enlightenment. Each angel transmits to the next lower angel the knowledge which he himself receives from above, but he transmits it only as a limited and fragmentary knowledge adapted to the capacity of the intelligence below him. The angel proceeds thus like our doctors who, while perceiving directly the consequences contained in principles, yet expound them by means of divers distinctions to bring them home to their hearers.[38]

In this way the elements which St. Thomas took over from the philosophical tradition arrange themselves in a harmonious synthesis. He confirms the angels in their biblical functions of heralds and messengers; though he refuses to reduce them, like the oriental philosophers, to a small number of separate intelligences moving and directing the celestial spheres, he still assigns these functions to angels, and ultimately we find again in the thomistic hierarchy of pure intelligences the Neoplatonic hierarchy adapted by the Pseudo-Dionysius. Yet St. Thomas Aquinas brings these conceptions of such diverse origin into a close relationship to his system and marks them deeply with the impress of his mind. By arranging the angelic hierarchies according to the growing darkening of intellectual illumination, he gives an entirely new organic structure to this world of separate intelligences, and the same internal principle placed in his system at the beginning of the universal order, governs also their distribution. By that very fact, the world of angels occupies in creation a place which makes it impossible to neglect its consideration without rendering the intelligibility of the universe impossible. The angels introduce, between the pure act of God and rational knowledge, resting upon sense-data, characteristic of man, an infinite number of intermediate degrees along which a less and less simple mode of knowing descends, parallel to a being becoming less and less pure act. No doubt, even an innumerable multitude of angels, being but finite creatures, is incapable of bridging the gulf which separates God from creation. But, though there will always be discontinuity in the possession of being, there is henceforth continuity of order: *Ordo rerum talis esse invenitur ut ab uno extremo ad alterum non pervenitur nisi per media*. Through the angels, as intelligences naturally full of intelligible essences, knowledge descends gradually from God, the source of all light, to man whom we see search for and gather the intelligible multiplied in sense-experience, until its ray is finally imprisoned in matter in the form of bare finality.

NOTES TO CHAPTER VIII.

1. On this point, cf. A. Schmid, *Die peripatetisch-scholastische Lehre von den Gestirngeistern*, in *Athenaeum*, Philos. Ztft., herausg. von J. von Froschammer, I., München, 1862, p. 549–589; J. Durantel, *La notion de la création dans saint Thomas*, Ann. de phil. chrét., April, 1912, p. 1–32; W. Schlössinger, *Die Stellung der Engel in der Schöpfung*, Jahrb. f. Phil. u. spek. Theol., XXV., p. 451–485, and XXVII., p. 81–117; of the same author, *Das Verhältnis der Engelwelt zur sichtbaren Schöpfung*, ibid., XXVII., p. 158–208. These two last studies consider the problem as such; they may, however, be consulted with advantage, because their conclusions rest mostly upon the authentic teaching of St. Thomas. By far the richest source of information on this matter is the second part of the work of Cl. Baeumker, *Witelo*, p. 523–606: *Die Intelligenzen*, and *Die Intelligenzenlehre der Schrift: De Intelligentiis*.

2. Cf. A. Schmid, *op. cit.*, p. 549ff; Cl. Baeumker, *op. cit.*, p. 523ff.

3. On these different points, cf. Zeller, IIIb, *ad loc*. The most important references are collected and brought up to date by Baeumker, *op. cit.*, p. 531–532.

4. For the dependence of Dionysius on the Neo-Platonists, see H. Koch, *Pseudo-Dionysius Areopagita in seinen Beziehungen zum Neuplatonismus und Mysterienwesen, eine litterarhistorische Untersuchung*, Mainz, 1900; H. P. Müller, *Dionysios, Proklos, Plotinos, Beiträge*, XX., 3–4, Münster, 1918. For the eventual influence of Dionysius, cf. J. Stiglmayr, *Das Aufkommen der pseudo-dionysischen Schriften und ihr Eindringen in die christliche Literatur bis zum Lateran konzil*, Feldkirch, 1895.

5. Cf. J. Turmel, *Histoire de l'angélologie des temps apostoliques à la fin du Ve siècle*, Rev. d'hist. et de litt. relig., III., 1898, and IV., 1899; esp. III., p. 407–434.

6. *De coel. hier.*, c. I. and VII.–X.

7. An extensive collection of references and texts dealing with this point will be found in Baeumker, *op. cit.*, p. 537–544 and notes.

8. *Ps.*, 103, 4.

9. *Sum. theol.*, I. 50, 1, ad *Resp*.

10. *Cont. Gent.*, II. 91, ad *Natura superior*.

11. *De spiritualibus creaturis*, qu. I. art. 5, ad *Resp*.

12. *De spirit. creat.*, qu. I. art. 1, 3°. Cf. this argument in St. Bonaventure, *Sent.*, dis. III., p. 1, a. 1, qu. 1, ad *Utrum angelus*.

13. *De spirit. creat.*, I, 1, 16; St. Bonaventure, *ibid.*, ad *Item hoc ipsum ostenditur.*

14. *De spirit. creat.*, I. 1, 17; *Sum. theol.*, I. 50, 2, 4; St. Bonaventure, *ibid.*, ad *Resp.*

15. *Sum. theol.*, I. 50, 2, ad *Resp.*; *De spirit. creat.*, qu. 1, art. 1, ad *Resp.*

16. *De spirit. creat.*, *ibid.*, ad 3^m.

17. *Ibid.*, ad 16.

18. *De spirit. creat.*, qu. I., art. 1, ad *Resp.*; *Sum. theol.*, I. 50, 2, ad 3^m; *Cont. Gent.*, II. 50, ad *Formae contrariorum*, 51 and 52; *per tot. Quodlib.*, IX., qu. IV., art. 1, ad *Resp.*

19. St. Bonaventure, *Sent.*, II., dis. 3, art. 1, qu. 1, ad *Item hoc videtur.*

20. On the agreement of St. Thomas with Avicenna on this point and his opposition to the majority of the doctors, cf. Baeumker, *op. cit.*, p. 543.

21. *Sum. theol.*, I. 50, 4, ad *Resp.*

22. *Cont. Gent.*, II. 93, ad *Id quod est*; *De spirit. creat.*, qu. un., art. 8, ad *Resp.*

23. *Sum. theol.*, I. 50, 3, ad *Resp.*; *Cont. Gent.*, I. 92, *per tot.*, *De Potentia*, qu. VI., art. 6, ad *Resp.* sub fin.

24. For the progressive synthesis which worked in the mind of St. Thomas here, see J. Durantel, *La notion de la création dans St. Thomas*, Ann. de phil. chrét., April, 1912, p. 19, note 2.

25. *De spirit. creat.*, qu. I., art. 8, ad 2^m.

26. *Sum. theol.*, I. 108, 3, ad *Resp.*

27. *Sum. theol.*, I. 54, 2 and 3, ad *Resp.*

28. *Cont. Gent.*, II. 96, ad *Sensibilia enim.*

29. *Sum. theol.*, I. 55, 2, ad *Resp.*

30. *De Verit.*, qu. VIII., art. 9, ad *Resp.*; *Sum. theol.*, I. 55, 2, ad *Resp.* and ad 1^m.

31. *De Verit.*, qu. VIII., art. 10, ad *Resp.*; *Sum. theol.*, I. 55, 3, ad *Resp.*

32. *De coel. hier.*, c. 7.

33. *Sum. theol.*, I. 108, 1, ad *Resp.*

34. *Sum. theol.*, I. 108, 6, ad *Resp.*

35. Cf. *Sent.*, IV. 48, 1, 4, 3, ad *Resp.*

36. *Cont. Gent.*, III. 80 ad *Sic ergo altiores intellectus*, and *Sum. theol.*, I. 108, 5, ad 4^m.

37. *Sum. theol.*, I. 108, 6, ad *Resp.*

38. *Sum. theol.*, I. 106, 1, ad *Resp.*, and 3, ad *Resp.*

CHAPTER IX. THE CORPOREAL WORLD AND THE EFFICACY OF SECONDARY CAUSES

IF we wish to understand the created Universe in its totality, we must evidently begin our research by the study of the pure intelligences; but we may well hesitate which path to take in order to pass to the inferior degrees of Being. Indeed, two different orders would here present themselves as possible, both corresponding to two directive principles of the universal order. The one would consist in following the hierarchy of created things considered in their order of decreasing perfection, and would pass consequently from the study of the angels to that of man. The other would mean leaving this point of view for that of the order of ends. This latter attitude is suggested by the biblical account of Genesis. Man whose position is immediately below the angels from the point of view of perfection, yet appears only at the close of Creation, the true end of which he is. It is for him that the incorruptible stars have been created, that God divides the waters by the firmament, lays bare the earth covered by the waters and fills it with animals and plants. Nothing could therefore be more proper than to follow up the study of purely spiritual beings by that of corporeal things and to finish up with that of man, the connecting link between the world of intelligences and the corporeal world.[1]

The order of natural philosophy is certainly the sphere in which St. Thomas has made the smallest innovations, at least if we confine our attention to Physics and Physiology in the strict sense of these terms. Here the Christian thinker adds nothing to the teaching of Aristotle, or so little that it would hardly be worth mentioning. He displays none of the curiosity of a man like Robert Grosseteste for the fruitful speculations of mathematical physics; no doubt the very spirit of his Aristotelianism would have stood in the way of it.

But it would not have prevented him from continuing the studies of his master, Albert the Great, in the region of zoology and of natural science; and yet here again he seems to draw back from them. The questions of the "Summa theologica" which are devoted to the commentary on the Six Days of Creation, offered him again and again an opportunity of exercising his natural ingenuity in one or other of these directions; but St. Thomas does not care to do so and rather reserves it for other matters. The essential point to his mind is to preserve intact the very letter of Scripture, with all due allowance for the fact that it is not a treatise on cosmography for the learned, but an expression of the truth for the use of simple people such as were those addressed by Moses, with, consequently, the occasional possibility of interpreting the text in different ways.[2]

In whatever manner or whichever different manners he considers it possible to reconcile the visible Universe with the account of Genesis, this Universe, as conceived by St. Thomas, is essentially that of Aristotle: viz. a series of seven concentric planetary spheres, contained within an eighth sphere, that of the fixed stars, and containing in their turn the Earth as their centre.[3] The matter of each of these celestial spheres is strictly incorruptible, because, in order to corrupt, it must be capable of change; but in order to change, it must be capable of becoming other than it is, which is precisely what is called "being in potency." But the matter of the celestial spheres, being, so to speak, saturated by its form, is no longer in potency in regard to any manner of being; it is all that it could be and is no longer capable of change except in the matter of position. To each sphere a moving Intelligence is assigned which maintains and directs its circular motion, but is not, properly speaking, either its form or its soul. Below the lowest sphere, that of the Moon, are arranged the spheres of the four elements: fire, air, water, and earth. By rights, each of these ought to be gathered up entirely in its natural site, where it is in a state of rest and equilibrium; in point of fact, the elements are more or less mixed and their tendency is to reach their natural site, a feature which causes the various movements to which we find them subject, as the fire always tending upwards, the earth tending downwards, and air and water keeping in an intermediate position, which is proper to them. All this cosmology lies within a framework well-known from other sources. Where St. Thomas is really in his element and free to perform the work peculiar to him, is in the metaphysical elaboration of the principles of natural philosophy. In this the Christian philosopher reveals his originality, because the relation which unites being and secondary causes with God is here in question and he feels himself directly interested in its precise determination.

We came to the conclusion in examining the very notion of "creation," that God alone is creator, since creation is the action proper to Him[4] and nothing exists which has not been created by Him. Perhaps it may not be amiss to recall this general conclusion at the moment of beginning the examination of the corporeal world, because it is an old and widespread error to think that its nature is bad in itself, that it is consequently the work of another principle, itself bad and other than God.[5] This is a doubly pernicious error, for, in the first place all existing things possess at least one common constitutive element, namely, their very being; consequently there must exist a single principle whence they derive this element and which causes them to be, of whatever kind they may otherwise be, whether invisible and spiritual, or visible and corporeal. As God is the cause of Being, His causality extends no less necessarily to bodies than to spirits. But a second argument, drawn from the end of things, may help to carry conviction: God Himself has no other end than Himself; things, on the contrary, have an end other than themselves, namely, God. This is an absolute truth which applies to every order of reality, to bodies no less than to spirits; but this fact must be linked with another, namely, that a being which exists for the sake of God, nevertheless, exists also for itself and for its own good. Thus in this sort of immense organism which is the Universe, every part exists, in the first place, for its own proper act and its own end, like the eye for the sake of seeing; but in addition, each of the inferior parts exists for the sake of the superior parts, as the creatures inferior to man for the sake of man; moreover, all these creatures, taken singly, exist only for the sake of the collective perfection of the Universe, and, finally, this collective perfection of creatures, taken in its totality, is there only as an imitation and representation of the glory of God Himself.[6] This radical metaphysical optimism leaves nothing out which in any manner whatever deserves to have the name of being, the corporeal world no more than the rest: matter exists for the sake of form, inferior forms for the sake of higher forms, the higher forms with the view to God. Therefore, everything that is, is good[7] and, consequently, also everything has God for its cause, whatever claims the objection may advance.

In elaborating this conclusion, we notice a first consequence which derives from it: God is the first and immediate cause of bodies, i.e. not of their form by itself, nor of their matter by itself, but of the indissoluble union of matter and form which constitutes them. What is meant by this, may be described as follows:

Experience permits us to apprehend immediately the existence of bodies which are the subjects of continual changes and movements. This is the concrete datum which metaphysical analysis aims to resolve into its constitutive elements. We should say then, in the first place, of any body that it possesses a constitutive principle in virtue of which it is what it is, and does what it does, without which we should have no means of apprehending it in itself as a being and should not even be able to give it a name. This positive principle of the body is also that which must be considered as its own perfection, i.e. as that part of being which defines it. We may then say that in exact proportion as it possesses perfection and being, it is "in act," and we shall give the term "form" to that principle which gives it its actuality. But we have, in addition, remarked that the bodies given us by experience, are subject to continual changes and movements. Now it is evident that, if the form explains what a body is, this form being the whole positive element of its being, it will not of itself explain that the body can cease to be what it is, in order to become something else. Side by side with the principle in virtue of which a body is what it is, we must postulate another, in virtue of which it becomes what it becomes. The term "potency" describes this margin of indetermination which constitutes its nature, and the term "matter" the principle which confers upon the body this possibility. What, now, is the movement itself which has its seat in that body? Simply the passage from potency to act under the impulse of an act which is already realised, or—what comes to the same thing—the introduction of a form into the matter apt to receive it. All these are terms and formulas which must not cause us to forget the concrete reality which they express, namely, an imperfect act which completes itself, or, still more simply, a being in process of realising itself. If this is so, then the body in question can be reduced neither to its matter nor to its form. For a form, pure and capable of subsisting by itself, like an Intelligence, cannot be applied to a body; and pure matter, being nothing but the possibility of becoming something, would really be nothing and could not, consequently, subsist. The proper expression to be used to describe the production by God of bodies and of their substantial principles, would be to say that God has "created" the bodies, but has "concreated" their form and their matter, i.e. the one in the other, indivisibly.[8]

Concerning the beings thus constituted, it is important to realise that God governs them by His providence, that He is intimately present in their substance and operations, and that yet the closeness of His concurrence leaves their own efficacy wholly intact. That, in the first place, the world is governed, is evident to the least sophisticated minds as soon as they direct their attention to the universal order of things. But the very idea of God to which we have been led by the proofs of His existence, forces this fact upon us, because God is postulated by reason as the first principle of the universe, and since whatever is the principle of a thing is also its end, God cannot but be the end of all things, hence relates them to Himself, directs them to Himself, which is precisely what "governing" means. The ultimate end, therefore, in view of which the creator administers the Universe, appears for that very reason as transcending things and external to them: here again, what is true of the principle is equally true of the end.[9]

The aspect, richest in metaphysical consequences, which this governance of things by God presents to our mind, is that of the conservation of things. By a series of arguments which lead to the very heart of his metaphysics of bodies, St. Thomas develops, first of all, regardless of consequences the postulates implied in this divine conservation. Then having, so to speak, left things with nothing belonging to them in their own right, he shows that this divine concurrence which seems to deprive them of their own efficacy and being, is really what, on the contrary, confers these upon things.

Every effect depends upon its cause and depends upon it in strict proportion to the extent in which the cause has really produced the effect. Let us, for instance, take the case of a workman fashioning an object, or of an architect building a house: the object or the house owe to their authors the external form and the configuration of the parts which characterise them; but that is all; for the material of which the thing is made exists already in nature, so that the maker did not have to make it but confined himself to utilising it. Now, the precise kind of causal relation is very well formulated by the relation of dependence which links together the two terms: the object, once made, subsists independently of the workman, because since it does not owe to him its being, it can naturally do without him in order to preserve it. Exactly the same observation applies to the order of natural beings; for each produces other beings by virtue of a form which it has itself only received but of which it is not the cause, with the result that each can indeed produce the form but not the being by which its effects subsist. Consequently we find that a child continues to live after the death of its father, in exactly the same manner as a house continues to stand after the architect has gone: in both cases we are dealing with causes which bring it about that a thing *becomes* what it is, but not that it exists.[10] Now, the situation is entirely different as regards the relation of things to God: in the first place, because God is not only the cause of the form taken on by things, but of the very being in virtue of which they exist, so that ceasing for a single instant to depend on their cause, they would cease to be altogether. The second reason is that there would be in a sense a contradiction in God making creatures which could do without Him.[11] For a "creature" is essentially something which has its being from someone else, in distinction to God who has His being only from Himself and subsists independently. For a creature to be able to subsist for a single instant without divine concurrence, it would have to exist in and by itself for that instant, i.e. it would have to be God.[12] Thus, the first effect of providence exercised by God upon things is the immediate and permanent influence by which He assures their conservation. This influence is, in some way, simply the continuation of the creative action, and any interruption of this continued creation by which God maintains all things in being, would instantly reduce them to nothingness.[13]

Proceeding further and following the divine influence into the very heart of things, we shall find that it extends beyond their existence, also to their causality. As, in fact, nothing is except by virtue of the divine Being, so nothing can do anything except again by virtue of divine efficacy. If, therefore, any being causes the existence of another being, it does so only because God confers upon it the power to do so—a truth, by the way, directly evident, if we bear in mind that being is the effect proper to God, since creation is His peculiar action and to produce being is, in the strict sense, to create.[14]

But we must go further still and assert that what is true of the productive efficacy of beings is equally true of their operations: God is for all beings that operate, the cause and reason of their operating. Why this further consequence? The answer is that to act means always, more or less, to produce, because whatever produces nothing, does nothing. Now, it was just stated that every genuine production of being, however minute, belongs properly to God alone: every operation therefore presupposes God as cause. In addition, a being acts only by virtue of the faculties it possesses and by applying the natural forces it can make use of, to their effects. But neither these faculties nor these forces originate in the first place from the thing but from God, who is their author as universal cause; so that, when all is said and done, God is the principal cause of all actions performed by His creatures[15] which are nothing but instruments in His hands.

So it is then finally at the very heart of things that God is everywhere present and acting by His efficacy; He supports them, animates them from within, guides them in their operations, applies them to their acts, so that they neither are nor do anything except by Him, just as they would neither exist nor act without Him. This is the teaching imparted by Scripture: "*Coelum et terram ego impleo*";[16] and again, "*Si ascendero in coelum, tu illic es; si descendero ad infernum, ades.*" The necessary conclusion to which the idea of God as the universal cause of all being leads us, is the same; the entire world, considered from this point of view, is nothing but a single instrument in the hands of its creator.

But it is just at this point, when St. Thomas has submerged created things in the divine presence and dissipated their activities in the divine efficacy, that he suddenly turns upon his irreconcilable enemies, those who deprived natural things of their proper operations. He does so with a smashing blow of which it is impossible to form an adequate idea, unless one observes its sudden delivery in the course of the arguments of the "Summa contra gentiles."[17] Nowhere is this constant feature of the thomistic method more impressively displayed, namely, *never to weaken any truth whatever under the pretext thereby the better to establish another truth*. For, though not a single word should be withdrawn from what has so far been asserted, another proposition has now to be established: thomistic philosophy, in which the creature is nothing and does nothing without God, yet sets itself in opposition to every doctrine which does not leave to secondary causes the full measure of being and efficacy which belongs to them by right. Numberless are the varieties and ramifications of the error which misconceives the action proper to secondary causes; it is not a question here of adopting or rejecting the solution of any particular difficulty, but rather of deciding for or against an entire philosophy. St. Thomas unmasks behind everyone of the doctrines he combats, the latent presence of platonism; if he rejects these doctrines, the reason is that in his eyes it is the business of philosophy to interpret the real world of Aristotle, not the world of appearances described by Plato. And, again, if he holds firmly to the real world of Aristotle, the reason is an assertion of sheer common sense beyond and behind which it is impossible to go. In the sensible world causes and effects follow with perfect regularity: a hot body always warms another in its vicinity, it never chills it; a human being never engenders anything but a human being; it is, therefore evident that the nature of the effect produced is inseparately bound up with the nature of the producing cause. Now it is this constancy in the relation of natural effects to secondary causes which makes it impossible to assume that the power of God simply takes their place; for if the action of God were not diversified in accordance with the different beings in which it operates, neither would the effects be diversified in the same manner as the things themselves, and the result would be that anything whatever would produce anything whatever.[18] The existence of laws of nature consequently renders it impossible to suppose that God has created beings deprived of causality.

What is perhaps even more remarkable is that those who deny to secondary causes all efficacy in order to reserve to God the privilege of causality, do no less wrong to God than to the things themselves. The work manifests by its excellence the glory of the maker, and what a poor universe would that world be which were completely deprived of efficacy! In the first place, it would be an absurd world. If you give someone the principal, you do not deny him the accessory. What would be the sense of creating heavy bodies but incapable of moving downwards? If God has conferred upon things resemblance to Himself by giving them being, He must also have given them the activity which flows from this being and must, consequently, have granted to them the actions proper to them. Moreover, a universe of inert things would imply a first cause less perfect than a universe of active things, capable of communicating to each other their perfections by acting upon each other just as God has communicated to them something of His own perfection by creating them, linked and ordered by the mutual actions which they exercise on each other. The sentiment which impels certain philosophers to withdraw all from nature in order to glorify God, is inspired by an intention, good enough in itself but nevertheless blind. In actual fact, *"detrahere actiones proprias rebus est divinae bonitati derogare,"* to deprive things of their proper actions is to detract from divine goodness.

The problem ultimately reduces itself to this, how to maintain without concession the two apparently contradictory truths: viz. that God does all that the creatures do, and yet the creatures do of themselves whatever they do. The point is consequently, how the same single effect can derive simultaneously from two different causes, God and the natural agent that produces it. This is at first sight an incomprehensible position from which the majority of philosophers seems to have recoiled, for it is difficult to see how one and the same action can proceed from two causes: if it is produced by a natural body, the cause cannot be God. Furthermore, if it proceeds from God, it is still less intelligible that it should at the same time be produced by a natural body, for the divine causality affects the very centre of the being and leaves nothing to be produced beyond its effects. The dilemma seems consequently inevitable, unless indeed we are content to place it into the very heart of things and leave it at that.[19]

In reality this contradiction which metaphysical thought encounters here, is not so entirely irreducible as it appears, and is perhaps at bottom merely superficial. It would indeed be contradictory to admit that God and natural things were both the causes of natural effects at the same time and under the same aspect. They are, in fact, causes at the same time, but not under the same aspect, as a comparison may help us to realise.

When a workman produces a thing, he must necessarily make use of utensils and instruments of all sorts. The choice of the instruments is guided by their shape, and he himself does no more than to move them in order to apply them and to cause them to produce their effects. When an axe splits a piece of wood, it is the axe that is the cause of the effect produced, and yet we can say with as much reason that the cause is also the carpenter who wields the axe. At the same time it is impossible to divide the effect produced into two parts, one of which is due to the axe and the other to the carpenter. It is the axe that produces the entire effect, and at the same time the entire effect is also produced by the carpenter. The real difference lies in this, that they do not produce the effect in the same manner, for the axe splits the wood only by virtue of the efficacy which is conferred upon it by the carpenter, so that, indeed, the carpenter is the primary and principal cause, whereas the axe is the secondary and instrumental cause of the effect produced. We must conceive an analogous relation between God as the first cause, and the natural bodies which we observe operating around us. But the relation is only analogous, because the divine influence penetrates the secondary cause far more completely than the workman can ever penetrate his utensil. God confers upon all things their being, their form, their movement and their efficacy; and yet this efficacy belongs all the same to them, once they have received it, and it is they that perform their operations. Even the lowliest being acts and produces its effect, although it does so by virtue of all the superior causes to whose action it is subjected and whose efficacy is transmitted to it in descending gradations. At the beginning of this whole series stands

God, entire and immediate cause of all the effects produced by things and of the whole activity developed
by them; at the lower end of the series is the natural
body, immediate cause of the operation proper to it
and performed by it, although it performs it simply by
virtue of the efficacy conferred upon it by God.

Considering from this point of view the operations
and movements that take place continually in the
universe, we observe that neither element in this double
causality can be considered as superfluous. In the first
place, it is evident that the divine operation is necessary
for the production of natural effects, since the secondary
causes owe all their own efficacy to the first cause which
is God. But it is not superfluous that God, who indeed
can produce by Himself all the natural effects, should yet
produce them by the intermediary of certain other
causes. These intermediaries which He has willed,
are not necessary to Him, because He could not do
without them; but it is for their own sake that He has
willed them, and the existence of secondary causes is
not evidence of a lack of power, but of the immensity of
his goodness.[20] The universe then, as conceived by
St. Thomas, is not a mass of inert bodies passively set in
motion by a force transmitted through them, but
an organism of active beings each one of which enjoys
the efficacy which God has delegated to it at the same
time as its being. At the first beginning of such a world,
we must therefore postulate not so much a power
that exercises its force, as an infinite goodness that
communicates itself to the world: Love is the deepest
spring of all causality.

This may perhaps be considered as the central point
of view whence the general order of thomistic metaphysical thought is most clearly apparent, the starting-
point of the various criticisms which he directs against
all other, then existing, systems. Looked at from
outside, this doctrine appears to certain of his adversaries like a vindication of the rights of the creature
against those of God, an accusation all the more insidious
as St. Thomas draws his inspiration ostensibly from
Aristotle and seems to this extent to yield to the

influence of pagan naturalism. Those who went furthest in this direction, have never forgiven him the insertion of "natures" and "efficient causes" between natural effects and God.[21] Seen from the inside, St. Thomas' metaphysics appear on the contrary as the exaltation of a God whose principal attribute is not power, but goodness. Certainly productive fertility and efficacy are divine things. Unless God communicated them outside Himself to the multiplicity of beings which He has created, not one of them would be capable of imparting to itself the smallest particle of it, and all efficacy is ultimately the participation in His power. Indeed, the divine power is in itself something so perfect and pre-eminent, that one can understand the hesitation felt by a religious mind, in attributing to himself even the least participation in it. But we have seen,[22] in examining the nature of the creative act, that its first source is the infinite expansiveness of the Good. Hence, the conception of a universe, willed by a Good communicating itself to it, must be different from that of a universe, willed by a Power which reserves unto itself all efficacy: all that this Power would have the right to retain for itself, Goodness would wish to give, and the greater the gift, the higher the mark of the love, capable of giving it satisfaction. The profound metaphysical intuition which joins together these two main pillars of the system, was to have seen that a universe such as that of Aristotle, requires as cause a God such as that of Dionysius the Areopagite. Our supreme glory is to be helpers of God by means of the causality which we exercise: "*Dei sumus adjutores*"[23]; or, as again Dionysius says: the most divine thing is to co-operate with God: "*omnium divinius est Dei cooperatorem fieri.*"[24] Hence the efficacy of secondary causes goes back, as to its source, to this original effusion which renders this co-operation possible, and no other universe would be equally worthy of such infinite Goodness.

A first consequence of this doctrine is to give its true meaning to what sometimes is called the "naturalism" or "physicism" of St. Thomas. If no metaphysic has been more constantly concerned to safeguard the rights of the creature, the reason is that this appeared as the only means of safeguarding the rights of God. So far from trespassing upon the privileges of the Creator, every perfection attributed to the secondary causes could not but increase his glory, since He is their first cause, and they an ever fresh occasion to glorify Him. Because there is causality in nature, we can go back, closer and closer, to the first cause, God. In a universe without secondary causes, the most evident proofs of the existence of God would, therefore, be impossible, and His highest metaphysical attributes would consequently be hidden from us. Conversely, all this throbbing of beings, of natures, of causes and operations which the corporeal world presents to us, can no longer be considered as existing and acting for its own sake. If God has imparted efficacy to them as the highest mark of their divine origin, what urges them and moves them to act is, therefore, a constant effort towards an assimilation to God. Every natural form carries at bottom within itself the desire to imitate, by its own operation, the creative fecundity and pure actuality of God, a desire unconscious indeed in the corporeal world which is the subject of our present provisional study, but no less an effort towards God which unfolds itself later in the sphere of human morality with its intelligence and its will. The foundation of the existence of physical knowledge of the corporeal world is, in the first place, the mystical knowledge of the divine life, for the natural laws of the communication of movements are but the imitation of the effusion of original creation, and the efficacy of secondary causes is but the analogue of its fecundity.

As soon as the significance of this principle is grasped, every trace of an antinomy between the perfection of God and that of the created being vanishes. On the contrary, a universe willed by God only by reason of its resemblance to the divine, can never be either too beautiful or too efficient, it can never realise itself too completely, can never tend too actively to its own perfection, in order to reproduce, as it ought, the image of its divine model. "*Unumquodque tendens in suam perfectionem, tendit in divinam similitudinem*":[25]   a principle of inexhaustible fertility in thomistic philosophy, since it governs at the same time human moral life and the metaphysics of nature: be perfect even as your heavenly Father is perfect.

From this point of view, the deep reason of the criticisms directed by St. Thomas against the earlier metaphysics is easily grasped. All teaching, other than that of Aristotle whence he draws his inspiration, falls in fact from his point of view into two classes, according to two ways of refusing to attribute to secondary causes the proper activity to which they can lay claim. On the one side, there is Platonism with all the innumerable systems derived from it: Avicenna, Ibn Gebirol, etc. According to this doctrine, every new element that appears in the corporeal world comes from outside it: it is a case of radical "extraneanism," whether the extraneous cause of forms or of the operations of the sensible world resides in the efficacy of Ideas, as with Plato, or in that of a separate Intelligence, as in the case of Avicenna, or in that of the divine Will, as in the case of Gebirol. In any case, the problem is subjected to the same solution, whether it is the case of explaining the physical operations of bodies, the cognitive operations of reason or the moral operations of the will; in all three cases, the entire efficacy is attributed to an extraneous agent which imparts *ab extra* the sensible form to the body, the intelligible form to the intellect or the virtue to the will. On the other hand, we have what might be called "Anaxagorism" with all the varieties that serve as its mark, an "intrinsicism" quite as radical as the "extraneanism" just discussed, which, nevertheless leads to the same result. From this second point of view, all the effects in question, instead of coming from outside, are on the contrary, already pre-formed and virtually realised within: "seminal reasons" contained in matter, developing under the stimulus of an external agent; innate ideas, contained in the soul, unfolding of themselves under the faint impact of sensation; natural virtues, outlined in the will which spontaneously perfect themselves in proportion as life offers the opportunities.

In the first case, the secondary cause operated nothing because it received everything from outside; in the second case, it hardly operates more, since the effects which it seems to produce, existed already virtually realised either within itself or in others, and its action amounts to nothing more than to remove the obstacles which prevented its development.[26] Both schools of thought were errors so closely akin that certain philosophers did not hesitate to combine them, as St. Augustine and those who claimed the authority of his teaching; for him knowledge comes to the soul from outside by way of divine illumination, while sensible forms develop within matter thanks to the "seminal reasons" contained within it. In point of fact, both schools derogate, though in different manners, from the order of the universe whose very texture is made up of order and of the nexus of causes. All causes are indebted to the infinite goodness of the first cause both for their being and for their being causes, as we shall see in the case, peculiarly important, of the human compound.

NOTES TO CHAPTER IX.

1. *Sum. theol.*, I. 65, 1 *proem.*
2. *Sum. theol.*, I. 66, 1, ad 2[m]: "Aërem autem, et ignem non nominat, quia non est ita manifestum rudibus, quibus Moyses loquebatur, hujusmodi esse corpora, sicut manifestum est de terra et aqua." Cf., in the same sense: "quia Moyses loquebatur rudi populo, qui nihil, nisi corporalia, poterat capere..." *ibid.*, 67, 4, ad *Resp.* "Moyses rudi populo loquebatur, quorum imbecillitati condescendens, illa solum eis proposuit quae manifeste sensui apparent..." *ibid.*, 63, 3, 2, ad *Resp.* "Moyses autem rudi populo condescendens...," *ibid.*, 70; 1; ad 3[m]; and also 70, 2, ad *Resp.* The following are the principles of thomistic exegesis: "Primo, quidem, ut veritas Scripturae inconcusse teneatur. Secundo, cum Scriptura divina multipliciter exponi possit, quod nulli expositioni aliquis ita praecise inhaereat, ut si certa ratione constiterit hoc esse falsum, quod aliquis sensum Scripturae esse credebat, id nihilominus asserere praesumat, ne Scriptura ex hoc ab infidelibus derideatur, et ne eis via credendi praecludatur." *Sum. theol.*, I, 68, 1, ad *Resp.* St. Thomas is here in complete agreement with St. Augustine, from whom he adopted the twofold principle: (1) to maintain firmly the literal truth of Scripture; (2) never to hold exclusively one of several possible interpretations

so as to uphold it when the contrary has scientifically been demonstrated.

3. Above the Heaven of the fixed stars begins the invisible world, the structure of which is naturally more on Aristotelian lines: viz. the Heaven of the waters or the Crystalline Heaven and the Heaven of light or Empyrean. *Sum. theol.*, I. 68, 4, ad *Resp.*

4. See Chapter VII., p. 135.

5. The constant preoccupation of St. Thomas to refute the manichean doctrine is due to the development of the Albigensian heresy against which the Dominican Order fought from its very beginnings.

6. *Sum. theol.*, I. 65, 2, ad *Resp.*

7. See Chapter VII., p. 151ff.

8. *Sum. theol.*, I. 66, 1, ad *Resp.* Pure matter can, therefore, not exist by itself, since it is only a being in potency; it is, however, not merely potentially good, but really and absolutely good, because it is ordered in view of a form and constitutes for that reason a good. There is, therefore, an aspect under which the Good is wider than Being. Cf. *Cont. Gent.*, III. 20, ad *Inter partes.*

9. *Sum. theol.*, II. 103, 2, ad *Resp.*; *Cont. Gent.*, III. 64.

10. This corresponds to the technical distinction between a *"causa fiendi"* and a *"causa essendi"*: man engenders a man, independently of himself: he is, therefore, his *"causa fiendi"*; the sun engenders light and the light ceases as soon as the sun disappears: the sun is its *"causa essendi."*

11. *Cont. Gent.*, II. 25, ad *Similiter Deus facere non potest.*

12. *Sum. theol.*, I. 104, 1, ad *Resp.*

13. "Nec aliter res (Deus) in esse conservat, nisi inquantum eis continue influit esse; sicut ergo antequam res essent, potuit eis non communicare esse, et sic eas non facere; ita postquam jam factae sunt, potest eis non influere esse, et sic desinerent esse, quod est eas in nihilum redigere." *Sum theol.*, I, 104, 3, ad *Resp.*

14. *Cont. Gent.*, III. 66.

15. "Causa autem actionis magis est id cujus virtute agitur, quam etiam illud quod agit, sicut principale agens magis agit quam instrumentum. Deus igitur principalius est causa cujuslibet actionis quam etiam secundae causae agentes." *Cont. Gent.*, III. 67.

16. Jerem., 23, 24. For the following text, Ps. 138, 8, see *Cont. Gent.*, III, 68; *Sum. theol*, I, 8, 1, ad *Resp.*

17. The following is the order of the chapters in which the balance of the argument is re-established: Cap. 65: "Quod Deus conservat res in esse"; cap. 66: "Quod nihil dat esse nisi inquantum agit in virtute divina"; cap. 67: "Quod Deus est causa operandi omnibus operantibus"; Cap. 68: "Quod Deus est ubique et in omnibus rebus"; cap. 69: "De

opinione eorum qui rebus naturalibus proprias subtrahunt actiones."

18. "Si enim nulla inferior causa, et maxime corporalis, aliquid operatur, sed Deus operatur in omnibus solus, Deus autem non variatur per hoc, quod operatur in rebus diversis, non sequetur diversus effectus ex diversitate rerum in quibus Deus operatur. Hoc autem ad sensum apparet falsum; non enim ex appositione calidi sequitur infrigidatio, sed calefactio tantum, neque ex semine hominis sequitur generatio nisi hominis; non ergo causalitas effectuum inferiorum est ita attribuenda divinae virtuti, quod subtrahatur causalitas inferiorum agentium." *Cont. Gent.*, III, 69.

19. *Cont. Gent.*, III. 70, ad *Quibusdam autem*.

20. "Patet etiam quod, si res naturalis producat proprium effectum, non est superfluum quod Deus illum producat. Quia res naturalis non producit ipsum, nisi in virtute divina. Neque est superfluum, si Deus per seipsum potest omnes effectus naturales producere, quod per quasdam alias causas producantur. Non enim hoc est ex insufficientia divinae virtutis, sed ex immensitate bonitatis ipsius per quam suam similitudinem rebus communicare voluit, non solum quantum ad hoc quod essent, sed etiam quantum ad hoc quod aliorum causae essent." *Cont. Gent.*, III, 70.

21. From this point of view the absolute antithesis of Thomism is the philosophy of Malebranche. There God only is cause and all efficacy is exclusively reserved to Him. For that reason the preface to "la Recherche de la vérité" begins with a protestation against the Aristotelian, and, therefore pagan, inspiration of thomistic Scolasticism.

22. See Chapter VII., par. 1: "The Nature of the Creative Act," p. 132.

23. St. Paul, *I Corinth.*, III. 9.

24. *De coelest. hierarch.*, c. 3. These texts are quoted in *Cont. Gent.*, III. 21.

25. *Cont. Gent.*, III. 21, ad *Praeterea, tunc maxime perfectum*.

26. "Utraque autem istarum opinionum est absque ratione. Prima enim opinio excludit causas propinquas, dum effectus omnes in inferioribus provenientes, solis causis attribuit; in quo derogatur ordini universi, qui ordine et connexione causarum contexitur; dum prima causa ex eminentia bonitatis suae rebus aliis confert non solum quod sint, sed etiam quod causae sint. Secunda opinio in idem quasi inconveniens redit: cum enim removens prohibens non sit nisi movens per accidens..., si inferiora agentia nihil aliud faciunt quam producere de occulto in manifestum, removendo impedimenta, quibus formae et habitus virtutum et scientiarum occultabantur, sequitur quod omnia inferiora agentia non agant nisi per accidens." *Quaest. Disp. de verit.*, qu. XI., art. 1, ad *Resp*.

CHAPTER X. THE UNION OF SOUL AND BODY

At the apex of the world of forms we find the separate Intelligences; at the lowest stage we have encountered sensible forms, entirely enclosed in matter, between the two is situated the soul, neither pure Intelligence, nor a simply material form. Our first task must be to define its condition.

It will not be surprising to find that the soul, as a subsisting form, is affected by the same imperfection that is characteristic of the angelic substance. By its very definition, the soul is entirely form and not susceptible to any admixture of matter.[1] Any matter alleged to exist in it would not be the soul itself but simply the first of the objects animated by the soul.[2] It is equally true that, like the angel, the soul is composed of potency and act; in it, as in all other creatures, the *quo est* differs from the *quod est*, existence from essence. The soul is accordingly a form quite different from God who is pure act; it possesses only such being as its nature permits, according to the general law that the quantity of being participated in by any creature, is measured by the capacity of the participating essence.[3] But here we find a new determination enabling us to distinguish between the soul and the separated intelligences which we know already to be infinitely distant from God: the human soul, being neither matter nor body, is in its turn, by reason of the nature of its own essence, capable of being united with a body. It will, no doubt, be objected that the body, united with the soul does not belong to the essence of the soul as such, and that consequently the human soul as such continues to be an intellectual form of the same species as the angel. But this objection merely shows the failure to realise clearly the new degree of imperfection which here appears in the hierarchy of created beings. To say that the human soul is naturally capable of union with a body does not mean that by a combination of circumstances unrelated to some fundamental feature of its own nature, the soul is merely accidentally united with the body; the capacity of union with the body is, on the contrary, essential to the soul and characteristic of its nature. We are therefore dealing no longer with a pure intelligence such as the angelic substance, but with a simple intellect, i.e. with a principle of intellection which requires a body to achieve its proper operation; and hence the human soul represents, in comparison with the angel, an inferior degree of intellectuality.[4] The truth of this conclusion will be fully apparent as soon as the mode is defined in which the soul is united with the body in constituting the composite human being.

What, accordingly, is this corporeal nature and of what kind are these composite beings? The body must not be taken as bad in itself; the Manicheans incurred the guilt not only of heresy in considering matter as bad and in attributing to it a creative principle distinct from God, but also of a philosophical error. For if matter were bad in itself, it would be nothing; and if it is something, then, in the very measure in which it is, it is not bad. Like everything else within the range of creation, matter is therefore good and created by God.[5]

Further: not only is matter good in itself, but it is also a good and a source of good for all forms capable of combining with it. It would mean abandoning entirely the thomistic perspective to conceive the material universe as the result of a lapse, and the union of soul and body as the consequence of some fall. The doctrine of St. Thomas is pervaded by a radical optimism, because it interprets the universe as created out of pure goodness, all parts of which, in the measure of their subsistence, are as many reflections of the infinite perfections of God. The views of Origen who taught that God had created the bodies only to imprison the sinful souls, are profoundly repugnant to the mind of St. Thomas. The body is not the prison of the soul, but a servant and instrument placed by God at its disposal; the union of the soul and the body is not a punishment of the soul, but a beneficent link by which the human soul will attain to its complete perfection. Nor is this a theory constructed on purpose to meet the particular case of the soul; this case is, on the contrary, governed by a metaphysical principle of universal range, viz. that the less perfect is ordered towards the more perfect as towards its end; it is therefore not against it, but for it. In man each organ exists by reason of its function, as the eye, to enable him to see; each inferior organ exists by reason of a superior organ and function, as the sense-organs for the sake of the intelligence or the lungs for the sake of the heart. Again all these organs exist in their turn for the sake of the perfection of the whole, as matter for the sake of the form or the body for the sake of the soul, for the parts are, as it were, the matter of the whole. Now, exactly the same situation obtains, if the disposition of individual beings is considered within this whole. Each creature exists for its own act and perfection; the less noble creatures exist with the view to the more noble; the individuals exist with the view to the perfection of the universe and the universe itself exists with the view to God. The *raison d'être* of a substance or of a given mode of existence lies therefore never in an evil, but in a good; it is therefore for us to discover what good the human body can afford to the rational soul that animates it.[6]

Since the sufficient reasons and final causes must be sought for in the good defining the essence and, consequently, in the form, the *raison d'être* of the body must be looked for in the soul itself. If the soul were an intelligence of the same degree of perfection as the angel, it would be pure form, subsisting and operating without the assistance of an external instrument: realising to the full its own definition and finally concentrating the total perfection of its essence in an unique individuality. It may be said that every angel defines in himself completely one of the degrees of possible participations in the perfection of God. The human soul, on the contrary, occupying a lower place in the scale of beings, belongs already to that order of forms which possess too little perfection to subsist separately. Whereas each angelic intelligence of a given degree subsists separately, a form corresponding to the human soul and realising fully its perfection neither does nor can so exist anywhere. Now, it is a constant principle that an unattainable unity is represented and imitated by a multiplicity. The individual human souls, whose constantly renewed succession assures the continuity of the species, make it possible for the degree of perfection corresponding to man to be continually represented in the universe. But, while the human representation of Divine perfection, required by the order of creation, is thus safeguarded, each soul, taken individually, is but the incomplete realisation of its ideal type. Inasmuch as it meets its own definition, it is therefore in act, and enjoys being that which it ought to be; but, inasmuch as it satisfies its own definition only imperfectly, it is in potency, i.e. it is not all that it might be; it is even in a state of deprivation, because it is conscious of the fact that it ought to be what it is not. A human soul, or any corporeal form, is therefore a certain incomplete perfection, but tending to complete itself, and feeling the need or entertaining the hope of doing so. Hence the form, moved by the privation of what it lacks, is the principle of operation in natural things; each being, to the extent to which it is, wills to be; it acts merely to maintain itself in existence and to establish itself more completely. Now, the intelligence of man is the weakest ray of light in the order of knowledge. The light illuminating him is so poor and feeble that no intelligible object is of itself apparent to it. Left to itself or placed in face of purely intelligible objects such as the angels easily apprehend, the human intelligence would remain blank or would discern nothing. Thus, this incomplete form is radically incapable of completing itself by its own strength; it is in potency in respect of all the perfection it lacks, but it has no means wherewith to make it actual; the operation needed to complete it, remains therefore beyond its reach. It would be condemned to sterility and inaction, unless it had an instrument, itself incomplete without the soul, but to be organised and animated by it from within, and so enabling the soul to enter into relation with an intelligible object which it can assimilate. In order to become conscious of what it lacks and, thus stimulated by the sense of its deprivation, to go in search of the intelligible hidden in the sensible, the human intelligence must be a soul and must avail itself of the advantages offered by its union with the body. Let us consider how this union can take place.

In the first place any solution of this problem must satisfy the following condition. The act proper to an intelligent soul is evidently intellectual knowledge: the problem is, therefore, to discover a mode of union between soul and body which should allow us to attribute intellectual knowledge, not merely to the soul, but to man as a whole. The legitimacy of this requirement cannot be doubted. Every human being observes by direct experience that it is he himself that knows, not merely a part of himself. We have consequently only two hypotheses from which to choose: Either man is nothing but his intellective soul—in which case it is self-evident that intellectual knowledge pertains to the whole man: or the soul is only a part of man—in which case the problem is to establish a sufficiently close union between them, to make the action of the soul attributable to the man.[7] Now, it is impossible to maintain that the soul, in itself, is man himself. For everything can be defined as that which performs the operations proper to that thing; thus man will be defined as that which performs the operations proper to man. Now, man performs not only intellectual acts, but also sensitive acts, and these latter can evidently not take place without changes in a bodily organ. His vision, for instance, presupposes a modification of the pupil by the coloured species, and the same applies to his other senses.[8] If therefore feeling is a true—although not the proper—operation of man, it is clear that man is not only his soul, but a composite of soul and body.[9] What is the nature of their union?

Here we must eliminate an hypothesis which considers body and soul to be a mixed being the virtues of which participate at the same time in the spiritual and the corporeal substances composing it. In a truly mixed being, the component parts no longer exist except virtually, once the mixture is complete, for if they existed actually, it would not be mixture, but simply a conglomerate. In a mixture the several component elements no longer exist separately. Now, intellectual substances not being composed of matter and form, are simple and consequently incorruptible[10] and could not, therefore, combine with the body to form a mixture in which their proper natures would cease to exist.[11]

Opposed to the theory which unites the soul with the body in such a way as to destroy the soul's essence, is the theory which distinguishes between them so radically as to leave nothing but an external contact and, so to say, a mere relation of contiguity between them. Such is the attitude of Plato who considers the intellect to be united with the body as the motive force of the body. But this mode of being is not sufficient to allow us to attribute the action of the intellect to the whole being constituted by intellect and body. For the action of the motive force can be attributed to the thing set in motion only *quâ* instrument, as when we attribute the action of the carpenter to the saw. If, therefore, intellectual knowledge is attributable to Socrates himself, because it is the action of this intellect which sets his body in motion, it follows that it is attributed to Socrates only as to the instrument. Now, Socrates would be a corporeal instrument, since he is composed of a soul and of a body; and as intellectual knowledge requires no corporeal instrument, it may legitimately be concluded that, in assuming the soul to be the mover of the body, we have no right to attribute the intellectual activity of the soul to the whole man. Moreover, it must be noted that sometimes the action of a part may be attributed to the whole, as we attribute to the man the action of his eye; but we never attribute the action of one part to another part, except by accident. We do not, for instance, say that the hand sees because the eye sees. If therefore Socrates and his intellect are two parts of the same whole, united as the thing moved is to its mover, it follows that the action of his intellect is not, strictly speaking, attributable to the whole Socrates. If, on the other hand, Socrates himself is a whole, composed of the union of his intellect with the rest constituting Socrates, without his intellect being united with the body otherwise than as mover, it follows that Socrates possesses only an accidental unity and being: but this cannot legitimately be asserted of the human composite being.[12]

In reality it is not difficult to perceive that we are here really dealing with an error which has already been refuted. If Plato refuses to combine the soul with the body except as the mover of the body, he does so because he locates the essence of man not in the combination of soul and body, but in the soul alone, using the body as its instrument. Therefore we find him asserting that the soul is in the body as the pilot on his ship. To state that man is a composite of a soul and a body, would amount—from the Platonic point of view—to saying that Peter is a composite of his humanity and of his clothes, the truth being, on the contrary, that Peter is a man who makes use of his clothes, as man is a soul making use of his body. But such a doctrine is clearly unacceptable. For man and animals are sensible and natural beings, i.e. physical composites, composed of matter and form. This would evidently not be the case on the assumption that the body and its parts do not form part of the essence of man or of the animal, since the soul as such is nothing sensible or material. We must, moreover, remember that, as already stated, the soul, apart from operations in which the body does not share, such as pure intellection, performs many operations which are common to it and to the body, such as the sensations and passions. We are therefore driven to conclude that man is not simply a soul using his body as a mover uses whatever he moves, but a true whole, composed of body and soul.[13]

Consequently there remains as the only possible mode of union between soul and body that proposed by Aristotle, when he considers the intellective principle as the form of the body. Further, if such an hypothesis should be found true, the intellection of the soul could be legitimately attributed to the man as the substantial unity of body and soul; and it cannot be doubted that this is the case. For, whatever causes a being to pass from potency to act is the proper form and act of the being. Now, the living body is such in potency only as long as the soul does not inform it. The human body truly deserves to be called such only while the soul animates and imparts life to it. The eye or the arm of a dead body are no more truly an eye or an arm than if they were painted on a canvas or cut in stone.[14] But, if the soul indeed assigns to the body its place in the species of human bodies, it is the soul that actually confers upon it the being it possesses; consequently, as had been supposed, it is the soul that is truly the form of the body.[15] The same conclusion can be reached, if, instead of considering the human body as animated and quickened by the soul, we start from the definition of the human species as such. To discover the nature of any being, all that is needed is to discover its operation. Now, the operation proper to man, is none other than intellectual knowledge; thereby he surpasses in dignity all other animals and therefore we find Aristotle identifying this operation, characteristic of the human being, with supreme happiness.[16] Consequently, the principle of intellectual operations assigns to man his place in his species; but the species of a being is always determined by its proper form; the fact, therefore, remains that the intellective principle, i.e. the human soul, is the form proper to man.[17]

Certain philosophers, however, feel a difficulty in acquiescing in this conclusion which they accept only under protest. They find it hard to admit that an intellectual form, eminent in dignity, such as the human soul, should be so directly united with the matter of the human body. In order to mitigate the shock of such a disproportion, they insert a number of intermediate forms between the highest substantial form of the human being, that is, the intellectual principle itself, and the first matter, informed by it. Matter, considered as subjected to its first form, becomes thus the proximate subject of the second form and so on up to the last. On this assumption, the proximate subject of the rational soul would not be the corporeal matter purely and simply, but the body already informed by the sensitive soul.[18] This opinion is easily intelligible from the point of view of the Platonic philosophers. They start from the principle that a hierarchy of genera and species exists and that, within this hierarchy, the superior degrees are always intelligible in themselves and independently of the inferior degrees: thus man generally, and abstracting from any particular man, is intelligible in himself; animal is intelligible independently of man and so forth. These philosophers argue, moreover, as if a distinct and separate being corresponding to the abstract respresentations formed by our intellect, existed in reality. Observing that mathematics can be considered apart from sensibles, the Platonists assert the existence of mathematical beings subsisting outside sensible things; in the same way, they posit man as such, above and outside particular human beings, and thus proceed up the scale to the Being, to the One, to the Good, placed at the highest degree of things. But, by considering in this manner universals as separate forms, in which sensible beings participate, they were necessarily led to say that Socrates is an animal in so far as he participates in the idea of "animal," and man in so far as he participates in the idea "man"—which amounts to assuming in him a multiplicity of hierarchically arranged forms. On the contrary, if we consider things from the point of view of sensible reality—which is the method of Aristotle and of true philosophy—we see that this cannot be so. Among all the predicates attributable to things there is one that applies to them in a particularly intimate and direct fashion: viz. being itself; and since it is the form that confers on matter its actual being, it follows necessarily that the form from which matter draws its being, belongs to it directly and before all else. Now, what confers substantial being on matter is none other than the substantial form. The accidental forms confer upon the thing they inform, a merely relative and accidental being: they make it into a white or a coloured being, but they do not make it into a being. If we therefore suppose a form which does not confer substantial being upon matter, but is simply added to a matter previously existing, being such by virtue of a previous form, the second form cannot be considered as a truly substantial form. This means that it is impossible by definition to insert between the substantial form and its matter a number of intermediate substantial forms.[19]

If this is the case, we must assume within each individual only one substantial form. Man owes to this single and unique substantial form which is the human form, not only his being man, but also his being animal, living, body, substance, and a being. The explanation is as follows: Every agent impresses its own resemblance upon the matter it acts upon: this resemblance is what is called a form. It may be noted, on the other hand, that the higher in dignity an active and operative virtue is placed, the greater is the number of other virtues synthesised and comprised by it. We must add, lastly, that it does not contain them as distinct parts which in their combination impart to it its dignity, but that, on the contrary, it gathers the other virtues up into the unity of its own perfection. Now, when a being acts, the form impressed on the matter is the more perfect, the more perfect the being, and since the form resembles the being producing it, a more perfect form ought to achieve in a single operation all that forms, inferior to it in dignity, require many operations to achieve, and even more than that. If, for example, the form of the inanimate thing can impart to matter the power to be, and to be a thing, the form of the plant can confer this upon it equally well, and in addition imparts life to it. If now the rational soul supervenes, it suffices of itself to give to matter being, corporeal nature, life and, in addition, reason. Hence, in man as in all other animals, the appearance of a more perfect form always entails the passing away of the previous form; in such a manner, however, that the later form possesses all that the former possessed.[20] In essence, therefore, this thesis contains an observation made already several times, which moreover a simple examination of the universe is sufficient to render obvious: viz. that the forms of natural things are distinct from each other only as the relatively perfect is distinct from the more perfect. The species and the forms determining them, are differentiated by the quantities of being, more or less considerable, in which they participate. Species are like numbers: by adding or subtracting a unit, we change their species. And better still: we may say with Aristotle that the vegetative soul is contained in the sensitive soul, and the sensitive soul in the intellectual soul, as the triangle is contained in the tetragon and the tetragon in the pentagon. The pentagon in fact contains virtually the tetragon, for it possesses all that the tetragon has and more besides; but it does not contain it in the sense that we can separately discern what belongs to the tetragon and what to the pentagon. Lastly, in the same way, the intellectual soul contains virtually the sensitive soul, since it has all that the sensitive soul possesses and more besides; but it does not contain the sensitive soul in the sense that we can distinguish in it two different souls.[21] Thus a single and unique substantial form, which is the human intellect, suffices to constitute man in his proper being, by conferring upon him at the same time being, body, life, sense and intellection.[22]

The immediate consequences of this conclusion are of the highest importance, and must at once be indicated. We see, first of all, why the term "man" cannot, strictly speaking, mean either the human body or the human soul, but the combination of soul and body taken as a whole. If the soul is the form of the body, it forms with it a physical compound of the same nature as all the other compounds of matter and form. Now in such a case, the form alone does not constitute the species, but the form and the matter combined;[23] we are therefore justified in considering the human compound as a single being to whom intellectual knowledge may legitimately be attributed. Moreover, the union of soul and body is not only so close that the soul interpenetrates and envelops the body to the extent of being present in each of its parts[24]—which goes without saying, if it is really the form of the body; but we must further assert that this union is a substantial union, not merely an accidental union. By elaborating the meaning of this assertion we shall reach a definition of the precise position, occupied by the human soul in the hierarchy of created beings.

The term "accidental composition" is given to a combination uniting the accident with its supporting subject; "substantial composition" to the combination resulting from the union of matter with the form investing it.[25] The mode of union between the beings we have just considered differs widely according as it is a question of their accidental or substantial union. The accidental union leads to one essence being grafted on another without the nature proper to either of them requiring the union. The substantial union, on the contrary, is one which combines two beings, each in-complete by itself, into one single complete being. Matter and form, incomplete realities if taken each by itself, become one single complete substance as soon as the form actuates the matter invested by it. This amounts to saying that man contains two incomplete beings in himself: matter which is the body, and a form which is the soul. The matter, being pure potency, requires, in order to be really a body and not simply matter, the actuality imparted to it by its union with the form. But neither is the soul a complete being; and this must unhesitatingly be asserted, not only of the soul as vegetative or sensitive, but also of the rational soul itself. The place occupied by it in the hierarchy of intellectual forms, is marked by the fact that the soul has a tendency towards union with the body; and this tendency is so far constitutive of its essence that the soul, separated from the body as it is between the death of a man and his resurrection, is in a state which, without violating its nature, is yet not in complete conformity with it. The soul, being an integral part of the human composition, is constituted in its full natural perfection only by its union with the body.[26]

We encounter therefore in the human soul an intellectual form of a definitely inferior order. Its defective and lower degree of actuality is no longer sufficient for it; intimately bound up with matter as it is, since its full definition covers the matter it informs, it is placed in the lowest degree of intelligent creatures;[27] it is not a body, but without its body it is not itself;[28] in short, its place is on the confines and, as it were, on the border-line between spirits and bodies.[29] Statements such as these are surprising only if the human soul is considered merely in its own dignity or by reference to the matter which it animates; but the difficulty disappears as soon as it is given its proper place in the totality of creation. Human intellectual knowledge, constrained to search for the intelligible within the sensible, is but the last reflection of a light which further on is lost in matter. The human intellect is the lowest of all intellects, i.e. the one furthest removed from the Divine intellect: *Humanus intellectus est infimus in ordine intellectuum et maxime remotus a perfectione divini intellectus.*[30]

But while it is important to insist on the close dependence of the human soul upon matter, it is no less important not to let it be so deeply involved in it as to lose thereby its true nature. The soul is not an intelligence; it remains nevertheless a principle of intellection. The lowest in the order of intellects, it is yet the first in the order of material forms, and thus we see it, as the form of the human body, exercise functions in which this body alone could not take part. If a doubt is raised whether such beings, at the same time dependent on and independent of matter, can naturally find a place in the hierarchy of created beings, it can be dispelled by a rapid induction. For it is clear that the nobler a form is, the more will it dominate over its corporeal matter; the less deeply it is involved in it, the more it surpasses it by its virtue and operation. Thus the forms of the elements, lowliest of all and nearest to matter, perform no operation beyond the qualities of activity and passivity, such as rarefaction and condensation and others of the same order which seem reducible to simple dispositions of matter. Above these forms we find mixed bodies the operation of which is not reducible to those of elementary qualities: if, for instance, the magnet attracts iron, it does so not by reason of any warmth or cold in it but because it participates in the virtue of the celestial bodies which constitute it in its proper species. Further above these forms we find the souls of the plants, the operation of which, superior to that of the mineral forms, results in nourishment and growth. Finally we reach the sensitive souls possessed by animals; their operations extend to a certain degree of knowledge, though it is confined to matter and is obtained exclusively by material organs. Thus we come to the human souls which, exceeding in dignity all preceding forms, are destined to rise above matter by a virtue and operation in which the body has no share. And such precisely is that virtue which in them is called intellect.[31]

Here we verify once more the continuity which characterises the creative activity and the universe produced by it: *si anima humana, inquantum unitur corpori ut forma, habet esse elevatum supra corpus, non dependens ab eo, manifestum est quod ipsa est in confinio corporalium et separatarum substantiarum constituta.*[32] Just as the separate intelligences form the transition from God to man, so the human souls effect the transition from pure intelligences to bodies deprived of intelligence. We are consequently always moving from one extreme to another by passing through some middle term, and in accordance with this directive principle we shall examine in detail the operations of the human composite being.

NOTES TO CHAPTER X.

1. Cf., on the contrary, St. Bonaventure, *Sent.*, II., dis. 17, art. 1, qu. II., ad *concl.*
2. *Sum. theol.*, I. 75, 5, ad 4^m, *De spirit. creat.*, qu. un. art. 1, ad *Resp.*; *De anima*, qu. un. art. 6, ad *Resp.*
3. *Sum. theol.*, I. 75, 7, ad 3^m.
4. *De potentia*, III. 5; *Sum. theol.*, I. 65, 1; *Cont. Gent.*, II. 6 and 15.
5. *Sum. theol.*, I. 47, 2, ad *Resp.*; I. 65, 2, ad *Resp.* We approach here very closely to the difficult problem of individuation. Without going into it, we merely observe that many of the criticisms against St. Thomas on the ground that it is impossible on his system to save individuality, because individuality is brought about by matter, misunderstand a fundamental principle of thomistic philosophy: viz. that matter renders possible the multiplicity of certain forms, but that it exists only in view of these forms. Matter is indeed the passive principle of individuation, but the form is the active principle of individuality. It must further be noted that there is more in the individual than in the species, and even that God alone can account for individuality as such; for since the individual is unique by definition, it does not resemble any active form, and since the effect resembles its cause, there is no secondary cause capable of accounting for it. Whatever is universal in the individual may be begotten; but whatever is individual in it can only be created by God: *"cuius esse est infinitum quod est omnis entis* (even individual) *comprehendens similitudinem."* (*Cont. Gent.*, II. 21.)
6. *Sum. theol.*, I. 76, 1, ad *Resp.*
7. *Sum. theol.*, I. 75, 3, ad *Resp.*
8. *Sum. theol.*, I. 75, 4, ad *Resp.*
9. *Cont. Gent.*, II. 55, ad *Omnis enim.*
10. *Cont. Gent.*, II. 56, ad *Quae miscentur.*
11. *Sum. theol.*, I. 76, 1, ad *Resp.*; *Cont. Gent.*, II. 56, ad *Quae autem uniuntur.*
12. *Cont. Gent.*, II. 57, ad *Animal et homo*; *De anima*, qu. I., art. 1, ad *Resp.*
13. *De anima, ibid.*
14. *Cont. Gent.*, II. 57, ad *Illud quo aliquid.*
15. *Eth.*, X. 7, 1177, a. 12.
16. *Sum. theol.*, I. 76, 1, ad *Resp.*; *Cont. Gent., ibid.*; *De spirit. creat.*, qu. un. art. 2, ad *Resp.*

17. Cf. on this point De Wulf, *Le traité des formes de Gilles de Lessines*
(Les philosophes belges), Louvain, 1901. As far as a conclusion
may be based on the actual condition of the texts, this conception is attributable to Alexander of Hales (*Summa*, p. II., qu.
63, m. 4). It is disputable as far as St. Bonaventure is concerned
(cf. Ed. Lutz, *Die Psychologie Bonaventuras nach den Quellen
dargestellt.* Münster, 1909, p. 53–61.)

18. *De anima*, qu. I., art. 9, ad *Resp.*; *Cont. Gent.*, II. 58, ad *Quae
attribuuntur*; *Sum. theol.*, I. 76, 4, ad *Resp.*

19. *Sum. theol.*, I. 118, 2, ad 2^m.

20. *De spirit. creat.*, qu. un., art. 3, ad *Resp.*

21. *Qu. de Anima*, qu. un., art. 9, ad *Resp.*

22. *Sum. theol.*, I. 75, 4, ad *Resp.*

23. *Sum. theol.*, I. 76, 8, ad *Resp.*; *Cont. Gent.*, II. 72; *De spirit. creat.*,
qu. au art. 4, ad *Resp.*; *De anima*, qu. un. art. 10, ad *Resp.*

24. *Sum. theol.*, I. 3, 7, ad *Resp.*; I. 40, ad 1^m; I. 85, 5, ad 3^m; *Cont.
Gent.*, II. 54, ad *Tertia*, and *Quodlib.*, VII. 3, 7, ad 1^m.

25. *Sum. theol.*, I. 75, 7, ad 3^m; I. 90, 4, ad *Resp.*; Ia IIae, 4, 5, ad 2^m.

26. *Sum. theol.*, I. 76, 5, ad *Resp.*

27. *Sum. theol.*, I. 118, 3, ad *Resp.*; Ia IIae, 4, 6, ad *Resp.*

28. *Sum. theol.*, I. 77, 2, ad *Resp.*

29. *Sum. theol.*, I. 79, 2, ad *Resp.* "Anima enim nostra in genere
intellectualium tenet ultimum locum, sicut materia prima in
genere sensibilium"; *De Verit.*, X. 8, ad *Resp.*

30. *Qu. de Anima*, qu. un. art. I., ad *Resp.*; *Sum. theol.*, I. 76, 1, ad
Resp.

31. *Qu. de Anima*, qu. un. art. I., ad *Resp.*

CHAPTER XI.
THE POWERS OF THE SOUL—
LIFE AND THE SENSES

A SINGLE substantial form exists in man, and consequently a single soul whence he derives at the same time reason, sense, movement and life. This single soul displays therefore manifold powers, a fact that will cause no surprise, if we recall to mind the position occupied by man in the totality of created beings. For the inferior beings are incapable of attaining naturally to complete perfection, but they reach a moderate degree of excellence by means of a few movements. Those superior to them are able to reach complete perfection by means of many movements. Still higher in the scale are the beings which attain to their complete perfection by a small number of movements, the highest degree being occupied by those which possess perfection without having to execute any movements to acquire it. In the same way, the worst state of health of all is that of a man who, unable to reach perfect health, yet succeeds in maintaining a precarious health with the help of some remedies; better is the health of those who attain a perfect state of well-being at the expense of many remedies; still better the condition of those who obtain it with a few; and best of all that of a man who is always well without any remedies at all. In the same way, it may be said that the things inferior to man may lay claim to some particular perfections; they perform therefore a small number of operations which are moreover fixed and determinate. Man, on the contrary, is able to secure a universal and perfect good, since he can attain to the Supreme Good; on the other hand, we find him placed in the lowest rank of beings capable of reaching beatitude, since he is the last of intellectual creatures. It is therefore right that the human soul should reach its proper good by means of many operations which presuppose a certain diversity of powers. Above him are the angels who attain to beatitude by a smaller number of means, and finally God in whom no power or action is to be found beyond His unique and single essence. It may be added that a very obvious consideration would lead directly to the same conclusion. Since man is placed at the meeting-point of the world of spirits and the world of bodies, it follows necessarily that the powers both of the one and the other are combined in him.[1] Let us see under what aspects these powers may be distinguished.

Every power, considered as such, is ordered by reference to its act. The reason of every power can consequently be found in the act towards which it is ordered, which amounts to saying that the powers are distinguishable in the same way as their acts. Now, it is clear that acts are distinguished by reason of their objects. To an object acting as principle and moving cause there necessarily corresponds a passive power undergoing its action; thus colour, in so far as it moves vision, is the principle of vision. An object acting as term and end, is correlated with an active power: thus the perfection of stature which is the end of growth, constitutes the end of the faculty of growth possessed by living beings.[2] We should reach the same conclusion by a consideration of the actions of warming or chilling. These two actions differ indeed inasmuch as the principle of the one is warmth and of the other cold; but they are distinguished above all by the ends to which they tend. For, since the agent acts only in order to impress its resemblance upon another being, warmth and cold act in order to warm or to chill. Thus, the actions and the powers, whence they spring, are distinguished according to their objects.[3]

If we apply this conclusion to the distinction of the powers of the soul, we shall find that they are arranged hierarchically in a certain order, for it is always in an orderly manner that the manifold issues from the one: *ordine quodam ab uno in multitudinem proceditur;*[4] and that this hierarchy of the powers of the soul is based on the degree of universality of their objects. The higher in dignity the position occupied by a power, the more universal is the object to which it corresponds. At the lowest point is that power of the soul, the only object of which is the body with which the soul is united: this power has been called "vegetative," for the so-called vegetative soul acts only on its own body. Another kind of power corresponds to a more universal object, viz. all sensible bodies, and no longer that one sensible body, united with the soul: this belongs to the so-called "sensitive" soul. Above this again is a power having a yet more universal object, namely, not merely sensible bodies in general, but the whole of being in its universality: this is the so-called "intellective" soul.[5]

Again, it is evident that, corresponding to the differences in the objects of the soul, there are differences in the mode of its operations. The action of the soul transcends the operations of corporeal nature, in proportion as its objects increase in universality, and from this point of view also we discover three degrees in it. In the first place, the action of the soul transcends the action of nature, operating in inanimate things. For the proper action of the soul is life; now, we call living a thing that in its operation moves of itself; the soul is consequently the principle of an intrinsic action, whereas all inanimate bodies receive on the contrary their movement from an external principle. The vegetative powers of the soul, even though exercised only upon the body directly united with the soul, place it therefore on a degree of being definitely superior to that of purely corporeal nature. At the same time it must be recognised that, though the mode of the vegetative operations of the soul cannot be reduced to the mode of action of bodies, yet the operations themselves are identical in both cases. Inanimate things receive from an external principle the same act which animate beings receive from their soul; hence there is room, above the vegetative actions of the soul, for actions of a superior order, going beyond those performed by natural forms both from the point of view of what they perform and from that of the mode of their performance. The common feature of these operations is that the soul tends naturally to receive in itself everything according to the mode of immaterial being.

We have to observe, in fact, that the soul, in so far as it is endowed with sense and intellect, *is* in a sense the universality of being. But though all things can be in the soul under the mode of immaterial being, there are yet degrees of immaterialness in the mode in which they enter the soul. At the first degree, things are in the soul, deprived of course of their own matter, yet according to their particular being and in the conditions of individuality which they owe to their matter. This degree corresponds to the sense, receiving the species produced by individual things, which, though received deprived of matter, are received nevertheless by a corporeal organ. The superior and most perfect degree belongs to the intellect which without any bodily organ receives species entirely devoid both of matter and of the conditions of individuality entailed by it.[6] The soul performs, accordingly, immanent operations of the natural order within the body to which it is united; it further performs operations of the sensible order, but already immaterial, by means of a bodily organ; it performs, lastly, operations of the intelligible order without any bodily organ. In this way the multiplicity of its actions and of the corresponding powers are hierarchically arranged. We have considered them in their order; the task remains to examine them in themselves. And since the order of generation is inverse to the order of perfection[7], we shall take first the least perfect power, the vegetative power.

As has been stated, the object of the vegetative power is the body receiving life from the soul as from its form. Now, the nature of the body requires the exercise of a threefold operation of the soul corresponding to a threefold subdivision of the vegetative power. By the first of these operations the body receives the being conferred on it by the soul: this is the operation of the generative power. We note, moreover, that inanimate natural things receive at the same time their specific being and their requisite size or quantity. But in the case of beings endowed with life, this does not happen. Generated from a seed, they are bound to possess at the beginning of their existence a being which is imperfect under the aspect of quantity. Consequently, apart from the generative power, there must necessarily be in them an augmentative power which develops them to the size that they should naturally possess. But this increase in being would be impossible, unless something transforms itself into the substance of the being to be increased, and is thereby added to it.[8] This transformation is the result of heat which elaborates and digests all external additions. The conservation of the individual requires therefore a nutritive virtue which continually replaces what has been lost, supplies what is lacking in the attainment of the perfect size, and what is needed to produce the seed required for reproduction.[9] Thus the vegetative power presupposes in its turn a generative power which confers being, an augmentative power ensuring due growth, and a nutritive power for the conservation of this being in its existence and in its proper quantity. Here, again, we must note a hierarchic order between these powers. The nutritive and augmentative powers produce their effects in the being in which they are placed; it is precisely the body united with the soul which the soul increases and maintains. The generative power, on the contrary, produces its effects not in this body but in another, since nothing can beget itself. This power consequently approximates to the sensitive soul in dignity more than the other two, since its operation is performed on external objects, although the operations of the sensitive soul display a superior excellence and higher degree of universality. Here we can verify once more the principle propounded by Dionysius[10] that the highest degree of an inferior order borders on the lowest degree of the next superior order. The nutritive power is subordinated to the augmentative, which in its turn is subordinated to the generative,[11] and with this latter we almost touch the sensitive power which finally liberates the individual from his subjection to his particular mode of being.

The sensitive power of the soul is the lowest form of knowledge within the universal order. Taken in its complete form and such as it ought to be to suffice for the existence of the animal, sensitive knowledge requires five operations, some of which presuppose in their turn a variety of hierarchically ordered operations. The simplest of all pertains to the "particular sense," the first in the order of sensitive powers corresponding to a direct modification of the soul by sensible realities. But the particular sense itself is subdivided into distinct powers according to the diversity of sensible impressions which it is capable of receiving. For sensibles act upon the particular sense by means of the species which they impress upon it; and unquestionably, though contrary to the general idea, these species are not taken in by the sense in a material form —if they were, the sense would become the sensible itself, the eye colour, or the ear sound—but all the same, certain kinds of sensations are accompanied by very marked organic changes on the part of the animal experiencing them. We shall start, therefore, from the principle that the senses receive the sensible species deprived of matter, and we shall class them in the order of the increasing immaterialness of the modifications they undergo.

We find, in the first place, certain sensibles the species of which, though received immaterially by the sense, yet modify materially the animal experiencing them. Of this order are the qualities effecting changes in material things themselves, namely, heat, cold, dryness, damp, and others of the same kind. Since therefore sensibles of this class produce material impressions in us and since all material impressions are made by contact, it follows necessarily that such sensibles must be in contact with us, for us to be aware of them; hence the sensitive power which apprehends them is called "touch." On the other hand, there are certain sensibles the impression of which does not by itself modify us materially, but is accompanied by accessory material changes. Sometimes this accompanying change affects at the same time the sensible and the sense organ: this is the case with taste. For though the tasted object does not modify the organ of taste to the extent of rendering it sweet or bitter, still it cannot be apprehended without both the object and the organ being in some manner modified. It seems in particular that the function of the saliva in wetting both the tongue and the object is required for effective tasting. This is in no way similar to the action of heat which warms the part of the body to which it is applied; we are dealing here simply with a material change as a condition of, not as constituting, sense-perception. Sometimes it happens that the material change associated with the sensation affects only the sensible quality itself. In that case it may consist in a sort of alteration or decomposition of the sensible, as when bodies exhale odours, or it may reduce itself to a simple local movement, as in the perception of sounds. Hearing and smelling involve therefore no material change in the sense-organ; they apprehend the material changes affecting the sensible at a distance and through an external ambient medium. We come finally to a last class of sensibles which act upon the sense without any material change accompanying their action: such are colour and light. The process by which species of the sort emanate from their object to act on the subject remains wholly spiritual,[12]* and we find in these, the noblest and most universal of

* i.e. immaterial.

all senses, an operation closely analogous to intellectual operations in the strict sense. Accordingly, comparisons between intellectual knowledge and sight, between the eye of the soul and the eye of the body are very frequent.[13] Such is the hierarchy of the five external sensitive powers, which form the basis of the four internal sensitive powers, the role and functions of which are easily discerned.[14]

For, while it is true to say that nature never does anything in vain and does not multiply beings without need, it is equally true that she never refuses to beings whatever they require. The sensitive soul must therefore perform as many operations as are needed for a perfect animal to live. At the same time it is evident that all operations which are irreducible to the same principle, presuppose the existence in the soul of as many different corresponding powers: what, in fact, is called a power is none other than the proximate principle of an operation of the soul. These principles being admitted, we have to note that the particular sense is not sufficient to itself. The particular sense judges the sensible corresponding to it, and distinguishes it from among other sensibles brought to its notice; it distinguishes for instance white from black or green, and from that point of view it suffices; but it cannot distinguish a white colour from a sweet taste. Sight can distinguish between one colour and all the other colours because it knows them all; but it cannot distinguish between a colour and a taste because it does not know tastes, for to discriminate between sensible realities, they must first be known. We must therefore necessarily assume a "common sense" to which all sense-perceptions must be submitted, as to their common centre, to enable it to judge of them and to distinguish between them. The common sense will further apprehend, besides the sensibles whose species are transmitted to it, also the operations themselves. For it is clear that we know that we are seeing. Now, such a knowledge cannot pertain to the particular sense which knows nothing but the sensible form affecting it; but after the modification has been imparted by that form to vision, the visual sensation imparts in its turn a second modification to the "common sense" which thereupon perceives the vision itself.[15]

Again, considering the conditions to be met by an animal in order to live a perfect animal life, it will be granted that it is not sufficient for it to apprehend sensibles when they are presented to it; a living being must also be able to represent them to itself, even when they are absent. For, since the movements and actions of an animal are determined by the objects apprehended, it would never set itself in motion to secure whatever it needs, if it were unable to represent to itself these objects in their absence. The sensitive soul of the animal must therefore be able, not only to receive the sensible species, but also to retain them and preserve them. Now, it is easy to observe that in the case of bodies, the same principles do not both receive and retain; what is damp receives easily and retains badly; what is dry, on the contrary, receives badly but retains well whatever it has received. Therefore, since the sensitive power of the soul is the act of a bodily organ, we must assume in it two different powers, one to receive the sensible species and the other to retain them. The power of retention goes by the name of "phantasy" or "imagination."

The sensible knowledge with which the living being is provided, requires thirdly the power of discriminating certain properties of things which sense, left to itself, would be incapable of apprehending. Not all the sensibles perceived offer to the animal an equal interest from the point of view of their retention; some are useful, others harmful. Man who is capable of comparing his particular knowledge and of reasoning about it, makes a distinction between the useful and the harmful by means of what has been called his "particular" or "cogitative reason." But the animal, devoid of reason, must apprehend directly in the things their usefulness or harm, although these are not

sensible qualities in the strict sense. Hence a further
sensitive power is necessarily needed; by means of it
the sheep knows that it must flee when it sees a wolf;
the bird is led to pick up a wisp of straw; yet the
sheep does not flee from the wolf, nor the bird gather
straw because the forms or colours of these objects
please or displease them, but because they perceive
them directly as opposed to or in conformity with
their natures. This new power is called "estimative"*
power and is the direct means for rendering possible
the fourth of the internal sensitive powers, namely,
"memory."

For the living being needs to be able to recall
actually to mind the species previously apprehended
by sense and inwardly retained by imagination.
Now, whatever we may be inclined to think at first
sight, imagination is insufficient for this purpose.
Imagination is, in a sense, a treasure house in which
forms perceived by sense are stored; but we have just
noted that the particular sense does not succeed in
apprehending all the aspects of sensibles; the useful or
the harmful as such escape its grasp; hence another
power is required to preserve their species.[16] It must
moreover be admitted that diverse movements presuppose diverse moving principles determining them.
In the imagination the movement is from the things
to the soul: it is the objects that impress their species
first upon the particular sense, then upon the common
sense, to enable the imagination to retain them. But
it is different in the case of the memory; there the
movement starts from the soul to end in the species
evoked by it. In the case of animals, the remem-
brance of the useful or the harmful causes the representations of previously perceived objects to arise; we
are there dealing with a spontaneous revival of the
sensible species, pertaining to memory proper. In the
case of man, on the contrary, an effort of search is
needed for the species stored in the imagination, to

* Synonymous with "instinct."

become afresh the object of actual consideration; here we are dealing no longer with simple memory, but with what has been called "reminiscence." It must be added that in either case, the objects present themselves bearing the character of past occurrences, another quality which lies outside the range of the particular sense.[17]

It will be seen at the same time that the consideration of the highest sensitive powers of the soul brings us to the very threshold of intellectual activity. The estimative power by which animals apprehend the harmful or useful, corresponds in man to the particular reason or the passive intellect,[18] just as the animal memory corresponds to the reminiscence of man. We have, however, not yet entered the sphere of the intellect strictly speaking. The passive intellect remains a power of the sensible order, because it collects only particular knowledge, whereas the characteristic of the intellect is the faculty of apprehending the universal. In the same manner, reminiscence differs from spontaneous revival, characteristic of the animal memory; it presupposes a sort of syllogistic dialectic, by which we proceed from one memory to another until we reach the one we have been searching for; but this search is concerned only with particular representations and so far the universality, required for intellectual knowledge, is completely lacking.[19] It may, therefore, be asserted that the sensitive powers of the soul are of exactly the same nature both in the animal and in man, at least if they are considered in what is properly speaking sensitive about them; the particular dignity which they possess in man, comes to them from the intellect on which they border, in reference to which they are ordered and the eminent dignity of which seems to be reflected back upon the operations proper to them.[20] The step we are now about to take, from the sensitive powers up to the intellectual powers of the soul, is therefore decisive.

NOTES TO CHAPTER XI.

1. *Cont. Gent.*, II. 72, ad *Non est autem*; *Sum. theol.*, I. 77, 2, ad *Resp.*
2. *Sum. theol.*, I. 77, 2, ad *Resp.*
3. *De anima*, qu. un. art. 13, ad *Resp.*
4. *Sum. theol.*, I. 77, 4, ad *Resp.*
5. *Sum. theol.*, I. 78, 1, ad *Resp.*
6. *De anima*, qu. un. art. 13, ad *Resp.*; *Sum. theol.*, I. 78, 1, ad *Resp.*
7. *Sum. theol.*, I. 77, 4, ad *Resp.*; *De anima*, qu. un. art. 13, ad 10^m.
8. *De anima*, qu. un. art. 13, ad 15^m.
9. *De anima*, qu. un. art. 13, ad 15^m.
10. *De div. nom.*, c. 7.
11. *Sum. theol.*, I. 78, 2, ad *Resp.*
12. *De anima*, qu. un. art. 13, ad *Resp.*
13. *Sum. theol.*, I. 67, 1, ad *Resp.*; *Sent.*, II., dist. 13, qu. 1, art. 2.
14. Avicenna distinguishes five powers. Cf. I. 78, 4, ad *Resp. sub fin.*
15. *Sum. theol.*, I. 78, 4, ad 2^m.
16. *Sum. theol.*, I. 78, 4, ad *Resp.*
17. *Sum. theol.*, ibid.; *De anima*, qu. un. art. 13, ad *Resp.*
18. *Cont. Gent.*, II. 73, ad *Si autem dicatur.*
19. *Sum. theol.*, ibid.; ad *Considerandum est autem.*
20. *Ibid.*, ad 5^m.

CHAPTER XII. THE INTELLECT AND RATIONAL KNOWLEDGE

THE intellect is the power which imparts the proper degree of perfection to the human soul; and yet the human soul is not, strictly speaking, an intellect. The angel whose whole virtue is concentrated in his intellectual power and in his will springing from it, is a pure intellect; therefore the name of "intelligence" has been given to him. The human soul, on the contrary, performing in addition vegetative and sensitive operations, could not well be described by that name. We must therefore simply say that the intellect is one of the powers of the human soul.[1] Let us examine its structure and principal operations.

Taken in its lowliest aspect, the human intellect appears as a passive power. The verb "pati" can be taken in three different senses. In the first sense, which is moreover its proper signification, it means that a thing is deprived of something which it ought to have according to its essence or which is the object of its natural inclination; for instance, if water loses its cold temperature as it is heated by fire, or if a man falls ill or becomes sad. In the second sense, less rigorously literal, it means that a being is deprived of something, whether this something ought or ought not to be possessed by it. From this point of view, the recovery of health no less than the loss of it is a "passion" (i.e. something suffered or undergone);* so it is to rejoice as well as to be sad. Lastly, in the third sense, the most general of all, the verb means that a being no longer loses or is deprived of one quality or receives another, but simply that something, being

---

* It is well to note that 'passion' in the moral sense—the sense in which it is normally used in English—is defined as 'an act of the sensitive appetite.'

in potency, receives that in respect of which it is in potency. From this point of view, everything passing from potency to act can be considered as "passive," even though such passivity should be a source of enrichment rather than a cause of impoverishment. Our intellect is passive in this last sense, and the reason of this passivity can be deduced directly from the relatively inferior position of man in the hierarchy of being.

For the intellect is in potency or in act according to the relation it maintains with universal being. In considering the nature of this relation, we find, at its highest degree, an intellect whose relation to universal being consists in being the very act of being, taken in its totality. We here recognise the Divine intellect, viz. the Divine essence itself in whom all being pre-exists originally and virtually as in its first Cause. Because it is actually the totality of being, the Divine intellect is at no point in potency, but, on the contrary, pure act. It is different in the case of a created intellect. For such an intellect to be the act of the universal being, it would have to be an infinite being which contradicts its condition of created being. The created intellect is therefore, by the mere fact of its existence, not the act of all intelligibles; as a merely finite and participated being, it is in potency in respect of all the intelligible reality which is not the intellect itself. Intellectual passivity is therefore the direct consequence of this limitation of being. Now, the relation of potency to act can present a twofold aspect. For there is a certain order of potentiality in which the potency is never deprived of its act; we are able to observe this fact in the celestial bodies. But there is another order of potentiality in which the potency, sometimes deprived of its act, has to pass into act to acquire it: such is the matter of corruptible beings. It will be seen at once that the angelic intellect is characterised by the former of these two degrees of potentiality; its proximity to the first intellect, which is pure act, is the cause of the angelic intellect possessing always in act its own intelligible species. The human intellect, on the contrary, coming last in the order of intellects and being as far removed as possible from the Divine intellect, is in potency in respect of the intelligibles, not only in the sense that it is passive when receiving them, but also in the sense of being naturally deprived of them. Therefore Aristotle asserts that, to start with, the soul is like a "tabula rasa" without any writing upon it. The necessity of assuming a certain passivity at the beginning of our intellectual knowledge rests therefore upon the extreme imperfection of our intellect.[2]

We must, on the other hand, admit the existence of an active power as no less absolutely required, if we wish to give an account of human knowledge. For, since the possible intellect is in potency in regard to intelligibles, it follows necessarily that the intelligibles must set this intellect in motion, to render any human knowledge possible. But it is evident that in order to impart movement, a thing must first be. Now, no intelligibles, in the proper sense of the term, would exist in an universe where only merely passive intellects were to be found. For the intelligible is not to be encountered, as a subsisting reality, within nature. Aristotle had proved against Plato that the forms of natural things do not subsist without matter; but the forms to be found in matter are evidently not intelligibles in themselves, since it is immaterialness that confers intelligibility; it follows therefore that the natures, i.e. the forms which our intellect knows in sensible things, must be rendered intelligible in act. But only a being in act is able to cause something in potency to pass from potency to act. We must therefore attribute to the intellect an active virtue which renders the intelligible, contained potentially in sensible reality, actually intelligible; and this virtue has been called "intellectus agens," or active intellect.[3] It is moreover easy to see that this fact dominates the whole structure of human knowledge. Since sensible things are endowed with actual existence outside our own soul, it is useless to posit an active sense; hence the sensitive power of our soul is entirely passive.[4] But as we reject the Platonic doctrine of ideas as realities subsisting in the nature of things, we require an active intellect to disentangle the intelligibles embedded in the sensibles. Since, finally, immaterial and actually intelligible substances exist, such as the angels or God, we must recognise that our intellect is incapable of apprehending these realities in themselves, but must rest content with acquiring knowledge by abstracting the intelligible from the material and sensible.[5]

Is this active intellect, the necessity of which has been established, a power of the soul or a superior power, extrinsic to the soul's essence and conferring upon it *ab extra* the faculty of knowing? It is easy to understand why some thinkers have held the latter view. It is evident that we must assume above the rational soul a superior intellect from which it holds its faculty of knowing. Something that is participated, mobile and imperfect, presupposes always a being which is such by its essence, immobile and perfect. Now, the human soul is an intellective principle only by participation: this is proved by the fact that it is not wholly, but only partially, intelligent; or again by the fact that it attains to truth by a discursive process, not by direct and simple intuition. The soul requires accordingly an intellect of a superior order which confers upon it the power of intellection; hence certain philosophers identify this intellect with the active intellect which they take to be a separate substance which, by illuminating the phantasms of sensible origin impressed on us by things, renders them intelligible.[6] But even if we conceded the existence of such a separate active intellect, we should still have to assume in the very soul of man a participated power of this superior intellect, capable of rendering the sensible species actually intelligible. For whenever universal principles exercise their action, we find particular principles of activity, subordinated to them, governing the proper operations of each being. Thus the active virtue of the celestial bodies which extends to the whole universe, does not prevent the inferior bodies from being endowed with virtues of their own, directing determinate operations. This is particularly easy to note in the perfect animals. There are animals of the inferior orders the production of which is adequately explained by the action of the celestial bodies: such are the animals produced by putrefaction. But the generation of perfect animals requires, apart from the activity of a celestial body, a particular virtue residing in the seed. Now, by far the most perfect operation performed by sublunary beings, is clearly intellectual knowledge, i.e. the operations of the intellect. Consequently, even assuming an active principle of all intellection, such as the illuminating virtue of God, we must necessarily posit in each man an active principle of his own, conferring on the individual in question actual intelligence: and this is what is called the "intellectus agens."[7] But this conclusion evidently amounts to the denial of the existence of one *separate* active intellect. For, since the intellectual knowledge of each man and each soul requires an active principle of operation, a plurality of active intellects must be assumed. We must consequently recognise as many active intellects as there are souls, i.e. ultimately as many as there are men; for it would be absurd to attribute one and numerically the same principle of operation to a number of different subjects.[8] Thereby all the errors, entailed by positing a single active intellect for all men, are fundamentally disproved, such as the denial of personal immortality, for example, or of the free-will. Let us proceed to examine the principal functions of this intellect.

We must, in the first place, assign memory to it. Not that all the philosophers are agreed on this point, even among those who claim the authority of Aristotle; Avicenna denies it, forced to the denial precisely by the doctrine of a single intellect, which we have just refuted. According to him, it would be conceivable for the passive intellect, bound to a bodily organ, to preserve the sensible species without apprehending them actually; but this would not apply in case of the active intellect. In this wholly immaterial power nothing can subsist except in an intelligible and consequently actual form. As soon as an intellect ceases actually to apprehend an object, the species of that object vanishes from the intellect; if it wishes to renew the knowledge of the object, it would have to appeal to the "intellectus agens" as to a separate substance, from which the intelligible species flows into the passive intellect. The repetition and exercise by the passive intellect of this movement of turning to the "intellectus agens," forms in it a sort of habit of or facility for carrying out this operation, and the possession of knowledge is reduced to this. To know, therefore, does not mean to retain the species which are not actually apprehended, and this eliminates from the intellect all memory in the narrow sense of that term. But such a conclusion hardly meets the requirements of our reason. For it is one of the main principles that *quod recipitur in aliquo recipitur in eo secundum modum recipientis*; now, the intellect is naturally more stable and immovable than corporeal matter. If we therefore find that corporeal matter not merely retains forms during the reception of them, but for a long time after it has actually received them, the intellect must *a fortiori* preserve unchangeably and indefectibly the intelligible species which it has apprehended. If we simply describe by the term "memory" the capacity of preserving the species, we must admit that there is a memory in the intellect. We must, however, note that if it is considered characteristic of memory to apprehend the past as past, then memory can exist only in the sensitive power of the soul. For the past as such consists in existence at a definite point in time—a mode of existence which can pertain only to particular things. But the apprehension of the material and of the particular pertains to the sensitive power of the soul. We can therefore conclude that, if the memory of the past belongs to the sensitive soul, there exists in addition a strictly intellectual memory which preserves the intelligible species and has as its proper object the universal, abstracted from all conditions determining it to such and such a mode of particular existence.[9]

Memory, such as it has just been defined, forms part of the intellectual operation itself; it is therefore, strictly speaking, not another power of the intellect.[10] This conclusion applies with equal truth to reason and to the intellect in the proper sense of those terms; they are not different powers of the soul, and it is easy to test this by examining the acts characteristic of them. Intellection is the simple apprehension of an intelligible truth; reasoning is the process of the mind proceeding from one object of knowledge to another in order to reach an intelligible truth. The angels, for instance, who possess perfectly the knowledge of such intelligible truth as their degree of perfection allows them to apprehend, discover it by a simple and in no way discursive operation; they are true intelligences. Man, on the other hand, attains to the knowledge of intelligible truth by passing from one object of knowledge to another; hence the name really applicable to him is not that of an intelligence, but rather of a rational being. It appears also that reasoning is to intellection as movement is to rest, or acquisition is to possession; the same relation obtains between these terms as between the imperfect and the perfect. Now, it is well known that movement starts from an antecedent immobility and ends in rest; the same holds good of human knowledge. Reasoning proceeds from certain initial terms which we apprehend purely and simply by means of the intellect: these are the first principles; its final term is equally the first principles to which it returns to check the conclusions of its argument. Intellection is to be found therefore both at the beginning and at the end of reasoning. Now, it is evident that rest and movement depend on one and the same power: this assertion can be proved down to natural things where we find the same nature setting things in motion and maintaining them in repose. *A fortiori* intellect and reasoning pertain to one and the same power. It is therefore clear that in man the terms of both intellect and reason describe one and the same power.[11]

Here we discern the precise point where the human soul borders on the separate intelligences in the hierarchy of created beings. It is obvious that the mode of knowledge characteristic of man is reasoning or discursive knowledge. But it is also clear that discursive knowledge requires two fixed terms, one at the beginning, the other at the end, both consisting in the simple apprehension of truth by the intellect. The intellection of principles opens as well as closes the processes of reason. Although therefore the knowledge proper to the human soul follows the line of reasoning, it nevertheless presupposes a certain participation in that simple mode of knowledge which is to be found in the intellectual substances of an higher order. Here again the words of Dionysius are proved true: *Divina sapientia semper fines priorum conjungit principiis secundorum.*[12] But they are true only if we deny the existence in man of an intellectual power distinct from his reason. For the universal hierarchy is based, not on the inferior possessing what the superior also possesses, but on the imperfect participation of the inferior in what is possessed by the superior. Thus the animal whose nature is purely sensitive, is devoid of reason; yet it is endowed with a sort of natural prudence or power of judgment which constitutes a certain participation in human reason. In the same way, man does not possess, as a special power, an intellect by which he attains simply, absolutely and without discursive steps to the knowledge of truth; but he participates in this mode of knowing by a kind of natural disposition which is the intellection of principles. In short, the human intellect, as it appears as the result of our discussion, is nothing but reason itself in so far as it participates in the simplicity of intellectual knowledge: *unde et potentia discurrens et veritatem accipiens non erunt diversae sed una...; ipsa ratio intellectus dicitur quod participat de intellectuali simplicitate, ex quo est principium et terminus in ejus propria operatione.*[13] Let us consider this operation itself, i.e. the mode by which human reason apprehends its different objects.

The fundamental problem the solution of which will govern all ultimate conclusions, is to know how the human intellect knows the corporeal substances which are naturally inferior to it.[14] According to Plato, the human soul possesses a natural and innate knowledge of all things. For no one can give exact answers except to questions which he knows; now, an entirely ignorant person will always reply correctly to questions, if only he is asked methodically: this we note in the "Meno."[15] Therefore, everyone possesses the knowledge of things even before acquiring knowledge; and this amounts to asserting that the soul knows all, including the body, by innate species, naturally possessed by it. But this theory encounters at once a serious difficulty. For, since the form is the principle of all action, it follows that each thing maintains the same relation both to the form and to the action produced by that form. If we assume, for instance, that an upward movement is produced by lightness, we should say that what is in potency in respect to this movement is potentially light, and that, what moves actually upwards, is actually light. Now, it is clear that man, in respect of both his senses and his intellect is often in potency regarding his knowledge; he is brought from potency to act either by sense objects acting on his senses or by teaching and discovery acting on his intellect. It must therefore be admitted that the rational soul is in potency in regard to the sensible species as well as to the intelligible. But when it is in potency in regard to the species, it evidently does not possess them actually; the soul consequently does not know all things by means of naturally innate species.[16] It is true that it is possible to possess actually a form and yet to be incapable of producing the action of this form owing to some exterior obstacle. Thus a light body may sometimes be prevented from rising upwards by some hindrance. Therefore Plato, observing that the soul is not always in actual possession of its knowledge, asserted that the human intellect is naturally full of all intelligible species, but is prevented by its union with the body from knowing them always actually.

Now, a simple observation suffices to show the falsity of this theory. If one sense fails, the whole knowledge of what this sense apprehends, vanishes with it. One sense the less—one branch of knowledge the less. A man born blind knows nothing of colours; yet he would know them if the intellect possessed, as naturally innate, the intelligible reasons of all things. But it is possible to go beyond the mere statement of this fact and show that such knowledge would be disproportionate to the human soul.

If we adopt the Platonic view, we are led to consider the body as a sort of veil or screen placed between our intellect and the objects of our knowledge; we should have to say that the soul does not acquire its knowledge with the help of the body, but in spite of it. Now, we have noted that it is natural for the soul to be united with the body. If, therefore, we accepted the Platonic position, we should have to assume that the natural operation of the soul, namely, intellectual knowledge, finds no greater obstacle than the bond with its body, which is yet conformable to its nature. But this is a view repugnant to reason. Nature, producing the soul for the sake of knowing, cannot have united with it a body which prevents it from knowing; rather, she must have given a body to the soul only to facilitate intellectual knowledge. This assertion loses all its paradoxical appearance, if we remember the low dignity and extreme imperfection of the human soul. There is a faculty of knowing in all intellectual substances, which draws its strength from the influence of the Divine light. In its first principle, this light is one and single; but the further intelligent creatures are removed from the first principle, the more this light is divided and scattered, like the rays diverging from a central point. Hence God knows all things by his simple and unique essence. The higher intellectual substances know, indeed, by means of many forms, but make use of only a limited number of them; moreover, they apprehend highly universal forms and, being endowed with an extremely effective faculty of knowing, discover the multiplicity of particular objects within these universal forms. In the inferior intellectual substances, on the contrary, we find a greater number of less universal forms, and being further removed from the first source of all knowledge, these forms no longer permit an equally distinct apprehension of the particular objects. If therefore the lower intellectual substances possessed only the universal intelligible forms, as they occur in the angels, they—being illuminated only by a very feeble and darkened ray of light—would never succeed in discovering the multiplicity of particular objects in such forms. The knowledge would therefore be only of a vague and confused generality; they would be like those ignorant people who fail to perceive in principles the innumerable implicated consequences seen by the learned. Now, we know that in the order of nature the human souls are the last of all the intellectual substances. Consequently, they had either to be given a merely confused and general knowledge, or to be united with bodies to enable them to receive from sense-objects the proper and particular knowledge of what these objects are. God has treated the human soul as we treat those crude minds which can learn only with the help of sensible illustrations. It is therefore for its own advantage that the soul has been united with a body to make use of it for the acquisition of knowledge: *Sic ergo patet quod propter melius animae est ut corpori uniatur, et intelligat per conversionem ad phantasmata;*[17] and again: *Competit eis* (animis) *ut a corporibus et per corpora suam perfectionem intelligibilem consequantur, alioquin frustra corporibus unirentur.*[18] In short, the soul will attain to a knowledge of its objects by turning for help to the body, not by turning away from it, as would be demanded by the Platonic theory of innate species.

Let us endeavour to describe in detail the mode in which this human intellect apprehends its objects. According to St. Augustine who points to the right solution, the intellectual soul discovers all things in the eternal essences, that is, in the immovable truth which is in God. *Si ambo videmus verum esse quod dicis, et ambo videmus verum esse quod dico, ubi, quaeso, id videmus? Nec ego utique in te, nec tu in me, sed ambo in ipsa, quae supra mentes nostras est, incommutabili veritate.*[19] St. Augustine was, in fact, of opinion that we ought always to avail ourselves of whatever truth the pagan philosophies might contain, and as he was himself imbued with Platonic conceptions, he constantly attempted to gather up whatever good he found in the Platonists, or even to correct and utilise whatever he found in them contrary to Faith. Now Plato described by the term "ideas" the forms of things considered as subsisting by themselves and separately from matter. The knowledge acquired by our soul, would reduce itself to its participation in the forms thus defined; just as corporeal matter becomes stone inasmuch as it participates in the idea "stone," so our intellect would know the stone, in so far as it participated in this same idea. But it is evidently contrary to Faith thus to assume separated forms, subsisting of themselves and endowed with a sort of creative activity. Therefore St. Augustine substituted for the ideas of Plato the essences of all creatures which he conceived as gathered up in the mind of God, in conformity to which all things were created and by the help of which ultimately the human soul would know all things. Now it must be said that this theory, taken in a certain sense, is inacceptable. In asserting with St. Augustine that the intellect knows all in the eternal essences and, therefore, in God, the expression "to know in" may mean that the eternal essences constitute the very objects apprehended by the intellect. But it cannot be admitted that in this life the soul can know all things in the eternal essences, and we have just seen the reason why, in the criticism of the innate Platonic ideas. Only the Blessed who see God and see all in God, know all in the eternal essences; on earth, on the contrary, the human intellect has as its proper object the sensible, not the intelligible. But the expression "to know in" may define the principle, instead of the object, of knowledge; it may mean "that whereby" we know and not "what" we know.[20] In this sense, it merely expresses a great truth, viz. the need of placing at the origin of our intellection the Divine light and the first principles of knowledge.

The soul, indeed, knows all in the eternal essences as the eye sees "in the sun," all that it sees "by means of the sun." It is important to be clear about the full meaning of that statement. We note that there is a principle of intellection in the human soul. This intellectual light in us is none other than a participated resemblance to the uncreated Light, and since the uncreated Light contains the eternal essences of all things, it may in a sense be said, that we know all in the Divine exemplars. Therefore, "to know in the eternal essences" would mean simply "to know by means of the participation in the Divine light" in which the essences of all things are contained. Hence the Psalm 4 says: *Multi dicunt: Quis ostendit nobis bona?* The Psalmist replies: *Signatum est super nos lumen vultus tui Domine.* And this means: *Per ipsam sigillationem divini luminis in nobis omnia demonstrantur.* But this faculty of knowing, given to us by God, is not sufficient by itself. We have seen that it is naturally devoid of the intelligible species which Plato attributed to it. Far from possessing innate knowledge, it is rather at first in potency in respect of all intelligibles.

Let us now add that this faculty does not give us a

knowledge of material things by the mere participation
in their eternal essences; it still needs the intelligible
species which it abstracts from the things themselves.[21]
The human intellect therefore possesses an adequate
and sufficient light to enable it to acquire the knowledge of the intelligibles to which it can attain by
means of sensible things.[22] We find the germs of all
knowledge in the intellect itself: *praeexistunt in nobis
quaedam scientiarum semina.*[23] These preformed germs
of which we have natural knowledge are the first
principles: *prima intelligibilium principia.*[24] What is
characteristic of these principles is that they are the
first concepts formed by our intellect when we come
into contact with the sensible. To say that they pre-
exist, does not mean that the intellect possesses them
actually, independently of the action which bodies
exercise on our soul; it simply means that they are the
first intelligibles which our intellect can reach in
starting from sensible experience. The intellection of
these principles is no more innate than the conclusions
of deductive arguments,[25] but, whereas we discover
the former naturally, we have to reach the latter by
an effort of search. A few detailed examples will help
us to understand this truth.

The principles may be complex, as that the whole is
greater than the part; or they may be simple, like the
idea of being, of unity and others of this kind. Now,
it is possible to say that these complex principles like
the one quoted, do in some manner pre-exist in our
intellect. For, as soon as the rational soul of man
understands the definitions of the whole and of a part,
it knows that the whole is greater than the part.
It is, therefore, naturally capable of acquiring this
knowledge directly. But it is no less clear that the
soul did not possess this knowledge as such, and that
the intellect left to its own resources would never have
acquired it. In order to know that the whole is greater
than the part, it is, as we said, necessary to know
the definitions of the part and the whole; but it is impossible to know them except by abstracting the

intelligible species from sensible matter.[26] If we there-fore cannot know what the whole is or what a part is without appealing to the perception of bodies, and if we cannot know that the whole is greater than the part without first possessing that knowledge, it follows that the apprehension of the very first intelligible conceptions presupposes necessarily the intervention of the sensible. This conclusion is still more evident, if we consider the simple principles of knowledge. We should be ignorant of what being or unity is, unless we had previously perceived sensible objects from which to abstract the intelligible species. The exact definitions of these principles would consequently be as follows: *primae conceptiones intellectus, quae statim lumine intellectus agentis cognoscuntur per species a sensibilibus abstractas.*[27] These principles are the first beginning of all our certain knowledge. We start from them in our search for truth, and, as has been pointed out above, our reasoning appeals to them in the last resort for a verification of its conclusions. On the other hand, our aptitude for the formulation of these principles upon contact with sensibles is, in human souls taken collectively, like an image of the Divine truth in which they participate. In this sense, but in this sense only, may we then say that, to the extent to which the soul knows all things by means of the first principles of knowledge, it sees all in the Divine truth or in the eternal essences of things.[28]

In thus positing the need of an intellectual light as a gift of God, and the impotence of this light, when left to its own resources, we have, in fact, indicated the conditions, both necessary and sufficient, of human knowledge. The conclusion to which we have constantly been led, is that intellectual knowledge takes as its starting point sensible things: *principium nostrae cognitionis est a sensu.* The only problem awaiting solution is to determine exactly the relation between the intellect and the sensible within knowledge. In opposition to Plato who makes our intellect participate in the separate intelligible forms, we find

Democritus who considered as the only cause of our knowledge the presence in our soul of the image of the bodies of which we think. According to this philosopher all action can be reduced to an influx of material atoms, passing from one body into another. He therefore imagines small images starting from the objects and penetrating into the matter of our soul. But we know that the human soul performs an operation in which the body does not share,[29] namely, the operation of the intellect. Now, it is clearly impossible for a corporeal matter to impress its mark upon and to modify an incorporeal substance like the intellect. The mere impress of sensible bodies would therefore not suffice to produce an operation like that of the intellect, and is insufficient to explain it. We must therefore appeal to some nobler principle of operation, without going so far as to appeal to the separate intelligibles of Platonism. This we do by keeping to the *via media* followed by Aristotle, between Democritus and Plato, i.e. by assuming an active intellect capable of extracting the intelligible from the sensible by means of abstraction, the nature of which we shall now proceed to describe in greater detail.

Let us assume that as the result of operations, described above,[30] a sensible body has impressed its image upon the common sense; and let us give the name of "phantasm" to this image. We have therewith not yet reached the full and perfect cause of intellectual knowledge; not even the sufficient cause, but at most the matter upon which this cause works.[31] For what is this phantasm? It is the image of a particular thing: *similitudo rei particularis.*[32] Or, speaking more correctly, the phantasms are the images of particular things, impressed on or preserved in the bodily organs: *similitudines individuorum existentes in organis corporeis.*[33] In short, from the point of view of both the object and of the subject we are so far still in the sphere of the sensible. Colours, for instance, have the same mode of existence as being both in the matter of an individual body and in the visual power of the sensible soul. In either case they subsist in a definite material subject. Hence colours are naturally capable of impressing their likeness upon the organ of sight. But, for the same reason it is evident that neither the sensible as such, nor consequently its phantasms, would ever succeed in penetrating into the intellect. The sensible is the act of a bodily organ; it is therefore capable of receiving the particular as such, i.e. the universal form existing in an individual corporeal matter.[34] The sensible species, the medium transmitting it and the sense itself are realities of the same order, since they belong all three to the class of the particular. The same may be said of the imagination where the phantasm is to be found. But it does not apply to the possible intellect. *Quâ* intellect, it receives universal species; the imagination, on the contrary, contains only particular species. There is therefore a difference of kind between the phantasm and the intelligible species, between the particular and the universal: *sunt alterius generis*.[35] And hence the phantasms, necessarily required to make intellectual knowledge possible, are yet but its matter, and serve so to speak merely as its instrument.[36]

In order to form a precise picture of the process of human intellection, the rôle assigned to the active intellect must be borne in mind. Man is placed in a universe where the intelligible does not occur in a state of purity, and in addition his intellect is such that the intuition of the intelligible is entirely outside his reach. The proper object with which the human intellect has to deal is merely the "quiddity," i.e. the nature existing in a particular corporeal matter. Thus our business is not to know the idea "stone," but the nature of a particular stone, and this nature is the result of the combination of a form and its proper matter. In the same way, the idea "horse" is not an object offered to our knowledge, but we have to know rather the nature of the horse as realised in such and such a particular material horse.[37] In other words, it is easy to distinguish in the objects of human knowledge a universal and intelligible element, associated with a particular and material element. The operation proper to the active intellect consists precisely in separating these two elements so as to present to the possible intellect the intelligible and universal, implicated in the sensible.

For, let us note that the object of knowledge is always proportionate to the faculty of knowing, which apprehends it. Now, three degrees may be observed in the hierarchy of the faculties of knowing. Sensible knowledge is the act of a bodily organ, viz. the sense. Therefore the object of all the senses is the form as existing in a corporeal matter. And, as corporeal matter is the principle of individuation, none of the powers of the sensitive soul are capable of knowing anything but particular objects. At the other end of the scale we find a knowledge which is neither the act of a bodily organ, nor in any way linked to any corporeal matter. Such is angelic knowledge. The object proper to this knowledge is consequently the form, subsisting outside all matter. Even when the angels apprehend particular objects, they perceive them only under immaterial forms, i.e. in themselves or in God. Now the human intellect occupies a position midway between these. It is not the act of a bodily organ, but it belongs to a soul which is the form of a body. Therefore the proper function of this intellect is to apprehend forms, undoubtedly existing individually in a corporeal matter, but also not to apprehend them in so far as they exist in this matter. But to know what exists in an individual matter without taking into account the matter within which the object subsists, means to abstract the form from the individual matter, represented by the phantasm.[38] This abstraction consists, in its simplest aspect, therefore in the intellect considering in each material thing what constitutes it in its proper species, leaving aside all the principles of individuation belonging to the matter. In the same way as we can consider separately the colour of a fruit without taking count of its other properties, so our intellect can consider separately, in the phantasms of the imagination, that which constitutes the essence of a man, of a horse or of a stone, without regard to what distinguishes, within these species, such and such an individual.[39] But the operation of the active intellect is not limited to separating in this way the universal from the particular; its activity is not merely to separate, but also to produce the intelligible. For it must not be thought that, in abstracting the intelligible species from the phantasms, the active intellect does nothing more than transfer bodily into the possible intellect the very form which previously was in the phantasm. To enable the sensible species of a thing to become the intelligible form of the intellect, it has to undergo a real transformation, and the active intellect must be turned upon the phantasms in order to illuminate them. This illumination of the sensible species is the true sense of abstraction. It is this process which abstracts from the species whatever intelligible element they contain,[40] and produces in the possible intellect the knowledge of what the phantasms represent, considering in them only the specific and universal, and setting aside the material and particular.[41]

The extreme difficulty of forming a clear conception of what St. Thomas here means, arises from the unconscious tendency to picture this operation to ourselves and to form a concrete image of it. But, there is no psycho-physiological mechanism behind this description of intellection as offered to us by the philosopher; we move in a different order, namely, that of the metaphysician, and the solution of the problem of knowledge here indicated by St. Thomas, is above all a solution of principle. We can understand it only by constantly reverting to the very data of the problem under discussion.

The question is, whether there exists in the universe an intellectual being who can attain only to the intelligible, when it is combined with the sensible. We know that the hypothesis is *a priori* probable, because it conforms to the principle of continuity governing the universe. The problem remains whether it is possible, and of what order the relations are which such an operation establishes between the intelligible in act as the superior term of the operation, and matter as its lower term; it is necessary for the solution of the problem to find the intermediate terms bridging the distance.

A first intermediate term is supplied by the sensible itself. It is, as was said, the combination of a form; and therefore of an intelligible, with a determinate matter. The sensible consequently contains the intelligible in potency, and some of it forms part of the metaphysical chemistry to which it owes its being, though determined in act to a particular mode of being. Passing now to man, we find in him an intelligible in act, namely his intellect, i.e. that part of himself which is the prolongation beyond the lowest orders of angelic being. But we also know that what this intelligible lacks, is determination; it is a light by which it is possible to see, but in which nothing can be seen. To give us sight, it must fall upon the objects; but for it to fall on objects, objects must exist which have a certain kinship with it. The intelligible in act, namely our intellect, will consequently die of inanition, unless it finds its own nourishment in the world where we are placed. But, it can find it only in the sensible: consequently the solution of the thomistic problem of knowledge is possible, provided that the sensible, determinate in act and intelligible in potency, is able to communicate its determination to our intellect, which is intelligible in act, but determinate in potency only.

In order to solve it, St. Thomas admits the existence in the same individual substance—not in two distinct subjects like the Averroists—of a possible intellect and an active intellect. If the assertion of the co-existence of these two powers of the soul in one subject is not contradictory, it may be said that the solution of the problem is reached, since such an hypothesis would meet all the requirements of the data. Now, this assertion is not contradictory. It is contradictory to say that the same thing is, at the same time and under the same aspects, both in act and in potency; but it is not contradictory to assert that is in potency under one aspect, and in act under another; this is even the normal condition of all finite and created beings. This is also the condition of the rational soul in reference to the sensibles and to the phantasms representing them. The soul is intelligibility in act, but it lacks determination; the phantasms have determination in act, but lack intelligibility; the soul will therefore confer intelligibility on them, wherefore it will be active intellect, and in turn receive determination, whereby it will be possible intellect. For the operation to be carried into effect, a single condition must be met, which is a metaphysical condition resting on the requirements of order: viz. the action of the active intellect rendering the phantasms intelligible must precede the reception into the possible intellect of this intelligible: *actio intellectus agentis in phantasmatibus praecedit receptionem intellectus possibilis*. As the sensible as such cannot penetrate into the intelligible as such, our intellect, desiring to receive the determination of the sensible, first makes the action of the sensible possible, by raising it to its own dignity. On this condition only—and this was the only problem to be solved—*parvum lumen intelligibile quod est in nobis connaturale sufficit ad nostrum intelligere.*[42]

Such is the mode by which the human soul knows bodies. This conclusion is true not only in so far as the acquisition of knowledge is concerned, but it holds equally for the use made of knowledge after it has been acquired. Any lesion of the common sense, of the imagination or memory suppresses at once both the phantasms and the knowledge of the corresponding intelligibles.[43] And lastly the conclusion enables us to understand how the human soul knows itself, as well as objects which it discovers beyond itself. For the intellect knows itself in exactly the same way as it knows other things. We know now the conditions of this action. The human intellect as it works in this earthly life, can know only by turning to the material and sensible; it knows itself therefore only to the extent that it passes from potency to act, under the influence of the species which the light of the active intellect abstracts from sensible things.[44] We see therefore both the multiplicity of operations required for such knowledge and the order in which they present themselves. Our soul attains to the knowledge of itself only in the measure in which it apprehends other things: *ex objecto enim cognoscit suam operationem, per quam devenit ad cognitionem sui ipsius.*[45] It knows first its object, then its operation, and lastly its own nature. Sometimes it perceives simply that it is an intellectual soul, since it apprehends the operation of its intellect. Sometimes it rises to a universal knowledge of what the nature of the human soul is by means of a systematic reflexion on the conditions required for such an operation.[46] But in either case the order of procedure of thought remains the same. *Est autem alius intellectus, scilicet humanus, qui nec est suum intelligere, nec sui intelligere est objectum primum ipsa ejus essentia, sed aliquid extrinsecum, scilicet natura materialis rei. Et ideo, id quod primo cognoscitur ab intellectu humano, est hujusmodi objectum; et secundario cognoscitur ipse actus quo cognoscitur objectum; et per actum cognoscitur ipse intellectus, cujus est perfectio, ipsum intelligere.*[47]

In order to determine the mode by which the human soul knows what it discovers beyond itself, all that is needed is to apply the results of the preceding analysis. Whether concerned with wholly immaterial substances, as the angels, or with the infinite and uncreated essence which we call God, the direct apprehension of the intelligible as such remains entirely beyond our reach.[48] We can claim therefore no more than the power to form a certain very imperfect representation of the intelligible by taking as our starting point nature or sensible quiddity. Therefore the first object apprehended by the soul is not God, any more than the human soul itself. It must begin, on the contrary, with the consideration of material bodies and it will never advance in the knowledge of the intelligible beyond the point up to which the sensible, as its point of departure, allows it to go. Here we find, therefore, the final justification of the method adopted to prove the existence of God and to analyse His essence. *Cognitio Dei quae ex mente humana accipi potest, non excedit illud genus cognitionis quod ex sensibilibus sumitur, cum et ipsa de seipsa cognoscat quid est, per hoc quod naturas sensibilium intelligit.*[49] This is a truth which cannot be sufficiently emphasised, since it governs the whole of philosophy. Failing to grasp it, we assign objects to the human intellect which it is naturally incapable of apprehending, and we misjudge the proper value and limits of our understanding. The most dangerous form of this illusion is the belief that reality is the better known to us, in porportion as it is in itself more intelligible and knowable. We know now, on the contrary, that our intellect is constructed for extracting the intelligible from the sensible; and we cannot without a sophism infer from the fact that it is capable of disentangling from individuating matter the universal form contained in it, that it is *a fortiori* capable of apprehending the pure intelligible. The intellect may be compared to an eye that would be both capable of receiving colours and also sufficiently luminous itself to render these same colours visible, Such an eye, able by hypothesis to perceive a light of average strength, would be quite unable to perceive one of greater intensity. There are, in fact, animals which are said to possess eyes which give out a light sufficient for illuminating the objects they see. Now, these animals see better at night than in daylight; their eyes are weak, a little light illuminates them, but much light blinds them. The same applies to our intellect. Faced by the supreme intelligibles, it remains blinded and bewildered like the owl which does not see the sun before its eyes. We must therefore be content with the little intellectual light which is natural to us and sufficient for the needs of our knowledge, but we must beware of asking of it more than it can give. The incorporeal is known to us only by comparison with the corporeal, and whenever we lay claim to some knowledge of intelligibles, we must needs turn to the phantasms impressed on us by bodies, though there are no phantasms of intelligible realities.[50] By doing so, we shall act as it behoves the lowly intellects that we are, and we shall accept the limits set to our faculty of knowing by the place we occupy in the hierarchy of created beings.[51]

NOTES TO CHAPTER XII.

1. *Sum. theol.*, I. 79, 1, ad 3^m; *De Verit.*, 17, 1, ad *Resp.*
2. *Sum. theol.*, I. 79, 2, ad *Resp.*; *Cont. Gent.*, II. 59, ad *Per demonstrationem*.
3. *De anima*, qu. un. art. 4, ad *Resp.*; *Sum. theol.*, I. 79, 3, ad *Resp.*
4. *Sum. theol.*, I. 79, 3, ad 1^m.
5. *De anima, ibid.* Following St. Thomas we shall keep the term "passive intellect" to describe the faculty of the human composite being which Aristotle indicates by that name, and the term "possible intellect" to describe that immaterial and immortal faculty which St. Thomas, in distinction to Aristotle, attributes to us.*
6. Cf. Horten, *op. cit.* and esp. Mandonnet, *op. cit.*, p. 172–174; as regards the Averroist doctrine of Siger of Brabant, p. 175ff.
7. *De anima*, qu. un. art. 5, ad *Resp.*
8. *Cont. Gent.*, II. 76, ad *In natura*; and *Sum. theol.*, I. 79, 4 and 5, ad *Resp.*
9. *Cont. Gent.*, II. 74; *De Verit.*, qu. X., art. 2, ad *Resp.*; *Sum. theol.*, I. 79, 6, ad *Resp.*
10. *Sum. theol.*, I. 79, 7, ad *Resp.*
11. *Sum. theol.*, I. 79, 8, ad *Resp.*

*Censor's note: This is not St. Thomas' opinion; cf. e.g., *Sum. theol.*, I. 79, 2 ad 2^m. The author proceeds to use "passive" where "possible" should be used in the text.

12. *De Div. Nom.*, c. VII.
13. *De Verit.*, qu. 15, art. 1, ad *Resp.*
14. On the thomistic theory of knowledge see esp. P. Rousselot, *Métaphysique thomiste et critique de la connaissance*, Rev. néoscolast., 1910, p. 476–509; Le Guichaoua, *A propos des rapports entre la métaphysique thomiste et la théorie de la connaissance, ibid.*, 1913, p. 88–101; Domenico Lanna, *La teoria della conoscenza in S. Tommaso d'Aquino*, Firenze, 1913, with bibliography; M. Baumgartner, *Zur thomistischen Lehre von den ersten Prinzipien der Erkenntnis*, Festg. f. G. v. Hertling, Freiburg i. B., 1913, p. 1–16; of the same, *Zum thomistischen Wahrheitsbegriff*, Festg. f. Cl. Baeumker, Münster, 1913, p. 241–260; A.-D. Sertillanges, *L'être et la connaissance dans la philosophie de saint Thomas d'Aquin*, Mélanges thomistes (Biblioth. thom.), III., Le Saulchoir, Kain, 1923, p. 175–197.
15. *Meno*, 82b ff.
16. *Sum. theol.*, I. 84, 3, ad *Resp.*
17. *Sum. theol.*, I. 89, 1, ad *Resp.*
18. *Sum. theol.*, I. 55, 2, ad *Resp.*
19. *Confess.*, XII., c. 25.
20. *Sum. theol.*, I. 84, 5, ad *Resp.*; St. Thomas perfectly understood the differences separating the theory of Aristotle from that of St. Augustine. Cf. esp. the remarkable passage: *De spirit. creat.*, art. 10, ad 8[m]; and *De Verit.*, XI., 1.
21. *Sum. theol.*, I. 84, 5, ad *Resp.*
22. *Sum. theol.*, IaIIae, 109, 1, ad *Resp.* But since its proper object is the intelligible, the intellect can know the particular, whence it extracts the intelligible, only indirectly and by means of a reflexion, the mechanism of which is analysed in *De Verit.*, qu. X., art. 4, ad *Resp.*
23. *De Verit.*, XI., 1, ad *Resp.*
24. *Cont. Gent.*, IV. 11, ad *Rursus considerandum est.*
25. *Ibid.*
26. *Sum. theol.*, IaIIae, 51, 1, ad *Resp.*
27. *De Verit.*, XI. 1, ad *Resp.* The interpretation of the thomistic teaching concerning the principles of knowledge, as given by J. Durantel, *Le retour à Dieu*, pp. 46, 156–157, 159, etc., is in formal contradiction with the texts of St. Thomas, *Cont. Gent.*, II. 78, *ad Amplius Aristoteles; De anima*, qu. un. art. 5, ad *Resp.*: "Quidam vero crediderunt. . . ." The remark on p. 161, note 3, suggests that the author does not admit that middle term between sensualism and Platonism, viz. that innate intellect without innate principles which constitutes precisely the doctrine of St. Thomas; and since "la théorie des principes premiers est le point central et caractéristique de la doctrine de la connaissance chez saint Thomas" (p. 156), the misunderstanding of this point leads to other misconceptions. As a result he considers the principles as Kantian categories which have their

origin in God (p. 162, agrees with p. 159: "car il faut. ...").
The cause is the misunderstanding of the thomistic expression
"determination," and its interpretation as the intrinsic development of a virtual content, instead of taking it, in the proper
sense of "determine," as the introduction of a content received
by the intellect *ab extra* and intellectualised by it.

28. *Cont. Gent.*, III. 47, ad *Quamvis autem*; esp. *Compend. theol.*, c.
    129; *De Verit.*, X. 6, ad *Resp., fin.*
29. See above, p. 216.
30. See above, p. 227.
31. *Sum. theol.*, I. 84, 6, ad *Resp.*
32. *Sum. theol.*, I. 84, 7, ad 2^m.
33. *Sum. theol.*, I. 85, 1, ad 3^m.
34. *Sum. theol.*, I. 85, 1, ad *Resp.*
35. *De anima*, qu. 4, ad 5^m.
36. *De Verit.*, X. 6, ad 7.
37. *Sum. theol.*, I. 84, 7, ad *Resp.* "In mente enim accipiente
    scientiam a rebus, formae existunt per quamdam actionem
    rerum in animam; omnis autem actio est per formam; unde
    formae quae sunt in mente nostra, primo et principaliter
    respiciunt res extra animam existentes quantum ad formas
    earum." *De Verit.*, X. 4, ad *Resp.*
38. *Sum. theol.*, I. 85, 1, ad *Resp.*
39. *Ibid.*, ad 1^m.
40. *Ibid.*, ad 4^m.
41. *Ibid.*, ad 3^m; *De anima*, qu. 4, ad *Resp.*; cf. *Comp. theol.*, c.
    81–83.
42. *Cont. Gent.*, II. 77.
43. *Sum. theol.*, I. 84, 7, ad *Resp.*
44. *Sum. theol.*, I. 87, 1, ad *Resp.*
45. *De anima*, III., ad 4^m, cf. *De Verit.*, X. 8, ad *Resp.*
46. *Sum. theol.*, I. 87, 1, ad *Resp.*
47. *Sum. theol.*, I. 87, 3, ad *Resp.*; cf. B. Romeyer, *Notre science de
    l'esprit humain d'après saint Thomas d'Aquin*, Arch. de phil., I. 1,
    p. 51–55, Paris, 1923.
48. *Sum. theol.*, I. 88, 3, ad *Resp.*
49. *Cont. Gent.*, III. 47, ad *Ex his ergo.*
50. *Sum. theol.*, I. 84, 7, ad 3^m.
51. Besides the works indicated, bearing directly upon the thomistic
    theory of knowledge, there are a number of classical works on
    the relation of the thomistic theory to the augustinian school in
    general. This is a problem which it is unwise to attack until after
    the direct study of the thomistic and augustinian texts, but to
    which one is inevitably led later, and which it is well worth
    while, historically and philosophically, to consider. See: J.
    Kleutgen, *Die Philosophie der Vorzeit*, Münster, 1860, 2 Vols.
    (French transl. *La philosophie scolastique*, 4 Vols., Paris, 1868–
    1890; Italian transl. in 2 Vols., 1866, Roma); Lepidi, *Examen*

philosophico-theologicum de Ontologismo, Lovanii, 1874; of the same, *De Ente generalissimo, prout est aliquid psychologicum, logicum, ontologicum*; Divus Thomas, 1881, no. 11; Zigliara, *Della luce intellettuale e dell' ontologismo secondo le dottrine dei SS. Agostino, Bonaventura e Tommaso*, Roma, 1874 (or also in Vol. II of *Oeuvres complètes*, trad. Murgue, Lyon, 1881, p. 273ff.). A general introduction to the question, sometimes contestable but always suggestive, may be found in *De humanae cognitionis ratione anecdota quaedam S. D. Sancti Bonaventurae*, ad Claras Aquas (Quaracchi), 1883, esp. *Dissertatio praevia*, p. 1–47.

CHAPTER XIII.
KNOWLEDGE AND TRUTH

WE have described the cognitive operations of the rational soul and have thereby in some manner indicated the place occupied by man in the hierarchy of created beings. We must stop at this point for a moment in order to realise by a special effort of reflexion the nature of human knowledge, as conceived by St. Thomas, and his notion of truth.

This is an undertaking which, though necessary, is beset with difficulties. Five centuries of history divide us from St. Thomas, full of new systems or new formulations of old problems through which we see Thomism, as it were, refracted. The—in itself very legitimate—pre-occupation to find in thomistic philosophy the answer to questions which were formulated only subsequently to it, is apt to lead us imperceptibly to alter the sense of the problem as St. Thomas himself posited it, to coax his text in the direction requisite for adapting it to new problems, and sometimes even to press it for an answer with so little discretion, in order to make his word bear the desired interpretation, as to endanger the equilibrium of his whole system. These are proceedings as little satisfactory to philosophy as they are to history. If we wish to find a thomistic solution to the problem of knowledge the first requisite is that it should be St. Thomas'. In order to ensure that it be his, and not Descartes' or Kant's answer, we must come to it, not with a Cartesian or Kantian problem—for problems raised by philosophers are part and parcel of the answers which they give to them—, but with the question, what would have been the form of the problem of knowledge, if by an organic development of its own principles, thomistic philosophy had ever been led to raise it.

Such a task lies definitely outside the sphere of the historian; yet he too has his share to contribute to it.

The setting out of a genuinely thomistic theory of knowledge presupposes that we know exactly what the two fundamental ideas "knowledge" and "truth" meant for St. Thomas. Only a precise determination of their sense allows us to conceive the part attributed to each of the elements involved in an act of knowing, and no theory of knowledge with any pretension to being thomistic, couild rightly claim to be constructed except in terms of such a definition. It would be a long, and in practice perhaps endless, undertaking to exhaust this problem and to treat it in all its details. But we can at least establish the principles on which its solution depends.[1]

The preoccupation to know what knowledge is, is by no means spontaneous in man. Almost all men live and die without worrying about philosophy, and yet use, all their lives, their faculties of knowing, without ever dreaming of being astonished at doing so. Yet we cannot examine the nature of the beings which are given to us by experience, without observing that the fact of knowing is not necessarily involved in the mere fact of existing. A few examples will explain what is meant. There are in the first place artificial beings, made by the hand of man, which are inert and incapable of spontaneous movement. If a bed, for instance, falls to the ground, it is not quâ bed, but quâ wood that it falls; or if, buried in the ground, it were to germinate, it is again not quâ bed, but quâ tree that it germinates. Next there are natural beings, endowed with an internal principle of movement, like lightness or heaviness, implied by their form, but which move only by virtue of this internal principle without the slightest adaptation of their movements to the conditions of the external world. Left to itself, a stone falls or a flame rises straight up, the one drawn downwards, the other upwards. There are many much more complex natural movements, like those of a plant animated by its vegetative life, spreading in space the growth of its roots, branches and leaves, but, here again, we are dealing with a motive force which is regulated and conditioned from within, without the external world doing anything more than permitting or preventing its development. An oak sprouts, if it can sprout, just as a stone falls, when it is dropped; when its growth is completed, it dies, having never been anything but an oak, i.e. all it could ever have become.

As soon as we enter the animal kingdom, the aspect of things changes completely. Directed as before by internal principles, the movements of animals are yet not wholly explicable by them alone. A dog can do other things than merely fall by his own weight or grow by his own vital principle; he can change his position in space in search of a prey, he can rush to seize it, run to bring it back, all of them actions which suppose that the prey in question, existing in the first place for its own sake, exists at the same time also for the dog. The goat does not exist for the shrub that it nibbles, but the shrub exists for the goat, in whatever other manner it may exist besides. This existence of one being for another, which begins with the animal world and develops with man, is precisely what is called "knowledge." That there is knowledge in the world is a fact. The question now is, under what conditions knowledge in general is possible.

We will state the problem in all strictness. What does it mean; a living being becomes aware of another being? Considered in itself, this being which knows, is in the first place its own essence, i.e. falls under a genus, is defined by its species and is individualised by all the properties which distinguish it from analogous beings. As such, it is what it is and nothing more: a dog, a goat, a man. But, in so far as it knows, we find it becoming yet something else beside itself, since the prey pursued by the dog, the shrub nibbled by the goat, the book read by the man, exist henceforth in some manner in the dog, in the goat and in the man. Since these objects are now in the subjects which know them, the subjects have necessarily in some manner become these objects. To know is, then, to be in a new and fuller manner than the previous being was, because it means essentially to cause to enter into that being, which at first was for its own self, another thing which previously existed for its (the thing's) self.[2] We express this fact by saying that to know something is a manner of becoming it.[3]

We have here to make a first observation, in order to bring out the full significance of this phenomenon. Whatever may be the ultimate interpretation of these facts, it is clear that we are here in presence of two kinds of being which are strictly different. There is a considerable gap between that which is never anything but itself, and that whose being is on the contrary capable of dilating and taking up within itself the being of other things; this is precisely the gap which separates the material from the spiritual. Whatever in a being is body or matter, has the effect of restricting and diminishing it; whatever spiritual element it contains, results, on the contrary, in enlarging and amplifying it. At the lowest rung of the ladder, there is the mineral which is only whatever it is; at the highest rung, or rather beyond every conceivable degree, there is God who is all; between the two, there is man who in a certain manner is capable of becoming all by means of his senses and his intelligence.[4] The problem of human knowledge is consequently at bottom that of the mode of existence of a spiritual being which yet is not pure spirituality.

A second observation will confirm this: there are not two conceivable solutions of the problem of knowledge, one for the intelligence and the other for the senses. Sensible knowledge and intellectual knowledge may be and are in fact two different kinds or two different phases of one and the same operation, but they must inevitably be accounted for by the same explanation. If we are to make an ideal division in the universal order, it would have to be made between the animal and the plant, not between animal and man. However restricted its range, the animal displays already an increase of being by reason of its sensations; it emerges therefore clearly, however imperfectly, from pure materiality.[5] Our task is then to describe the cognitive operations in such a manner as to reduce to the same principle and to judge by the same rules both intelligence and sensation.

Starting from this point, the main theses of thomistic epistemology begin to take shape. So far we have only considered what is required on the part of the knowing subject, for knowledge in general to be possible; but it is a matter of course, that corresponding requirements have to be met on the part of the object known. We have no business to describe just any universe and then to ask what our knowledge may be, in order that this universe may become knowable to us; but we must take the converse course: given the fact that there is knowledge, what must things be like to give us an explanation of the fact that we know them.

A first condition of the possibility of such knowledge is that things too may participate in some degree in immateriality. If we assumed a purely material universe, deprived of every intelligible element, it would, by definition, lack transparancy to the mind. Since this is not the case, the reason must be that, apart from the intellect which can in some way become a thing, there must be, in the thing, some aspect under which it is capable of becoming, in some way, mind. The element of an object which can be assimilated by thought, is precisely its form. To say that the knowing subject becomes the object, is consequently the same thing as to say that the form of the knowing subject enriches itself with the form of the object known.[6] We are, from the metaphysical point of view, familiar with the possibility of this close kinship between thought and thing, since the universe, down to its least parts, is a participation in the supreme intelligible which is God; we observe in addition, that this kinship is necessarily required for certain facts such as ideas and sensations to be even conceivable. It is not enough to provide for a point of contact between thought and thing; what is also required is that the thing be such as to be capable of making contact.

Once this twofold assimilation is seen to be possible, what becomes of the notion of knowledge? The same fact presents itself to us under two different aspects, according as we envisage it from the point of view of the contribution of the object known, or from that of the contribution of the knowing subject. To describe knowledge by adopting one of these complementary standpoints and then to use expressions as if we were envisaging it from the other, leads to inextricable difficulties.

Let us first consider it from the point of view of the object, for this is easier to grasp. If we are to remain faithful to the principles just stated, we must admit that the being of the object itself is imposed upon the being of the subject which knows it. Since, in fact, to know a thing is to become it, it follows necessarily that at the moment when the act of knowing takes place, a new being is formed, wider than the former, precisely because it contains in a richer unity the being which knows, such as it was before it knew, and that which it has become, enriched as it is by the object known. This synthesis involves, consequently, the fusion of two beings, which coincide at the moment of their union. Sense differs from the sensible and intellect differs from the intelligible; but neither the sense differs from the sensed, nor the intellect from the object actually grasped by it; literally the sense, taken in its act of sensing, fuses with the sensible taken in the act by which it is sensed, and the intellect taken as the act of knowing fuses with the intelligible taken in the act by which it is known: "*sensibile in actu est sensus in actu, et intelligibile in actu est intellectus in actu.*"[7]

The direct corollary of this fact is the thomistic thesis that every act of knowledge presupposes within the knowing subject the presence of the object known. The passages in support of this are numerous and explicit and their meaning can all the less be called in question as they do no more than formulate differently the fundamental thesis which asserts in the act of knowing the coincidence of the sense or of the intellect

with its object. We have, however, to meet a complication which requires the introduction of a new datum
into our analysis, viz. the sensible "species" in the
knowledge by sense, the intelligible "species" in the
knowledge by the intellect.

We start with the fact that the knowing of an object
is the actual presence of the object in the thought, though
the object must not invade it to the extent that the
thought ceases to be thought. In fact, things happen as
described; for if they happened otherwise, we should not
even be there to raise the question of a theory of knowledge. The sense of sight perceives the form of a stone,
but does not become petrified; the intellect conceives
the idea "wood," but does not turn to wood; it remains,
on the contrary, what it was before and preserves even
its dispositions to become yet other things. If this new
factor is borne in mind, the problem of knowledge
presents itself under a more complex form, viz. on what
conditions can the knowing subject become the object
known, without ceasing to be itself?

To meet this difficulty, St. Thomas introduces the
notion of the "species." Whatever order of knowledge
may be considered, there always is a subject, an object
and an intermediary between object and subject. This
holds even in the case of the most immediate forms of
sensation, such as touch and taste,[8] and becomes more
evident in proportion as we ascend in the scale of knowledge. To solve the problem, all that is needed is,
therefore, to conceive an intermediary of such a kind
that, without ceasing to be the object, it should yet be
capable of becoming the subject. Given this condition,
the thing would not invade thought, as in fact, it
does not, and would yet be the thing known, by the
presence of its "species" within the thought that
knows it.

In order to conceive of such an intermediary which
the very fact of knowledge forces us to assume, we have
to abandon the attempt to picture it to ourselves in
a concrete image. We can, at best, imagine sensible
species analogous to the sensible qualities, which convey

them through space; but, when dealing with an intelligible form, its protrusion towards our thought cannot but be equally of an intelligible nature. We must not even speak here of "protrusion," for we have left the range of physical facts and are in the sphere of metaphysics. The operation which we are analysing takes place wholly outside space, and the intelligible part of a thing, which is in space, thanks to its matter, need cross no space to reach the intellection of our thought, which is in space only by reason of our body. There is no more fatal obstacle to our understanding of the problem than to imagine it concretely; all that is needed is to grant to thought and to things what they require in order to be able to perform what in fact they do perform, viz. something by means of which the object can coincide with our intellect, without the object destroying itself or our intellect ceasing to be what it is.

The "species" to which this function is assigned, must in the first place be conceived as being nothing but the intelligible or sensible part of the object itself under another mode of existence. In practice it is almost impossible to speak of it except in terms as if the species were an image, equivalent or substitute of the object, and St. Thomas himself does not hestitate to do so. But it is of capital importance to grasp that the species is not one thing and the object another; the species is the object itself "per modum speciei," that is to say, the object considered in its action and its efficacy exercised upon a subject. Only on this condition is it possible to assert that it is not the species of the object, but the object by means of its species, that is present in thought; and, since the active and determining principle of an object is its form, it is the form of the object which becomes through its species, the intellect which knows it. The whole objectivity of human knowledge rests ultimately upon this fact that what is introduced in our thought in place of the thing, is not a superadded intermediary or a distinct substitute, but the sensible species of the thing itself which, rendered intelligible by the active intellect, comes to be the form of our possible intellect.[9] A last consequence of this same principle will complete the evidence of the continuity of the species with the form of the object.

We said that it is necessary to introduce the notion of a "species" into the analysis of knowledge, in order to safeguard the individuality of subject and object. Let us now assume that, to secure still better their individuality and distinctness, we grant to the species, linking subject and object, an independent existence. The immediate result of this would be that the object of knowledge would cease to be the intelligible form of the thing known itself, and would become the intelligible species substituted for it. In other words, if the species were things distinct from their forms, our knowledge would bear on the species instead of on the objects.[10] This consequence would be unacceptable for two reasons: first, because, in that case, our knowledge would cease to bear upon external realities and would attain only to their representations in our consciousness; therewith we would fall into the platonic error which holds that our knowledge is a knowledge of ideas, instead of being a knowledge of things; and secondly, because there would be no longer any conceivable criterion of certitude, each person remaining the sole judge of truth, in so far as all that would matter would be what part of it may be grasped by his thought, instead of what part of it exists independently of his thought. Seeing, however, that there exists a demonstrable knowledge concerning things, and not mere opinions, the objects of knowledge must necessarily be the things in themselves, and not merely individual images distinct from them. The species then is not what thought knows of the thing, but that by which thought knows the thing itself,[11] without the interposition of any intermediary, between thought and its object in the act of knowing.

Let us now shift our position so as to envisage the same act from the point of view of thought: under what aspect does it appear to us then?

The first thing that strikes the attention is that the

act of knowing is an act immanent to the subject. What is meant by that is that it takes place within the subject for his exclusive benefit. Grasping this, we shall see the unity of the intellect and of its object, on which so much stress has been laid, presenting itself from a new and clearly marked point of view. So far relying on the fact that knowing was an act common to both the knower and the known, we were able to speak indifferently of the thought becoming the object of its knowledge and of the object becoming the knowledge which the thought acquired of it. Now we see clearly that the thing, by becoming an object of intelligence in thought, becomes nothing either more than or different from what it had been before. "To be known" has, for an object unaware of it, no significance; as far as it is concerned, it is as if nothing had happened; the being of the knowing subject alone has gained something in the process.

There is something further. As the act of knowing is entirely immanent to thought, however much we may say that the thought becomes the object, the fact remains that the object has to conform to the manner of being of the thought, to enable the thought itself to become it. Thought, consequently, retains its being, having, in addition, that of the object, only because the object assumes in thought a being of the same order as that of thought. "*Omne quod recipitur in altero, recipitur secundum modum recipientis.*" For iron or a tree to be in thought quâ known, they must be there without their matter, by their form alone, i.e. according to a mode of universal and spiritual being. This mode of being assumed by things in the thought that assimilates them, has been called "intentional" being.[12] This means, on further thought, a profound transformation of the concrete datum by the mind that receives it. What experience supplies, is a particular man, both form and matter; what the sense and then later the intellect receive of him, is a form more and more relieved of all marks of materiality, namely, his intelligible form.

Nor is this all: the act of knowing frees itself still

further and more definitely from the object by producing the interior "verbum" or concept. The term "concept" is, in fact, given to the representation of the perceived object, as conceived by the intellect, i.e. created within itself, and expressed by a word.[13] The sensible, and then further the intelligible species by which (not which) we know, is still the form itself of the object; but the concept is the representation of the object which the intellect produces under the action of the species. Here then we are dealing with a real substitute of the object, which is no longer the substance of the knowing intellect, nor the thing known itself, but an "intentional being," the subsistence of which is impossible outside thought,[14] expressed by a word and fixed by a definition.

We are now in a position better to understand the complex relation linking our knowledge with its object. Between a thing taken in its proper nature, and the concept formed of it by the intellect there are two resemblances which require to be kept distinct. There is in the first place, the resemblance to the thing of the thing within us, that is, the resemblance of the form which is the species: this is a direct resemblance, formed by the object of itself and impressed upon us by it, as indistinguishable from it, as is the action of the seal upon the wax from the seal itself; a resemblance consequently indistinguishable from its original because it is not a representation of it, but its impress and, so to speak, its prolongation. Secondly, there is the resemblance to the thing which we in ourselves conceive of the thing: this, instead of being its very form, is now only a representation of the thing.[15] The next question is, what guarantee we have of the faithfulness of the resemblance of this concept to its object.

It is impossible to doubt that the concept of a thing, this first product of the intellect, is something actually distinct from the thing itself. Their dissociation takes place almost experientially before our very eyes, since the concept "man" for example, exists only in the intellect that conceives it, while the men themselves continue to exist in reality, even after ceasing to be known. It is no less clear that the concept is not, either, the species itself directly induced in us by the object, because, as we have seen, the species is the cause of the concept in us.[16] But in the absence of an identity between the knowledge and the object known, or even between the intelligible species and the concept, we can at least assert the identity between the object and subject which latter produces in himself the resemblance to the object. The concept is certainly not the thing, but the intellect which conceives the concept, is, on its part, actually the thing of which it forms the concept. The intellect which produces the concept "book" does so only because it has first become the form of a book, thanks to the species which is nothing but this form itself; and so the concept necessarily resembles the object. Just as at the beginning of the operation the intellect formed a unity with the object, because it formed a unity with its species, so also at the end of the operation, the intellect contains a faithful representation of the object, only because before producing it, it had, in some manner, become the object itself. The concept of an object resembles it, because the intellect had to be fertilised by the species of the object itself to be able to produce the concept.[17]

The operation by which the intellect engenders the concept, is a natural operation; in performing it, it performs therefore simply what it is natural to it to perform, and the process being as described, we may conclude that its result is necessarily infallible. An intellect expressing the intelligible merely because the object has first impressed it upon the intellect, cannot err in its expression. If we describe by the term "quiddity" the essence of this thing thus known, we can say that the quiddity is the proper object of the intellect and that the intellect can never be deceived in apprehending it. If we abstract, for the sake of simplicity, from accidental causes of error which may falsify experience, we observe that this is indeed the case. *De jure* and almost always *de facto*, a human intellect confronted with an oak, forms the concept "tree," and confronted with Socrates or Plato, forms the concept "man." The intellect conceives the essences as infallibly as hearing perceives sound or sight perceives colour.[18]

Thus the concept is necessarily in conformity with its object and yet its presence in the intellect does not as such constitute the presence of a truth. All that can be said for the moment is that it is there, and that the intellect itself which has formed it, does not know how it has done so. This concept is not born of a reflection of the intellect, examining the intelligible species and endeavouring then to manufacture an image resembling it, for the unity of the intellect and of the species, as it guarantees the objectivity of knowledge, also renders the assumption of any such dissociation impossible.[19] The most obvious consequence of this continuity in the operation is that, if the concept is conforming to the object, the intellect which produces this concept, is unaware of the conformity. This simple and direct apprehension of reality by the intellect presupposes therefore no conscious or original activity on its part. It is the operation of a mind that acts according to its nature and under the impetus of an external reality rather than the free activity of a mind that dominates and enriches this reality. For this conformity of the concept to the object to become known and to assume the form of a truth within consciousness, it is required that the intellect should add something of its own to the external reality which it has assimilated. This addition begins at the moment when, not content with apprehending a thing, the intellect forms a judgment upon it and says: "this is a man" or "this is a tree." In this case, the intellect really adds something new, an affirmation which exists only in it, not in the things, but offers the possibility of asking whether or not it corresponds to reality. The formula which defines truth as an adequation of the thing and of the intellect, *adaequatio rei et intellectus*, expresses simply the fact that the problem of truth has no sense until after the intellect has made the separation between itself and its object. Up to that point,

while it forms but one thing with the thing ("species")
or acts under its direct pressure ("conceptus"), to be
in conformity with the thing would mean simply
to be in conformity with itself. But now comes
the judgment, as an original act of the intellect which
is posited as such in thought: now we are dealing
indeed with two distinct realities confronting each other,
and consequently there is room for raising the question
of their relation. Truth is simply the accord between
the intellect which judges, and the thing. Error, on the
contrary, is nothing but the discord between them. [20]

Taking this central point to start from, the main
theses of the thomistic epistemology will be seen to join
up and the texts which commentators are in the habit of
setting in opposition to each other, will be found to
harmonise. In the first place, it is true that the first
object known is indeed the thing itself: *id quod intelligitur
primo est res*, provided that it is present in thought in
the form of its species: *res, cujus species intelligibilis est
similitudo*. [21] By saying, in this precise meaning, that
the object is the first thing known, the intention is not to
oppose the knowledge of the object to the concept
expressing it, but to the knowledge of the intellectual
act which conceives and of the subject performing that
act. The formula "id quod intelligitur primo est res"
means therefore: thought forms first of all the concept
of the object, then, reflecting on this object, it becomes
aware of the act by which it has apprehended it, and
finally, aware of the existence of its acts, it discovers
itself as their common source: *et ideo id, quod primo cognoscitur ab intellectu humano, est hujusmodi objectum; et secundario cognoscitur ipse actus, quo cognoscitur objectum; et per
actum cognoscitur ipse intellectus, cujus est perfectio ipsum
intelligere*. [22]

Secondly, it is equally true to say that the first object
of the intellect is not the thing, but its concept. This
is true, provided it is taken in the only sense that is
given to this proposition in the thought of St. Thomas.
What is known in the proper and absolute sense of that
term, is not the thing considered in its own subjective

existence, since it remains what it is, whether I know it or not; it is simply and solely that same thing insofar as it has become mine by the co-incidence of my intellect and its species, whence springs the act of the concept. To assert that the immediate object of thought is the concept does not therefore mean to deny that it is the thing, but on the contrary, to affirm that it is indeed the thing, inasmuch as its intelligibility constitutes wholly that of the concept.[23]

Once these directive lines of thomistic teaching are grasped, it becomes possible to conceive a critique of knowledge which would follow them closely, which we perhaps already possess more fully than we are wont to imagine.

We should have to place in the foreground of such a teaching a criticism of the Critique whose business it would be to examine whether the fundamental argument of idealism does not involve a false statement of the problem of knowledge. There is, indeed, no bridge for thought to pass into things and idealism is consequently true, if initially the presupposition is accepted that things exist by themselves and the intellect by itself, i.e. that their contact is impossible. It is contradictory to enquire whether our ideas are or are not conforming to things, if things are known to us only by their ideas; the argument is irrefutable and, here again, idealism is true, provided it is more than a mere "petitio principii." St. Thomas, it has been said, has never called attention to this difficulty. But perhaps he has not done so simply because he had previously solved another which idealism in its turn has never raised, the solution of which renders the very formulation of the idealist problem impossible. St. Thomas has, indeed, not asked himself the question under what conditions mathematical physics are possible; but he had, on the other hand, asked himself the question under what conditions we can have the general idea of any physical body whatever; and the very possibility of our knowledge in general is perhaps pre-formed in the conformity of the humblest of our concepts to its object. In a philosophy according to which the presence in us of the things is the very condition of our conceiving ideas, it is, contrary to the idealist thesis, possible to know whether our ideas are or are not in conformity with things. The true thomistic answer to the critical problem lies, therefore, in a pre-Critique in which the enquiry about the possibility of knowledge in general takes precedence over the enquiry about the possibility of a particular knowledge. To expect from St. Thomas a direct refutation of the Kantian Critique, is to ask him for the solution of a problem which, from his point of view, had no right to exist.

The ground having been freed by this preliminary clearing, it would perhaps appear that from St. Thomas' point of view a complete theory of knowledge must coincide with a critique of knowledge. There is knowledge; this knowledge is valid, at least under certain conditions,[24] for every mind which is not content to resign itself to scepticism: how comes it that an agreement is reached between different minds and that, beyond the conflict of opinions, there exists a truth? The intellect, in search for this impersonal foundation of given truths, reflects upon its act and judges that this foundation lies in the object known. This is a legitimate conclusion which effects a considerable economy of thought, for the most immediate touchstone conceivable to discover what is true concerning any object, is that object itself. In short, the simplest hypothesis to explain the fact that thoughts agree upon things, is to assume that their common point of reference is the things. But is it possible to conceive in its turn the act of a thought attaining to things? For an answer, the regressive analysis which has led us up to the concept, must go back from the concept to the intellect. Is there in us a principle of such a kind as to produce a concept whose conformity to the object is guaranteed? Certainly, if it is true that we possess an intelligence, i.e. in the last resort, if it is true that we are not shut in within our own being, but capable of becoming other beings by means of representations.[25] The only possible keystone of a thomistic theory of knowledge is that adequacy of the intellect to things which defines truth; and this may be rightly asserted in a philosophy in which to become things is the proper nature of the intellect: *secundum hoc cognoscit veritatem intellectus, quod supra se reflectitur.* When, reflecting upon itself, the intellect which judges things, realises itself as conceiving them only by reason of its union with them, no scruple need restrain it from asserting as valid, judgments which merely unfold the content of its concepts. The initial fact of knowledge which this analysis does no more than deepen, implies the existence of an intellect whose objectivity is guaranteed fully by its own legitimate exercise.

NOTES TO CHAPTER XIII.

1. Apart from works referred to in Chapter XII, full references to this question will be found in: P. Mandonnet et J. Destrez, *Bibliographie thomiste*, p. 36–39. There is not one of all the works which we know that does not contain some facts or ideas worthy of note; but many of them are useless for beginners and may even start them off on a wrong tack. This applies even more to many a book or article that has appeared since the closing of the *Bibliographie thomiste*; a great deal is passed off under the guise of St. Thomas which belongs really to St. Augustine, Descartes and sometimes even to Kant. We should, therefore, advise those who are more concerned to go right than to go far, to keep to a small number of works, if they are interested to discover the original thomistic position rather than to interpret it in the sense of what the Germans call an "Umdeutung," however ingenious it may be. Such works to be consulted are, for instance: A.-D. Sertillanges, *L'idée générale de la connaissance d'après saint Thomas d'Aquin*, Rev. des sciences philos. et théol., 1908, t. II., 449–465; M.-D. Roland-Gosselin, *Sur la théorie thomiste de la vérité, ibid.*, 1921, t. X., p. 222–234 (see also the important notes, *ibid.*, t. XIV., p. 188–189 and 201–203); L. Noël, *Notes d'épistémologie thomiste*, Louvain, 1925. After a great many hesitations, it seems that we are approaching a final settlement of the problem, but no one knows better than those actually engaged upon its solution how many risks of error attend almost every step.

2. In thomistic language: since a being is defined by its form, a being that knows, is distinguished from a being that does not know by the fact of possessing, apart from its own form, also the form of the thing it knows: "Cognoscentia a non cognoscentibus in hoc distinguuntur, quia non cognoscentia nihil habent, nisi formam suam tantum, sed cognoscens natum est habere formam etiam rei alterius; nam species cogniti est in cognoscente. Unde manifestum est, quod natura rei non cognoscentis est magis coarctata et limitata. Natura autem rerum cognoscentium habet majorem amplitudinem, et extensionem; propter quod dicit Philosophus, III de Anima, quod *anima est quodammodo omnia.*" *Sum. theol.*, I. 14, 1, ad *Resp.*

3. This is the meaning of the famous formula of John of St. Thomas: "Cognoscentia autem in hoc elevantur super non cognoscentia, quia id quod est alterius, ut alterius, seu

278 *The Philosophy of St. Thomas*

prout manet distinctum in altero possunt in se recipere, *ita quod in se sunt, sed etiam possunt fieri alia a se.*" Joannes a sancto Thoma, *De anima*, qu. IV, art 1. The formula is not St. Thomas' own, but faithfully expresses the substance of his thought. As regards its interpretation, cp. the controversy between M. N. Balthasar and P. Garrigou-Lagrange, Rev. néo-scolastique de phil., 1923, t. XXV., p. 294–310 and 420–441.

4. *In lib. de Anima*, III, lect. 13; ed. Pirotta, no. 790. Cf. "Forma autem in his, quae cognitionem participant, altiori modo invenitur quam in his, quae cognitione carent. In his enim, quae cognitione carent, invenitur tantummodo forma ad unum esse proprium determinans unumquodque, quod etiam naturale uniuscujusque est.... In habentibus autem cognitionem sic determinatur unumquodque ad proprium esse naturale, per forman naturalem, quod tamen est receptivum specierum aliarum rerum: sicut sensus recipit species omnium sensibilium, et intellectus omnium intelligibilium. Et sic anima hominis fit omnia quodammodo, secundum sensum et intellectum, in quo, quodammodo, cognitionem habentia ad Dei similitudinem appropinquant, in quo omnia praeexistunt." *Sum. theol.*, I. 80, 1, ad *Resp.* "Patet igitur, quod immaterialitas alicujus rei est ratio, quod sit cognoscitiva, et secundum modum immaterialitatis est modus cognitionis. Unde in 2 de Anima dicitur quod plantae non cognoscunt propter suam materialitatem. Sensus autem cognoscitivus est, quia receptivus est specierum sine materia, et intellectus adhuc magis cognoscitivus, quia magis separatus est a materia et immixtus. ... Unde, cum Deus sit in summo immaterialtatis..., sequitur quod ipse sit in summo cognitionis." *Sum. theol.*, I. 14, 1, ad *Resp.* Cf. *In lib. de Anima*, II., Lect. V., ed. Pirotta, no. 283.

5. "Hujusmodi autem viventia inferiora, quorum actus est anima, de qua nunc agitur, habent duplex esse. Unum quidem materiale, in quo conveniunt cum aliis rebus materialibus. Aliud autem immateriale, in quo communicant cum substantiis superioribus aliqualiter." *In lib. de Anima*, II., 5, ed. Pirotta, no. 282.

6. See above preceding Note 2.

7. "Unde dicitur in III lib. de Anima, quod sensibile in actu est sensus in actu, et intelligibile in actu est intellectus in actu. Ex hoc enim aliquid in actu sentimus, vel intelligimus, quod intellectus noster vel sensus informatur in actu per speciem sensibilis vel intelligibilis. Et secundum hoc tantum sensus, vel intellectus aliud est a sensibili, vel intelligibili, quia utrumque est in potentia." *Sum. theol.*, I. 14, 2, ad *Resp.* Cf. *In lib. de Anima*, III., Lect. 2, ed. Pirotta, nos. 591–593 and 724.

8. *In lib. de Anima*, II., lect. 15, ed. Pirotta, nos. 437–438. See M.-D. Roland-Gosselin, *Ce que saint Thomas pense de la sensation immédiate et de son organe*, Rev. des sciences philos. et théol., 1914, t. VIII., p. 104–105.

9. Cf. the striking formula by which St. Thomas describes this operation: "Cum vero praedictas species (*scil.* intelligibiles) in actu completo habuerit, vocatur intellectus in actu. Sic enim actu intelligit res, cum species rei facta fuerit forma intellectus possibilis." *Compendium theologiae*, cap. 83. The term "similitudo" by which St. Thomas often describes the species (for inst. *Cont. Gent.*, II. 98), must be taken in the full sense given to it at that time, viz. a participation of the form which represents it, because it is nothing but the prolongation of that very form. The "similitudo formae" is not a picture or even a cast of it, otherwise knowledge would only apprehend the shadow of objects. "Sciendum est autem quod, cum quaelibet cognitio perficiatur per hoc quod similitudo rei cognitae est in cognoscente, sicut perfectio rei cognitae consistit in hoc quod habet talem formam per quam est res talis, ita perfectio cognitionis consistit in hoc, quod habet similitudinem formae praedictae." *In metaph.*, lib. VI., lect. 4, ed. Cathala, no 1234. Cf. 1235–1236. We arrive at the thomistic definition of truth, because to have the "similitudo" is equivalent to having the form.

10. "Quidam posuerunt, quod vires cognoscitivae, quae sunt in nobis, nihil cognoscunt, nisi proprias passiones: puta, quod sensus non sentit nisi passionem sui organi; et secundum hoc intellectus nihil intelligit, nisi suam passionem, id est speciem intelligibilem in se receptam: et secundum hoc species hujusmodi est ipsum *quod* intelligitur. Sed haec opinio manifeste apparet falsa ex duobus," etc. *Sum. theol.*, I. 85, 2, ad *Resp.* "Intellectum est in intelligente per suam similitudinem. Et per hunc modum dicitur, quod intellectum in actu est intellectus in actu; in quantum similitudo rei intellectae est forma intellectus, sicut similitudo rei sensibilis est forma sensus in actu; unde non sequitur quod species intelligibilis abstracta sit id quod actu intelligitur, sed quod sit similitudo ejus." *Ibid.*, ad 1m.

11. "Manifestum est etiam, quod species intelligibiles, quibus intellectus possibilis fit in actu, non sunt objectum intellectus. Non enim se habent ad intellectum sicut *quod* intelligitur, sed sicut *quo* intelligit.... Manifestum est enim quod scientiae sunt de his quae intellectus intelligit. Sunt autem scientiae de rebus, non autem de speciebus, vel intentionibus intelligibilibus, nisi sola scientia rationalis" (*scil.* logic). *In lib. de Anima*, III., lect. 8, ed. Pirotta, no. 718.

12. *In lib. de Anima*, II., lect. 24, ed. Pirotta, nos. 552 and 553.

13. "Dico autem intentionem intellectam (*sive* conceptum) id quod intellectus in seipso concipit de re intellecta. Quae quidem in nobis neque est ipsa res quae intelligitur neque est ipsa substantia intellectus, sed est quaedam similitudo concepta intellectu de re intellecta, quam voces exteriores significant; unde et ipsa intentio verbum interius nominatur, quod est exteriori verbo significatum." *Cont. Gent.*, IV. 11.

14. *In lib. de Anima*, II. 12, ed. Pirotta, nos. 378–380; *Sum. theol.*, I. 88, 2, ad 2*ᵐ*.

15. "Intellectus, per speciem rei formatus, intelligendo format in seipso quamdam intentionem rei intellectae, quae est ratio ipsius, quam significat diffinitio.... Haec autem intentio intellecta, cum sit quasi terminus intelligibilis operationis, est aliud a specie intelligibili quae facit intellectum in actu, quod oportet considerari ut intelligibilis operationis principium: licet utrumque sit rei intellectae similitudo. Per hoc enim quod species intelligibilis quae est forma intellectus, et intelligendi principium, est similitudo rei exterioris, sequitur quod intellectus intentionem formet illius rei similem. Quia quale est unumquodque, talia operatur, et ex hoc quod intentio intellecta est similis alicui rei, sequitur quod intellectus, formando hujusmodi intentionem, rem illam intelligat." *Cont. Gent.*, I. 53, ad *Ulterius autem*.

16. "Id autem quod est per se intellectum non est res illa cujus notitia per intellectum habetur, cum illa quandoque sit intellecta in potentia tantum, et sit extra intelligentem, sicut cum homo intelligit res materiales, ut lapidem vel animal aut aliud hujusmodi: cum tamen oporteat quod intellectum sit in intelligente, et unum cum ipso. Neque etiam intellectum per se est similitudo rei intellectae, per quam informatur intellectus ad intelligendum. Intellectus enim non potest intelligere nisi secundum quod fit in actu per hanc similitudinem, sicut nihil aliud potest operari secundum quod est in potentia, sed secundum quod fit actu per aliquam formam. Haec ergo similitudo se habet in intelligendo sicut intelligendi principium, ut calor est principium calefactionis, non sicut intelligendi terminus. Hoc ergo est primo et per se intellectum, quod intellectus in se ipso concipit de re intellecta, sive illud sit definitio, sive enuntiatio, secundum quod ponuntur duae operationes intellectus, in III Anima (Com. 12). Hoc autem sic ab intellectu conceptum dicitur verbum interius, hoc enim est quod significatur per vocem." *De potentia*, qu. XI., art. 5, ad *Resp*. Cf. *ibid.*, qu. VIII., art. 1, ad *Resp*.

17. See *De natura verbi intellectus* from: "Cum ergo intellectus, informatus specie, natus sit agere..." down to: "Verbum igitur cordis...," esp. the expressive formula: "Idem enim lumen quod intellectus possibilis recipit cum specie

ab agente, per actionem intellectus informati tali specie diffunditur, cum objectum (*scil.* conceptum) formatur, et manet cum objecto formato." In the impossibility of establishing the identity of the concept and object, St. Thomas maintains at least the continuity of the intelligibility of things with what it allows the intellect to introduce into the concept. This is the reason why the texts which declare the immediate object of the intellect to be the concept and not the thing, in no way contradict the objectivity of the concept. On the contrary, if our intellect had an immediate intuition of the object (like the sight has of colour), the concept subsequently formed of this intuition, would be the image only of the intuition and, consequently, only an indirect image of the object. In considering the concept, the immediate object of the intellect, as the product of the intellect inasmuch as fertilised by the object itself, St. Thomas intends therefore to guarantee the strictest continuity between the intelligibility of the object and that of the concept. From this point of view the necessity of positing the species as a principle, not as an object of knowledge, is fully apparent. There is the object, which is not in itself apprehended by an intuition; there is the species which is nothing but the object and, therefore, not apprehended either by an intuition; there is the intellect informed by the species which thus becomes the object, which also has no direct intuition of what it has thereby become; there is lastly the concept, the first conscious representation of the object: no intermediate representation separates, therefore, the object from the concept expressing it, and this is the fact which imparts to our conceptual knowledge its objectivity. The whole weight of the doctrine lies, therefore, upon the twofold capacity of our intellect (1) to become the thing and (2) to produce the concept while thus fertilised. See: *De natura verbi intellectus*, ad *Ex dictis manifestum est.* ... Cf. *De intellectu et intelligibili*, ad *Et ideo intelligere nostrum*.

18. "Quidditas autem rei est proprium objectum intellectus: unde sicut sensus sensibilium propriorum semper est verus, ita et intellectus in cognoscendo quod quid est." *De verit.*, qu. I., art. 12, ad *Resp.* Cf. *Sum. theol.*, I. 16, 2: "Cum autem omnis res sit vera secundum quod habet propriam formam naturae suae, necesse est quod intellectus in quantum est cognoscens sit verus, in quantum habet similitudinem rei cognitae, quae est forma ejus in quantum est cognoscens."

19. "Sed sciendum est quod cum reflexio fiat redeundo super idem; hic autem non sit reditio super speciem, nec super intellectum formatum specie, quia non percipiuntur quando verbum formatur, gignitio verbi non est reflexa." *De nat.*

verbi intell. "Non enim intellectus noster inspiciens hanc speciem (*scil.* intelligibilem) tanquam exemplar sibi simile, aliquid facit quasi verbum ejus; sic enim non fieret unum ex intellectu et specie, cum intellectus non intelligat nisi factus unum aliquid cum specie, sed in ipsa specie formatus agit tanquam aliquo sui, ipsam tamen non excedens. Species autem sic accepta semper ducit in objectum primum." *Ibid.*

20. "Veri enim ratio consistit in adaequatione rei et intellectus idem autem non adaequatur sibi ipsi, sed aequalitas diversorum est; unde ibi primo invenitur ratio veritatis in intellectu ubi primo intellectus incipit aliquid proprium habere quod res extra animam non habet, sed aliquid ei correspondens, inter quae adaequatio attendi potest. Intellectus autem formans quidditates (*scil.* per conceptum), non habet nisi similitudinem rei existentis extra animam, sicut et sensus in quantum accipit speciem rei sensibilis; sed quando incipit judicare de re apprehensa, tunc ipsum judicium intellectus est quoddam proprium ei, quod non invenitur extra in re. Sed quando adaequatur ei quod est extra in re, dicitur judicium verum esse. Tunc autem judicat intellectus de re apprehensa quando dicit quod aliquid est vel non est." *Qu. disp. de Verit.*, qu. I., art. 3, ad *Resp.*

21. *Sum. theol.*, I. 85, 2, ad *Resp.*

22. *Sum. theol.*, I. 87, 3, ad *Resp.*

23. *De potentia*, qu. VIII., art. 1, and qu. IX., art 5. We fail to see wherein lies the disagreement of P. Roland-Gosselin with H. J. Maritain on this point (*Rev. des sciences phil. et théol.*, 1925, t. XIV., p. 202). The identity between the species (and hence of the object) and the intellect which M. Maritain rightly asserts, is in no wise contradicted by the non-identity, equally rightly asserted by P. Roland-Gosselin, between the object and the concept. What we fail to see is how passages affirming the one, can be quoted to deny the other. Perhaps the source of the misunderstanding lies in the twofold use of the term "similitudo" to which we have called attention: the conformity to the object of a "similitudo" expressed by the object does not arise, as it is the object itself; the conformity to the object by a "similitudo" of this object expressed by thought is certain, considering the conditions under which thought expresses it, but it is no longer identical with the object. P. Roland-Gosselin is therefore right in saying: "Et c'est toujours, pour saint Thomas, la resemblance du verbe à la chose dont il se distingue (la resemblance et non pas l'identité) qui rend raison de son objectivité." *Op. cit.*, p. 203. Certainly, but this resemblance of the "verbum" to the thing presupposes in its turn the identity between the species

and the intellect which conceives the "verbum," otherwise it would be not the thing itself that the "verbum" (or concept) expresses.

24. See on this point the important work of P. Roland-Gosselin: *La théorie thomiste de l'erreur*, in *Mélanges thomistes* (Bibl. thom., III.), 1923, p. 253–274.

25. "In intellectu enim est (*scil.* veritas), sicut consequens actum intellectus, et sicut cognita per intellectum; consequitur namque intellectus operationem secundum quod judicium intellectus est de re secundum quod est cognoscitur autem ab intellectu, secundum quod intellectus reflectitur supra actum suum, non solum secundum quod cognoscit actum suum, sed secundum quod cognoscit proportionem ejus ad rem: quod quidem cognosci non potest nisi cognita natura ipsius actus; quae cognosci non potest, nisi cognoscatur natura principii activi, quod est ipse intellectus, in cujus natura est ut rebus conformetur; unde secundum hoc cognoscit veritatem intellectus quod supra seipsum reflectitur." *Qu. disp. de Verit.*, qu. I., art. 9, ad *Resp.*

CHAPTER XIV.
APPETITE AND WILL

WE have so far considered only the cognitive powers of the human soul. The soul, however, is capable not only of knowing, but also of willing and desiring. This again is a feature which it has in common with all natural forms: it assumes a particular character here only because the human soul is endowed with knowledge. For every form entails a certain inclination; fire, for instance, inclines by reason of its form to rise upwards and to produce fire in such bodies as come into contact with it. But the form of beings endowed with knowledge is superior to the form of bodies devoid of it. In these latter the form determines each body to the particular being proper to it; in other words, it confers on it its natural being. The inclination resulting from such a form has therefore properly been called its "natural appetite." Beings, endowed with knowledge, on the contrary, are determined to the proper being natural to them, by a form which, while certainly their natural form, is yet at the same time capable of receiving the species of other beings: thus the sense receives the species of all sensibles and the intellect the species of all intelligibles. The human soul is consequently able to become in a sense all things, thanks to its senses and its intellect. Herein it resembles up to a certain point God Himself in whom the exemplars of all creatures pre-exist. If therefore the forms of beings endowed with knowledge, belong to a higher degree than those devoid of it, it follows that the resulting inclination also is superior to the natural inclination. At this point we encounter the appetitive powers of the soul by which the animal inclines to what it knows.[1] Moreover, the animate beings, participating in the Divine goodness more amply than inferior things, require a greater number of operations and means to acquire their proper perfection. They resemble those people who, as mentioned earlier, are able to acquire perfect health but only on condition of employing a sufficient number of remedies.[2] The natural appetite, determined to a single object and a merely moderate perfection, needs but a single operation to reach it. The appetite of the animal, on the other hand, must be diverse and capable of extending to everything that the animal requires. Therefore its nature needs necessarily an appetite which falls in with its faculty of knowing and allows it to incline towards all the objects which it apprehends.[3]

It is consequently apparent that the nature of the appetite is closely bound up with the degree of the knowledge from which it springs. It is therefore no matter of surprise to find as many appetitive powers ascribed to the human soul as it possesses cognitive powers. Now, the soul apprehends objects by means of two powers, an inferior power, namely the sensitive, and a superior power, the intellectual or rational. The soul consequently tends to its objects by two appetitive powers, a lower appetite called "sensuality," itself divided into the "irascible" and the "concupiscible" appetite; and a higher appetite, called "will."[4] It cannot, further, be doubted that these are three distinct powers of the human soul. The natural, sensitive and rational appetites are distinct from each other as three irreducible degrees of perfection. For, the closer a nature is to Divine perfection, the clearer is the evident resemblance to the Divine creator in it. But what characterises the Divine dignity is that He who possesses it, sets in motion, inclines and directs all, without being Himself moved, inclined or directed by anything else. Therefore, the nearer a nature is to God, the less is it determined by Him and the more is it able to determine itself. Insensible nature which, by reason of its materialness, is infinitely distant from God, will therefore incline to one particular end, and yet it could not be said that there is anything in it that gives it the inclination towards this end, except just the inclination itself. Such is the movement of the arrow directed to its target by the archer, or of the stone tending to fall to the ground.[5] Sensitive nature, on the contrary, being nearer to God, contains in itself something that inclines it, namely, the desirable object which it apprehends. The inclination itself is, however, not in the power of the animal subject to the inclination, but the inclination is determined by the object. In the previous instance the object of the inclination is exterior and the inclination determined; in this case, the object is interior, though the inclination is still determined. Thus, animals before some pleasant object, cannot help desiring it, since they are not masters of their inclinations, and so we can say with St. John Damascene, that they do not act, but are being acted upon: *non agunt sed magis aguntur.* The reason of this inferiority is that the sensible appetite of the animal is bound up, like the sense itself, with a bodily organ; the likeness of this appetite to the dispositions of matter and to corporeal things results in a nature which is less capable of moving than of being moved.

But rational nature, much closer to God than the others, cannot fail to possess an inclination of a superior order, distinct from the other two. Like all animate beings, it contains inclinations towards determinate objects, in so far, for instance, as it possesses the form of a natural body which, being heavy, tends downwards. Again, like the animals, it possesses an inclination moved and determined by the external objects which it apprehends. But it has in addition an inclination, not necessarily moved by the desirable objects it apprehends, an inclination, which may or may not incline as it pleases, and the movement of which, consequently, is not determined by anything except by the movement itself. This privilege belongs to it, inasmuch as it employs no bodily organ in its operation; by its immaterialness it is removed from the nature of mobile things and approximates to the nature of a mover and agent. But no being can determine its own inclination towards an end, unless it previously knows the end and the relation of the means to it. This knowledge, however, belongs only to rational beings. This appetite, not necessarily determined from outside, is therefore closely linked with rational knowledge: hence the name given to it, is that of "rational appetite" or will.[6] Accordingly the dinstinction between the will and sensuality arises in the first place from the fact that the one determines itself, whereas the other is determined in its inclination, —a distinction which presupposes two powers of different orders. And since this diversity in their mode of determination requires in its turn of difference in their modes of apprehending objects, it may be said, in the second place, that they differ like the degrees of knowledge which correspond to them.[7]

We shall examine each of these powers in itself, beginning first of all with the sensitive appetite or sensuality. A natural object, it was said, is determined in its natural being; it can therefore only be what it is by nature; it possesses therefore but one inclination towards a determinate object, and this inclination does not require the power of distinguishing between what is desirable and what is not. It suffices that the author of nature has provided for this by imparting to each being its requisite inclination. Sensitive appetite, on the contrary, though it does not tend to what is universally desirable or good, which reason alone apprehends, tends at least to every object which is useful or pleasant to it. As the corresponding sense has for its object some particular sensible, so the sensitive appetite aims at some particular good.[8] All the same, we are dealing here with a faculty which considered in its own nature, is wholly appetitive, and in no way cognitive. Sensuality receives its name from the movement of sense, as sight is so called from seeing, and in general, as a power receives its name from its act. For, sense-movement, defined strictly and in itself, is nothing but the appetite consequent upon the apprehension of the sensible by sense. But this apprehension, in distinction to the action of the appetite, has not the character of a movement. The operation of a sense apprehending its object, is completed when the apprehended object has passed into the power apprehending it. The operation of the appetitive virtue, on the contrary, terminates as soon as the being endowed with the appetite, inclines to the desired object. The operation of the apprehending powers therefore resembles repose, while that of the appetitive powers resembles rather a movement. Sensuality therefore does not in any way pertain to the sphere of knowledge but solely to that of appetite.[9]

Within the sensitive appetite, as a sort of generic power described by the term sensuality, two powers must be distinguished which constitute its species: the "irascible" and the "concupiscible." For the sensitive appetite has this in common with natural appetite that both tend always towards an object conformable to the being desiring it. But it is easy to observe, within the natural appetite, a twofold tendency, corresponding to the two operations performed by the natural being. By the first of these operations a natural thing endeavours to secure whatever is needed to preserve its nature; thus a heavy body moves downwards, as to its natural position. In the second operation it displays a certain active quality directed to the destruction of everything that may be contrary to it. And it is necessary for corruptible beings to exercise an operation of this kind, for, unless they possessed the force to destroy whatever is inimical to them, they would immediately be destroyed themselves. Thus natural appetite tends towards two aims: to acquire whatever is conformable to its nature, and to win a sort of victory over each of its enemies. Now, the first operation is rather of a receptive kind; the second of a more active kind; and since acting depends on a principle different from that of receiving, different powers must be assumed to underlie these different operations. The same applies to the sensitive appetite. By its appetitive power the animal tends to whatever is friendly to its own nature and helpful to its preservation; this is the function performed by the concupiscible powers, the proper object of which is everything that may be apprehended by the senses as agreeable. On the other hand, the animal evidently desires to obtain a victory and domination over everything opposed to it, and this function is performed by the irascible power, the object of which is not the agreeable, but on the contrary the hostile and difficult.[10]

The irascible is therefore obviously a power different from the concupiscible. For the ground of desirability is not the same for what is attractive as for what is hostile. Generally whatever is difficult or inimical, cannot be overcome without the sacrifice of some pleasure or the danger of some suffering. The animal will forego even the most alluring pleasure in order to fight, and will not give up the struggle in spite of the pain caused by its wounds. The concupiscible tends to receive its object, for it desires only to be united with whatever delights it. The irascible, on the contrary, is directed to action, since it endeavours to destroy whatever threatens it with danger. Now, what has been said of the natural appetite is equally true of the sensible: receiving and acting pertain to different powers. This applies even to knowledge, since we were led to distinguish between the active and the passive intellect. We must therefore recognise the irascible and the concupiscible as two distinct powers. But, the distinction does not prevent them from being in ordered relation to each other. The irascible is, in fact, ordered in reference to the concupiscible, of which it is the guardian and defender. It is essential for the animal to be able to overcome its enemies so that the concupiscible power may enjoy in peace the objects pleasing to it. In fact, animals fight always for the sake of securing some pleasure; they fight for the pleasure of love or of food.

The movements of the irascible consequently both originate and end in the concupiscible. Anger begins in sadness and ends in the joy of revenge which belongs to the sphere of the concupiscible; hope is born of desire and completed in joy. Thus the movement of sensuality always proceeds from the concupiscible to the concupiscible by passing though the irascible.[11]

Is it possible to observe a difference in the degree of perfection between these two powers, distinct, yet so closely allied? Can we assert the superiority of the irascible or of the concupiscible in the same way as we noted the superiority of the sensible appetite over the natural appetite? If we consider the sensitive power of the soul by itself, we observe in the first place that, both from the point of view of knowledge and from that of appetite, it contains certain faculties which belong to it by right, through the mere fact of its sensible nature, and others which it possesses, on the contrary, by a sort of participation in that higher power which is reason. Not as if the intellectual and the sensible intermingled at certain points; but the higher degrees of the sensible, border on the lower degrees of the rational, according to the principle formulated by Dionysius: *divina sapientia conjungit fines primorum principiis secundorum.*[12] Thus, imagination belongs to the sensitive soul as perfectly conforming to the proper degree of its perfection, for what perceives sensible forms is also naturally capable of preserving them. The case is perhaps different with the estimative faculty. We must bear in mind the functions which we assigned to that power of the sensible order: it apprehends species which the senses are incapable of receiving, since it perceives objects as useful or harmful, and beings as friends or enemies. The judgments thus passed upon things by the sensitive soul, impart to the animal a sort of natural prudence, the results of which are analogous to those obtained by reason in very different ways. Now, it seems that the irascible is superior to the concupiscible, in the same manner as the estimative power is superior to the imagination. When the animal tends, by virtue of its concupiscible appetite, to the object yielding it pleasure, it acts simply in a way which is perfectly proportionate to the proper nature of the sensitive soul. But the fact that the animal under the stress of its irascible appetite, comes to forget its pleasures in order to desire a victory, unattainable except by pain, is the result of an appetitive power extremely close to an order superior to the sensible. Just as the estimative power obtains results analogous to those of the intellect, so the irascible obtains results analogous to those of the will. We can therefore place the irascible above the concupiscible, even though its end is to safeguard the act of the latter; we must see in it the noblest instrument with which nature has endowed the animal to maintain its existence and to ensure its own preservation.[13]

This conclusion, inevitable in regard to the animal, applies no less to man, endowed with will and reason. The powers of the sensitive appetite are exactly of the same nature in man and in the animal. The movements carried out are the same; they differ only in their origin. Considering the sensitive appetite, such as it is in animals, we note that it is moved and determined by the judgments of their estimative power; thus the sheep fears the wolf because it judges him naturally to be dangerous. But we have seen above[14] that the estimative faculty is replaced in man by a cogitative faculty which collates the images of particular objects. The movements of our sensitive appetite are, consequently, determined by our cogitative power. And, since in the case of man, this particular sensible reason is moved and directed by universal reason, we may legitimately assert that our appetites are placed under the direction of our reason. Nothing is, moreover, easier than to convince ourselves of this fact. Our syllogistic arguments start from universal premises to conclude in particular propositions. When a sensible object is perceived by us as being good or bad, useful or harmful, we may

say that the perception of this "usefulness" or "harm-
fulness" in the particular instance is conditioned by
our intellectual knowledge of usefulness and harmful-
ness in general. Such and such an object may be
made to appear as pleasing or dangerous, agreeable or
painful by our reason acting on the imagination
through the appropriate syllogisms. By reasoning
we are able to soothe our anger or to allay our fear.[15]
Lastly, the sensitive appetite cannot execute any
movement in man with the help of the moving power
of the soul, unless it has previously obtained the
consent of the will. In animals the irascible or
concupiscible appetites determine certain movements
directly: the sheep fears the wolf and immediately
takes to flight. In this case no superior appetite is
able to inhibit such movements of sensible origin.
But it is not the same in man; his movements are not
released inevitably by the inclination of his appetites,
but on the contrary always await the superior orders of
his will. In all ordered motive forces, the inferior
forces act by virtue of the superior; the sensitive
appetite which is of an inferior order, would be unable
to determine any movement without the consent of
the superior appetite. In the same way as in the
celestial spheres the lower spheres are moved by the
higher, so the appetite is moved by the will.[16]

We are here on the threshold of voluntary activity
and of free-will, properly speaking. To cross it, we
need merely attribute to the appetite an object,
corresponding under the aspect of universality to that
of rational knowledge. What confers on the will its
proper degree of perfection is the fact that its first
and main object is the desirable and good as such;
particular beings can become the objects of will only
to the extent of their participating in the universal
reason of good.[17] Let us examine in detail the relations
between the appetite and this new object.

It is a fact worth noting that every appetitive power
is determined necessarily by its proper object. In the
animal, as being devoid of reason, the appetite is

inevitably drawn towards an object apprehended by the senses as desirable; seeing the desirable the animal is unable not to desire it. The same applies to the will. Its proper object is the general good, and to desire it is for the will an absolute natural necessity. This necessity results directly from the definition of the will. For the necessary is that which cannot not be. When this necessity is imposed on a being by virtue of one of its essential principles, whether material or formal, it may be said that this necessity is natural and absolute. It is in this sense that we say of any compound, combining contrary elements, that it must necessarily decay, or of a triangle that its angles are necessarily equal to two right angles. In the same way again, the intellect must necessarily, by definition, conform to the first principles of knowledge. Lastly, in the same way, the will must necessarily conform to the good in general, i.e. to the ultimate goal, which is beatitude. Such a necessity is not only not repugnant to the will, but it is the formal constitutive principle of its essence. In the same manner, therefore, as the intellection of principles underlies all our speculative knowledge, so the conformity of the will to the last end underlies all the operations of our will. Nor can it be otherwise. Whatever a being possesses by reason of the needs of its own nature and as an unalterable possession, is necessarily the foundation and principle of all the rest, of its properties no less than of its actions. For the nature of everything and the origin of every movement are always to be found in an unalterable principle.[18] Hence the conclusion: the will wills necessarily good in general; this necessity means nothing else but that the will cannot but be itself, and this unalterable conformity to the good as such, constitutes the first principle of all its operations.

Does it follow from the fact that the will cannot not will good in general (*bonum secundum communem boni rationem*[19]), that it wills necessarily *all* that it wills? Evidently not. Let us go back to the parallel between appetite and knowledge. The will, as was said, conforms naturally and necessarily to the ultimate end which is the Supreme Good, as the intellect conforms naturally and necessarily to the first principles. Now, there are propositions which are intelligible to human reason, but are not linked to these principles by a necessary connexion. Such are "contingent" propositions, i.e. all those which it is possible to deny, without contradicting the first principles of knowledge. The unalterable conformity of the intellect to these principles does not therefore oblige it to accept such propositions. But there are, on the contrary, propositions called "necessary," because they follow necessarily from the first principles whence they may be deduced by demonstrative reasoning. To deny these propositions would amount to denying the principles from which they follow. As soon therefore as the intellect apprehends the necessary connexion linking these conclusions with their principles, it must necessarily accept the conclusions, as it accepts the principles from which they are deduced; but its assent is only necessary when a demonstration has brought home to it the necessity of this connexion. It is the same with the will. A very large number of particular goods are such that it is perfectly possible to be happy without possessing them; they are, therefore, not bound up with beatitude by a necessary connexion and the will is consequently not obliged by natural necessity to will them.

If we consider, on the contrary, such goods as are related to beatitude by a necessary connexion, we find among them evidently all the goods by which man is attached to God, in whom alone true beautitude consists; the human will cannot therefore not adhere to them. But it is here a question of a necessity of right, not of fact. In the same way as conclusions impose themselves necessarily only upon those who see them as implications of the principles, so man would indefectibly adhere to God, and to whatever is of God, if he had a clear view of the Divine essence and of the necessary connexion of the particular goods with Him. This is the case of the Blessed who are confirmed in grace; their will necessarily adheres to God because they see His essence. In this life, on the contrary, the vision of the Divine essence is refused us; our will, consequently, necessarily wills beatitude, but nothing more. We fail to see with compelling evidence that God is the Supreme Good and the only beatitude, nor do we perceive with convincing certainty the link of a necessary connexion between God and what is truly of God. Thus the will not only does not will necessarily whatever it wills, but it does not will necessarily even the Supreme Good; and, since its imperfection is such that it finds never any but particular goods, it may even be said that—with the exception of good in general—it is never obliged to will what it wills.[20] This truth will be yet more obvious when we have determined the relation between the intellect and the will within the human soul.

It is not without relevance to our understanding of what free-will is, to consider whether one of these two powers (viz. the intellect and the will) is nobler and of superior dignity than the other. Now, intellect and will can be considered either in their very essence, or as particular powers of the soul, performing definite acts. Essentially the intellect has the function of apprehending being and truth in their universality; the will is by essence the appetite for the good in general. Compared from this point of view, the intellect appears as nobler and more eminent than the will, because the object of the will is comprised and included in that of the intellect. The will tends to the good, inasmuch as it is desirable; but the good presupposes being; for there is no desirable good except where there is a being which is good and desirable. But being is the proper object of the intellect; the essence of the good desired by the will is the same as that which the intellect apprehends; so that, if we compare the objects of the two powers, that of the intellect appears as absolute, that of the will as relative.

And, since the order of the powers of the soul follows the order of their objects, we must conclude that, taken in itself and absolutely, the intellect is the more eminent and nobler of the two.[21]

We shall reach the same conclusion if we compare the intellect in relation to its universal object, with the will as a particular and determinate power of the soul. Being and universal truth, the objects of the intellect, contain in effect the will, its act and even its object, as so many particular beings and truths. In respect of the intellect, the will, its act and its object are matters for intellection, exactly like stone, wood and all the beings and all the truths which the intellect apprehends. But, if we consider the will according to the universality of its object which is the good, and consider the intellect, on the contrary, as a special power of the soul, the previous order of perfection is reversed. Every individual intellect, every intellectual knowledge and every object of knowledge constitute particular goods, and are ordered as such under the universal good which is the proper object of the will. Viewed in this aspect, the will presents itself as superior to the intellect and as capable of setting it in motion.

Understanding and will, consequently, mutually include one another and by that very fact they mutually set each other in motion. One thing may set another in motion, because it is the end of that other. In this sense, the end moves him who realises it, since he acts with the view to its realisation. The intellect therefore moves the will, since the good, apprehended by the intellect, is the object of the will and sets the will in motion as its end. But it can also be said that one being moves another when it acts upon the latter and modifies the state in which it is; thus whatever changes another thing moves what is changed, and the mover sets in motion the moved. In this sense, the intellect can be said to be moved by the will. In all active powers that are reciprocally ordered, the power concerned with a universal end, moves the powers aiming at particular ends. This can easily be observed both in the natural state and the social order. The heavens whose action has as its end the preservation of the inferior bodies which come to be and pass away, move all these inferior bodies, which act only with the view to preserving their species and their own individuality. In the same manner, a king whose action is directed to the general good of the whole kingdom, moves by his commands those who preside over the government of each town. Now, the object of the will is the good and end in general; the other powers of the soul are ordered simply in view of particular goods, like the visual organ whose end is the perception of colours, and the intellect whose end is the knowledge of truth. The will, consequently, sets in motion and action both the intellect and all the other powers of the soul, except the natural functions of the vegetative life which are not subject to the decisions of our free-will.[22]

It is now easy to understand our free-will and the conditions under which it performs its functions. In the first place, it may be taken as evident that man is free. Some philosophers, however, contend that the freedom of man amounts merely to an absence of constraint. This is, indeed, a necessary, but by no means sufficient condition of our freedom. For it is obvious that the will can never be constrained. Constraint means violence, and the violent is, by definition, whatever runs counter to the natural inclination of a thing. The natural and the violent are mutually exclusive, and it is inconceivable for a thing to possess simultaneously both these characters. But the act of the will is nothing but the inclination of the will to its object; if constraint or violence entered into the will, they would, therefore, immediately destroy it. Consequently, in the same way as natural action is according to the inclination of a nature, so voluntary action is according to the inclination of the will; and just as it is impossible for a thing to be both violent and natural, so it is impossible for a power of the soul to be both constrained (i.e. subject to violence) and voluntary.[23]

But we have seen that this is not all, and that the will, free by definition from all constraint, is equally free from necessity. To deny this truth, is tantamount to suppressing in human actions everything which confers on them an either blameworthy or meritorious character. For it is clear that we cannot deserve praise or blame in the performance of actions which it is not in our power to avoid. But, a doctrine which leads to the suppression of merit and, consequently, of all morality, must be considered as un-philosophical: *extranea philosophiae*. For if there is nothing free in us, and if we are necessarily determined to will, then reflexion and exhortations, precepts and punishments, praise and blame, in short all the objects of moral philosophy vanish at once and lose all meaning. Such a doctrine is, as we said, un-philosophical, as are all the opinions which destroy the principles of any part of philosophy, such for instance as the proposition: *nothing is in motion*, because this would make any natural philosophy impossible.[24] But the denial of our free-will, unless it is explained by the incapacity of some persons to master their own passions, rests on nothing but sophistry, and especially on ignorance of the movements performed by the powers of the human soul and of the relations between them and their object.

The movement of every power of the soul can, indeed, be considered from two points of view: that of the subject and that of the object. Sight, considered in itself, may be moved to see more or less clearly according as some change occurs in the disposition of the visual organ. Here the movement occurs in the subject. But it may also be found in the object, as it happens when the eye perceives a white body which is then replaced by a black one. The former kind of modification concerns the exercise itself of the action; it causes the act to be or not to be better or less well performed. The latter change affects the specification of the act, for the quality of the act is determined by the nature of its object. In considering the exercise of the movement of the will under these two aspects, we note in the first place that the will is not subject to any necessary determination as regards the performance itself of the act.

We have shown earlier that the will moves all the powers of the soul; therefore it moves itself as it moves all the rest. It will perhaps be objected that it is thus both in potency and in act at the same time and under the same aspect; but this difficulty is merely apparent. Let us consider, for instance, the intellect of a man searching for a truth; he moves towards knowledge, for he passes from what he knows actually to what he is as yet ignorant of and knows only potentially. So when a man wills something actually, he moves himself also to will something else which he wills only potentially, or strictly speaking something which he does not yet will. Thus, if a man desires health, this will to recover his health moves him to take the requisite medicine. For as soon as he wills his health, he begins to consider the means to acquire it and the result of this deliberation is that he wills to take the medicine. What happens in such a case? The deliberation precedes the will to take the remedy; but the deliberation itself presupposes the will of the man who has willed to deliberate. And since the will has not always willed to deliberate, it must have been moved by something. If it has been moved by itself, we must necessarily assume an earlier deliberation, resulting in its turn from an act of the will. And as it is impossible in this way to regress *ad infinitum*, it cannot but be admitted that the first movement of the human will must be explained by the action of some external cause which caused the will to begin to will. What cause could this be? The first mover of the intellect and of the will must be, one would think, beyond both the will and the intellect. It must therefore be God Himself. But this conclusion introduces no necessity into our voluntary acts of will. God is indeed the first mover of all movable things, but He moves each according to its nature. He who moves the light body upwards and the heavy body downwards, moves also the will according to its own nature; He imparts to it therefore no compulsory movement, but, on the contrary, a naturally indeterminate movement which can direct itself towards different objects. If we therefore consider the will in itself, as the source of the acts it performs, we find nothing but a succession of deliberations and decisions, each decision presupposing a previous deliberation and each deliberation in its turn presupposing a decision. If we go back to the first origin of this movement, we find God who imparts it to the will, but imparts it only as an indeterminate movement. From the point of view, therefore, of the subject and of the exercise of the action, there is no necessary determination within the will.

Let us now consider the aspect of the specification of the act, which is the aspect of the object. Here again we do not find any necessity. For what is the object capable of moving the will? The good apprehended by the intellect as suitable: *bonum conveniens apprehensum*. If, therefore, a good is offered to the intellect, but the intellect, though seeing in it a good, yet fails to consider it as suitable, this good will not suffice to move the will. On the other hand, deliberations and decisions influence our acts, and our acts are individual and particular things. It is therefore not sufficient for an object to be good in itself and suitable in a general way, in order to move our will; it is further required that we should apprehend it as good and suitable in such and such a particular case, taking all the particular circumstances which we can discover, into account. Now, there is but one object that presents itself as good and suitable under *all* aspects: that is beatitude. Boëthius defines it as: *status omnium bonorum congregatione perfectus;*[25] it is therefore evident that this object moves our will of necessity. But, we must be careful to observe that this necessity itself affects only the determination of the act; it is therefore strictly limited to this, namely that the will cannot will the contrary of beatitude. This reservation might be differently expressed by saying: if the will performs its action, while the intellect thinks of the beatitude, the action will be necessarily determined by this object; the will would not wish for any other. But the exercise itself of the act remains free. If we cannot will beatitude while thinking of it, we can yet will not to think of the beatitude; the will remains mistress of its act and can use it as it likes with regard to any object: *libertas ad actum inest voluntati in quodlibet statu naturae respectu cujuslibet objecti.*[26]

Let us assume, on the other hand, that the good offered to the will is not a good according to all the particular circumstances giving it its character. In such a case, not only does the will remain free to perform its action or not, but even the determination itself of the act will not include any necessity. In other words, the will could, as always, will not to think about this object; and further we could also will a different object, even while thinking of this one. It is sufficient for the new object to appear as good under some aspect. What are the reasons leading the will to prefer certain objects from among all the particular goods offered to it? We can adduce three main reasons. In the first place, one object may exceed the others in excellence; in choosing it, the will moves therefore in conformity with reason. Again, as the result of internal dispositions or some external circumstance, the intellect may fasten upon some particular character of a good and not upon some other; the will conforms then to this thought, which is of quite accidental origin. Lastly, account must be taken of the disposition of man as a whole. The will of a man in a state of irritation will not come to a decision like the will of a man in a calm state of mind, for the object that suits the one will not suit the other. As the man is, so is his aim. A healthy person does not take his food like a sick one. But the disposition leading the will to consider one thing as good or suitable rather than another, may have a twofold origin. If it is a question of a natural disposition outside the range of the will, there is a natural necessity for the will to conform to it. Thus all men desire naturally to be, to live and to know. If, on the contrary, it is a question of a disposition which does not naturally pertain to man, but is on the contrary dependent on his will, the individual is not necessarily constrained to conform to it. Supposing, for example, that a passion causes us to consider some particular object as good or bad, our will is capable of reacting against this passion, and thereby of transforming the judgment which we pass on the object. We may soothe our anger in order not to be blinded by it in framing our judgment on some matter. If the disposition in question is a habit, it will be more difficult to free ourselves from it, for it is less easy to cast off a habit than to restrain a passion. It is, however, not impossible, and there again the choice of our will remains exempt from all necessity.[27]

Let us summarise the preceding conclusions: To suppose that the will can be constrained is a contradiction in terms and an absurdity; it is consequently entirely free from constraint. Is the will free from necessity? On this point we must make distinctions. As far as the exercise of the act is concerned, the will is always free from necessity; we are even able not to will the Supreme Good, because we are able not to think it. As far as the determination of the act is concerned, we are able not to will the Supreme Good or the objects of our natural dispositions, even while we think of them; we can also freely choose between all particular goods, including those which acquired dispositions on our part make us think to be such, without any of them being able to determine the movement of our will. Expressed still more shortly: the will is always free to will or not to will any object; it is always free, when it wills, to determine itself to such and such particular objects. From this point onwards the constitutive elements of the human act begin to appear in outline; the task remains to determine more accurately their relations by examining the operations by which man tends towards beatitude which constitutes his Supreme Good and ultimate goal.

NOTES TO CHAPTER XIV.

1. *Sum. theol.*, I. 80, 1, ad *Resp.*
2. See above, p. 221.
3. *De Verit.*, XXII. 3, ad *Resp.* and ad 2^m.
4. *De Verit.*, XV. 3, ad *Resp.*
5. *De Verit.*, XXII. 1, ad *Resp.*
6. *De Verit.*, XXII. 4, ad *Resp.*
7. *Sum. theol.*, I. 80, 2, ad *Resp.*; *De Verit.*, XXII. 4, ad 1^m.
8. *De Verit.*, XXV. 1, ad *Resp.*
9. *Sum. theol.*, I. 81, 1, ad *Resp.*; *De Verit.*, XXV. 1, ad 1^m.
10. *Sum. theol.*, I. 81, 2, ad *Resp.*
11. *De Verit*, XXV. 5, ad *Resp.*; *Sum. theol.*, ad *loc.*
12. *De Div. Nom.*, c. VII.
13. *De Verit.*, XXV. 2, ad *Resp.*
14. See chap. XI., p. 231.
15. *De Verit.*, XXV. 4, ad *Resp.*
16. *Sum. theol.*, I. 81, 3, ad *Resp.*
17. *De Verit.*, XXV. 1, ad *Resp.*
18. *Sum. theol.*, I. 82, 1, ad *Resp.*
19. *Sum. theol.*, I. 59, 4, ad *Resp.*
20. *De Verit.*, XXII. 6, ad *Resp.*; *De Malo*, III. 3, ad *Resp.*; *Sum. theol.*, I. 82, 2, ad *Resp.*
21. *Sum. theol.*, I. 82, 3, ad *Resp.*
22. *Sum. theol.*, I. 82, 4, ad *Resp.*
23. *Sum. theol.*, I. 82, 1, ad *Resp.*
24. *De Malo*, VI., art. un., ad *Resp.*
25. *De Consolat.*, lib. III., prosa 2.
26. *De Verit.*, XXII. 6, ad *Resp.*
27. *De Malo*, VI., art. un., ad *Resp.*

CHAPTER XV.
THE HUMAN ACT

THE creative act is usually thought to have had no other effect but that of producing all being from non-being. But this is an incomplete and one-sided view of creation. Its efficacy is not exhausted by the bringing forth from God of all beings. At the same time as created things receive the impulse which places them in a state of being, relatively independent and external to that of the Creator, they receive a second impulse leading them back to their starting-point and impelling them to re-ascend as far as possible to their first source. We have so far considered the order in which intelligent creatures issue forth from God, and have defined the operations characteristic of them; the task remains to determine the goal to which these operations tend and in view of which they are disposed.[1]

In reality, this problem presents itself in all its difficulty in reference to man and to him alone. The fate of the angels was definitely fixed from the first moment following on their creation; not as if they had been created in a state of bliss;[2] but, once created, as is probable, in a state of grace, those among them who so willed, turned to God by a single act of love securing to them at once eternal happiness,[3] while conversely the bad angels by a single act of their free-will turned for ever away from Him.[4] Again, as far as the creatures, inferior to man, are concerned, i.e. those devoid of intellectual knowledge, the solution of the question is equally simple; without either intelligence or will, they can attain to their ultimate goal—which is God—inasmuch as they participate in some resemblance to their Creator. Endowed with being, life and sensible knowledge, they are in various degrees as many images of God who has created them, and the possession of this likeness amounts for them to the attainment of their final end.[5] The truth of this conclusion is evident. For it is clear that the end always corresponds to the beginning. If, therefore, we know the beginning of all things, we cannot possibly be in ignorance of their end. Now, we have shown earlier that the first beginning of all things is a Creator transcending the universe He has created. The end of all things must therefore be a good, since a good alone can act as end, and moreover a good external to the universe; this end is accordingly none other than God. The question remains how creatures, devoid of intelligence, can have an end which is external to themselves. In the case of an intelligent being the end of his operation is what he proposes to do, or the aim he has in view; but in the case of a being without intellect, the only manner of having an end, is either to possess it in effect without knowing it, or to represent it. In this sense "Hercules" may be said to be the end of a statue intended to represent him. In the same sense the Supreme Good external to the universe can be said to be the end of all things, insofar as it is possessed or represented by them, because all created things tend to a participation in it and to represent it as far as in them lies.[6]

But this does not apply to man endowed with free-will, i.e. with intelligence and will. The inclination imparted to him by God at creation is not natural; it is an inclination of the will, and it follows therefrom that this creature, the image of God, like all the others and a more perfect image than many of them, is master of the choice of his acts. We must consequently enquire what his ultimate goal is and by what means he may be able to attain to it.

A. THE STRUCTURE OF THE HUMAN ACT

It has been established earlier that man is a being endowed with will, as is inevitable in an agent at once rational and free. The source of this freedom is also known; it is the result of the discrepancy which is bound to occur in this life between our will and its objects. By its essence the will tends towards the universal good; but in reality it is constantly confronted with particular goods. These particular goods which are unable to satisfy its desire, do not therefore constitute for it compelling ends, with the result that the will remains completely free in respect of them. *Si proponatur aliquod objectum voluntati quod sit universaliter bonum et secundum omnem considerationem, ex necessitate voluntas in illud tendit, si aliquid velit: non enim poterit velle oppositum. Si autem proponatur sibi aliquod objectum quod non secundum quamlibet considerationem sit bonum, non ex necessitate voluntas fertur in illud.*[7] But, though we are now in possession of the general principle which governs the whole of our rational activity, we have still to show its mechanism and to examine how it works in practice.

Let us take as our starting-point the conclusion which we just recalled to mind. It cannot be grasped unless we assume, on the one hand, the will and, on the other, an object to which it tends. This movement of the will which sets itself in motion and imparts motion to all the other powers of the soul in the direction of its object, is called "intention." It is further of importance to state precisely, at this starting-point of human activity, the respective parts played by the intellect and by the will. They act one on the other, but in different relations. For, consider the objects of these two powers: that of the intellect is none other than being and universal truth. But being and universal truth constitute the first formal principle which it is possible to indicate, and the formal principle of an act is also what assigns it to a definite species. For instance, the act of heating is such only by reason of its formal principle being heat. Now, the intellect moves the will by presenting to it its object, namely being and universal truth, and thereby it assigns to the act of will its proper species, in distinction to the acts performed by the sensitive or merely natural powers. There is therefore here a real and effective movement imparted by the intellect to the will. But, conversely, the will moves the intellect in the sense that it may, in certain cases, effectively communicate movement to it. For, if we compare all our active faculties among each other, we find that the one which tends to an universal end appears as necessarily directing those which tend to merely particular ends: for everything that acts, acts in view of an end; thus the art, whose proper object is a certain end, directs and moves those arts which merely furnish the means to that end. Now, the object of the will is precisely the good, i.e. the general end. Therefore, since every power of the soul tends to its own particular end, as sight to the perception of colours or the intellect to the knowledge of the true, the will whose object is the good in general, must be able to make use of all the powers of the soul and in particular of the intellect, because it follows the intellect.[8]

Thus the will moves all the faculties to their ends, and to it belongs especially that first act, the "intention": *in aliquid tendere*. In making the act of intention, the will turns to its end as to the completion of its movement; and since, in willing the end, it necessarily also wills the means, it follows that the intention of the end and the willing of the means constitute one and the same act. The reason of this is easy to understand. The means is to the end as the intermediate stage is to the completion. In natural beings, the same movement passes through the intermediate stage and reaches its termination; the same applies also to the movements of the will. To-will-a-remedy-with-the-view-to-health is to accomplish a single act of the will. The means is willed only because of the end; the willing of the means is therefore identical with the intention of the end.[9]

The proper object of the intention is thus the end willed in itself and for itself; the intention is therefore a simple act and, so to say, an indivisible movement of our will. But the action of the will becomes extremely complex as soon as we pass from the intention of the end to the choice of means. The will tends in a single act both to the end and the means, once it has exercised its option for such and such determinate means; but the option in favour of such and such means does not properly belong to the voluntary act of the intention. This option is the result of choice, preceded in its turn by deliberation and judgment.

Human actions are always concerned with the particular and the contingent; but, in passing from the universal to the particular, we pass from what is unchangeable and certain to what is uncertain and variable. This—it may be said incidentally—is the reason why our knowledge of what should be done, is so fatally beset with uncertainty. Now, reason never ventures upon a judgment in doubtful and uncertain questions without first submitting it to deliberation; this deliberation has been called "consilium." It has just been observed that the object of this deliberation is not the end as such. The intention of the end, being the very principle whence the action started, cannot be called in question. If the end should come to be the object of deliberation, it could not be *quâ* end, but merely in so far as it may be considered in its turn as the means to a further end. Whatever acts as end in a deliberation, is therefore capable of acting as means to another and may as such become the burden of discussion.[10] In any case, the deliberation must terminate in a judgment, for, without it, it would continue indefinitely and we should never come to a decision. Limited as it is by its initial term, viz. the simple intention of the end, it is equally limited by its final term, viz. the first action which we deem needful. Thus the deliberation may end by a judgment of practical reason, and the whole of this process of voluntary movement takes place in the intellect alone, without the intervention of the will for any other purpose than to set it in movement and, in a sense, to release the process.

Supposing now that the will has to deal with results obtained by such deliberation: since practical reason is

a matter of particular and contingent action, it generally ends in two or more judgments each of which offers
us a line of action appearing as good under some
aspect. The consideration on the part of the intellect
of several actions presented to the will as possible,
has its counter-part in the will in the shape of a movement of approval of whatever good is contained in each
of these actions. By approving of and fastening upon
it, the will has a sort of experience of the object on
which it dwells: *quasi experientiam quamdam sumens
de re cui inhaeret*,[11] and, in doing so, it adds its consent.
The act by which the will applies itself and adheres to
the result of the deliberation we shall therefore call
"consensus."

But the deliberation cannot end in this consent.
Since it leads to several judgments, arousing in the will
several consents, the will must still, by an act of
decision, choose one of these consents by preference
over the others. Deliberation leads us to observe
that several means can bring about the end we have
in view; each of these means pleases us, and in so far
as it does so, we give it our adherence; but we select
one out of these several means, and this selection
belongs by right to the act of choice (*electio*). It may,
however, happen that only a single means is offered
by reason and that, in consequence, only one means
pleases us. In such a case, choice may be said to
coincide with consent.[12]

What is this choice? It is an act, part of which
pertains to the reason or intellect, while another part
pertains to the will. Hence it has been called by
Aristotle: *appetitivus intellectus, vel appetitus intel-
lectivus*.[13] In its fullest sense, it is, in fact, simply the
complete act by which the will determines itself, comprising at the same time the deliberation of reason and
the decision of the will. Reason and understanding
are required for the purpose of deliberation, in the
manner explained, and for a judgment on the means
which seem preferable, the will is required to bring
about the consent given to these means, and the

option in favour of one of them. But it is still to be determined whether, taken in its proper essence, the act finally concluding the deliberation pertains to the understanding or to the will. To reach a decision on this point, it must be remarked that the substance of an act depends both on its matter and on its form. Now, among the acts of the soul, an act which, in its matter, pertains to a certain power, may yet have its form and, consequently, its specific quality from a power of a superior order; for the inferior is always ordered with reference to the superior. If, for example, a man performs a feat of physical strength out of his love of God, this feat is indeed, in its very matter, an act of physical strength, but in its form an act of love, and therefore substantially an act of love. Applying this argument to the act of choice: the understanding furnishes in some sort the matter of the act by offering its judgments to the acceptance of the will; but, to give the very form of choice to the act, a movement of the soul is needed towards the good which it elects. Choice constitutes therefore, in its very substance, an act of will.[14]

Such is the structure of the human act in general outline. In that act we see the intellect and the will interacting upon each other; yet it would be a mistake to confuse them in the unity of the same act. They perpetually intercross but never mix. This can easily be observed by distinguishing spontaneous acts from acts commanded. Every act of will is either spontaneous, as the act by which the will tends to its end as such, or commanded, as happens when reason intimates its order: "Do this!" It is clear, moreover, that nothing is more in our own power than acts of the will and that we can, consequently, always intimate to ourselves such an order.[15] What happens in such a case? Reason may simply say: "This is what has to be done"; and evidently, reason alone intervenes in such an instance. But it may also happen that it orders: "Do this," and thus moves the will to will it; the intimation of the order here belongs to the intellect, and the moving force of the order belongs to the will.[16] Let us, on the other hand, consider the operations of reason implied in an human act. If it is a question of the exercise itself of a rational act, this can always be the object of an imperative, as, for instance, the order by which we tell someone to pay attention or to appeal to his reason. For if the possible object of such an act is in question, we must be careful to distinguish two cases: on the one hand, the intellect may simply apprehend a certain truth concerning any question; this depends solely on our natural intelligence and in no way on our will. It is not a matter of our free-will to see or not to see a truth at the moment of our discovering it. But the intellect may also give its assent to what it apprehends.[17] If then what is apprehended, belongs to the class of propositions to which the intellect must, by its very nature, give its assent—for instance, the class of first principles—it is not in our power to give or to withhold our assent. If, on the contrary, the propositions apprehended do not convince our intellect, to the extent that it can still either not affirm them, or deny them, or suspend at least its refusal or acceptance, it is evident that in such a case both assent and denial remain in our power and fall into the domain of our will.[18] But in every case, it is the understanding alone that apprehends the truths, accepts or declines them and issues orders, whereas the movement received or transmitted by the intellect, comes always from the will. Every movement, therefore, remains voluntary, even when it seems to issue from the intellect; all knowledge remains intellectual, even when it originates in a movement of the will.

B. HABITS

We have just defined the human acts in themselves and, as it were, in the abstract, but it is not in the abstract that they present themselves. They are performed by individual concrete human beings; and these human beings are not pure substances;

they have also their accidents. Each acting subject, instead of being a schematic agent constituted theoretically by an intellect and a will, is further influenced in his actions by certain ways of acting peculiar to him, by permanent dispositions affecting him, the most important of which are his habits and virtues. We must consider first the nature of habits.

Man, as we know, is a discursive being, and his life must have a certain duration to enable him to attain to his end. Now, this duration is not that of an inorganic body whose mode of being remains unaltered in the course of its existence; it is the duration of a living being. Each effort made by man to reach his goal, instead of lapsing again into nothingness, is registered in him and leaves its mark on him. The soul of man, as well as his body, has a history; it preserves its past to benefit by it and to utilise it in a perpetual present: and the most general form of this fixation of past experience is called "habit." Habit, as conceived by St. Thomas, is in fact a quality, that is to say, not the very substance of man, but a definite disposition, added to and modifying it. The characteristic feature of habit and of this disposition as such among all the other species of quality, is that it is a disposition of the subject in reference to his own nature; or, in other words, the habit of a being determines the manner in which he realises his own definition.

It is a consequence of this that no habit can be described without the use of the qualification of good or bad as part of the description; for what defines a thing is its form; but the form is not only the essence of it, but also its *raison d'être*: the form is at the same time the end of the thing. To explain how the habit of a being determines the manner of his realising his own definition, means therefore to explain how he realises his essence and how far he is from his proper goal. If his habit approximates him to the ideal type to which he tends, this habit is good; if, on the contrary, it removes him from the ideal type, it is bad; a habit may consequently be defined in general as the disposition according to which a subject is well or ill disposed,[19] and if habits are qualities and accidents, they must be those nearest to the nature of the subject, or those that come nearest to being part of his essence and constituent elements of his definition.[20]

What are the conditions required for the development of a habit? The first condition which at bottom implies all the others, is the existence of a subject in potency in respect of several different determinations, so that several different principles are able to combine in producing one of these determinations.[21] This means that God, for instance, being wholly act, could not be the subject of any habit; it means further that the celestial bodies, the matter of which is entirely and definitely fixed by their form, leave equally no room for that absence of determination necessary for the development of an habit; it means lastly that the qualities of elementary bodies, as necessarily and inseparably tied to these elements, also offer no occasion for it. In fact, the true subject of an habit is a soul like the human soul, for it admits of an element of receptivity and potency, and as it is the principle of a number of operations, thanks to the number of faculties possessed by it, it meets all the conditions required for the development of habit.[22] But it is possible to indicate with more detail the soil on which it grows within the human soul itself: for it cannot reside in the sensitive powers of the soul, because, in themselves and independently of reason, they appear determined to their action by a sort of natural instinct and as lacking in that indetermination which is needed for the growth of habit. There remains therefore only the intellect in which it can be placed. That multiplicity of indeterminate powers, capable of combining and organising themselves into the most diverse schemes, is to be found in the intellect alone. And lastly since potency is the decisive factor in the formation of habit, we may complete our determination by assigning to it that part of the intellect which is called the possible intellect. It goes without saying that the will as a faculty of the rational soul and as based in its free indetermination on the universality of reason itself, is capable on that very ground of becoming also the subject of an habit.

As a result we perceive both what the nature of habit is and the quite special position which it occupies in the anthropological conceptions of St. Thomas. While studying the faculties of the soul by themselves, we necessarily considered them from a static and inorganic point of view. The conception of habit, on the contrary, introduces into his thought a dynamic element of progress and organisation. In its deepest sense, habit, as St. Thomas understood it, appears as an exigency of life in the human intellect, and through the intellect in the whole human soul. We use the term "exigency" advisedly, for wherever the conditions required for the development of habit occur, its development is not merely possible, but necessary. At least it is so, if every nature is to possess all the instruments needed for the attainment of its goal. Now, whereas a natural form necessarily reaches its goal by reason of the very determination which ties it down to one single operation, the intellectual form with its universality and indetermination, would never attain to its end unless some complementary disposition inclined it towards it. It is precisely habit that constitutes this complementary nature, these superadded determinations which set up definite relations between the passive intellect and its objects or possible operations.[23] This means that a given real intellect is inseparable in practice from the totality of its habits, whether they enrich or degrade the intellect. Habits represent so many instruments which the intellect has acquired and between which it is moreover always free to choose as master; but the intellect has acquired these habits, because it had necessarily to do so, to meet the conditions required by the very nature of its operations.

For, setting aside habits which are nothing but simple dispositions towards being, such as the habit of matter to receive a form, we note that the various kinds of habit are directed to certain operations, either cognitive or voluntary. Some of them are in some way natural and as it were innate. Such is the intellection of first principles. Everything happens as if our intellect were born with a natural disposition to know them from our very first experience of sensible things. Again, if we place ourselves at the point of view of the individual and not of the species, each of us might be said to carry in him at birth the beginnings of a cognitive habit. For our sensitive organs, the collaboration of which is indispensable to the act of cognition, predispose us to know more or less effectively. The same applies to the will, with this difference however, that it is not the habit itself which exists already in outline, but only certain constitutive principles of the habit, such as the principles of rectitude which are sometimes called "seeds of the virtues." *Per contra*, certain kinds of habit of the will exist already in outline in the body, since there are men who according to their natural complexion and individual temperament are born with a predisposition to gentleness or chastity or some other habit of this kind. As a general rule, however, habit results much less from our natural dispositions than from our acts. Sometimes a single act suffices to break the passivity of the faculty in which the habit is developing; such is the case of a directly evident proposition sufficing to convince the intellect completely and to impose on it the acceptance of a certain conclusion for good and all. Sometimes, again—and this is much the most frequent case—a number of analogous and repeated acts is required to set up an habit in a power of the soul. For instance, a probable opinion is not at once accepted, but it becomes an habitual belief when the active intellect has impressed it by a large number of acts on the possible intellect; and even then the possible intellect must repeat the acts in reference to the inferior faculties, if this belief is, for example, to be deeply impressed on the memory. The active power therefore generally needs time to master completely the matter to which it is applied; as with fire which does not instantaneously consume all its inflammable material nor succeeds in setting it alight at once, but gradually deprives it of its opposing dispositions until it finally masters and assimilates it completely.[24] Thus the repetition of acts more and more penetrating a matter with their form and a power of the soul with some new disposition, increases progressively that habit, just as the cessation of the acts or the performance of contrary acts undermines and breaks it down.[25]

C. GOOD AND EVIL. — THE VIRTUES.

Having once understood the nature of habit, the nature of the virtues is also established, for virtues are forms of habit disposing us more permanently to good actions. For, as was said above, habit is a disposition to the better or to the worse. Since habit measures the greater or lesser distance of the individual from his proper goal and causes him to conform more or less to his proper type, a careful distinction must be made between an habit disposing him to perform an act conforming to his nature, and one disposing him to an act in disagreement with his nature. The former are good habits, and such are also the virtues; the latter are bad habits, and these are vices.[26] To obtain an exact definition of virtue, we have to ask the question which are the acts conforming to man's nature; we shall then know also wherein the morally good and bad consists and how to distinguish between vice and virtue.

Operations and actions are like the beings that perform them: *unaquaeque res talem actionem producit, qualis est ipsa*; and the excellence of things is always measured by the degree of their being. Man, then, as a defective and imperfect being, is bound to perform incomplete and defective actions, and therefore good and bad are always combined in them, though in variable proportions.[27] The good in human actions may be considered from four points of view. In the first place, human action belongs to the genus "action," and as every action is judged by the perfection of the being performing it, there is, apart from everything else, in the very substance of any action of whatever kind an intrinsic value corresponding to a certain degree of excellence and goodness. Secondly, actions depend for their goodness on their species, and as the species of every action is determined by its object, it follows that every action may be called good or bad from this new point of view, according as it is or is not applied to a suitable object.[28] In the third place, human actions are good or bad by reason of the accompanying circumstances. For in the same way as a natural being receives not only the fulness of its perfection from its substantial form which places it in a certain species, but receives in addition a number of accidents, such as in the case of man, his stature, his colour and others of the same kind; so in the case of actions. An action receives its goodness not only from its species, but also from a fairly large number of accidents. These accidents are the due circumstances, the lack of which suffices to make an action bad.[29] Lastly, the goodness of an human action depends on its end. For, we recalled the fact that the order of goodness corresponds to the order of being. Now, there are beings which, as such, do not depend on others; and, to estimate their operations, it is sufficient to consider in itself the being whence the operations spring. But there are others whose being, on the contrary, depends on some other being; their operations can therefore only be judged by taking into account the cause whence they depend. We must consequently take count—and this is the essential point— of the relation in which human actions stand to the first Cause of all goodness, namely God.[30]

This last point requires to be elaborated. In every voluntary action, two different acts must be distinguished, viz. the interior act of the will and the external act. Each of these two acts corresponds to an object proper to it. The object of the interior act of the will is none other than its end, and the object of the external act is whatever this act is relevant to. But it is clear that of these two acts, one directs the other. The external act receives, in fact, its specification from the object which constitutes its point of application; the internal act of the will is specified by the end, as by its proper object. But whatever in this case the will contains, imposes its form on what constitutes the external act; for the limbs of the body are merely the instruments which the will employs in its action, and external acts have a moral significance only in so far as they are voluntary. Therefore, if we wish to reach the highest principle whereby to specify acts as good or bad, we must assert that human acts formally receive their species from the end to which the internal act of the will is directed, and at most materially, from the object to which the external act is applied.[31]

But what is this end to be? Dionysius supplies the proper answer to this question. The good of man, he says,[32] is to be in accord with reason; evil, on the contrary, is everything contrary to reason. For the good of everything is what is suitable to it, given its own form; and evil is whatsoever contradicts and consequently tends to destroy the order of that form. Since therefore the form of man is his rational soul itself, it follows that every act in conformity with reason is good, and every act which is contrary to reason, evil.[33] Thus, whenever a human act contains something contrary to the order of reason, it falls by that very fact into the species of bad actions: as, for instance, the action of stealing which consists in seizing the goods belonging to another. But it is at the same time evident that, if the end or the object of an act contains nothing relevant to the order of reason, such as when a man picks up a wisp of straw, such an act must be pronounced to be morally indifferent.[34]

If, on the other hand, we consider each of these acts as conforming to reason, it will appear such in so far as it appears ordered in view of an end and of a series of means, which on enquiry reason declares to be good. Thus the various particular good acts performed by man, may be defined as the sum total of acts ordered with a view to their ends and justifiable by reason.

The condition which takes precedence over all others required to constitute the moral goodness of a human act, is evidently the subordination of the act to its legitimate end. As has been seen, the movement by which the will tends to a certain end, is described as the "intention"; it would consequently appear that the morality to which we are led, is essentially a morality of intention. This conclusion would in certain respects be correct, provided it is not taken in too narrow and exclusive a sense. In itself, the intention by which the will turns towards its end, can be considered as the germ of the complete voluntary act. The reason is that, because I will the end, I also will the means, I choose, and I act; as, therefore, the intention is, so also is the act produced by it, good, if the intention is good, bad, if the intention is bad, though neither to the same degree nor in the same manner. If the intention is bad, the act is irremediably bad, since each of the parts constituting the act are brought into existence to be placed at the service of evil. When, on the contrary, the intention is good, this initial orientation of the will towards the good, cannot but impregnate the entire resulting act; yet it is not sufficient to define the act entirely. We could not, without manifest abuse, place on the same level two acts whose intention may be equally good, but of which one is mistaken in its choice of means or fails to apply them, whereas the other selects the most appropriate means and secures impeccably their application. A moral act, therefore, always gains by being inspired by a good intention, for, even if failing in the accomplishment of its object, it retains none the less the merit of having intended to do good, and often even deserves more than it accomplishes. Still, a morally perfect act is nevertheless an act which fully satisfies the demands of reason, in its end no less than in each of its parts, and, not content with merely willing the good, actually achieves it.

Such being the nature of moral good, it is easy to understand the nature of virtue: virtue consists essentially and originally in a permanent disposition to act in conformity with reason. But the complexity of the human being forces us at once to complicate the conception of the virtue proper to him. For, it is certain that reason is the first principle of all human acts, and that all other principles of human acts of whatever kind, conform to reason. If therefore man were a pure spirit, or if the body with which his soul is united were completely subject to him, it would be sufficient to see what we have to do in order to do it; the thesis of Socrates would be true and there would be no virtues but intellectual virtues. But we are not pure spirits; nor is it even true, after the original fall, that our body is perfectly subject to us. For man to act well, reason must not only be well disposed by the habit of intellectual virtue, but his appetite or faculty of desiring must be well disposed by the habit of moral virtue. Moral virtue must therefore be distinguished from intellectual virtue and be added to it; and just as the appetite is the principle of human acts in so far as it participates in reason, so moral virtue is a human virtue to the extent to which it conforms to reason.[35] It is therefore as absolutely impossible to reduce these two orders of virtue to each other as it is to isolate one from the other. Moral virtue cannot do without all intellectual virtue; for moral virtue must determine a good act; but an act presupposes a choice and we saw in studying the structure of the human act, that choice presupposes deliberation and the judgment of reason. Again, the intellectual virtues not directly relevant to action, may be able to do without moral virtues, but not so prudence which is bound to result precisely in acts. This intellectual virtue does not simply determine what has to be done in a general way—for that, it would suffice of itself without the help of moral virtues—but it has to descend to the details of particular cases. Now, there again, it is no longer a pure spirit that has to judge, but a compound of soul and body. A person in whom concupiscence dominates, considers good whatever he desires, even if this judgment contradicts the universal judgment of reason, and to neutralise this sophistry of the passions, man must safeguard himself by moral habits through which it will become almost co-natural to him to judge soundly of his end.[36]

Among the intellectual virtues four stand out in importance: intelligence, knowledge, wisdom, and prudence. The first three are purely intellectual and are grouped under wisdom, as the lower powers of the soul are grouped under the rational soul. For truth can either be evident, or known in itself and directly, or known indirectly by inference. In so far as it is known in itself and directly, the true acts as principle. The immediate knowledge of the principles is the first habit and the first virtue of the intellect on its first contact with sensible experience; it is the first permanent disposition formed and the first perfection acquired; intelligence is therefore called the virtue which fits the intellect for the knowledge of directly evident truths or principles.

The truths, on the other hand, which are not directly evident, but deduced or inferred, depend no longer on the intellect, but on reason. Now, reason may tend to conclusions which are the final conclusion of a particular kind, i.e. provisional conclusions, or they may be the absolute final and highest conclusions of all. In the first case, reason is called knowledge; in the second, wisdom. And since knowledge is a virtue enabling reason to judge sanely of a certain order of knowables, there may, nay, there must, be a number of different kinds of knowledge in the human mind. But as wisdom is concerned with the ultimate causes and with both the most perfect and the most universal object, only one knowable of this kind exists and consequently only one wisdom. And this is ultimately the reason why these three virtues are distinct not by simple juxtaposition, but are ordered hierarchically. Knowledge, as the habit of conclusions deduced from principles, depends on intelligence which is the habit of principles. And both knowledge and intelligence depend on wisdom which contains and dominates them, since it judges both the intelligence and its principles, and knowledge and its conclusions: *convenienter judicat et ordinat de omnibus, quia judicium perfectum et universale haberi non potest, nisi per resolutionem ad primas causas.*[37]

Thanks to these three virtues, the possible intellect which previously could be compared to a blank tablet, acquires a series of progressive determinations which enable it to perform the operations of knowledge. But up to this point, the intellect can do no more than perform this operation; to bring it yet nearer to its perfection, a supplementary determination is needed to give it the capacity not only to know, but also to utilise the virtues which it has acquired. It is not enough for man merely to think, he must also live and live rightly. Now, to live rightly means to act rightly; and to act rightly he needs to take count not only of what he has to do, but also of the manner of doing it. It is not enough just to take a decision; what matters is, to take a decision reasonably, not by blind impulse or passion. The principle of such a deliberation is supplied not by the intelligence, but by the end aimed at by the will; for in human acts, the end has the same function as that fulfilled by the principles in speculative knowledge. But to will a suitable end, depends also on a virtue, but on a moral, not intellectual virtue. Once the end is willed, on the contrary, the consideration and choice of means suitable to the end are a matter for intellectual virtue. It follows that an intellectual virtue must exist which enables reason to arrive at a suitable determination of means leading to the end in view: this virtue is prudence, *recta ratio agibilium*; and this is a virtue necessary for living rightly.[38]

The moral virtues impart to the will the same

perfections as those conferred by the intellectual virtues upon knowledge. Some of these virtues regulate the contents and nature of the operations themselves, independently of our personal dispositions at the moment of acting. Such in particular is justice which ensures the moral value and rectitude of all those operations which involve ideas of what is or is not due; for example, operations of sale and purchase pre-suppose the recognition or denial of a debt towards our neighbour; they belong therefore to the domain of justice. Other moral virtues, on the contrary, concern the quality of acts, considered in regard to him who performs them; they deal therefore with the internal dispositions of the agent at the moment of acting, and in a sort, with his passions. If the agent is carried away by passion to commit an act contrary to reason, he needs to appeal to the virtue which restrains and controls his passions: this is the virtue of temperance. If the agent, instead of being carried away by some passion, weakens in his action (say, by fear of danger or of effort), another moral virtue is required to confirm him in the resolutions dictated by his reason: this is the virtue of fortitude.[39]

These three moral virtues together with the one intellectual virtue of prudence, are usually described as "principal" or "cardinal" virtues, for they alone imply both the faculty of acting rightly and the performance of the good act itself, and consequently they realise by themselves perfectly the definition of virtue.[40]

Thus the conception of virtue in its most perfect form gradually takes shape: it owes its quality of moral good to the rule of reason, and it has as its matter the operations or the passions: *virtus moralis bonitatem habet ex regula rationis*.[41] And it is due to this also that the intellectual and moral virtues consist in a mean between two extremes. The act regulated by moral virtue, conforms to right reason, and reason has the effect of assigning the right mean, equidistant from excess and from deficiency in each particular case. Sometimes it happens that the right mean fixed by reason is also the right mean of the thing itself; so it is

in the case of justice which regulates operations concerned with external acts and has to assign to each his
due, neither more nor less. Sometimes, on the contrary,
the right mean fixed by reason is not that of the thing,
but a mean which is such only by reference to us. This
applies to all the other moral virtues which affect not
operations, but our passions. Having to consider the
internal dispositions which differ from man to man, and
even in the same person at different moments,
temperance and fortitude fix the just mean, conforming
to reason, by reference to us and to the passions actua-
ting us. It is the same, finally, with the intellectual virtues.
Every virtue aims at determining a measure and a good.
But the good of the intellectual virtue is the true, and
the measure of truth is the thing. Our reason attains to
truth when whatever reason affirms as existing, does
exist, and what reason declares not to exist, does not
exist. It commits an error by excess when it asserts
the existence of what does not exist; it errs by deficiency when it denies the existence of what exists;
truth therefore is the right mean, determined by the
thing itself, and this very truth confers on virtue its
moral excellence.[42]

Acts of will dictated by reason, habits, and especially
virtuous habits, are the inner principles which direct our
moral action; it remains for us to determine the external
principles which regulate it in a sense *ab extra*, i.e. the
laws.

D. THE LAWS

All the preceding considerations lead to the conception
of a moral behaviour wholly dependent upon itself and
—to use an expression unknown to thomistic diction—
entirely "autonomous." This autonomy of thomistic
morality is beyond doubt; however, to form an exact
idea of it, it is necessary to consider the laws which are
imposed upon and direct the human will, leaving for
later discussion how an accord can be secured between a
self-directing will and this external legislation which
imperiously prescribes the end to be aimed by the will.

The first question here presents itself: what is a law? It is a rule which prescribes or forbids an action; in short, it is the rule of an action. If this is true, the idea of a law assumes at once an universal extension: where-ever any thing is done, there must be a rule in conformity with which things are done and, consequently, also a law. Such a definition, however, is vague and incomplete and needs to be supplemented.

In point of fact, if we attempt to disengage the essential character of what we describe by the term "law," beyond the mere idea of a simple rule, we encounter the far deeper quality of an "obligation." Whenever an activity submits to a rule, it sets such a rule up, so to speak, as a measure of its legitimacy, adopts it as its principle and undertakes the obligation to respect it. Now, do we know of any other regulative principle of actions but reason? Reason, indeed, in all domains, appears as the rule and measure of what is done, so that law, if it is really nothing but the formula of this rule, presents itself at once as an obligation founded upon the demands of reason.[43] This is a definition which we note is at least founded upon custom and in accord with conscience universally. The unreasonable prescriptions of a tyrant may well usurp the title of laws but are not real laws; wherever reason is lacking, there can be neither law nor equity, but pure and simple iniquity.[44]

Moreover, an imperative order of reason is of itself not sufficient for the existence of a law; it is required further that such an order should aim at a determined end, other than our merely individual ends. For saying that law is a prescription of reason determining what is to be done, brings it at once into contact with practical reason whose proper function it is to prescribe the acts that are to be performed. But this practical reason depends in its turn on a principle which directs it and to which it must conform; for it prescribes such and such an act only with the view to guide us to such and such an end, and, if therefore an end exists which is common to all our acts, this latter constitutes the first principle on which all decisions of practical reason depend. Now it is not difficult to discover this principle. A being acting rationally strives always to attain to its good, and the good at which each one of its acts aims beyond the particular ends realised, is the supreme Good which completely satisfies the being, if it is permitted to attain to it, possession of which would dispense it from the attainment of all the others.[45] Even without having fully defined the object pursued, we may therefore say that the will aims, through all the multiplicity of its particular acts, at a single end which is the beatitude. Every law, inasmuch as it is the prescription of practical reason, is consequently the rule of an action aiming at the attainment of happiness.

To these determinations we may add a last condition which, however external it may appear at first sight, constitutes, nonetheless, an important element in the definition of law. since law aims essentially at the realisation of a good without any reservation, it cannot be limited to the good of particular individuals; what it prescribes is the absolute good, hence the common good, and consequently also a collective good. That is the reason why the authority required to set up legitimately a law can only belong to him who is charged with the care of the interests of a collectivity, or to the collectivity itself. It is, therefore, not simply practical reason decreeing what is to be done with the view to happiness that constitutes the origin of law, for the reason of the individual person is constantly ordering what he is to do in order to be happy, without such orders being laws; but it is practical reason decreeing what the individual person is to do with a view to the good of the community of which he forms part. The people, or the people's representative invested with the regular powers to guide the collectivity which he rules to its normal end, possess alone the qualifications to set up and promulgate laws.[46]

What is true to a people, is also true of the whole community of beings, ruled with the view to their common good by a sovereign whose decisions are governed by reason. We shall, therefore, have as many laws as we have such communities. The first and vastest of all is the Universe. The entirety of beings created by God and maintained in existence by His will, can be considered as an immense society of which we are citizens; and not only we, but also all animals and all things. There is not a single creature, animate or inanimate, which does not act in conformity with certain rules and in view of certain ends. Animals and things follow these rules and tend towards these ends without knowing them; man, on the contrary, is conscious of them and his moral justice consists in accepting them voluntarily. All laws of nature, all the laws of morality and of society must therefore be considered as so many particular instances of one and the same law, viz. the divine law. But the law by which God wills the universe to be governed is necessarily eternal as God is Himself; *eternal law* is, therefore, the name given to this first law which is the source of all other laws.[47]

As rational creature, man has the strict duty to know what the eternal law demands of him, and to conform to it. This would be an insoluble problem, were this law not somehow inscribed upon his very substance, so that he needs but observe himself carefully to discover it. The inclination, in us as in all things, which carries us towards certain ends, is the unmistakable mark of what the eternal law imposes on us. Since it is this law that causes us to be what we are, we need but yield to the legitimate tendencies of our nature to obey it. The eternal law which each of us shares in and discovers inscribed in our own nature, is given the name of *natural law*.[48] What are its prescriptions?

The first and most universal of all is the one proclaimed by all living beings by the very fact of their yielding to it: to do what is good and to avoid what is bad. This is a statement which may have become a truism and may be suspected to claim the entire content of morality under the pretext of formulating its first law; but it merely states the least contestable and most universal experience. It is a fact that every living being moves under the impulse of its desires and aversions. What has been given the name of "good" is nothing but the object of desire, and what is called "bad" is but the object of aversion. If we suppose an object which everything desires, this would, by definition, be the Absolute Good in itself. Therefore, if we say that we must do what is good and avoid what is bad, we do not arbitrarily decree a moral law; we simply read a natural law which is inscribed in the very substance of beings, and display the hidden spring of all their actions. "It must be done because we must do it"; this precept is so far a mere statement of fact.

Hence it is evident that the precepts of the natural law are in exact correspondence with our natural inclinations and follow the same order. Man is in the first place a being, like all others; he is further, more especially a living being, like all the other animals; he is lastly, by a privilege of nature, a rational being. Hence flow the three great natural laws which are imposed on him according to each of these aspects.

In the first place, man is a being. On this ground, he desires the preservation of his being; i.e. he desires to preserve himself by securing the integrity of every-thing that belongs by right to his nature. What is usually called the "instinct of self-preservation" means simply what this law expresses: each strives with all his power, and must strive, towards whatever can preserve his life or protect his health. The tendency to preserve in his being is consequently the first precept of the natural law imposed on man.

The second precept covers all laws which result from the fact that he is an animal and exercises animal functions: to reproduce himself, bring up his offspring and other natural obligations of this kind. The third, imposed on him as a rational being, prescribes to him the pursuit of everything that is good according to the order of reason: to live in communities, in order to pool the efforts of all and help one another; search for truth in the order of natural sciences or, better still, concerning the supreme Intelligible which is God; correspondingly not to harm those with whom he is called upon to live, to avoid ignorance and to try to dispel it—all these are imperative prescriptions of the natural law which in its turn is but one aspect of the eternal law willed by God.[49]

In this sense, the natural law is literally written upon the human heart and cannot be cancelled from it. But the question may well be asked: If this is so, how does it come about that not all men live the same life? The explanation is that a third series of precepts intervene between the natural law and the actions performed by each of us. This is *human law*. What is the reason for its existence?

As long as it is only a question of formulating the most general and abstract principles of human conduct, mankind comes easily to an agreement. No one calls in doubt the need for doing good, avoiding evil, acquiring knowledge, dispelling ignorance and for obeying in all things the dictates of reason. The real difficulty begins with the question what is good and what is bad, and what ought to be done to meet the requirements of reason. A gaping chasm opens between the universal principles of the natural law and the infinitely detailed complexity of particular actions which are supposed to conform to the natural law. No individual reflexion can bridge this gap which it is precisely the function of human law to fill.

From this follow two important consequences concerning the nature of this law. In the first place, it is evident that human law cannot lay claim to any principle of its own, but is confined strictly to the definition of the manner of applying the natural law. Princes or states, in legislating, merely deduce from the natural law the particular consequences required by social life. Secondly, and for this very reason, it is clear that anyone following spontaneously the natural law, is in a sense predisposed to the acceptance of and obedience to the human law. Once promulgated, human law may be a hindrance to the lawless and the revolutionary, but the just man will conform to it with perfect spontaneity, as if civil law did not exist for him.[50]

Having the object of prescribing the particular acts which natural law imposes on individuals with the view to the common good, human laws are an obligation only to the extent of their justice, i.e. in so far as they meet the conditions of their own definition. Such laws may be hard to bear and may impose upon the citizen painful sacrifices, but this does not diminish the strict duty to obey them. *Per contra*, if the state or the ruler impose laws with no other object but to satisfy their own greed or their thirst for glory, if they promulgate laws without having the authority to do so, or if they distribute burdens among citizens inequitably, or, lastly, if the burdens which they claim the right to impose, are excessive or disproportionate to the good which they are to secure, then such laws are said to be unjust and no one can be held in conscience to obey them. There may, of course, be a temporary obligation to observe them in order to avoid scandal and disorder, but sooner or later they must be modified. As to those laws which are contrary in any way whatever to the rights of God, no one should obey them under any pretext, because, according to the words of Scripture, it is better to obey God than man.[51]

The true nature of natural, human and divine law enables us to understand the precise meaning which should be given to the notion of "sanction." Only too often rewards and punishments are considered as accidental helps to moral progress and as simple artifices employed by the legislator to turn men towards the good and away from evil. The witness of human law and of social order where, indeed, as we have seen, sanctions play exactly this part, tends to disguise from us their real nature and the place they occupy in the universal order. On the same ground, they lose their meaning and are justly excluded from the moral order by every conscience which considers as good only such acts as are performed out of sheer love of the good.

The fundamental relation existing between an act and the sanction attached to it, is best seen in the domain of purely natural beings, viz. of those which act in virtue of their natural form alone, and not in virtue of the will. We have already observed that even such beings observe a rule, although they do not know it, and that this rule is in a sense inscribed upon their very substance[52]; they do not act, but are acted on. Now, the mere fact of obeying the nature which God has given to them and of acting in conformity with it, places such beings in a position similar to that of rational persons, governed by a law. It is universal legislation, promulgated by God to nature, which the words of the Psalm expresses: *Praeceptum posuit et non praeteribit.*[53] But it happens that certain bodies, by reason of the position and function imposed on them in the general economy of the universe, are prevented from meeting the requirements of their nature, from acting as it demands and, consequently, from attaining to their end. The consequence is that they suffer both in their operations and their substance, die and destroy themselves. The death of an animal or the destruction of an object are not the accidental complements of the disorder which prevents them from acting upon and following their nature; it is not even a consequence of it; but they are just part of the situation in which the animal or object is placed as the result of this very disorder, and they are, again, precisely what re-establishes order in the disorder which has created this situation. In point of fact, nothing can withdraw itself from the law, since everything which attempts to do so, destroys itself in proportion as it succeeds, bearing thereby witness to the fact that the legislation which it aimed at violating, cannot be broken.

In both the continued existence of the body which obeys the law, and this destruction of the body which defies it, we have before us in concrete and, so to speak, material shape, all the essential features of the moral sanction. Man, subject to the divine law like the rest of the universe, is at the same time endowed with a will, thanks to which it depends on him whether he submits to the order or rebels against it. But it does not depend on him whether that order exists or not, nor whether its effects come about or not in the universe. God may leave to the will of man the responsibility of securing on certain points the respect for the law, but He does not leave to human caprice the law itself which is the expression of the divine order. The will which submits to the law, and that which sets itself up in opposition, may indeed seem for a time immune from the consequences of their acts, but they must necessarily in the last resort end in the position in which they have placed themselves in respect to the eternal law. It is precisely the function of a "sanction" to bring them to this position. The only difference between the effect of the natural law and the sanction is that the former results naturally from the observation or the transgression of the law, whereas the latter is the effect of a will which reacts to the act of another will. The good which in the order of bodies flows necessarily from an action conformable to the natural law, is freely conferred by God upon the will of man who has freely observed it. The evil which is imposed necessarily upon a disordered body, is inflicted freely by God upon the evil will of man who has revolted against this order. This intentional character of reward and punishment is also what constitutes the good and evil imposed upon individuals as sanctions in the proper sense of the term[54]; but we must not forget that in both cases a sanction is nothing more than the strict observance of the law, the satisfaction of order and the realisation of a perfect equilibrium between acts and their consequences. As far as man refused to fulfil the divine law, so far must he ultimately undergo it: that precisely contitutes his punishment.[55]

Understood in this sense, restored to the purity and rigour of its meaning, the notion of "sanction" introduces no heteronomy into the order of morality. The reward to be gained or the punishment to be escaped are not what imparts to an act its morality or immorality; the act I perform is not good because it will have its reward, but it will have its reward because it is good. For the same reason I do not do good with the view of escaping punishment, but it is enough to do the one in order to escape the other, as it suffices to do good in order to reap the reward. There is, of course, no need to deny that the hope for reward and the fear of pain are not very effective helps to moral progress. But man is in the same position as regards the divine law, as the citizen is as regards civil and human laws: to avoid having the law inflicted upon him, he needs but observe it. We are wont to come to love gradually the good which at first we desire for the sake of some other thing, or of what we think is another thing, and come to will it for its own sake, as the universal good and order in which our individual good is unshakeably assured. Herein consist ultimately that liberty of the children of God, obeying Him like a father whose law of love imposes upon the child only its own good.

NOTES TO CHAPTER XV.

1. On the Ethics of St. Thomas in general see A. de la Barre, *La morale d' après saint Thomas et les théologiens scolastiques; mémento théorique et guide bibliographique*, Paris, 1911; Sertillanges, *La philosophie morale de saint Thomas*, 1916; H. D. Noble, *La vie morale d' après saint Thomas d'Aquin, Première série: La conscience morale*, Paris, 1923. E. Gilson, *Saint Thomas d'Aquin (Les moralistes chrétiens, textes et commentaires)*, Paris, J. Gabalda, 3rd ed. 1925.

2. *In II. Sent.*, dist. IV., art. 1.

3. *Sum. theol.*, I. 62, 5, ad *Resp.* The reason of this fact lies in the perfection of the angelic nature. The angel lives naturally by direct intuition and has no discursive knowledge; he can therefore attain to his end by a single act. Man, on the contrary, must search for it; he requires therefore time and a life of a certain duration to reach his end. The length of human life rests therefore upon his mode of knowledge: "Homo secundum suam naturam non statim natus est ultimam perfectionem adipisci, sicut angelus: et ideo homini longior vita data est ad merendum beatitudinem, quam angelo." *Ibid.*, ad 1ᵐ. Cf. I. 58, 3 and 4; I. 62, 6, ad *Resp.*

4. *Ibid.*, 63, 6, ad *Resp.*

5. *Sum. theol.*, IaIIae, 1, 8, ad *Resp.*

6. *Cont. Gent.*, III. 17; *Sum. theol.*, I. 103, 2, ad *Resp.* and ad 2ᵐ. Cf. Chap. IX, p. 197.

7. *Sum. theol.*, IaIIae, 10, 2, ad *Resp.*

8. *Sum. theol.*, I. 82, 4, ad *Resp.*; IaIIae, 9, 1, ad *Resp.*; *Cont. Gent.*, I. 72; III. 26; *De Verit.*, qu. XXII. 12, ad *Resp.*; *De Malo*, VI. 1, ad *Resp.*

9. *Sum. theol.*, IaIIae, 12, 3, ad *Resp.*; and 4, ad *Resp.*; *De Verit.*, qu. XXII., art. 14, ad *Resp.*

10. *Sum. theol.*, IaIIae, 14, 1, ad *Resp.*, and 2, ad *Resp.*

11. *Sum. theol.*, IaIIae, 15, 1, ad *Resp.*

12. *Sum. theol.*, IaIIae, 15, 3, ad 3ᵐ.

13. *In VI Ethic.*, cap. II., n. 5, lect. II.

14. *Sum. theol.*, I. 83, 8, ad *Resp.*; IaIIae, 13, 1, ad *Resp.*; *De Verit.*, qu. XXII., art. 15, ad *Resp.*

15. *Sum. theol.*, IaIIae, 17, 5, ad *Resp.*

16. *Sum. theol.*, IaIIae, 17, 1, ad *Resp.*

17. On the distinction between "assenting" which is applied rather to the intellect, and "consenting" which by reason of the suggested union between the power and the object, is applied on principle to the will, see *Sum. theol.*, IaIIae, 15, 1, ad 3ᵐ.

18. *Sum. theol.*, IaIIae, 17, 6; ad *Resp.*; *De Virtut.*, qu. 1, art. 7, ad *Resp.*

19. *Sum. theol.*, IaIIae, 49, 2, ad *Resp.*; Aristotle, *Metaph.*, IV. 20, 1022b, 10.

20. *Sum. theol.*, IaIIae, 49, 2, ad *Resp.* This is also the justification why we demand stability in order to speak of an habit. All habits are dispositions, but not all dispositions are habits; a disposition is merely passing, while an habit is a permanent disposition. Even then we are not dealing with anything definite or immutable; a disposition becomes more and more, or less and less an habit, in proportion as it is less and less, or more and more easy to lose it. An habit is an organism which develops: "Et sic dispositio fit habitus, sicut puer fit vir" (*ibid.*, ad 3ᵐ).

21. *Sum. theol.*, IaIIae, 49, 4, ad *Resp.*

22. *Ibid.*, 50, 2, ad *Resp.*; *I Sent.*, 26, 3, ad 4 et 5.

23. *Sum. theol.*, IaIIae, 49, 4, ad 1ᵐ; *In III Sent.*, 23, 1, 1, 1; Pègues, *Commentaire français littéral de la Somme théologique*, VII., p. 562–570.

24. *Sum. theol.*, IaIIae, 51, 2 and 3, ad *Resp.*

25. *Ibid.*, 52, 2, ad *Resp.*, and 53, 1, ad *Resp.*

26. *Sum. theol.*, IaIIae, 54, 3, ad *Resp.*, and 55, 1–4.

27. *De Malo*, qu. II., art. 4, ad *Resp.*; *Sum. theol.*, IaIIae, 18, 1, ad *Resp.*

28. *Sum. theol.*, IaIIae, 18, 2, ad *Resp.*, and 19, 1, ad *Resp.*

29. *Sum. theol.*, IaIIae, 18, 3, ad *Resp.* For the study of these circumstances see *ibid.*, 7, 1–4.

30. *Sum. theol.*, IaIIae, 18, 4, ad *Resp.*

31. *Sum. theol.*, IaIIae, 18, 6, ad *Resp.*

32. *De Div. Nom.*, c. IV.

33. *Sum. theol.*, IaIIae, 18, 5, ad *Resp.*; *Cont. Gent.*, III. 9; *De Malo*, qu. II., art. 4, ad *Resp.*; *De Virtut.*, qu. I., art. 2, ad 3.

34. *Sum. theol.*, IaIIae, 18, 8, ad *Resp.*; *De Malo*, qu. II., art. 5, ad *Resp.*

35. *Sum. theol.*, IaIIae, 58, 2, ad *Resp.* On the adequacy of this division, see *ibid.*, 3, ad *Resp.*

36. *Sum. theol.*, IaIIae, 58, 4–5, ad *Resp.*

37. *Sum. theol.*, IaIIae, 57, 2, ad *Resp.* and ad 2ᵐ.

38. *Sum. theol.*, IaIIae, 57, 5, ad *Resp.*

39. *Sum. theol.*, IaIIae, 60, 2, ad *Resp.*, and 61, 2, ad *Resp.*

40. *Sum. theol.*, IaIIae, 56, 3, ad *Resp.*, and 61, 1, ad *Resp.*

41. *Sum. theol.*, IaIIae, 64, 1, ad 1ᵐ.

42. *Sum. theol.*, IaIIae, 64, 2 and 3, ad *Resp.*; *De virtutibus cardinalibus*, qu. un. 1, ad *Resp.*; *De virtutibus in communi*, qu. un. 13, ad *Resp.*

43. *Sum. theol.*, IaIIae, 90, 1, ad *Resp.*

44. *Ibid.*, ad 3m.

45. See chapter XVI., The Last End.

46. *Sum. theol.*, IaIIae, 90, 3, ad *Resp.*

47. *Cont. Gent.*, III. 115; *Sum. theol.*, Iallae, 91, 1, and 93, 3.
48. *Sum. theol.*, Iallae, 91, 2, ad *Resp.*
49. *Sum. theol.*, Iallae, 94, 2, ad *Resp.*
50. *Sum. theol.*, Iallae, 91, 3, ad *Resp.*, and 95, 1, ad *Resp.*
51. *Act.* IV., 19; *Sum. theol.*, Iallae, 96, 4, ad *Resp.*
52. See Chapter IX, p. 190.
53. Psalm CXLVIII., cited in *Sum. theol.*, Iallae, 93, 5, ad *Resp.*
54. "Sicut res naturales ordini divinae providentiae subduntur, ita et actus humani.... Utrobique autem convenit debitum ordinem servari vel etiam praetermitti; hoc tamen interest quod observatio vel transgressio debiti ordinis est in potestate humanae voluntatis constituta, non autem in potestate naturalium rerum est quod a debito ordine deficiant vel ipsum sequantur. Oportet autem effectus causis per convenientiam respondere. Sicut igitur res naturales, cum in eis debitus ordo naturalium principiorum et actionum servatur, sequitur necessitate naturae conservatio et bonum in ipsis, corruptio autem et malum, quum a debito et naturali ordine receditur, ita etiam in rebus humanis oportet, quod, cum homo voluntarie servat ordinem legis divinitus impositae, consequatur bonum, non velut ex necessitate, sed ex dispensatione gubernantis, quod est praemiari, et e converso malum, cum ordo legis fuerit praetermissus, et hoc est puniri." *Cont. Gent.*, III. 140. Cf. *Sum. theol.*, Iallae, 93, 6.
55. "Quum, igitur actus humani divinae providentiae subdantur, sicut et res naturales, oportet malum quod accidit in humanis actibus sub ordine alicujus boni concludi. Hoc autem convenientissime fit per hoc quod peccata puniuntur; sic enim sub ordine justitiae, quae ad aequalitatem reducit, comprehenduntur ea quae debitam quantitatem excedunt. Excedit autem homo debitum suae quantitatis gradum, dum voluntatem suam divinae voluntati praefert, satisfaciendo ei contra ordinem Dei; quae quidem inaequalitas tollitur, dum contra voluntatem suam homo aliquid pati cogitur secundum ordinationem. Oportet igitur quod peccata humana puniantur divinitus, et eadem ratione bona facta remunerationem accipiant." *Cont. Gent.*, III. 140.

CHAPTER XVI.
THE LAST END

THE entire order of creatures derives from a single cause and tends towards a single end. It is, therefore, to be expected that the regulative principle of moral actions is identical with that of physical laws. The deep cause which causes a stone to fall, a flame to rise, the heavens to revolve and men to will, is one and the same cause. Each of these beings acts only in order to attain by means of its operations the perfection which is proper to it and thereby to realise its end which is to represent God: *unumquodque tendens in suam perfectionem, tendit in divinam similitudinem.* Only that, as each being is defined by its own essence, it must be added that each will also have its own peculiar manner of realising their common end.

Since all creatures, even those devoid of intellect, are ordered towards God as to their last end, and since all things attain to their last end in the measure of their participation in His likeness, creatures endowed with intelligence cannot but attain to it in a manner peculiar to them, namely by the operations proper to them as intelligent creatures and with a knowledge of their end. It is therefore evident that the last end of an intelligent creature is to know God.[1] This conclusion is inevitable and other arguments, equally direct, confirm us in the sense of its necessity. We shall reach, however, full conviction only when we have understood the way in which this last end gathers up and organises all the intermediate ends and how all particular happiness is nothing but the premiss to this beatitude.

Man, as a being endowed with will and freedom, acts always, as explained earlier, with the view to an end which imparts to his acts their specific quality; which means that his acts arrange themselves under diverse species according to the ends which constitute

both their principles and completion.[2] But there is no
doubt that, besides the multiplicity of particular ends,
a last end of human life, taken in its totality, exists.
For the ends are ordered and willed for the sake of each
other; unless therefore a final end existed, we would
have to regress *ad infinitum* in the series of ends,
and, as in the series of movers and moved things, if it
were infinite, nothing would be desired and no action
could ever be completed. Every action takes its
starting-point from an end and comes to rest in it:
the existence of a final end must therefore be necessarily admitted.[3] It is apparent, moreover, that all
that man wills, he wills in view of this last end. The
last end moves the appetite in the same manner in
which the first mover moves all other moveable things.
Now, it is evident that when a secondary thing imparts
movement, it can do so only inasmuch as it has itself
been set in motion by the first Mover. In the same
way, consequently, the secondary ends are desirable
and move the appetite only in so far as they are ordered
towards the last end which is the first of all desirable
objects.[4] Wherein consists this last end?

A search for the aspects under which men conceive
it, would discover the most diverse and strange notions.
Wealth, health, power, etc., all the goods of the body
in short, have been considered as constituting the
Supreme Good and last end. But these are only so
many palpable errors. For man himself cannot be the
last end of the universe; he is but a particular being,
ordered, like all the others, in view of a superior end.
The satisfaction and preservation of his body therefore
cannot form the Supreme Good and last end. And
even if it were conceded that the end of reason and of
the human will were the preservation of the human
being, it would not follow therefrom that the last end
of man consists in some bodily good. For the human
being is composed of body and soul, and though it is
true that the being of the body depends on the soul,
it is not true that conversely the being of the soul
depends on the body. On the contrary, the body is

ordered in view of the soul, as matter is ordered in view of the form. In neither case, therefore, could the last end of man which is beatitude, be identified with some good of the corporeal order.[5]

Does it consist in pleasure or some other good of the soul? If we mean by "beatitude" not the attainment or possession of beatitude—which indeed pertains to the soul—but what actually beatitude consists in, it must be said that beatitude is none of the goods of the soul, but subsists outside of, and infinitely above, the soul. *Beatitudo est aliquid animae; sed id in quo consistit beatitudo, est aliquid extra animam.*[6] It is in effect impossible that the last end of man could be his soul or anything whatever belonging to it. The soul, considered in itself, is only in potency; its knowledge and its virtue are in need of being brought from potency to act. But, whatever is in potency is to its act, as the incomplete is to the complete; potency exists only in view of the act. It is therefore clear that the human soul exists in view of some other thing and that, consequently, it is not its own last end. But it is yet far more evident that no good of the human soul constitutes the Supreme Good. The Good which is the last end can only be a perfect good which fully satisfies the appetite. Now, human appetite which is the will, tends, as was shown before, to the universal good. On the other hand, it is obvious that every good inherent in a finite soul such as ours, is, by that very fact, but a finite and participated good. It is consequently impossible for any of these goods to constitute the Supreme Good of man and to become his last end. It may be asserted further as a general thesis that the beatitude of man cannot consist in any created good. It can consist only, as just stated, in a perfect good, fully satisfying the appetite—it would not, in fact, be the last end, if, once attained, it left anything to be desired—and since nothing can fully satisfy the human will except the universal good which is its proper object, it follows of necessity that every created and participated good is incapable of constituting the Supreme Good and last end. Human beatitude consists therefore in God alone,[7] as in the first and universal good and the source of all other goods.

With this knowledge of what beatitude consists in, let us consider what is its essence. The exact meaning of the question is this: the term "end" may have two senses. It may mean an actual thing which it is desired to obtain; thus money is the end pursued by the miser; but it may also mean the acquisition or possession or finally the enjoyment of what is desired; thus the end which the miser seeks is the possession of money. These two senses must be carefully kept apart in considering beatitude. We know what it is in the first sense, namely, the uncreated Good which we call God who alone in His infinite goodness is able to satisfy perfectly the will of man. But what beatitude consists in, taken in the second sense, is a matter that has now to be examined.

It seems at first sight that, viewed under this aspect, beatitude is a created good. Doubtless the cause or object of beatitude is, as just established, something uncreated. But the essence itself of beatitude, i.e. the acquisition and the enjoyment by man of the last end, is necessarily something human, and consequently something created.[8] We may add that this something is an operation and an act, since beatitude constitutes the highest perfection of man and perfection implies an act, as potency implies imperfection.[9] Lastly, this operation belongs to the human intellect to the exclusion of every other power of the soul. For it cannot be claimed that beatitude could be reduced to an operation of the sensitive soul; we have shown that the very object of beatitude does not consist in bodily goods, and these are the only goods which are accessible to the sensitive operations of the soul; they are consequently completely incapable of conferring beatitude.[10] It appears, on the other hand, that of the intellect and the will, which are the rational part of our soul, the intellect is the only power capable of grasping directly the object of our beatitude and of our last end.

For we must distinguish, within beatitude, what constitutes the very essence of it, from the delight which is certainly always linked with it, but is in the last resort only a mere accident of it.[11] In view of this, it becomes clear that beatitude cannot consist essentially in an act of will. For all men desire, it is true, their last end, the possession of which represents in their eyes the supreme degree of perfection and therefore beatitude; but it is not for the will to apprehend any end. The will tends to absent ends when it desires them, and to present ends when it delights and finds rest in them. But to desire an end would not seem to be the same as apprehending it; it means simply moving towards it. And as regards the delight, this arises in the will only by reason of the very presence of its object. In other words: the will rejoices in an object only on condition that it is present, and it must not be argued, as if the object became present, simply because the will delights in it. The essence itself of the beatitude consists accordingly in an act of the intellect; only the delight accompanying it, can be considered as an act of the will.[12]

These arguments all presuppose the principle that, if beatitude is attainable by a human operation, it could be attained only by the most perfect and highest operation. This same principle enables us to assert further that beatitude must consist in an operation of the speculative intellect rather than of the practical intellect. For the most perfect power of the intellect is that of which the object is the most perfect, viz. the essence of God. Now, this essence is the object of the speculative, not of the practical intellect. The act constituting beatitude must therefore be of a speculative nature, and this amounts to saying that this act must consist in contemplation.[13] Still, its object remains to be determined. Would this contemplation, as the source of beatitude, consist, for example, in the study and consideration of the speculative sciences? To reply to this question, we must distinguish between two beatitudes accessible to man, the one perfect, the other imperfect. The perfect beatitude is that which attains to the true essence of beatitude; imperfect beatitude does not reach this, but participates, at some particular points, in some of the characters peculiar to true beatitude. Now, it is certain that true beatitude cannot be reduced in its essence to a knowledge of the speculative sciences. In our study of speculative sciences, the range of our vision cannot extend beyond the first principles of the sciences, for the whole of every science is virtually contained in the principles whence it is deduced. But the principles of speculative science are known to us only by means of sensible knowledge; the study of these sciences cannot therefore carry our intellect beyond the point to which the knowledge of sensible things can advance it. All that is needed therefore is to consider whether the knowledge of the sensible could constitute the highest beatitude of man, i.e. his highest perfection. The answer is evidently in the negative. The higher cannot find its perfection in what is inferior to it as such. The lower can contribute to the perfection of the higher only in so far as it participates, however inadequately, in a reality beyond, and which is even beyond that, to the perfection of which it contributes. It is evident, for example, that the form of a stone or of any other sensible object is inferior to man. If, therefore, in sensible knowledge, the form of a stone confers some perfection on the human intellect, it does so not inasmuch as it is simply the form of a stone, but in so far as this form participates in some reality of a higher order than the human intellect: say, the intelligible light or something else of that kind. All knowledge capable of imparting some perfection to the human intellect presupposes therefore an object superior to the intellect, and this is eminently true of the absolutely perfect human knowledge which the beatific contemplation would confer on it. Here we gather the fruits of the conclusions which we have reached earlier concerning the value and range of human knowledge. Its proper object is the sensible: the human intellect cannot therefore find its beatitude and highest perfection in the study of the sensible to which the speculative sciences are limited.[14] But it may find there the imperfect beatitude, the only one accessible to us here on earth. Just as the sensible forms participate in some resemblance to the higher substances, so the study of the speculative sciences is a sort of participation in the true and perfect beatitude.[15] For by them our intellect is brought from potency to act even though they cannot bring it to its full and ultimate actuality.

This means that the essential and true beatitude is not of this world; it can only be found in the full view of the essence of God. In order to see the truth of this conclusion, it is important to keep the following two principles in mind. The first is that man is not perfectly happy as long as there is something to be desired and searched for. The second is that the perfection of a power of the soul is always measured by the nature of its object. Now, the object of the intellect is *quod quid est,* i.e. the essence of a thing. The perfection of the intellect is consequently measured by the more or less deep knowledge of the essence of its object. If, for instance, a given intellect knows the essence of a certain effect without this knowledge enabling him to know the essence of its cause, one might say that it knows the existence of the cause, but not its nature, the *an sit,* but not the *quid est*: in short, it could not be straightway said that it knows the cause. A natural desire therefore subsists in that man who knows that the effect has a cause, to know what that cause is. This is the source of curiosity and of that "wonder" which, according to the Philosopher, is at the root of all enquiry. Someone seeing an eclipse of the sun judges at once that this phenomenon has a cause; but since he is ignorant of the cause, he wonders, and because he wonders searches for it; and this search will only end when he discovers, in its very essence, the cause of the event. Let us now recall what the human intellect knows of its

Creator. We saw that strictly speaking, it knows no other essences but those of a few sensible and created objects, and that it advances from this knowledge to that of the existence of God, but without ever attaining to the essence of the first Cause, in its perfection. Man, therefore, feels the natural desire to know fully and to see directly the essence of this cause. But he desires beatitude naturally, though he does not, *quâ* man and without the light of Revelation, know what beatitude is; at least he knows it only to the extent to which God can be known by starting from sensible things. He will therefore never reach his last end and his highest perfection except by his union with God, the only object whose contemplation can entirely satisfy the highest powers of his soul and raise him to complete perfection.[16]

This beatitude, transcending man and nature, is, however, no adventitious term invented in order to harmonise morality with religion; there, is, between terrestrial beatitude, accessible to us in this life, and the celestial beatitude to which we are called, an intimate harmony and almost continuity. The last end is not the negation of our human ends; on the contrary, it gathers them up in sublimating them, and conversely our human ends are like so many partial imitations and imperfect substitutes of our last end. There is not a single thing of those that we desire, the desire for which, if interpreted and regulated by reason, is not capable of receiving a legitimate meaning. We desire in this life health and the goods of the body; but health and bodily perfection are in fact conditions favourable to the operations of knowledge by which we reach the most perfect human happiness. We desire in this life external goods, such as wealth; but the reason is that it allows us to live and to achieve the operations of contemplative as well as active virtue; if wealth is not essential to beatitude, it may be at least its instrument. We desire here even the company of our friends and we are right, for as a matter of happiness in this present life, a happy man has need of friends; not to make use of them; the wise man suffices unto himself; not to derive pleasure from them; the wise man finds his perfect pleasure in the exercise of virtue: but in order to have the material for the very exercise of virtue. His friends serve him as the recipients of his benevolence, and for the expansion of the perfection of his goodness. Conversely, we said, all goods are ordered and sublimated in the celestial beatitude. Even seeing God face to face in the beatific vision, even, when the soul has become like some separate intelligence, the beatitude of man is not that of a soul wholly separated from its body. This combination we find again even in the glory of heaven itself: *cum enim naturale sit animae corpori uniri, non potest esse quod perfectio animae naturalem ejus perfectionem excludat.* The body *before* beatitude is the minister of the soul and the instrument of such inferior operations as smooth our path to it; *in* beatitude, the soul, on the contrary, in rewarding its servant, confers upon it incorruptibility and allows it to share in its immortal perfection: *ex beatitudine animae fiet redundantia ad corpus, ut et ipsum sua perfectione potiatur.*[17] Re-united with this hitherto animal body, now spiritualised by the soul's glory, the soul has no further use for the material goods which had been disposed here below for the sake of our animal existence; it has no need even of friends other than God who comforts it out of His eternity, truth and love. Yet perhaps it is not forbidden us to think that the joy of heaven is not a solitary joy and that celestial beatitude, fulfilled in the vision which the Blessed enjoy of their mutual happiness, is further enhanced by eternal friendship.[18] Thus the thought of St. Thomas prolongs nature into the supernatural, for having assigned the description of man as a whole, not only of the human soul, to philosophy as its object, it outlines the destiny, not of the soul alone, but of the whole man. The beatitude of the Christian, as conceived by St. Thomas, is the beatitude of man in his entirety.

NOTES TO CHAPTER XVI.

1. *Cont. Gent.*, III. 25.
2. *De Virtut.*, qu. I., art 2, ad 3; qu. II., art. 3, ad *Resp.*
3. *Sum. theol.*, IaIIae, 1, 4, ad *Resp.*
4. *IV Sent.*, dist., 49, qu. 1, art. 3; *Sum. theol.*, IaIIae, 1, 6, ad *Resp.*
5. *Cont. Gent.*, III. 32; *Comp. theol.*, II. 9; *Sum, theol.*, IaIIae, 2, 5, ad *Resp.*
6. *Sum. theol.*, IaIIae, 2, 7, ad *Resp.*
7. *Cont. Gent.*, IV. 54; *Sum. theol.*, IaIIae, 2, 8, ad *Resp.*; *Comp. theol.*, I. 108; II. 9.
8. *Sum. theol.*, I. 26, 3, ad *Resp.*; IaIIae, 3, 1, ad *Resp.*
9. *Sum. theol.*, IaIIae, 3, 2, ad *Resp.*
10. *Cont. Gent.*, III., 33; *Sum. theol.*, IaIIae, 3, 3, ad *Resp.*; *Comp. theol.*, II. 9.
11. It is moreover to be noted that, though beatitude does not consist in the joy accompanying it, the joy is a necessary accompaniment of beatitude. Cf. *Sum. theol.*, IaIIae, 4, 1, ad *Resp.*
12. *Cont. Gent.*, III. 26; *Sum. theol.*, I. 26, 2, ad 2^m; IaIIae, 3, 4, ad *Resp.*; *Quodlib.*, VIII. 9, 1.
13. *Sum. theol.*, IaIIae, 3, 5, ad *Resp.*
14. *Cont. Gent.*, III. 48; *Sum. theol.*, IaIIae, 3, 6, ad *Resp.*
15. *Sum. theol.*, IaIIae, 3, 5, ad *Resp.*; and 3, 6, ad *Resp.* "Et ideo quidam philosophi attendentes naturalem perfectionem hominis, dixerunt ultimam felicitatem hominis in hoc consistere quod in anima hominis describatur ordo totius universi." *De Verit.*, XX. 3, ad *Resp.*
16. *Sum. theol.*, I 32, 1; IaIIae, 3, 8, ad *Resp.*; *De Verit.*, VIII. 1, ad *Resp.*; *Quodlib.*, X. qu. 8, ad *Resp.*
17. *Sum. theol.*, IaIIae, 4, 6, ad *Resp.*
18. *Sum. theol.*, IaIIae, 4, 8, ad *Resp.*

CHAPTER XVII.
THE SPIRIT OF THOMISTIC
PHILOSOPHY

WE have so far presented a number of separate expositions of the most important problems on which Thomistic Philosophy touches, and even in thus severally discussing these problems, we have endeavoured to indicate the link of continuity of their solutions. It may, however, perhaps not be superfluous, on reaching the end of this exposition, to take a bird's-eye view of the ground covered, and to set forth, as accurately as possible, the constant element in the philosophical attitude of St. Thomas Aquinas.

Doubtless, the powerfully marked systematic character of his teaching will have been noted or at least felt; it constitutes a world-system, an all-round explanation of the universe, offered from the point of view of reason. This systematic quality is the result, in the first place, of the woof of thomistic thought being entirely woven of a small number of principles which continually intercross, and perhaps of its being drawn wholly from different aspects of the same idea, the idea of being. Human thought rests satisfied only when it succeeds in mastering an existence; yet a being never leads our intellect to the mere sterile statement of a datum, but, on the contrary, invites the intellect to search all around it and spurs on our spiritual action by the very multiplicity of the aspects discovered in its object. In so far as this being is indistinguishable from itself, it is one, and in this sense it can be said that being and oneness are the same thing, since no essence can be broken up without losing at the same time its being and its unity. But the very fact that a being presents itself by definition as inseparable from itself, is the basis of the truth which can be asserted of it: to assert the true is to assert what *is*, and to attribute to each thing the very being which defines it. The being of the thing therefore defines the truth of the thing, and the truth of the thing is the foundation of the truth of thought. We think truly concerning a thing when we attribute to it the being which the thing is; in this way harmony is established between our thought and the thing's essence, and the truth of our knowledge rests on this harmony, just as the intimate harmony subsisting between the thing's essence and the eternal thought of God is the foundation of the truth of the thing outside of our own thought. The series of relations of truth is therefore but one aspect of the series of relations of being. Precisely the same applies to the good. Every being is the basis of a truth in so far as knowable; but in so far as defined by a certain quantity of perfection, and consequently insofar as it *is*, it is desirable and presents itself to us as a good; hence the movement arising within us to possess it whenever we find ourselves in its presence. Thus being itself, without any external additions, asserts itself in its unity, its truth and its goodness; whatever the relations of identity which our thought may assert at any one of the moments of synthesis constituting the system, whatever the truth affirmed or the good desired by us: it is always to the being that our thought returns as to the fixed harmony of being with itself, whether our mind assimilates the object by means of knowledge or enjoys its perfection by means of the will.

But being itself is not a conception whose content can be defined once and for all and posited *a priori*; there is not only *one* manner of being, and these diverse manners require statement. The one most directly given, is our own, and that of the corporeal things in the midst of which we live. Each one of us *is*, but in an incomplete and defective manner; within the range of experience directly accessible to us, we find only substantial composites, analogous of ourselves, forms interlocked with matter by so indissoluble a bond that this interlocking itself defines these beings, and that the creative action of God, in positing them, results directly in the union of matter and form which constitutes them. But, however imperfect a being of this kind, it yet possesses perfection to the extent to which it possesses being; even here we discover the transcendental inseparable relations, which have been defined, but we note at the same time that for a reason, the deep nature of which is still to be determined, these relations are not fixed, settled or defined. Everything happens, as a matter of experience, as if we had to struggle to establish these relations, instead of peacefully enjoying them as a good given to us. We *are*, and we are identical with ourselves; yet not completely. A sort of margin separates us from our proper definition; none of us realises fully the human essence or even the full conception of his own individuality; hence, instead of a plain and simple manner of being, there is a continual effort to maintain ourselves in being, to preserve and realise ourselves. So it is with all the sensible beings which we find around us; the world is perpetually labouring under forces, agitated by movements and in a continual state of becoming, just as man is ceaselessly travelling to pass from one state to another state.

The fact of this universal becoming is formulated in the distinction of potency and act, governing all beings within our experience; the distinction claims nothing more than to formulate this experience. As Aristotle who notes the universality of its application together with the impossibility of explaining it, so St. Thomas uses this distinction more frequently than he explains it. For it is a sort of postulate, a formula to be concreted in a fact, the acceptance of a property, not of being as such this time, but of the mode of a definite being presented to us by experience. Every essence, not completely realising its definition, is act in so far as it realises it, and potency in so far as it does not; it is deprivation to the extent to which it suffers under not realising it. Inasmuch as the essence is in act, it is the active principle releasing the movement towards realisation; and from the actuality of the form start all the efforts of this kind; it is the origin of movement, the reason of becoming, it is cause. Here, therefore, again, whatever of being is contained in things, is the ultimate reason of all natural processes which we observe; it is being as such that communicates its form as efficient cause, that produces change as moving force, that assigns to the change a reason as final cause. What is given us are beings, ceaselessly moving under the stress of a fundamental need to save and to complete themselves.

Now, it is impossible to reflect upon an experience of such a kind without perceiving that it fails to contain the sufficient reason of the facts which it presents. This world of becoming, in striving to be, these celestial spheres seeking themselves perpetually at each successive point of their orbits, these human souls capturing and assimilating being by their intellect, these substantial forms searching without interruption new matter in which to realise themselves, do not contain within themselves the reason of what they are. If such beings contained the explanation of themselves, they would lack nothing, or, conversely, they should lack nothing in order to explain themselves, but in that case they would cease from the movement to find themselves, they would rest in the completeness of their realised essence, they would cease to be what they are.

We must therefore search for the sufficient reason of the universe in a being who *is* wholly what he is, outside the world of potency and act and beyond becoming. But this being, inferred by thought, would manifestly be of a nature different from the being with which we are acquainted, for unless he were radically different from the being of our experience, there would be no advantage in positing him. The world of becoming postulates a principle, exempt from becoming and situated entirely outside it. But then a new problem presents itself: if the being postulated by reason is radically different from that given to us, how can we know him, in starting from our experience, and of what use could he be to explain it? We could never either infer or argue from one being concerning another unless they both "were" in the same sense. And indeed, our thought would never suffice to infer him, unless the reality with which we are linked, constituted in its hierarchic and analogical structure, a sort of ladder leading us up to God. Precisely because every operation is the realisation of an essence and because every essence is a certain quantity of being and perfection, the universe presents itself to us as a society of superior and inferior beings in which the very definition of each essence places each directly into its proper rank within the degrees of this hierarchy. The explanation of the operation of each individual requires, therefore, not only the definition of the individual itself, but further the definition of the essence which is defectively embodied in it; nor does the species suffice for itself, since the individuals representing it are continually striving to realise themselves; hence we must either abandon the attempt to account for it or look for the sufficient reason beyond the species, in a higher degree of perfection. Henceforth the universe appears as essentially a hierarchy. The philosophical problem consists now in setting out its exact arrangement, assigning to each class of beings its true position in it. To do so, one principle of universal value must never be lost sight of: viz, that the more or the less can be estimated and classed only in reference to the maximum, the relative only by reference to the absolute. Between God, who is Being pure and simple, and complete nothingness are thus placed pure intelligences, the angels, *prope Deum*, and material forms, *prope nihil*; between the angel and material nature, the human creature is inserted, as a frontier and skyline between spirits and bodies, so that as the angel diminishes the distance separating man from God, so man fills the gap separating the angel from matter. There is a correspondence between each of these degrees and the mode of operation proper to it, since each being operates according as it is in act, and since its degree of actuality is identical with its degree of perfection. In this way the ordered hierarchy of beings is completed by the ordered hierarchy of their operations, the lowest of a superior degree always bordering on the highest of the next inferior; the principle of continuity thus details and determines the principle of perfection. In reality these two principles merely express the superior law which governs the communication of being. There is no being except the Divine Being in whom all creatures participate, and the creatures differ from each other only by the greater or lesser dignity of the degree of participation realised by them.[1] Their perfection therefore necessarily measures the distance which separates them from God, and they are necessarily differentiated by the hierarchical order in which they are placed.

But if this is so, it is this analogy which alone allows us to infer a transcendent God, though our intelligence only starts from the sensible; it is again this analogy that alone allows us to hold that the universe has its being from a transcendent God, without being either identical with Him or superadded to Him. For the very resemblance of the analogue requires explanation and is explained only by what the analogue imitates: *non enim ens de multis aequivoce dicitur, sed per analogiam, et sic oportet fieri reductionem in unum.*[2] But while it possesses enough being from its model to require the model as a cause, it possesses it in such a manner as to prevent the cause of its being from becoming involved in its own. Hence the term "being" signifies two different modes of existence whether it is applied to God or to the creatures, and therefore no problem of addition or subtraction can arise on this point. The being of the creatures is but an image and an imitation of the Divine being; just as reflections flicker round a flame, multiply, decrease and vanish without the flame itself being affected, so the likenesses freely created by the Divine substance owe all the being they have to this substance, subsist only in it, and yet borrow nothing of a mode of being *per se* which is not theirs, and neither add nor detract the smallest fraction from it. These two principles of analogy and hierarchical order, which make creation by a transcendent Creator possible, also enable creature and Creator to be kept in relation and to form those ties between them which become the constitutive principles of the created essences and the laws of their explanation. Whatever the physical side of things ultimately may be, it must necessarily be subordinated to the metaphysics of essences and quality. If creatures are, by reason of their origin, likenesses, we must expect analogy to explain the structure of the universe, as it explains the creation of them. To give an account of the operation of a being, means to show that the operation is founded in its essence; and to give a sufficient reason of this essence, means to show that a certain likeness of the pure act, corresponding precisely to what the essence in question is, must find a place in our universe. Why lastly is such a likeness required by a universe such as ours? Because the various likenesses of any one model cannot be essentially different from each other except in being more or less perfect; a closed system of images of an infinite being must therefore present real degrees of likeness within the limits assigned to the system by the free choice of the Creator: the metaphysical explanation of a physical phenomenon is always tantamount to indicating the place of an essence in a hierarchy.

In this meaning of a hierarchy it is easy to see the influence of the Pseudo-Dionysius on the mind of St. Thomas. This influence is incontestable, and explains to some extent why the author of the "Summa theologica" has sometimes been classed among the disciples of Plotinus. But this thesis can be accepted only if its range is exactly defined. The Areopagite furnishes the framework of the hierarchy, impresses the need of such an hierarchy deeply on the mind, leaves the conviction that it is impossible not to consider the universe as a hierarchy; but he leaves the task of filling this hierarchy to St. Thomas, and even in sketching its degrees, he is unaware of the law which governs their order and distribution. Can it further be said that the contents of this universal hierarchy is conceived by the author of the two "Summae" in a neo-platonic spirit? Even if we grant the exception— and that only with many reservations—of the pure spirits, it is easy to see that this is not so. The God of St. Thomas is in general outline the God of St. Augustine, and it is not enough for St. Augustine to have been influenced by Neo-platonism for his God to be identified with that of Plotinus. Between the Plotinian speculation and the theology of the Fathers, Jehovah is interposed, a personal God, acting by intelligence and will, who freely creates outside Himself the real world chosen by His wisdom from among an infinity of possible worlds. Between this freely created world and its Creator lies an impassable gulf and no other continuity but that of order. Strictly speaking, the world is an ordered discontinuity. How is it possible not to see that here we are at the very antipodes of Neo-platonic philosophy? To make St. Thomas into a Plotinian or even a Plotiniser, is to confuse him with the disciples of Averroes and Avicenna, that is, with the adversaries whom he fought against with all his energy.

The distance between the two philosophies is no less striking, when we pass from God to man. We said that the God of St. Thomas is not the God of Plotinus, but the Christian God of St. Augustine; we can add that the man of St. Thomas is the man not of Plotinus, but of Aristotle. The opposition is particularly marked as far as the central problem is concerned, viz. the relation of body and soul and the theory of knowledge resulting therefrom. On the one side, the assertion of an extreme independence and almost complete aseity of the soul, with platonic reminiscence, and even a momentary return to the One in ecstatic union; on the other, the very emphatic assertion of the physical nature of the soul and most watchful care to close all approaches to a direct intuition of the intelligible, leaving open only the path of sensible knowledge. Platonism places mysticism on the line of a natural prolongation of human knowledge; in the thomistic philosophy mysticism is added to and co-ordinated with natural knowledge, but without continuing it. All that we know of God is contained in what our reason learns by reflecting on the data of sense; if a neo-platonic doctrine of knowledge is to be found in the Middle Ages, it has to be sought elsewhere than in the system of St. Thomas.

This is to be seen still more clearly, if leaving aside the consideration of this particular problem, the thomistic hierarchy of the universe is examined directly and in itself. We have said much about God and creative virtue, of the angels and their functions, about man and his operations. But, in the successive consideration of the universality of creatures endowed with intellect, and of the first Intelligence itself, the nature as well as the range of the knowledge which it has been given us to acquire, have varied considerably according to the greater or lesser perfection of the reality which was its object. Anyone wishing to get a clear grasp of the spirit of thomistic Philosophy, must therefore, after running his eye over the ladder of being, proceed to a revision of the values which class each order of knowledge in its appropriate rank.

What is knowing? It means the apprehension of an essence, and there is no other knowledge but this. But it is at once clear that we are ruthlessly debarred from every knowledge, in the strict sense of the term, of the higher degrees of the universal hierarchy. Of God and even of the pure intelligences we know that they exist, but not what they are. There is further no doubt that the sense of this deficiency of our knowledge of God leaves us with a burning desire for a higher and fuller knowledge. It remains nonetheless true that, if knowing consists in grasping the essence of the object known, God, the angels and, in a general way, everything pertaining to the order of the purely intelligible, escape by definition the grasp of our intellect. This is the reason why we have to substitute for the lacking intuition of the Divine essence a number of concepts which, in their combination, imitate, though confusedly, what would be a true idea of the Divine being. After gathering together all that we have been able to assert concerning this object, all that we obtain is a collection of negations or analogies: nothing more.

Where then is human knowledge, so to say, at home and dealing with its proper object? Only at the point where it comes into contact with the sensible. There reason feels on its own ground, though even here it is unable to penetrate entirely to reality, since the individual as such eludes its hold owing to the matter which it presupposes. Whether describing man, i.e. the human compound, animal and its operations, the celestial bodies and their virtues, mixed substances or the elements, rational knowledge continues to be proportionate to the various orders of the objects explored; but its content, though incomplete, is at least a truly positive content. And yet Thomism in its profoundest and most original aspects is not an effort to extend natural science or to establish it on a more solid foundation. Though identifying the object proper to the human intellect with the sensible, St. Thomas does not consider its study as the highest function of our faculty of knowledge. Though the proper *object* of the intellect be the sensible, its proper *function* is to disengage the intelligible from the sensible[3]; out of the particular object, illuminated by its light, it draws the universal, thanks to that Divine resemblance which is naturally impressed on it as the mark of its origin; in the proper and emphatic sense of the term, it is born and made for the universal. Hence the effort towards that object which yet remains for it most strictly inaccessible: the Divine essence. Here reason knows least, but even the humblest truth that it does know, exceed in dignity and price all other certitudes.[4]

If we wish, therefore, to find the true sense of Thomism, we must penetrate beyond the philosophical theses which in their close texture constitute its teaching, to the spirit and the very soul of St. Thomas.

What we find at the very base of this imposing structure of ideas, is a deep religious life and the secret fervour of a soul in seach of God. Long and subtle controversies have recently been witnessed on the question whether, from the thomistic point of view, man can feel the natural desire for his supernatural end. It is the business of the theologians to decide issues of this kind and to agree upon the formula which, without violating the transcendance of God, yet allows man not to be separated from Him. All that the historian can state is that St. Thomas has provided in his philosophical structure many cases of toothings which with their gaps indicate what nature expects from grace to be completed. At the foundation of this philosophy, as of all Christian philosophies, there lies a sense of deep misery and the need of a consoler who cannot be but God: *naturalis ratio dictat homini quod alicui superiori subdatur, propter defectus quos in seipso sentit, in quibus ab aliquo superiori eget adjuvari, et dirigi, et quidquid illud sit, hoc est quod apud omnes dicitur Deus.*[5] It is a natural sentiment which exalts grace in a Christian soul and is carried to its climax by the perfection of charity, when this soul is the soul of a saint. The ardent desire for God which bursts forth in lyrical accents in a St. John of the Cross, here clothes itself in the language of pure ideas; but their impersonal formulation must not let us forget that they are fed by this desire and in their turn have the task to appease it.

It would be a will-o'-the-wisp to search behind the system, as has sometimes been suggested, for an interior life, in its essence specifically different from the system itself. It must not be thought that the wise ordering of the "Summa theologica" and the steady progress of reason adding stone after stone to this immense edifice, are in the case of St. Thomas merely the product of a superficial activity, beneath which a richer, deeper, more religious life freely pulsates. Not that the elevation or depth of his mystical life could be called in question; for ecstacies or mystical rapture and the beatific vision itself are the supreme completion of this same intellectual activity, both nurse and nurseling of that love for which Philosophy and speculative Theology only prepare the way. The interior life of St. Thomas, as far as the secret of so powerful a personality can be revealed to us, has therefore been precisely as it should be, to find expression in his teaching. Nothing could be more earnestly sought or be inspired by a more burning will than these proofs fashioned of ideas so exactly defined, wrought in formulas of such perfect precision, marshalled in a development so minutely balanced. Such mastery of expression and of the organisation of philosophical ideas cannot be achieved without a full surrender of oneself; the "Summa theologica" with its abstract limpidness and impersonal transparency *is* the interior life of St. Thomas itself, crystallised under our eyes and, as it were, fixed for eternity. The best means for the re-evocation of its deepest and most intense elements, is to re-order, in the same order which he himself imposed, the elements, so diverse, of this immense structure, to study its internal framework, to re-kindle in us the sense of its necessity; nothing but such a will to understand, awakened in us by that of the thinker himself, will allow us to feel that this light is the glow of an ardour kept under restraint, and to find beneath the ordered ideas the powerful effort which fused them together.

And only then the thomistic philosophy appears in its full beauty. It appeals by the force of sheer ideas, by the faith in the value of proofs and the self-abnegation before the demands of reason. This aspect of his teaching will strike those whom the unquestionable difficulties of a first initiation prevent from realising it, perhaps more forcibly, if they bear in mind what the religious mind of St. Thomas was. If it were true that the teaching of St. Thomas is animated by a spirit different from that which inspired his religious life, the difference ought to be visible, if the manner in which he prayed is compared with that in which he thought. But study the prayers of St. Thomas which have been preserved, and the religious value of which is so deep that the Church has inserted them into her Breviary: it will be found without difficulty that their fervour is neither in emotional exaltation, nor in impassionate exclamations, nor in that taste for spiritual delight characteristic of other forms of praying. The fervour of St. Thomas finds expression wholly in his will to ask of God *all that* he ought to ask of Him, *as* he ought to ask it of Him. There is a true fervour, deep, sensitive, in the rhythmic balance and the assonance of the words despite their austere precision; but the fervour of a spirituality which in its movements is governed by the order and very rhythm of the thought: *Precor ut haec sancta Communio non sit mihi reatus ad poenam sed intercessio salutaris ad veniam. Sit mihi armatura fidei, et scutum bonae voluntatis. Sit vitiorum meorum evacuatio, concupiscentiae et libidinis exterminatio, caritatis et patientiae, humilitatis et obedientiae, omniumque virtutum augmentatio; contra insidias inimicorum omnium tam visibilium quam invisibilium firma defensio; motuum meorum tam carnalium quam spiritualium perfecta quietatio; in te uno ac vero Deo firma adhaesio, atque finis mei felix consummatio.*[6] This spirituality desires not so much to receive satisfaction as light; the rhythm of the phrase and the sonorousness of the words alter in no way the order of the ideas; yet no one of any sensitiveness of taste can fail to perceive behind the cadence of the words a religious emotion and almost a poem.

For by virtue of that very reason which he served with so ardent a love, St. Thomas has become a poet, and, if we may believe an unbiassed judge, the greatest poet of the Latin tongue of the whole Middle Ages. It is noteworthy that the great beauty of the works attributed to this poet of the Eucharist, results almost entirely from the incomparable accuracy and closely packed thought of the words that he uses; the "Ecce panis angelorum" or the "Adoro te devote, latens deitas quae sub his figuris vere latitas," which have been food for the worship of so many faithful for centuries, are truly concentrated theological treatises. But nothing is perhaps more characteristic of Thomistic poetry than that "Pange lingua" which inspired Rémy de Gourmont to lines of as pure a style as those which they describe: "St. Thomas d'Aquin est toujours d'un égal génie et son génie est fait surtout de force et de certitude, de sécurité et de précision. Tout ce qu'il veut dire, il l'affirme, et avec une telle sonorité verbale que le doute, apeuré, fuit."[7]

> "Pange lingua gloriosi | corporis mysterium
> Sanguinisque pretiosi | quem in mundi pretium
> Fructus ventris generosi | Rex effudit gentium.
>
> Nobis datus, nobis natus | ex intacta Virgine
> Et in mundo conversatus, | sparso verbi semine
> Sui moras incolatus | miro clausit ordine...."

We thus pass from the philosophy of St. Thomas to his prayer, and from his prayer to his poetry without any sense of change in the order of ideas. For there is no change. His philosophy is as rich in beauty as his poetry is heavy with thought; we may say of the "Summa theologica" no less than of the "Pange lingua" that St. Thomas is always equal in genius, a genius of force and certitude, of firmness and precision. All he wishes to say, he affirms with such decisiveness of thought that "doubt, affrighted, flies."

Never perhaps has a more exacting intellect responded to the call of so religious a heart. St. Thomas conceives man as eminently apt for the knowledge of phenomena, but does not hold that the most adequate human knowledge is also the most useful or the highest to which we can lay claim. He places man's reason into the sensible as in its proper domain, but while considering it fitted for the exploration and conquest of that domain, he urges it to turn its glance rather to another which is no longer merely the domain of man but that of the children of God. Such is the thought of St. Thomas. If it be admitted that a philosophy should be estimated not by the elements it borrows, but by the spirit which animates it, we shall not see in his teaching either Plotinianism or Aristotelianism, but above all Christianity. His thought has tried to express in rational language the whole destiny of the Christian, but, in reminding him often that he has in this life to follow a path of exile without light or horizon, he has never ceased to direct his steps towards those heights whence he can descry, rising out of the haze of the distance, the confines of the Promised Land.

NOTES TO CHAPTER XVII.

1. "Necesse est igitur omnia quae diversificantur secundum diversam participationem essendi, ut sint perfectius vel minus perfecte, causari ab uno primo ente quod perfectissime est"; *Sum. theol.*, I. 44, 1, ad *Resp.*

2. *Cont. Gent.*, II. 15.

3. "Contemplatio humana secundum statum praesentis vitae non potest esse absque phantasmatibus..., sed tamen intellectualis cognitio non consistit in ipsis phantasmatibus, sed in eis contemplatur puritatem intelligibilis veritatis"; *Sum. theol.*, IIaIIae, 180, 5, ad 1ᵐ. Cf. *De Verit.*, XIII. 3, ad *Resp.*: "intellectus qui summam cognitionis tenet, proprie immaterialium est."

4. *Cont. Gent.*, I. 5, ad *Apparet.*

5. *Sum. theol.*, IIaIIae, 85, 1, ad *Resp.*

6. It is interesting to compare with this prayer of St. Thomas that of St. Bonaventure which follows upon it in the Breviary and forms a remarkable contrast to it.

7. R. de Gourmont, *Le latin mystique*, Paris, Crès, 1913, p. 274–275. All the texts bearing upon the spiritual life of St. Thomas are collected in the work of Fr. Sertillanges, *Prières de saint Thomas d'Aquin*, L'art catholique, Paris, 1920.

INDEX OF NAMES

SUBJECT INDEX

A NOTE ON THE TYPE

The text of this book is set in Bembo cut by the Monotype Corporation (England) in 1929. It is copied from the type cut by Francesco Griffo of Bologna for Aldus Manutius, the famous Venetian printer-publisher. The first book set in the type was Cardinal Pietro Bembo's *De Aetna* (1495)—hence the modern name of the face.